A History of Hurling

Séamus J. King

Gill & Macmillan

Gill & Macmillan Ltd
Goldenbridge
Dublin 8
with associated companies throughout the world

© Séamus J. King 1996
0 7171 2199 2
Index compiled by Warren Yeates
Design and print origination by Graham Thew Design
Printed by ColourBooks Ltd, Dublin

5 4 3 2 1

Contents

Preface

Hurling is an ancient game peculiar to the Irish. It has a long ancestry, with its earliest literary reference purporting to date it from the Battle of Moytura in 1272 BC. The game played by the warriors before this battle has changed in many ways and differs substantially from the compelling spectacle in Croke Park on the first Sunday in September, but the basic characteristics remain the same, the propulsion of a ball with a stick from one end of a field to the other with the intention of scoring a goal. Through the centuries since then this object has remained constant even if the goalposts have changed, or the size of the playing area, or the number of players on a side, or the fact that points have become more common than goals in the last century or so.

To attempt writing a history of this game is a daunting task, some might say an impossible one. Any such work must of its very nature be imbalanced. Over the centuries down to the foundation of the GAA our knowledge of the game is at its very best sketchy, at its worst non-existent. Brother Ó Caithnia, in his book Scéal na hIomána, did a major service to the public in tracing the history of hurling from earliest times to 1880. His book is the result of an assiduous trawling of mythological, literary and historical sources to provide us with an account of a game that has been played continuously down through the centuries and that achieved a rich flowering under landlord patronage during the two centuries before 1800.

This book makes no attempt to cover that period in any such detail. The first chapter traces the references in mythology and the laws to give a sketchy picture of how the game came through the mists of mythology to be legislated for under the Brehon Laws and legislated against in Anglo-Norman law. The second chapter describes how the landlords took over the game during the seventeenth and eighteenth centuries so that the countryside rang with the sound of spirited contests between teams of rival landlords and inter-barony contests. This 'Golden Age of Hurling' came to an abrupt end with the revolutions at the end of the eighteenth century, which brought about a growing suspicion between landlord and tenant, broke their relationship of shared activities, and sent them their separate ways. With the loss of such patronage hurling went into a decline that was aggravated by the Famine and had almost disappeared by the time Michael Cusack decided to 'bring back the hurling.' Chapter 3 complements the first two chapters in seeking to understand the nature of the game that was played during this period before the foundation of the GAA, and continues with the major rule changes since then.

The main part of the book is devoted to the revival of hurling following the foundation of the GAA and the development of the game since then. In doing so it has concentrated on the senior hurling championship and on the counties and the players who have figured in this competition. The study will show how hurling is concentrated in a small area of the country and how three counties — Cork, Kilkenny and Tipperary — have dominated the championship. It will also reveal how the hurling area has remained constant and how attempts to expand it have come to naught.

A chapter is devoted to other hurling competitions organised by the GAA. To cater for the growing popularity of the game and the fact that all players were not of senior hurling standard, the junior championship was introduced in 1912. To satisfy the needs of younger players the minor championship was begun in 1928 and the under-21 in 1964. Other major introductions were a second senior hurling competition, the National League, in 1926 and the inter-provincial series in 1927. Another development was the beginning of the inter-club championship in 1970. These competitions are given only cursory treatment, with the winners included in the results section.

A chapter devoted to the geography of hurling tackles the question of why the game is limited to such a small area of the country and why it hasn't translated beyond this area in spite of many serious efforts to spread it during the past century. Two further chapters deal with hurling styles and the future of the game. In the first of these an attempt is made to come to grips with the much-talked-of but little-defined subject of different hurling styles. Afficionados of the game have identified particular county styles and have claimed significant differences in style between counties. On the question of the future of hurling the changes that have taken place in the modern game are discussed as well as where the game is heading. The book concludes with a compilation of records for all inter-county championships as well as other major hurling competitions. It is hoped that this will serve as an important reference chapter for the whole work.

There are a few gaps in the work, the most obvious being the failure to give any space to club activity — as Séamus Ó Ceallaigh did in his monumental work on the GAA in Limerick — with the exception of a brief treatment of the club championship and occasional reference to major clubs in the course of describing the senior hurling championship. The only excuse for this omission is lack of space. To have attempted to write about the hundreds of clubs involved would have made the book unwieldy.

Neither does the book include profiles of players, with a very few exceptions, in the way achieved by Brendan Fullam in his two books, *Giants of the Ash* and *Hurling Giants*. Again, space would have prevented anything but a very cursory treatment of a very few stars. There would have been the added problem of having to make a selection.

Finally, the constraints of space forced the exclusion of an account of the game abroad among the Irish diaspora. Since the foundation of the GAA, attempts have been made to promote the game abroad by sending star teams on exhibition tours and by organising it among Irish exiles in Britain, the United States and further afield.

Within these constraints, however, the reader should find a comprehensive account of the history of hurling, particularly since 1884. The book fills a vacuum in the literature of the game, and whereas it does not claim to be a complete record of what happened in the history of hurling, it does provide a chronological sequence of the major events since that date.

Acknowledgments

There are a number of people whose help and encouragement were very important to me in the writing of this book. Pride of place must go to a friend and colleague, Séamus Leahy, who was always ready to read drafts and offer valuable suggestions. Others who have read chapters of the work and made important corrections and additions were Séamus O'Doherty, Liam Ó Donncha, Marcus de Búrca, David Power, and Jerry Healy. I wish to thank Billy Quirke of Enniscorthy for his help with the Wexford chapter and for his submission on the Wexford hurling style. In like manner Father Paddy Gantley was very helpful with the Galway dimension of the book. Jim Cronin of Cork and Tom Ryall of Kilkenny were immensely helpful and forthcoming on many requests for information and opinion. Justin McCarthy of Cork put his huge interest in and knowledge of the game of hurling at my disposal. Con Murphy from the same county also gave me of his time and made important written submissions. Ger McKenna gave me information on Kerry hurling, while Brendan Harvey of Belfast was my knowledgeable information on Ulster hurling and shinty. Paddy Buggy and Eddie Keher made valuable contributions on Kilkenny's hurling style. Before he died Noel Drumgoole gave me his opinion on Dublin hurling and his thoughts on the setback of 1961. Jimmy Butler Coffey, with his experience of the thirties, filled me in on Limerick hurling at its peak. Pat Daly of Croke Park was also very helpful. Dr Kevin Whelan, who has written on the geography of hurling, gave me valuable assistance. Mick Dunne kindly supplied the results of the All-Stars games. Mary Guinan-Darmody in Tipperary County Library was always very helpful and co-operative. There are many others, too numerous to mention, who made the writing of this book easier than it might have been, and I should like to acknowledge my debt to them. Finally, I should like to thank my family, particularly Ruadhan, who put some chapters on disk, and Eileen McCormack, who did the rest.

Maps

1

Remote Origins to the Sixteenth Century

Hurling has such a distant ancestry that it's impossible to pin down its origins. According to the evidence of Irish myth and legend, the game had its devoted followers more than a thousand years before Christ.

The first recorded mention dates it to the battle fought at Moytura, near Cong, County Mayo, in 1272 BC between the native Fir Bolg and the invading Tuatha Dé Danann, who were demanding half the country. When the request was refused a battle was inevitable, and it was fought on the first day of the sixth week in summer. While the sides were preparing for the fray it was agreed to have a hurling contest between twenty-seven of the best players from each side.

The match began. Many a blow was dealt on legs and arms 'till their bones were broken and bruised and they fell outstretched on the turf and the match ended.' The Fir Bolg won and then fell upon their opponents and slew them. The source for this account is Leabhar na Nuachongbhála or the Book of Leinster, the compilation of which began in 1152, more than two thousand years after the event described.

No-one knows where the game of hurling originated. It is probably true to say that since time immemorial people have been striking a ball with a stick for recreation. There is a carved panel in the National Museum of Greece dating from the fifth century BC that shows two figures facing each other in a crouched position, holding two crooked sticks with a ball between them as if waiting for the signal to begin the game. There is no information about the nature of the game, and there are no similar panels to tell us anything of its later history.

So, whether the game originated in Greece or among the Celts we can't be sure. All that we can be certain of is that no further panels give it a

Greek history but that a game similar to that in the Greek panel developed and flourished in Ireland. Significantly, there is no other game comparable to it anywhere else in Europe. It would appear, however, that hurling was alive and well when the Celts arrived on the shores of Ireland and that it had originated with some earlier group of settlers.

Which brings us back to a possible Greek origin. According to Leabhar Gabhála Éireann or the Book of the Conquest of Ireland, five peoples are represented as taking Ireland before the Celts. The fourth group of invaders were known as the Fir Bolg. Their name has often been explained as being due to the fact that they were forced while in Greece to make arable land by covering rocks with earth, which they carried in *boilg* or bags, or alternatively that it was because they brought bags of clay from Ireland to Greece as a protection against venomous reptiles, or because they used these bags to make vessels in which to sail to Ireland.[1] It is now understood, however, that the name refers to the Celtic tribe usually known as the Belgae.

Even if the Fir Bolg weren't responsible for the introduction of the game and adopted it from the previous settlers, there is still a possible Greek connection. According to Leabhar Gabhála Éireann, the settlers who preceded the Fir Bolg were led by Neimheadh, son of Agnoman, of the Greeks of Scythia.[2]

So we return to the Battle of Moytura. The Fir Bolg may have won the match but they lost the battle with Tuatha Dé Danann, who eventually won the right to settle in Ireland. One of their kings, Lú, who lived before the tenth century BC, was a patron of public sports and started the annual Aonach Tailteann or Tailteann Fair. The name is preserved in the name of Teltown, County Meath, and, according to the Annals of the Four Masters, the first fair was held in the 'year of the world 3370'. The fair used to be held on the first of August or Lúnasa, which derives its name from the circumstances of its origin, Lú-násadh or Lú's fair.

Such fairs were common in early Ireland and many of them were held for promulgating laws, for the purpose of buying and selling, and for other kinds of business. In the case of Tailteann, however, it appears to have been of the nature of an Olympic Games. To it the men of all Ireland came together to indulge in such sports as chariot-racing, horse-racing, and hurling. The fair was held continuously down to the time of the last High King of Ireland, Ruairí Ó Conchúir, in the twelfth century. The name was revived in 1924, when the idea of holding a great Celtic cultural festival every five years, which had originated with Michael Davitt and Michael Cusack, eventually saw the light of day. The programme of events included not only hurling and football but also handball, cycling, golf, tennis, aquatic and equine spots, dancing, chess, billiards, and air racing. Many famous American athletes and some notable American handball players took part. The games were held again in 1928 and 1932 but died out afterwards because of financial, organisational and political difficulties.

In the centuries before and after the beginning of the Christian era there are many other references to hurling in the myths and legends of Ireland. Six centuries before Christ, the king of Leinster's son, Maon, who was born dumb, is said to have recovered his speech in a most unusual way. In spite of all the attentions of the wisest men of the day he entered adult life as a mute and was forced to accept the regency of his uncle. However, he had one consolation in that he played hurling. One day during a game he received a blow on his shin from an opponent's hurley, so fierce that it brought a yelp of pain from him. His companions were amazed and, like Archimedes after his discovery in the bathtub, began to shout 'Labhraidh Maon, Labhraidh Maon.' The name Maon, meaning dumb, was quickly forgotten and in its place Labhraidh, the speaker, king of Leinster, entered into his inheritance.

According to the Annals, Cathaoir Mór, the semi-legendary king of Leinster, lived in the second century AD. His son and heir, Rosa Failí, bestowed various gifts on the other sons in accordance with the wishes of the dead father. One of these sons, Criofann by name, received fifty camáin and balls together with fifteen sets of chessmen and the right of adjudication over the youth of the province of Leinster.[3]

However, it is in the story of Cú Chulainn—also contained in the Book of Leinster—that hurling gets its first great exposure. His godfather was Lú, better known as Lú Lámhfhada, the man who started the Tailteann Fair and who was famed for his magical power. And Cú Chulainn had a skill with the camán that suggested that he had been taught to play 'above a mortal pitch'. When he was born he was given the name of Setanta by his father, Sualdamh, an Ulster nobleman, and his mother, Deichtire, who was a sister of the king, Conchúr. They lived in a remote part of Ulster, and the boy's only entertainments were his hurley and his spear. He had no playmates, and he longed for the company of other boys.

When he was about eight years old and had perfected his hurling skills he heard about a school at Eamhain Mhacha for the sons of noblemen that was supervised by Conchúr and in which there was intensive training in hurling and athletics. He decided he wanted to go, but his parents wouldn't hear of it because of his age. But he wouldn't take no for an answer, continued to plead with his parents, and eventually wrung from them permission to travel.

It was a long journey to his destination so he shortened it by playing his favourite game. He hurled the ball a long distance ahead of him. Then he flung his hurley after it, striking it in mid-air so that it travelled another long distance ahead. While the stick and ball were still in the air he threw his spear after them and raced like the wind to catch all three before they hit the ground. As might be imagined from all this, he arrived at Eamhain Mhacha in no time.

A game of hurling was in progress when he arrived at the school. Having watched for a while, he decided to join in the action. But no stranger was allowed in these games unless he had first sought the protection of the players. Having taken possession of the ball, Setanta steered it with his hurley to the end of the field, moving so fast that no-one could stop him. He turned around for the boys' acclamation, only to find a converging crowd of furious faces. Instead of expressions of admiration he received a shower of hurleys, which he warded off with his own. Next he had to protect himself from a rain of spears. Turning defence into attack, he charged into them, knocking most of them to the ground and scattering the rest. Some fled for protection to the palace, where Conchúr was playing a game of chess. The king grabbed Setanta, who was in hot pursuit.

After introductions, Conchúr called the boys together, introduced them to his nephew, and ordered them to give the newcomer their protection. They all returned to the field of play to resume the game. Conchúr himself went to watch them. Setanta got possession of the ball and raced away with it, scattering the boys out of his way and outshining them all in skill and courage. His uncle was proud of him and became convinced that the boy would grow up to be a great warrior. His acceptance in the school was complete, and he soon became the star pupil. No other boy could beat him at running, wrestling, hurling, or spear-throwing.

One day Conchúr received an invitation to a feast at the house of Culann, his blacksmith. As Culann had never met Setanta, the king decided to bring the boy along. When he was leaving for the visit Setanta was in the middle of an important game of hurling and promised to follow his uncle as soon as the game was finished. When Conchúr and the other guests had been received into Culann's house, the host asked if all the guests had arrived. The king, forgetting about Setanta, said they had. So Culann released a savage hound to guard the house during the feast.

When Setanta finished the game he hurried off to follow his uncle, bringing his hurley, ball and spear with him. To shorten the journey he threw them ahead of him and in this manner arrived at the house of

Culann. He was so interested in his sport that he failed to notice the hound, which suddenly sprang at him with gnashing teeth. At this point his hurley and spear were still in mid-air, and the only defensive weapon he had was the ball. He flung it with all his might down the hound's throat. The animal was halted in his tracks, choked, and collapsed to the ground, growling as it expired.

On hearing the commotion, all those inside the house fell silent. Conchúr suddenly remembered Setanta, and a look of horror crossed his face. All the guests believed Setanta was killed. The servants were despatched to find out, but when they arrived on the scene they were amazed to find Setanta standing over the dead hound. Conchúr was overjoyed to find him alive. However, when Culann heard of the death of his hound he was angry and complained of the loss of the best watchdog in the land. Setanta promised to find another dog for his host; in the meantime he promised that he himself would guard the house of Culann and become his watchdog. And with that Conchúr said that in future he would be known as Cú Chulainn, the hound of Culann.

One of the celebrated stories from the old sagas and romances is that of Diarmaid and Gráinne. Although she was already betrothed to Fionn mac Cumhaill, Gráinne fell in love with Diarmaid. In one translation of the story of 'Tóraíocht Dhiarmada agus Ghráinne' the following speech is put in Gráinne's mouth:

> Of a day when a hurling match was played on the green of Tara, between Mac Lú and the Fiann on the one side and Cairbre of the Liffey and the men of Tara on the other, I sat high up at the window of my sunny chamber to see the game. Thou didst remain sitting with some other that day, not meaning to take part in the play. But at last, when the game began to go against thy friends, I saw thee start up and, snatching the hurley from the man nearest to thee, thou didst rush into the thick of the crowd and before sitting down thou didst win the goal three times on the men of Tara. At that hour my eyes and my heart were turned to thee and well I knew thee today in this banquet hall, though I knew not thy name till the druid told me. At that same hour too I gave thee my love, what I never gave, and never will give, to any other.

The laws laid down in ancient Ireland by the brehons or judges are known as the Brehon Laws. They date from the seventh or eighth centuries AD and touch every aspect of life, from the fosterage of children to the distraining of cattle, from bee-keeping to hurling.

What the laws tell us about hurling is as follows. Only officially recognised games of hurling came within the ambit of the law: otherwise it might have been possible to claim that an injury had occurred in a match when it had not. The four essentials for a valid game were a hurley, a ball, a goal, and a field. To strike a player a deliberate blow of the hurley was a crime punishable by law. To knock down a wall or fence or any portion thereof and not replace it was a further breach of law. This was a practical consideration to protect people's livestock.

According to Ó Caithnia, 'early lawyers made a distinction between three hurling phenomena: a match (*fianchluiche*), a bout of "pucking around" or "slogging" (*ruidilse cluiche*) and specifically dangerous fouls (*colchluiche*). Scholars have sought for many decades to distinguish between these three (bracketed) Irish terms. Apparently the law dealt differently with injuries arising out of all three forms of play. A match was clearly more dangerous than a bout of "pucking around" but the specific fouls (four are named) were most dangerous of all. These four fouls, insofar as modern scholars can interpret them, seem to correspond (as they ought to) to fouls still known and occasionally practised in hurling, or known to have been practised at one time but not now because of alterations in the game.'[4] The first is the sandwich foul, when two or more players jostle and shoulder one man between them. The second is still with us, the two-way pull or cross-swiping. The third is very much with us today: throwing the hurley, for whatever purpose, among a group of players. The fourth foul is called *taithe tuilche*, which probably meant lying on the ball. This might appear a strange practice until one realises that in a game where no goal was scored the team that had kept the ball nearest the opponents' goal for most of the game secured victory. This could be achieved by the man in possession of the ball lying on the ground and having his comrades lie on top of him. As a further rule stipulated that only a man in possession of the ball could be touched, and as he was covered and untouchable and the men over him, not being in possession, could not be touched, the game ended in stalemate. In such a situation the men on the ground won the match.

The Normans in the second half of the twelfth century brought Ireland into the mainstream of events in western Europe, and the success of the invasion was to begin the involvement of England in Ireland that has remained with us to the present.

There are no references to hurling in early Norman Ireland until the proscription contained in the Statute of Kilkenny, issued in 1366. For the authorities, hurling appears to have become a threat to the security of the colony: the law was passed in order to wean the Normans from a game from which 'great evils and maims have arisen.' The general purpose of the statute was to deal with the problem of 'degeneracy' among the English settlers. In the preamble to the legislation it was stated:

> By now many English of the said land, forsaking the English language, fashion, mode of riding, laws and usages, live and govern themselves according to the manners, fashion and language of the Irish enemies, and also have made divers marriages and alliances between themselves and the Irish enemies aforesaid; whereby the said land and the liege people thereof, the English language, the allegiance due to our Lord the King, and the English laws there are put in subjection and decayed and the Irish enemies exalted and raised up contrary to right.

This statute was passed to provide 'for the good government of the said land and quiet of the people and for the better observance of the law and the punishment of evil doers.' It was not directed at the native Irish but at the English colonists, with the intention of consolidating them and of restraining them from adopting Irish customs, which would weaken their loyalty to London.[5] One of the best-known parts had to do with hurling:

> Whereas a land which is at war requires that every person do render himself able to defend himself, it is ordained and established that the commons of the said land of Ireland, who are in divers marches of war, use not henceforth the games which men call hurlings with great clubs of a ball on the ground, from which great evils and maims have arisen, to the weakening of the defence of the said land, and other games which men call coitings, but that they apply and accustom themselves to use and draw bows and throw lances and other gentle games that appertain to arms, whereby the Irish enemies may be the better checked by the liege commons of these parts; and if any so practise the contrary, and of this be attaint, that he be taken and imprisoned, and fined at the will of our lord the king.

The statute assures us that hurling was common among the colonists; and the fact that a law had to be brought in against it would indicate its widespread nature. According to Ó Maolfabhail, similar ordinances directed against other field games began to appear early in the fourteenth century and indicate a concerted campaign under the aegis of the English Crown against such pastimes.[6] For the authorities, men engaged in the practice of hurling were not practising archery, and men skilled in archery should always be available for the king's armies.

The Statute of Kilkenny did not have the desired effect, for hurling had to be outlawed again by the Galway Statute of 1537. But men of the Pale continued to play the game in spite of prohibitions, fines, and imprisonments. The following article from the Statute of Galway is so urgent and precise that it suggests a certain irritation on the part of the legislator at the persistence of time-wasting recreations:

> It is ordered, enacted and statuted that what so ever man is found, of what degree or condition so ever he be of, playing at quoits or stones but only to shoot in long bows, short crossbows and hurling of darts or spears, to lose at every time so found in doing the same, eight pence and also at no time to use not occupy the hurling of the little ball with hockey sticks or staves, nor use no handball to play without the walls, but only the great football, on pain of the pains above limited.[7]

But this statute did not have the required effect either, as is indicated by a letter sent nine years later by King Henry VII to 'our Town of Galway' to impress on the citizens the necessity of cultivating the English way of life. In this letter the citizens are exhorted 'to the furthering of your weal, profit and commodity, and to the extirpation of all abuses hitherto used or accustomed amongst you,' to 'shave their over lips and suffer the hair of their heads to grow till it cover their ears; and that every one of them wear English caps.' Also that every inhabitant 'endeavour themself to speak English, and to use themself after the English fashion: and specially that you, and every of you, do put forth your child to school to learn to speak English, and that you fail not to fulfil these our commandments, as you tender our favour and will avoid our indignation and high displeasure.' Although the reference to games does not mention hurling, it does state 'that every man provide, with all speed, long bows and English arrows, and haunt shooting, and specially every holiday; and to leave all other unlawful games.'[8]

To an extent a fifteenth-century grave-slab in Inishowen, County Donegal, sums up this period. It carries a relief engraving of a broadsword, a ball, and a camán. The inscription is in honour of Manas mac Mhoireasdain of Iona, who was probably a gallowglass who came to Ireland to fight for an Irish chieftain. If he took pride in his ability with the broadsword he was equally proud of his hurling.

By the end of the sixteenth century both had declined in popularity. With the advent of gunpowder the broadsword as well as the archer had become obsolete; and with the advent of religious and social changes, hurling suffered in the political upheaval that followed. There are no more statutes against the playing of hurling or exhortations in favour of archery practice. The new world of the Reformation and plantations was a very different place. In future any prohibitions against hurling were to be in the interest of sabbatarianism rather than militarism. Under the new puritan dispensation, 'Dicing, Dauncing, vaine players or Enterludes, with other idle Pastimes, etc. commonly used on the Sabbath-day'[9] were to be forbidden.

2

A Popular Game in the Seventeenth and Eighteenth Centuries

Writing in 1909, Rev. St John D. Seymour relates two legends concerning Loughmore Castle, which lies half way between Thurles and Templemore in County Tipperary. According to one of them there is a remarkably level stretch of green field between the road and the railway at the Templemore end of the castle. Along one side of this is a very low mound. It is said that one of the Baron Purcells was so enamoured with the game of hurling that he kept a private team of hurlers; this field was their playing ground, and the mound served as a kind of grandstand for the spectators.

The legend goes on to relate that the best hurler in the squad was one Londergen, whose favourite feat was to stand at one end of the castle, throw up a ball, and strike it with his hurley high over the roof. Quick as lightning he would rush to the far end of the building and strike the ball back before it had time to reach the ground and so would cause it to pass and repass nine times in all over the castle without allowing it to fall to the ground.[1]

No date is given to indicate when these events were taking place. We know that the last of the Baron Purcells died in 1723, and with his death the title became defunct. Life had been difficult for him during his later years, as he was on the losing side at the Battle of the Boyne and was one of the signatories of the Treaty of Limerick. However, the time may have been a happier one after the restoration of King Charles II to the English throne in 1660 and the appointment of the Duke of Ormond as Lord Lieutenant of Ireland. The lands of the Purcells were wrested back from the Cromwellian grantees, and when Nicholas came of age in 1673 he was the inheritor of the title and the property. It may be reasonable to speculate that the years up to 1690 were a period of tranquillity for the Purcells and a time when hurling contests could take place.[2]

From the evidence at our disposal it appears that hurling was alive and flourishing in the seventeenth and eighteenth centuries. With the decline of the old Irish chieftains the game was cultivated by the new landlords, whether Old Catholic gentry like the Purcells of Loughmore or the new Protestant planter class. The eighteenth century in particular saw the growth of organised hurling, similar in many respects to the development of cricket in England. Gentry and landowners fielded teams of their tenants. Such games were well attended and involved heavy wagering. There are records of such contests from many counties, mainly in Munster and Leinster.

Teams would consist of twenty or more players, and wagers of up to 100 guineas were commonplace. The result depended on who scored the first goal, but there would frequently be return challenge matches, and the concept of the 'best of three' was not unknown, nor was the principle of changing ends after a goal had been scored. There was no set size for the field of play, nor of the goals, but the players seem to have been divided into defenders, midfielders, and forwards. On many occasions teams wore distinguishing clothing—sashes, belts, caps, or ribbons. And the game could be dangerous.[3]

The most common type of game in Leinster and Munster was *camán*, also called summer or Leinster hurling. This was a summer game that used what is now regarded as a typical hurling stick, a broad camán, and a ball of hair or leather that might be lifted with the hand or struck with the stick. This game might be played across country. It was a different game from *camánacht* or winter hurling, played generally in winter and on a restricted field of play. This resembled hockey or the Scottish game of shinty, in that it used a thin, crooked stick and a hard ball that was played solely with the stick.

According to Ó Maolfabhail,[4] summer hurling was associated with the spread of English from the south-east of the country. There are many newspaper references to summer hurling in the eighteenth century, and these bear witness to the spectator nature of the game, while *camánacht*, which was generally confined to the north of the country, seems to have been more of a player's game.

Edward MacLysaght in *Irish Life in the Seventeenth Century* gives us a clue to why the Irish landlord classes should take an interest in sport and particularly in hurling. He instances as typical of his class Sir William Temple of Staplestown, who found Ireland an agreeable place of residence. Once the gentry felt they would be allowed to remain

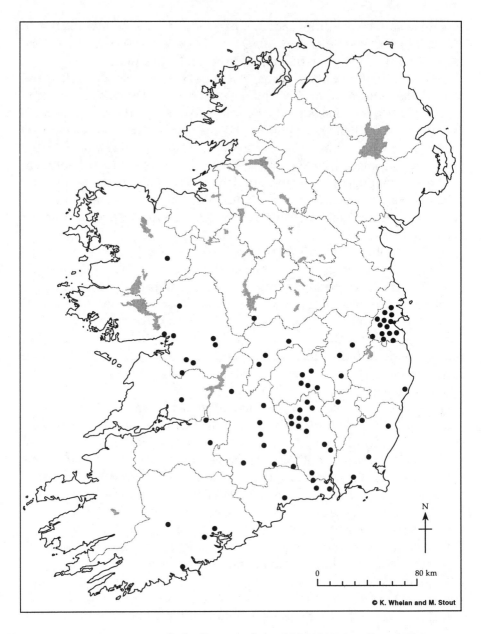

Early hurling matches, 1694–1814

undisturbed in possession of their estates, however acquired, they gave little thought to politics. 'They enjoyed life in the best way that suited their own inclinations: some lived for sport, some devoted themselves to agricultural improvements and buildings; others, emulating in a small way the first Earl of Cork, established rural universities: while the old-fashioned survivors of the bygone order attempted to keep up a pale shadow of the traditional past, with its harpers, its hospitality and its bands of irresponsible retainers.'[5] What better way of keeping them occupied than a good game of hurling!

Direct references to hurling in the seventeenth century are infrequent, but the game was certainly played. As part of the popular culture it would not be given exposure in the notices of the period: these would be confined to the activities of the upper classes. However, where the game impinged on the lives of the elite it was given mention.

One of the first references comes in 1620 from Seathrún Céitinn, who is rather scathing on the activities of the young men of his time.

> The foolish, conceited young men of today, however, do not consider the quirks of fate when they are enjoying themselves and leading a wild life, playing ball, shooting darts and arrows, and contending and hurling, drinking and playing, swearing and babbling.[6]

The reverend gentleman would see these activities, including hurling, as an occasion of sin and devoid of 'decency, diligence, gravity, modesty, orderliness, prudence, reason, self-control, sobriety and thrift.'[7]

Lord Orrery, who was then styled President of Munster, in a letter dated 9 July 1667 mentions a great meeting of Irish Catholics in Clanwilliam on the edge of the Barony of Kilnamanagh in County Tipperary 'under pretence of a match of hurling'[8]—again a member of the elite frowning on the activities of the populace. However, there is a direct reference to landlord involvement in an account given by an Englishman who visited the south of Ireland in 1673:

> The Irish gentry are musically disposed, and therefore many of them play singular well upon the Irish harp: they effect also to play at tables [backgammon]. The common sort meet oftentimes in great numbers in plain meadows or ground to recreate themselves at a play called bandy, with balls and crooked sticks, much after our play of stoe-ball ...[9]

Another English writer, Thomas Dineley, who has left an account of a journey from Dublin to Limerick, thence to Youghal and back to England,wrote:

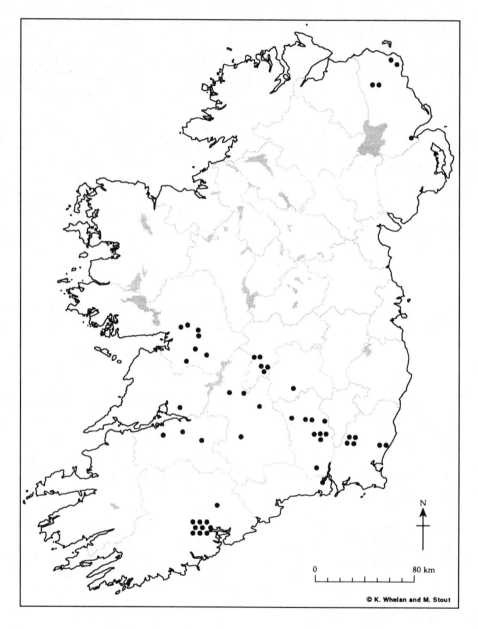

All-Ireland Club Hurling Championship Finalists, 1971-96

Gameing and laziness they are much addicted to, their chiefest games are five-cards, all fours, etc. In the meadows, at bandy and stoe-ball etc., at which they will play away all, to their very cloaks, which are the last moveable.[10]

The two references to 'bandy' are really to hurling. Bandy was a popular game in England, played with a ball and stick. The word means 'bent'.

One of the most detailed descriptions of hurling comes from the pen of John Dunton, who came to Ireland in 1698 and opened a bookshop. He travelled a little through the country and left accounts of his experiences. The following describes what he saw in Kildare:

And now I think I may say something to you about the sports used among the Irish on their holidays. One exercise they use very much is their hurling, which has something in it not unlike the play called Mall. When the cows are casting their hair, they pull it off their backs and with their hands work it into large balls that grow very hard. This ball they use at the hurling which they strike with a stick called a commaan about three foot and a half in the handle. At the lower end it is crooked and about three inches broad, and on this broad part you may sometimes see one of the gamesters carry the ball tossing it for 40 or 50 yards in spite of all of the adverse players: and when he is like to lose it, he generally gives it a great stroke to drive it towards the goal. Sometimes if he misses his blow at the ball, he knocks one of the opposers down, at which no resentment is to be shown. They seldom come off with broken heads or shins in which they glory so much. At this sport one parish or barony challenges another; they pick out 10, 12 or 20 players of a side, and the prize is generally a barrel or two of ale, which is brought on to the field and drunk off by the victors on the spot, though the vanquished are not without a share too. This commonly is upon some very large plain, the barer the grass the better, and the goals are 200 or 300 yards one from the other; whichever party drives the ball between the other's goal wins the day. Their champions are of the younger and more active among them, and their kindred and mistresses are frequently spectators of their address. Two or three bagpipes attend the conquerors at the barrel's head and then play them out of the field. At some of these meetings two thousand have been present.[11]

A further piece of evidence of the existence of the game in the seventeenth century comes from a most unlikely source. The Cosbys were an Elizabethan family that settled in Stradbally, County Laois, in 1563. The first of the line was notorious for his cruelty to the Irish. A descendent of his was Dudley Cosby, who died in 1729. His son, Pole, wrote thus about him in his autobiography:

> He danced on the ropes as well as any rope dancer that ever was. He was a fine tennis and five player, a most extraordinary fine hurler and very fond of all those things, and practised them very much when he was young and able ...[12]

So the planter stock had fallen in love with hurling, just as their predecessors the Scullys had. Significantly, Dudley Crosby and Nicholas Purcell would have been contemporaries, and the distance between Stradbally and Templemore is not very great. It is conceivable that they had a contest between their estate teams, with a hefty wager on the winner.

One of the earliest newspaper references to hurling in the eighteenth century appears in 1708. It is as follows:

> Tully Fair next St. Swithin's Day, the 15th of July and always after will be kept on that part of the lands of Tully next the Curragh. About three in the afternoon will be a hurling match on the Curragh, between 30 men from each side of the Liffey for 30 shillings. A barrel of ale, tobacco and pipes will be given to the hurlers.[13]

Most of the hurling matches mentioned in the notices were played between May and November. The venues were chiefly Dublin and the Munster-Leinster border. Frequent mention is made of gentlemen, and sometimes the attendance of the nobility is noted. For instance, in 1741 a match between Tipperary and Cork was played in which each side was patronised by a local man of standing.

The style of hurling referred to is Leinster or summer hurling, and the notices are chiefly in the English newspapers. There is one reference to summer hurling outside the Munster-Leinster area and that is in County Galway. It comes from the pen of Coquebert de Montbret, a Frenchman in the employment of the diplomatic service of the revolutionary French government who was stationed in Ireland from 1789 to 1791, at a time when France had no diplomatic representation in England. He was a shrewd and sympathetic observer, and during his time in Ireland he travelled widely through the country on foot, accompanied by his young son. His thoroughness can be gauged from the fact that he seems to have acquired a fair knowledge of Irish at a time when this was considered to be a badge of inferiority. His diaries are often merely notes, disjointed and hurriedly written. Writing in the neighbourhood of Loughrea, County Galway, he says:

It is the month of August that the playing of hurley commences. Each team is divided into three groups, the back guard the goal, and strive to prevent the ball from passing there. Another group is in front to prevent the enemy's ball from repassing from their side, that is the middle; the third or the whip is on the field between the middle and their opponents' back to force the ball to pass under the goal. The game is played only in Munster and Connacht, in Leinster football is played. In Ulster the Presbyterians are scandalised by Sunday play.[14]

The French observer goes on to state that the game is usually played in a commonage or turlough. The hurling ball is made of cow's hair knitted tightly together and with a leather covering. The sides wear different-coloured hats. It is frightening the way they used to make for each other. The ordinary people gather to watch the play and amuse themselves by dancing.

There are other references from this period to show that hurling flourished in Galway. One match was played in Meelick in 1798. It was quite common for Meelick to cross the Shannon and play a team in Offaly or Tipperary. In a letter to the editor of the *Irish World* on 15 September 1888 'A Galway Man' had this to say about the area:

Many readers of *The Irish World* residing in this country can call upon pleasant memories of hard-fought games some 30 or 40 years ago between the men of Tipperary and Galway on the verdant sod of the Shannon's banks, stretching from Portumna to Meelick, having for a background the ancient castle of Redwood, standing out in bold relief against the green hillsides of noble Tipperary.

According to Pádraic Ó Laoi, 'At Kilkerrin near Clonbeirne hurling matches were played in Madden's field, which has been used for centuries as a hurling field.'[15] Michael Cusack had learned of this hurling tradition in south-east Galway from his early teaching days in Lough Cultra school, not far from Gort. Later, in 1883, when he began to reorganise athletics in the country so that they would be open to everybody, his call was answered in the town of Killimor through the exertions of F. W. Lynch and Patrick Larkin and a few others, and the game of hurling was organised in the area. But this is to anticipate events.

The quotation above would seem to conflict with the evidence of the newspaper notices, which were confined to the Leinster-Munster area. A poem in praise of Robaird Elliott of Clonmore, County Kilkenny,[16] mentions the game; and tradition has it that the poet Donncha Rua Mac

Conmara, who was in his prime about the same time, was a hurler of prowess. The story of his life mentions a hurling match between the pupils of the school in which he may have been teaching in County Waterford and the other youths of the district.[17] Brian Merriman also mentions hurling in his famous poem 'on the smooth plain of every true hurling at dancing, sporting, racing, and diversion.'

There is another reference to hurling in the famous song 'Príosún Chluain Meala', which probably refers to the Whiteboy period. The youthful prisoner thinks of his fate and of former happy times; now his camán lies warping and mouldering under his bed while he is languishing in the prison in Clonmel. In one verse, given in an English version by J. J. Callanan and published in 1830, the poet says:

> Next Sunday the patron
> at home will be keeping
> and the young active hurlers
> the field will be sweeping.

Many of the newspaper references to hurling are advertisements for the games and appear in *Finn's Leinster Journal*. There are few reports of the games themselves; one such is in the *Hibernian Journal* for 17 October 1792:

> Yesterday, Tuesday, a hurling match took place in the Phoenix Park, which was honoured with the presence of Her Excellency, the Countess of Westmoreland, and several of the nobility and gentry, besides a vast concourse of spectators. Much agility and athletic contention took place, and great diversion was afforded, until the spectators forced into the playing ground. Colonel Lennox, Mr. Daly, and several other gentlemen, most obligingly used their endeavours to prevent any interruptions to the players, but to no effect. This active contest ended without either side claiming triumph and remains to be yet decided.

There is a reference in the *Dublin Courant* of 19 May 1748 to a grand hurling match on the commons of 'Crumbling' between the provinces of Munster and Leinster for a considerable wager. We are told that Leinster won and that the sides had a return the following month and Leinster won again. *Faulkner's Dublin Journal* has a report on the return game in its edition of 4 June 1748:

> A few weeks ago there was a grand match of hurling at Crumlin Commons between the Provinces of Leinster and Munster, in which the former came off victorious. In consequence of this, last

Tuesday [31 May] a chosen set from Munster engaged an equal number of their conquerors at the same exercise and made their utmost efforts to retrieve their honour, but all to no purpose: for Leinster after about an hour's struggle gained a complete victory.

The paper even adds a triumphalist verse:

Southern powers, in vain 'gainst East unite,
The South is doomed to thread the Northern flight,
Gallea to Britain quits the glorious field,
To Leinster, Munster ever forced to yield.[18]

In the following year there is another reference to this rivalry in the *Dublin Courant* of 20 May, according to which 'a great Match was played at Crumlin between the Munster and Leinster hurlers, which continued until night obliged them to give over.'

The *Universal Advertiser* for 17 July 1753 advertises a hurling match again at Crumlin 'for a Silver Laced Hat, value £1-2-9 by any 24 men, they subscribing their names to the Clerk of the Course before the day of the hurling and paying a British 6ď each.'

The Dublin correspondent of the *Corke Journal* records on 22 September 1755 that there was a grand match of hurling 'between the Gentlemen of the counties of Dublin and Kildare played lately on the common of Lyon at which the Marquis of Huntington, Lord Lieutenant and a most brilliant appearance of nobility and gentry were present.' Two years later almost to the day the *Universal Advertiser* announced a hurling match on Irishtown Green near Dublin between 'Married Men and Bachelors for 50 gns. a side, exactly at 4 o'clock. The Green is to be corded.' Obviously a fine crowd expected.

Finn's Leinster Journal reports in July 1768 on a dispute that arose at a hurling match on the commons of Gowran, County Kilkenny, in which one Anthony Langford received a stroke of a hurley that fractured his skull; he was carried to the County Hospital, with little hopes of recovery. Several others were also wounded.

The same paper announced the following month a grand hurling match to be played between Kilkenny and Tipperary at the fair-green of Urlingford for 20 guineas. 'Some of the principal Gentlemen of both counties are concerned.' A month later the same paper is advertising a grand hurling match on the green of Gurteen, near Durrow, between the hurlers of the baronies of Galmoy and Ossory for 100 guineas a side. In the same month the paper announced: 'The grandest match that was ever hurled in Ireland will be played on Thursday the 8th day of September between the provinces of Munster and Leinster, for 68 guineas, at the noted green of Lisduff near Urlingford.'

An unusual notice appears in the *Freeman's Journal* in October 1768 of a hurling match for 20 guineas a side between the gentlemen of the County of Meath and those of the County of Kerry that was played out in the long fields, Bloomsbury, London, and after a hard struggle was won by the Meath Gentlemen.

In July 1769 *Finn's Leinster Journal* advertises two games. One is to be played at Galberstown, near Thurles: 'Three baronies against all Ireland for 100 guineas a side, play or pay. The Ball is to be thrown up at precisely 4 o'clock.' The second notice is for a game to be played on 16 July on the noted green of Quonthobus near Urlingford for a wager of 20 guineas. The names of the teams are not given. This game didn't take place, and there is a notice in the *Journal* two weeks later stating that it would go ahead on 30 July. 'Some of the Gentlemen of the Counties of Kilkenny and Tipperary are concerned. There will also be a Bridle and Saddle run at the said green before the Ball is thrown up, which will be 5 o'clock.'

Tipperary and Kilkenny are reported as playing at Tibrachney, County Kilkenny, in October 1770. Kilkenny won. The *Dublin Evening Post* carries the following report on 12 August 1779: 'Notwithstanding that Mr. Sheriff Worthington dispersed a surprising multitude of people gathered on Sunday for a hurling match in the Phoenix Park, they had the audacity last Sunday evening to assemble again, and repeat their innocent diversion, so well-suited to the Sabbath, and so disgraceful to the authorities of the Park, which could easily suppress them, if properly executed.' There is a report of a bad game at Churchtown, near Carrick-on-Suir, in September 1788 between Tipperary and Waterford. It was played on a piece of ground as bad as ever was chosen: 'A miserable match it was: play commenced at nightfall and lasted only 10 minutes.'

One of the most detailed accounts of a hurling match in the eighteenth century, which took place about 1770, is to be found in a manuscript written in 1831 by Father Matt Horgan, then parish priest of Blarney. He states that he received the account from a few of his parishioners whose fathers had been eyewitnesses to the event.

> The leaders of the respective teams were Rowland Davies of Dawstown, Blarney, a landlord's son and Denis Horgan of Ballynaraha, in the same parish, who was son to a prosperous farmer. Forty days were required to publish the terms of the impending contest and to assemble the players. Davies invited every hurler from Blarney to the western coast, brought them together and exercised them the day before the day appointed.

The plain on which the match was fought was by the river Awmartin, a little north-west of Garrycloyne Chapel and a few miles north of Blarney. The playing field was almost three-quarters of a mile in length, without fence, hollow or slough, surrounded by hills which sloped gently to its verge.

Tents were pitched on both sides of the river, well filled with provisions to feed the spectators and the match was held on a fine day in the month of July, when the grass was dry and short and the ground elastic underfoot.

Davies had his men clad in the most becoming manner. On the head was worn a green cap fringed with a band. A green ribbon bound the collars and wrists of the shirts and a red sash was around the waist. A white trouser was worn but the feet were bare lest any covering on them might retard the speed of the player.

The number of players allowed on each side was fifty and by noon Davies' men were drawn up in order before the tents, whence they marched to the centre of the plain, where they formed into line. The music of the pipes, under a green flag flying, swelled the gentle breeze. Davies stood at the head dressed in a similar costume to those of his men and distinguished only by his cap which was silk, fringed with deep gold lace and decorated by a feather. He was then about twenty-two years of age and deemed the manly figure in County Cork.

In contrast Horgan contented himself with selecting men from around Cork city and the districts of Whitechurch, Carrignavar and Glenville. They were all well known to him as being youthful, active and well-acquainted with each other from their frequent meetings at local hurling matches. A few famous hurlers from the Youghal and Midleton districts heard of the forthcoming match, offered to try their fortunes and were duly enlisted by him in the team.

Horgan's men were on the eastern side of the little river and at a given signal he marched them into the field. Their dress was plain, simple and becoming. They were of a hardy appearance, well inured to labour and, seemingly, not discouraged by the splendid appearance of their opponents.

Another signal was sounded and both sides formed with extended lines, having each three divisions. The strongest and ablest men were placed in the main body, consisting of twenty-six men and the more youthful and active constituted the two wings, twelve on each side. At both extremities of the plain, two lofty poles had been erected between which the ball should be impelled to decide the victory. The teams, consisting of one hundred handsome looking men, with hurleys in hand, stood facing each other until the plain was cleared.

On casting lots, Horgan won and decided to play facing the southern goalposts though the sun's rays were shining in their faces. Then the round, elastic, well-covered ball was thrown in and the battle commenced. Both teams flew like lightning to oppose each other and such feats of activity, strength and exertion were never witnessed on that plain.

The two captains were in the midst of the fray and did everything possible to encourage the men. The game continued for two hours and nobody succeeded in obtaining the much coveted goal. Sometimes the men of the east bore the ball south but O'Sullivan from Beara and Healy from the Shoornagh Valley proved invincible. They are described as having the strength of heroes and successfully repelled all attacks.

At length when the players showed signs of exhaustion, Davies called for a cessation. This was granted and all went to their tents for some refreshments. They rested their wearied limbs for a time and resumed the game with renewed vigour. Now the McForien Duv (O'Sullivan) from Kerry, O'Leary from the Rooves, O'Donovan and McCarthy McDanial from Dripsey, Barrett from Drimoleague and many other men from the west bore down all before them but they met Barry of Dunbulloge, Buckley of Moah, Keily and MacCody of Cuil, Murphy of Rath and the Millers' brave son, who was born and reared on the banks of the Dubhglaise (Douglas). The shock was tremendous, many were levelled to the ground and the shouts of the spectators ascended to the high heavens, so that it would appear some great battle conflict between the nations in progress. The Millers' brave son had to withdraw, being hurt in the shock between McForien Duv of the seagirt hills and himself.

The sun was now approaching the western hills and both sides strengthened themselves for a deciding effort. Young Cronin from the Boggeragh watched keenly for a chance and stood at a little distance from his opponent. When the ball came he impelled it before him with such velocity that no enemy could outstrip him until he directed it between the two lofty poles and gained the victory.

Davies was so proud of his team winning that he forgave Horgan the wager. He entertained both sides and their friends at his hospitable mansion from which they departed the next day, each to his own part of the country. Some years later Rowland Davies died in Antigua in the West Indies to the grief of everybody who knew him. The hurleys used on the day, whether broken or whole, were kept by the players during their lives as a memorial of that well-fought struggle on the banks of the Awmartin.[19]

All these references are to summer hurling. The heyday of this inter-barony or inter-provincial hurling was in the middle of the eighteenth century, when great crowds attended. The matches were organised by the gentry and big landowners, who fielded teams of their tenants. When betting had been particularly heavy, trouble ensued.

In the earlier decades of the century the games were played on weekdays, because of the strict application of the Lord's Observance Act, which had been passed by the Irish Parliament in 1695 and prohibited 'hurling, commoning [ground hurling] and football on the Lord's Day with the penalty of twelve pence for each offence.'

On the other hand, the decline in camánacht was already noticeable. There are few references to it in the seventeenth and eighteenth centuries, and it began to wane rapidly in the nineteenth century. It seems to have persisted longest where English influence from Dublin was weak and where therefore the traditional Irish way of life was general. When that way of life came under pressure in the nineteenth century through the oppression of poverty and famine the traditional game of camánacht began to disappear. Information in the parish survey carried out by the Ordnance Survey between 1825 and 1840 shows that sport and recreation of all kinds were on the decline as a result of economic hardship as well as the exertions of the clergy of all denominations in putting down what they considered the wild behaviour associated with the games. It would appear that the Catholic Church was joining the Protestant churches in the desire for orderliness and respectability.

Towards the end of the eighteenth century a change came about in the relationship between the landlords and the people that led to the former abandoning their patronage of the game. A number of reasons have been suggested; among these are the European phenomenon of the abandonment of popular culture by the nobility. Peter Burke[20] gives a vivid account of this development:

The nobles were adopting more 'polished' manners, a new and more self-conscious style of behaviour, modelled on the courtesy books ... Noblemen were learning to exercise self-control, to behave with a studied nonchalance, to cultivate a sense of style and to move in a dignified manner as if engaging in a formal dance

... Noblemen stopped eating in great halls with their retainers and withdrew into separate dining-rooms ... They stopped wrestling with their peasants, as they used to do in Lombardy, and they stopped killing bulls in public as they used to do in Spain. The noblemen learned to speak and write 'correctly' according to formal rules and to avoid technical terms and the dialect words used by craftsmen and peasants.

One can imagine the change in Ireland—a Cosby or a Purcell coming to the conclusion that they were superior persons, and their need to avoid contamination from the 'people'. Mixing with retainers in a game of hurling was no longer possible; even riding up and down the field wielding a whip during the game and keeping the yokels in check was no longer the done thing. Placing wagers and sharing the barrel of ale after the game would be completely detrimental to their new image.

Another reason for the change was that such gatherings, as advertised in the newspapers, might be suspected of seditious undertones in the changing political climate of the last years of the century. This had come about as a result of Whiteboy activity and later of the United Irishmen and the Rising of 1798. The developments in Wexford and the south-east destroyed the political relationship between landlord and tenant. Another aspect of the events was the great slaughter of thousands of men of hurling age in the south-east. The Act of Union and the Napoleonic wars altered the way of life of many landlords, turning them into absentees and bringing to an end the great days of barony hurling and landlord patronage.

3

--- The Rules of the Game ---

Hurling as we know it today is a different game from what it was in the time of Cú Chulainn or during the golden age of hurling in the eighteenth century. And yet the basic ingredients stay the same: a camán, a sliotar, and the desire of one group to get the ball into a goal and of another group to keep it out. The number of players may have changed, so too the size of the crowds, the speed of the game, and the nature of the venue, but the stick, the ball and the attempts to score a goal have remained constant.

Of the many references to hurling in newspapers and journals from past centuries, one from the eighteenth-century newspaper *Pue's Occurrences* describes a match between Galway and Clare, played at Gort on 16 October 1759:

> There was a grand Hurling Match in the neighbourhood of Gort in the county for a considerable sum of Money between the counties of Galway and Clare; the Hurlers of the latter made a very handsome Appearance. They marched from Gort to the Turlough, two miles distant, preceded by the Band of Musick, a French Horn, a Running Footman and a Fellow in an Antic or Harlequin Dress. None of the hurlers were in the least hurt, the greatest Harmony having subsisted. The County of Clare Hurlers were elegantly entertained at Crushenehaire the Night following and a Hundred guineas was proposed to be Hurled for, but the Time and Place not yet agreed. The above procession closed with many Carriages and Horsemen, the numerous company at the Turlough made a fine appearance.[1]

The description suggests that the match had all the colour and excitement of the modern inter-county championship. The handsome appearance of the Galway team hints that their mode of dress was somewhat superior to that of Clare. The carriages and the horsemen suggest a well-heeled bunch of supporters; the band recalls the Artane Boys' Band on All-Ireland final day. The only serious difference is the prize that was played for, 100 guineas, a very substantial sum in those days.

But we are told nothing about the rules of the game in this or in similar reports. One of the greatest authorities on the history of the game, Liam Ó Caithnia, points out that eighteenth-century hurling had no book of rules as we understand the term today, partly because technical fouls were unknown and partly because the standard rules were so well known. He goes on, however, to express the belief that a set of rules would have to be agreed on for all games of any consequence, and they would be something like the following.

There was an equal number of players, usually twenty-one, on each side. The goal was different from today's, being usually a flexible stick with each end stuck in the ground. It was about three feet wide and high enough to allow a grown man to run through. The ball had to be carried through the bow, in either direction, to score; it could not be struck through the goal as it is today. Goalkeepers were unnecessary and forbidden, and points were unknown. The first team to score a goal won the game. Often two games out of three decided the match, these games being played in one evening or on three different evenings.

Ó Caithnia goes on to say that each player had to wear a distinguishing colour or dress. The game was partly professional, in the sense that players received prizes, whether of cash or otherwise, for their efforts. Wagers were also allowed. There were sidelines, but they were there not to keep the players in, as there were no sideline cuts, but rather to keep the spectators from encroaching. There was no such thing as a referee: the captains were responsible for controlling the play and the conduct of the players.

The teams also lined out differently from today. The captain stood forty yards in front of the goal and was forbidden to stand nearer it unless the ball went closer to it than he was. On each side of him were three players; the seven together were called the *cúl báire* or the 'back'. The four players on the outside of the seven had to be first-class runners and fearless attackers. To the three in the middle fell the responsibility of saving the goal at all costs, since once that was crossed the match was all over.

Standing in the middle of the field and acting in a way similar to the scrum in rugby was the 'phalanx'. They used longer and much heavier hurleys than the other fourteen players, which could only be swung by keeping the dominant hand near the boss. The phalanx were heavy, slow-footed men, who always played as a single unit, standing close together. They never took the ball away on a solo run, never lifted it on the boss, and never managed a long puck. Their duty was to keep the ball moving in short jabs, and they were entitled to strike on their right side only, never on the left, which was offside. A man who was clearly offside might justifiably be struck across the shins with a hurley! Because these players always moved in packs there was always danger from swiping hurleys when they came to grips with their opposite numbers. There was little of an attractive nature in the play of the phalanx and little that was challenging or exciting.

Between the *cúl báire* and the phalanx were the remaining seven players on the team. They stood slightly closer to the phalanx than to the *cúl báire*. The central three were known as the 'whips' and the end pairs as *na heitill* or the 'flies'. The duty of the whips was to wait for any ball that was jabbed or hooked out from the two phalanxes. When such a ball was hooked out the whip sprang on it, whipped it away, and drove it out to the flies on the right or the left. The moment the flies got hold of it they darted away at top speed, ball on boss, in an attempt to score a goal by crossing the goal-line with the ball. The flies did not strike the ball forward, as they would in today's game, because there were no forwards. If the ball were struck forward then possession would be given away. In fact it was considered offside to be standing nearer the opponents' goal than the ball was. The ball divided the field between the two teams, and the entire team stood behind the ball. The result was that there were no free pucks, no sideline cuts, and no puck-outs, because any of these strokes would be giving the ball away to the opposing side.

The flies carried the ball forward on their hurleys. If a fly was challenged he passed the ball back over his shoulder to the fly that followed. If he kept going forward he had to contend with the opposing phalanx and the opposing flies who had got back in time to defend the goal with their *cúl báire*. The result was that it was very difficult to score a goal, and in fact very few goals were scored. Occasionally if a fly was halted in his tracks he struck the ball forward, past the goal. The reason for this was that since the captain had to be forty yards from his goal, the opposing fly would hope to beat the captain and his fellow-defenders in the run for the ball, retrieve it, and carry it through the goal for a score and the match.

Although no helmets were worn, injuries were few and far between. The games were orderly because the landed classes were endlessly associated with hurling teams and hurling men and were openly and actively involved as players, captains of teams, trainers, managers, and powerful patrons. Moreover they gambled, according to their fashion, at every match, and their presence was a guarantee of strictly enforced rules. As Ó Caithnia continues, 'but more than all these things combined, more than the fields that they gave to practice, more than the hurleys and the balls and the outfits they so proudly presented to their hurling followers, more than all these things together, the landed gentry of the eighteenth century—but not the nineteenth—gave to hurling what it needed above all else and what they alone were capable of giving it, crowd-control, disciplined, restrained loyalty. They have been accused of trampling down the crowds, of the over use of the whip, of merciless disregard for the exuberant supporters of the great and colourful teams of the day. Perhaps so, but such accusations were never made by the peasantry—the ones who should know best, for win or lose or draw, at least the match would be finished provided only the moneyed class were there. No wonder the eighteenth century has been called the Golden Age of Hurling.'[2]

Wrestling and jostling were allowed, however roughly, but not the use of timber on an opponent. Handling the ball was strictly forbidden at all times, but the ball must be carried or tapped on the boss of the hurley. When neither team scored, the side that brought the ball nearest to the opponents' goal was the one that was deemed to have won. Lying on the ball was also strictly forbidden. The decision of the umpires was to be accepted at all times. The winning team in the first-of-three match had the right of nominating the pitch for the second match.

According to Ó Caithnia, 'two rules not included here are those concerning tripping and hooking because the evidence relating to them is doubtful. It seems probable, but not certain, that the rule of tripping came with the introduction of football in the late seventeenth century. There is very little evidence of the practice of hooking but the most probable explanation of this is that early hurling did not lend itself much to the habit of hooking. The doubt remains, however, for the "explanation" is not wholly convincing.'[3]

The fascinating thing about these rules is the many similarities to be found in modern rugby. It has already been mentioned that the opposing phalanxes served a purpose similar to the scrum. The whips did the same job as the out-half in getting the ball out to the wing, where the flies ran with it. The ball wasn't kicked forward, lest possession be lost, unless there was a chance that the cúl báire could be beaten in the run to the line. The ball was passed backwards, and occasionally a maul developed between the two phalanxes. Finally, the phalanx consisted of heavy, slow-footed men, while the flies were men of speed and agility, ready to run at the slightest chance.

One of the first sets of rules for hurling was adopted at a meeting of the Killimor Hurling Club, County Galway, on 22 February 1885. There was a long tradition of hurling in east Galway, and the Killimor Club was conscious of the fact that if the GAA were to progress there was an urgent need to standardise play by drawing up a set of rules. The rules they drew up and adopted 'until a general meeting of the GAA be held on next November' were as follows:[4]

1. Each team, when hurling, must wear a different colour for the purpose of distinction.
2. Three umpires to be appointed on each side who have the power to order any hurler to cease playing, who in their opinion is under the influence of strong drink, who loses his temper or strikes an opponent intentionally. Should the hurler refuse to do so, the opposing team may claim the prize that is being played for.
3. Should any hurler, when jostling, use his hurl so as to bring it into contact with his opponent with a view to injuring him, he must cease hurling when told to do so by any of the umpires. Penalty the same as Rule 2.
4. No hurler can get a substitute, except he meets with an accident which in the opinion of the umpires renders him unable to play.
5. No hurler is allowed, when playing to handle the ball, which must, in order to secure a count, be hurled over or through the goal.
6. Should the ball go outside the goalposts it is to be taken back by one of the umpires and placed at a distance of no more than thirty yards from the said goal.
7. The time and number of the goals to be agreed on by the captains before commencing play, and the majority of the goals constitutes the winner.
8. Bystanders to have no voice in any decision and should they interfere with the hurlers in any way, they may be considered by the umpires and judges as preventing the game from being fairly played, the aggrieved hurlers may claim the prize.
9. In cases of dispute, the umpires and/or three of the judges combined must decide by ballot. From this decision there is no appeal.
10. On the decision being declared, the stakeholder must hand over the prize to the captain of the winning team.

Although these rules were published only in 1885, Pádraig Puirséal in his book *The GAA and Its Time* expresses the opinion that they were in existence as early as 1869. The rules dealt only with the conduct of the players on the field and the place of the umpires and judges. They did not give details of the playing area, the height and width of the goalposts, the number of players on each side, or the regulations on sidelines, wides, and frees.

By the time these rules were published the GAA had drawn up its own set, adopted at a meeting in Thurles on 17 January 1885 and published in *United Ireland* on 7 February 1885. They addressed a number of issues not covered in the Killimor Rules. The ground was to be as near as possible 200 yards long and 150 yards wide. There were to be boundary lines at least five yards from the perimeter fence. The upright posts of the goals were to be 20 feet apart and the crossbar 10 feet from the ground. A goal was scored when the ball was driven between the posts and under the crossbar. The ball was not to be lifted off the ground with the hand when in play. The number of players was to be not less than fourteen and not more than twenty-one at any time.

There was to be an umpire for each side as well as a referee, who was to decide in cases where the umpires disagreed. It was the referee's job to keep the time and to throw up the ball at the beginning of each half. The time of play was to be one hour and twenty minutes, and sides were to be changed at half-time. Before play the hurlers were to draw up in two lines in the centre of the field opposite each other and catch hands, or hurleys across, then separate. The referee should then throw the ball along the ground between the players or high over their heads.

No player was to catch, trip or push from behind. The penalty for the offence was disqualification and a free puck to the opposing team. No player was to bring his hurley intentionally in contact with the person of another player, with the same penalty for doing so. When the ball was driven over the sidelines it was to be thrown in towards the middle of the ground by the referee or by one of the umpires, but if it rebounded into the ground it was considered to be in play. When the ball was driven over the end lines and not through the goal the player defending the goal should have a free puck on the ground twenty yards from the goalposts. Players whose goal it was should stand on the goal-line until the ball was struck. Hitting both right and left was allowed.[5]

It would be too much to expect that old rules and old traditions would easily and suddenly be set aside and the new rules accepted. According to the historians of the GAA, early matches under the rules 'led to exciting scenes, in which not only players but also spectators become participants.

Physical violence between members of teams was not unknown; the encroachment of spectators on to the playing field often terminated a match abruptly and the referee enjoyed no particular immunity from rough handling. His person was by no means sacrosanct. The occasions on which he was subject to physical violence, however, were rare. He was sometimes more patriotic than efficient, and the umpires were not always free from the suspicion of bias. Teams walked off the field when dissatisfied with the referee's decision and matches were often replayed for no other reason than that they were unfinished owing to the fault of the players themselves or their enthusiastic supporters. The cry was raised that the Sabbath was being desecrated, that publicans were making fortunes and that faction fighting was being revived. All kinds of horrors and calamities were being predicted. Notwithstanding everything, however, the games were being played with enthusiasm and in time the impetuous Celtic temperament began to respect the laws which were made by themselves and framed to prevent violence, to teach self-restraint and coolness and to develop hurling on scientific lines.'[6]

It will come as a surprise to many to learn that wrestling was permitted in hurling matches up to the end of 1886. Two players who came into collision at once got into hand grips. Only one fall was allowed. If players attempted a second fall on the occasion, the referee intervened.

The Second Annual Convention of the GAA, in November 1886, revised a number of the rules. For full-sized teams, of twenty-one players, the field should be 196 yards long and 140 yards wide. There should be an umpire at each goal to watch the goals and points. The goalposts should be 21 feet apart and the crossbar $10\frac{1}{2}$ feet from the ground. Beside the goalposts, side point posts were also provided for the first time. For certain breaches of the rule, including striking another player with the hurley, the referee was given the power to send the offender off for the whole or part of the balance of the game.

The time of the play was now to be one hour and the sides were to change at half time. No player from the opposite side was to advance closer than twenty-one yards until the ball had been pucked out, and no player from the striker's side was to be further out from his own goal than the centre of the field until the ball was pucked. The match would be decided by the greater number of goals and where no goals were scored by the greater number of points. The ball could be struck with the hand or kicked. It might be caught off the ground, and the player so catching it might puck it in any way that he pleased, but he must not carry it, except on the hurley, or throw it.

In spite of all the rules, it remains difficult to envisage one of the early games. One of the first great hurling matches was that between North Tipperary and South Galway in the Phoenix Park, Dublin, on 16 February 1886. It was reported as a fine game of vigorous hurling and lasted eighty minutes. Only one score, a goal, was registered, and the match was refereed by Michael Cusack. Tipperary won, and the teams were twenty-one a side.

Apart from specifying the length and breadth of the field and of the goals, the duration of the game, and how it should be started and restarted when the ball went out of play, there was very little on the rules of the game itself. And who decided how many were to play on each side, since the rule laid down between fourteen and twenty-one? The conclusion must be drawn that the rules in early games were of a very tentative nature and had to draw strongly on the traditional local ones. North Tipperary and south Galway probably had much in common by virtue of geographical proximity, but the same cannot be said for games between more distant places.

Whatever about the rules, the two fundamental requisites for the game were the hurley and the sliotar. The basic shape of the hurley has not changed much down through the ages: it remains a crooked stick. The word 'camán', incorporating the word for crooked, *cam*, recognises its essential nature. From examples in the National Museum it would appear that the evolution has been from a narrow crooked stick to a broader one. (It is significant that the width of the hurley had to be controlled some years ago because those being used by goalkeepers were getting wider and wider. Under the regulation the width could not be more than 5 inches or 13 cm. A similar regulation had to be brought in to control the width of the cricket bat during the evolution of that game.)

Ash is regarded as the traditional and the ideal wood for the making of hurleys. It has a flexibility that is necessary for withstanding the impact of two hurleys coming into contact with each other. But although ash is by far the most common type of wood used today, this was not always so. According to Ó Caithnia, 'almost every kind of wood grown in Ireland was used for the making of hurleys: ash, holly, rowan, sally (black and white), box, poplar, blackthorn, whitethorn, larch, hazel, elder, elm and so on.'[7] At one time an attempt was made to get a cheap supply of hurleys in the United States by making them out of hickory, but they splintered easily in clashes.

To preserve their hurleys, players have always banded them with some form of light metal. This banding of hurleys has a long history. According to mythology, it even goes back to the time of Cú Chulainn, when the better-off players banded their hurleys in expensive metals such as bronze. On the other hand, ordinary folk used tin and even wire.

The hurleys also differed in shape, with a narrow-bossed hurley used by the phalanxes of a 21-man eighteenth-century team and the *cúl báire*, the whips and the flies using a light, broad-bossed stick. One of the significant developments of today is the standardisation of the shape. There is little regional variation, at least to the eyes of the non-player. The chief development during the twentieth century has been away from the longer boss, which facilitated moving the ball along the ground, to the shorter, stubbier and more compact stick that makes lifting and striking in the air much easier and more certain. In fact the evolution in the shape of the hurley came with the change in the game from about the late sixties, from the slower game that emphasised ground hurling, hip-to-hip combat, and encounters of strength. The longer-bossed hurley was ideal for this style of play. With the development of a higher level of athleticism and speed in players, a different game was called for. This emphasised possession, which demanded getting the ball into the hand, and this in turn required a more manageable stick that made it easier to pick the ball up off the ground.

One of the most notable authorities on the game today and one who has been involved in the making of hurleys for a number of decades is Justin McCarthy of Cork. He is convinced that there are still regional variations in the making of hurleys. He would recognise the Wexford hurley as very distinctive, with a stubbier and more compact boss than that in use in Tipperary, Cork, or Limerick. The Wexford style of stick is also preferred in Galway. Both teams emphasise the skills of getting the ball into the hand, either by grabbing it from the air or picking it quickly off the ground. While we associate this type of play with Kilkenny also, McCarthy believes the hurley used in that county has a longer boss than the Wexford one and is more suited to ground hurling, even though they prefer the picking game. Another variation he has observed from his journeys around the hurling counties is that the Clare hurley tends to be longer than the Cork one, being on average over 37 inches to a more usual 36 inches in Cork.

The sliotar has been reduced dramatically in size and in weight since the foundation of the GAA. In earlier days the ball was made from cattle or horse hair. When the animals were coating in the summer, the short body hairs were collected and rolled between the palms of the hand. When the hair became matted, consolidated and compact it was covered with horsehair cord. The result was a durable ball. Sometimes the ball was begun by using a small piece of cork as a core.[8] Wooden balls were used in Culdaff, County Donegal, in 1816, and at Miltown, near Tuam, towards the end of the last century, while a wooden ball covered with leather was the traditional kind used in the parish of Bannow, County Wexford, about the end of the last century.[9]

At the time of the foundation of the GAA the size of the ball varied from locality to locality, but in general it was substantially larger than today's. A good example of one still in existence was used in 1886 in a match between Holycross-Ballycahill of County Tipperary and St Finbarr's of Cork in a tournament in Cork. The ball is almost twice the size of the modern one, cased in leather, and weighs 6 or 7 ounces. The leather is believed to be pigskin. Horse-skin was also used, as can be testified from a statement of account issued by the Holycross club in 1909. The price of the ordinary balls, presumably pigskin, was 2s 6d (12½p), but the horse-skin ball was 3s (15p).[10]

The ball appears to have remained at this size until the nineteen-twenties at least. According to the *Official Guide* for 1919/20, the weight of the ball is given as 6–7 ounces (180–200 grams) and the circumference 11½–12½ inches (29–32 cm).[11] It appears, however, that the ball was already getting smaller. There is a ball from the Sam Melbourne Collection dating from 1921 that is very similar in size to today's, weighing 76 grams.[12] This trend is confirmed by the *Official Guide* for 1943, where the weight is given as 3½–4½ ounces (100–130 grams) and the circumference as 9–10 inches (23–25 cm).[13] This is the weight and size given in the 1988 *Official Guide*, the only difference being that the measurements are now metric.[14]

The modern sliotar has now a core of cork, covered in layers of thread and cased in pigskin leather. The thread around the cork is very important, preventing the breaking up of the cork, which would reduce the ball's pressure and its resilience. The leather casing is held together by waxed stitching and it has a water-resistant coating.

Two problems associated with the sliotar in wet conditions in the past were an increasing weight and a general softening of the ball. Both these changes had adverse effects on play. It became more difficult to strike the ball long distances or to control it properly with the hurley. These problems were caused by the large rim, which was necessary for stitching the ball, and the fact that the leather was not resistant to water. The sewing rim has been reduced to the minimum in the modern ball by machining it down; this and the water-resistant coating have dramatically reduced the problems associated with playing in wet conditions. The reduction in the rim has had another important effect: it has increased the control of the ball, as it sits more easily on the hurley and can be manipulated with greater effect. Also, there is less air-resistance in shots, and this is most noticeable in puck-outs. In general, the modern ball has contributed to the overall speeding up of the game.

The rule changes that have been made over the past forty years have contributed greatly to making hurling a faster game and a more enjoyable spectator sport. Some spectators of the older school might disagree. One of the excitements of the old game was the charge on the goalkeeper and the bundling of him, the ball and anything else that stood in the way into the back of the net. The lucky goalie was the one who threw the ball outside the goalpost before the charge arrived. The story is told of the All-Ireland junior hurling final in 1915 between Tipperary and Offaly at Athlone. Towards the end Offaly were attacking strongly, and backs and forwards were bundled into the Tipperary net. The Tipperary back Felix Cronin found the ball under him and threw it out wide. When the referee untangled the mess he found no ball, and no score was given. In spite of the excitement on such occasions, the protection of the goalkeeper was welcomed by most. As the rule stands today, he cannot be deliberately tackled in the small square, but he is fair game once he is outside it.

A few other rule changes since the publication of the first set in 1885 are worth mentioning. Until 1899, when a ball went over the sideline a throw-in followed. In that year the sideline puck was introduced. Separate point posts were abolished in 1910, and goalposts were fixed at 21 feet apart. In the same year goal nets were made compulsory for championship matches. The free puck, for sending the ball across one's own end line, was increased from 50 to 70 yards. Teams were reduced from twenty-one to seventeen in 1892 and to fifteen in 1913. In that year counties were required to register their colours; and ten years later numbered jerseys were introduced. The following year these were made compulsory, as were programmes for major games. Extra time was made compulsory for replays in 1926. The length of the pitch was reduced from 170 to 160 yards in 1935.

Another rule change that has been welcomed was the elimination of the third-man tackle and the frontal charge. This used to be perfectly allowable, to prevent another player tackling a team-mate in possession, and contributed to a lot of off-the-ball carry-on. The frontal charge allowed a defender for instance to charge an incoming forward and up-end him with a shoulder to the chest. It was quite dangerous and could lead to serious injury, because, as in the third-man tackle, the receiver might be in full flight and not at all expecting it.

These two changes and the introduction of large parallelograms and the semi-penalty changed the game considerably. Ultimately they favoured the forwards and forced the backs to devise different means of dispossessing them. Under the new rules the traditional back—strong, heavy and with a 'Thou shall not pass' mentality—gave way to a more mobile player who had to take on the forward in a race for possession and, if he lost the contest, had to try to outwit him by brain rather than brawn. Another development was the differentiation between technical and personal fouls and the penalty of sending off for a succession of personal fouls. This rule is not being observed, probably because referees are loath to take the ultimate sanction. It probably suggests the need for a lesser penalty, such as sending off for a certain period during a game.

The hand pass has been an area of much discussion in recent decades. It was always allowed, and some players, such as Seán McLoughlin of Tipperary, were experts in getting scores from it. Players and pundits alike began to question the whole idea of scores from the hand in a game of hurling. After some years of debate the hand-pass score was disallowed in 1981, except in one circumstance: if a player is passed a ball and, using his hands in place of the hurley, strikes it to the net or over the bar, the score stands. In contrast, a player can kick the ball into the net or over the bar. It seems slightly incongruous to disallow from the hand but allow from the foot. Somehow it appears as if the legislators forgot about the foot when they were eliminating the hand!

A number of other developments have speeded up the game. In the good old days it was possible to slow down a good run of play by one's opponents by having a player go down injured. This used to lead to long delays. The rule was changed and the stopping of a game because of injury forbidden. In spite of the rule, some referees still hold up play until the injured player is ready to resume. The reduction in the number of substitutions, first to five and then to three, has also speeded up the game.

Other changes include the sending back of all players except the centrefield players for the start of the game. When the forwards had to wait after the throw-in, occasions for free-for-alls developed out of the throwing in of the ball. In 1970 the time for All-Ireland games was expanded to eighty minutes, and this continued until 1975, when the seventy-minute final was introduced. Since then this has been the length of all championship matches. The placing of the ball by the player, as opposed to the referee or the linesman, for all frees and sideline pucks was also a welcome development.

Two other developments that were recommended but never made the rule-book were that all players wear helmets and the introduction of thirteen-a-side in college games for an experimental period. The introduction of the helmet never became a rule because of opposition from the players, some of whom found it difficult to adjust to wearing one.

Another criticism of the helmet, nothing to do with the safety factor, is that it takes an important ingredient out of the game by obscuring individual characteristics under the cover of anonymity. There is a point in this criticism: had such a rule been in vogue in his time we would have been denied the dramatic vision of John Horgan's blond locks sweeping in the wind.

The thirteen-a-side experiment in college games was never taken up. To many it would have been one more step in speeding up the game by giving more space in the goal area and facilitating faster forward play. Without a full-forward and full-back the extra speed would have allowed for greater exploits and more dramatic scores. It would have forced the backs to greater mobility and reduced still more the difference between backs and forwards. And there would have been one additional welcome advantage: many club and county teams would find it much easier to find thirteen than fifteen players, and this would help the weaker clubs.

4

The Revival of Hurling

A n article appeared in the *United Ireland* of 11 October 1884 under the heading 'A word about Irish athletics'. Though unsigned, it was from the pen of Michael Cusack, and it ran to about seven hundred words. Its message was simple: the national pastimes of the people were an essential element of a successful nation.

> Voluntary neglect of such pastimes is a sure sign of national decay and of approaching dissolution. The strength and energy of a race are largely dependent on the national pastimes for the development of a spirit of courage and endurance ... The corrupting influences which have been for several years devastating the sporting grounds of our cities and towns are fast spreading to our rural population.

Foreign and hostile laws, Cusack believed, caused the Irish to abandon their pastimes, and when an attempt was made to revive athletics it did not originate with those who had sympathy with Ireland or with the Irish people. 'Accordingly labourers, tradesmen, artisans and even policemen and soldiers were excluded from the few competitions which constituted the lame and halting programme of the promoters.'

According to the article, all athletics meetings had to be held under the auspices and the rules of the Amateur Athletic Association of England, so that the management of such meetings 'has been entrusted to persons hostile to the dearest aspirations of the Irish people.' He called on the people to take the management of their games into their own hands, to encourage and promote in every way every form of athletics that was peculiarly Irish, and to remove with one sweep everything foreign and iniquitous in the existing system. And they should draft rules for the guidance of the promoters of athletics meetings.[1]

This clarion call for independence in athletics was to be of enormous importance for the future of national pastimes. It was to change the face of Irish athletics, lead to the formation of an association for the preservation and cultivation of national pastimes, and ultimately ensure the revival of hurling.

The call was unequivocally answered in the following week's issue of *United Ireland*. The answer came from one of the most respected athletes in Ireland, Maurice Davin of Deerpark, Carrick-on-Suir. He called for the publication of a rule-book on Irish games. He laid particular emphasis on the need to promote weight and jumping events, which tended to be left out of sports programmes; he also advocated Irish football, 'a great game and worth going a long way to see when played on a fairly laid-out ground and under proper rules.' He was keen to see both hurling and football revived under standard rules. He concluded by saying that if a movement were to come into existence for the purpose of reviving and encouraging Irish games and of drafting rules, 'I will gladly lend a hand if I can be of any use.'[2]

Cusack replied, in his own name, on 25 October. He referred to his friend Maurice Davin as 'the spotless in the midst of the speckled.' He spoke of the national pastimes that were excluded from sports programmes, including weight-throwing, jumping, hurling, Irish football, wrestling, and bowling. He was prepared to offer his advice 'in the event of a meeting being held to draft laws for the promotion and conservation of every form of Irish sport.' He claimed to have had conversations with many representative Irishmen, 'and they all agree that the suggestions you offered a fortnight ago should at once be acted upon.' He concluded by saying that the consensus was that a meeting should be held in Thurles on Saturday 1 November. Steps were being taken to 'summon by circular representative Irish men for that place and time.' He hoped it would be responded to by those who desired to see genuine Irish athletics revived.[3]

The circular was sent out from 4 Gardiner's Place, Dublin, on 27 October. It requested attendance at the Commercial Hotel, Thurles, at two o'clock on 1 November 'to take steps for the formation of a Gaelic Association for the preservation and cultivation of the national pastimes and for providing amusements for the Irish people during their leisure hours.' The proposed movement had the approval of Michael Davitt, Justin McCarthy MP, William O'Brien MP, T. Harrington MP, 'and other eminent men who are interested in the social elevation of the race.' The letter was signed by Maurice Davin and Michael Cusack.

Before considering the events that took place in Thurles on that November day it is necessary to give the background to Cusack's initiative and the state of hurling in the eighteen-eighties. Put simply, the game had declined dramatically from the position of eminence it held in the eighteenth century.

There were many reasons for this decline. As a result of the French Revolution and the Rising of 1798 the landlords had gradually withdrawn their patronage of the game. This was part of a general withdrawal from social involvement with their tenants and the common people, covering the areas of language, manners, attitudes, and pastimes. The expanding population began to seem a threat to the landlords' security.

The spread of Sunday observance[4] was another damper on the game. Gradually the Catholic Church adopted the sabbatarianism of the Protestant churches and began to frown on games on Sundays as something frivolous and a waste of time. As a result the clergy, who might have taken up the leadership abandoned by the landlords, left the people to fend for themselves.

The Great Famine was another disaster for the national pastimes. The drop in national morale and the destruction of a rural society in many areas caused a dramatic decline in traditional pastimes. The Kilkenny Young Irelander J. T. Campion deplored the passing of the old sports in 1857. Twenty years later A. M. O'Sullivan, the Home Rule MP, recalling the effect of the Famine on the ordinary people, wrote:

> Their ancient sports and pastimes everywhere disappeared and in many parts ... have never returned. The outdoor games, the hurling match ... are seen no more.[5]

Michael Doheny offers other reasons for the decline of the game. In a series of newspaper articles subtitled 'A glance at the history of Ireland from the passage of the Act of Union to the period of the monster meetings', he had this to say:

> As I have said the sport is fast dying away. Its decay is owing to several causes, among these are leading: first, the introduction of the dance drew down on the hurling the opposition of the priest. In some instances, too, of late, family and faction fights are renewed at the hurling, which still more imperatively called for the reprobation of the clergy. And finally, there was yet another cause which operated more effectively than any or, perhaps, all others, namely, the disinclination of the farmers to allow the hurling on their grazing lands. It was curious to observe how this feeling

gradually gained on the people. In the space of 20 years it was so extended that what was at first a rare exception, indeed, became a universal and unrelenting rule. That evils were growing up with the sport were undoubted: but the evils could be averted and crushed out by the same power and agency that were sufficient to put down the hurling itself. And putting down the hurling was so far crushing out the national heart. Woe to them who lend themselves to the unholy work of unnerving a people and accommodating them to the fetters of their masters. A few feeble attempts have been made in this country to revive hurling but without success, because politicians seek to make it subservient to their selfish and most unworthy purposes.[6]

The decline of hurling continued unabated, as another writer, P. F. O'Brien, attests when writing in 1884:

In seriousness, hurling was a good old game. I myself remember when hurling had not yet wholly died out; when the boys of the parish after Sunday mass had many a tussle and 'puck'. The most of the hurlers are now beyond the Atlantic wave and the remainder go whistling vacantly around the roads at home. Our schoolboys have permanently settled down to cricket, but our farmers' sons no longer interest themselves in the rounding of the boss or the feel of a hockey.[7]

However, Marcus de Búrca is of the opinion that even though the native games were nearer than ever to extinction, they did not die. According to him, 'Dublin Castle itself is authority for the statement that by the late 1850's hurling was being played all over Munster. Other sources establish hurling in the 1860's and 1870's in Cork, Tipperary, Limerick, Kerry and even Dublin City.'[8] The game continued to be played in the north of Ireland in the nineteenth century, particularly in County Antrim. Shaw Mason, in his parochial survey of Ireland, refers to the parish of Ballintoy, on the north coast of Antrim:

We have no patrons or patron-days, except that on Christmas day and on the first of the year, a great concourse of people assemble on the stand, at Whitepark, to play common or shinty.

A further survey was undertaken by the Ordnance Survey between 1825 and 1840. References to the playing of *camánacht* or commons abound for Counties Antrim and Down. One reference to Magheragall, County Antrim, has this to say:

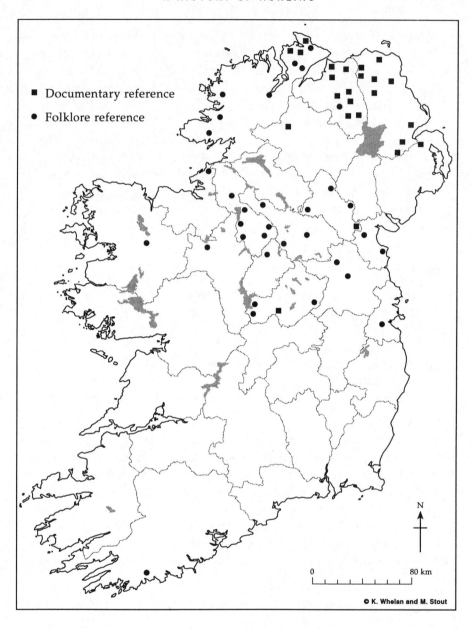

- ■ Documentary reference
- ● Folklore reference

N

0   80 km

© K. Whelan and M. Stout

The distribution of commons

Their principal amusements are dancing, cards and the cock-fighting. A sort of hurling or 'common-playing' as it is called in the north is still kept up there, chiefly among the Catholics.

This memoir was written about 1830, and it is interesting to recall that the same place, Loughguile, won an All-Ireland club championship in 1983. Another area where the game was still strong at this time was east Galway. As we have seen, teams from Meelick and Killimor crossed the Shannon to play the men of Tipperary. Michael Cusack had learned of this tradition from his early teaching days in Lough Cultra school, not far from Gort. When later he founded the Metropolitan Hurling Club in Dublin the Gaels of east Galway issued a challenge to the Dublin men. A challenge cup was put up, and the Fair Green in Ballinasloe was chosen as the venue.

The match was arranged for Easter Monday, 13 April 1884. Before it started the Killimor captain, F. W. Lynch, and the Metropolitan captain, Michael Cusack, settled the rules of the match. They agreed to play for four half-hours, no tripping or wrestling to be allowed. A big crowd turned up, which constantly encroached onto the pitch. In spite of the agreed set of rules, the game was a disappointment and it came to a premature end when Killimor scored a goal. Cusack called off his team, claiming that Killimor were too rough. The Galway men claimed victory, and this was honoured by bonfires and lights all the way from Ballinasloe to Killimor.

When Cusack began to lay plans for the founding of the GAA he saw the need for support from leaders of church and state. From his association with east Galway he knew of the sterling qualities of the Bishop of Clonfert, Dr Patrick Duggan. He therefore wrote to William Duffy of Loughrea, whom he had befriended while the latter was holidaying in Dublin a few years before, and asked him to arrange a delegation to call on Dr Duggan and ask him to become patron of the association. The arrangements were made, and on 15 August a deputation consisting of Michael Cusack, three Loughrea men—William J. Duffy, John P. McCarthy, and John Sweeney—Peter J. Kelly of Killeenadeema and Michael Gleenan of Kilchreest called on the bishop. Dr Duggan was seventy-one years old, was in rather bad health, and had already offered his resignation to the Pope. However, he was delighted to hear of the founding of the association and promised to do all he could to promote its success. But he declined to act as patron and advised them to ask Dr Croke, Archbishop of Cashel, 'a fine Gael, young, vigorous and energetic,' to become the first patron. And so, Cusack came to Thurles.

The report of the meeting on 1 November that appeared in the *United Ireland* of 8 November called it 'well attended'. It was far from that. It took place in Hayes's Commercial Hotel, which proved fully capable of accommodating all those who turned up. Indeed, when the meeting began at three o'clock the billiard room sufficed. The exact number is still in dispute. Seven founding fathers are officially recognised. Cusack later indicated that nine people were present; a study of contemporary newspaper accounts and subsequent claims might give a figure as high as fourteen.

The seven recognised founders are as follows. Michael Cusack, a teacher from Dublin who had been born in Carron, County Clare, and Maurice Davin, an athlete and farmer from Deerpark, Carrick-on-Suir, had jointly called the meeting. James K. Bracken was a building contractor and monumental mason from Templemore, County Tipperary. John Wyse-Power was a journalist, editor of the *Leinster Leader* and an 'associate of the extreme section of the Irish Nationalists.' Joseph P. O'Ryan was born in Carrick-on-Suir and practised as a solicitor in Callan and Thurles. John McKay was a Belfast man who was then working as a journalist with the *Cork Examiner*. District Inspector St George McCarthy, born in Bansha, County Tipperary, was a member of the RIC, stationed in nearby Templemore. Others who are reputed to have been there are Frank Moloney, Nenagh, William Foley, Carrick-on-Suir, and Thurles residents T. K. Dwyer, Charles Culhane, Michael Cantwell, William Delehunty, and John Butler. There is a strong Kilkenny tradition that Henry Joseph Meagher, father of the famous Lory, Jack Hoyne, who played on Kilkenny's first All-Ireland winning side in 1904 and a third Tullaroan man, Ned Teehan, were also present.

It is difficult to account for the small attendance at the meeting, and no satisfactory explanation has ever been given. One argument is that the short notice, a mere five days, was a factor. Another is that Thurles was not a satisfactory venue and that Cork would have been more attractive. Cusack himself seems to have been somewhat embarrassed by the small attendance and was at pains in the period after the meeting to emphasise all the letters of support he had received. In all he claimed that the number was sixty-odd, and some weeks after the meeting he had the text of eight of the letters of support published in the *Nation*.

When the meeting convened, Maurice Davin was elected chairman. He explained that the laws under which athletic sports were held in Ireland were designed mainly for the guidance of Englishmen and that they did not deal with the characteristic sports and pastimes of the Celtic race. 'It therefore became necessary to form an association which would resuscitate and draft laws for the guidance of those who are patriotic enough to devise schemes of recreation for the bulk of the people, and more especially for the humble and hard-working who seem now to be born to no other inheritance than the everlasting round of labour."[9]

Michael Cusack replied and urged the necessity of the association. He gave the background to the meeting and concluded by saying that he had received offers of support from a number of people, including Morrison Miller, honorary secretary of the Caledonian Games Society, Kinnersley Lewis of Wales, Professor Roehrig on behalf of the Irish in America, and a Mr Lynch, solicitor, of Melbourne for the Irish in Australia.

The business of the meeting was brief. Cusack, McKay and Wyse-Power were elected joint secretaries, with the power to add to their number. The new association was named the Gaelic Athletic Association for the Preservation and Cultivation of National Pastimes. It was agreed that the objects of the association be submitted to Archbishop Croke of Cashel and to Charles Stewart Parnell and Michael Davitt with a view to securing their patronage. The meeting was adjourned to give the elected officers time to draft the laws under which the work of the association was to be carried on.

The choice of Croke, Parnell and Davitt as patrons represented a recognition of the major forces in the national movement of the day, and all willingly accepted within a few days of each other. Of the three replies, that of Archbishop Croke was the longest and the most significant, and indeed it became the unofficial charter of the association. In it he said:

> One of the most painful, let me assure you, and, at the same time, one of the most frequently recurring reflections that, as an Irish man I am compelled to make in connection with the present aspect of things in the country, is derived from the ugly and irritating fact that we are daily importing from England, not only her manufactured goods, which we cannot help doing, since she has practically strangled our own manufacturing appliances, but, together with her fashions, her accents, her vicious literature, her music, her dances and her manifold mannerisms, her games also and her pastimes, to the utter discredit of our own grand national sports and to the sore humiliation, as I believe, of every genuine son and daughter of our old land. Ball-playing, hurling, football-kicking, according to Irish rules, casting, leaping in various ways, wrestling, handy-grips, top-pegging, leap-frog, rounders, tip-in-the-hat and all the favourite exercises and amusements amongst men and boys may now be said to be not only dead and buried but in several localities to be entirely forgotten and unknown ... Indeed, if we continue travelling for the next score years in the

same direction that we have been going in for some time past contemning the sports that were practised by our fore-fathers, effacing our national features as though we are ashamed of them and putting on, with England's stuffs and broadcloths, her masher habits and such other effeminate follies that she may recommend, we had better, at once and publicly abjure our nationality, clap hands for joy at the sight of the Union Jack and place 'England's bloody red' exultantly above the green.

The association had been set up for the preservation and cultivation of Irish athletics, and until 1887 the playing of hurling and football was to take second place to organising athletics meetings. Cusack's great desire was for nationalists to control athletics and to open them to every social class. After the association organised its first big sports meeting, in Clonmel in February 1885, there was a succession of very successful and well-attended meetings around the country. There was enormous enthusiasm, because the great majority of those participating were doing so for the first time, as they had been barred from taking part up to now or had refused to take part because the sports were controlled by a foreign body.

At this stage hurling had a very low profile. The rules were drawn up and adopted at the Thurles meeting on 17 January 1885. An important decision also taken at this meeting was the 'Parish Rule': the principle of one club for each parish. Goals were the only scores allowed in the early days; later the point was to be introduced for the ball going over the crossbar. There was also a 'forfeit point', given if a defender carried the ball over the goal-line. If the same defender struck the ball over his own crossbar three forfeit points were awarded to his opponents. The forfeit point was to disappear at the 1886 convention, after which the side points make their appearance for the first time. Wrestling was to be permitted until 1886, where two players who came into collision immediately came to hand grips. The number of players was twenty-one until 1892.

During the early years a goal had no equivalent in points. After some years five points, and later three points, were declared equal to a goal. Play was limited to an hour after 1886.

During the year following the foundation of the association hurling was played mostly at local and parish level. It was to take some time for the new rules to be learned and accepted in the hurling area. At first there were disputes and conflicts over the interpretation of the rules, but gradually they had a rejuvenating effect on existing clubs and led to the establishment of new clubs. Cusack's Metropolitan Club was the first and most famous of the Dublin hurling clubs, and the spread of hurling in the city was attributable to its example. New clubs were founded in Drumcondra, Inchicore, and other Dublin villages. The first club to be established outside the city was that of Clara in County Offaly, which came into existence on 15 December 1884.

During 1885 the new association spread rapidly, in Cusack's words, 'like a prairie fire.' The two Galway clubs, Killimor and Ballinakill, played a hurling match at Feagh, near Tynagh, for a plate of 10 sovereigns on the Twelfth Day. Killimor won by two goals to nil, and the game attracted a crowd of six thousand. The first hurling match in County Tipperary was played in Riverstown between Nenagh and Silvermines in March. F. R. Moloney refereed. 'The battle was grim and the Mitchels (Nenagh) were sore and sorry in the finish.'[10] The 'Mines' won the contest, which lasted eighty minutes. A return match was later played at Captain Carroll's field in Capparoe. On this occasion F. R. Moloney read Dr Croke's letter accepting the patronage of the association to the spectators after the contest, amid great enthusiasm.

Steps were taken to revive hurling in Belfast. The MP for Wexford, Mr Barry, offered a £25 challenge cup for competition among the hurlers in that county. There was a match in Lusmagh, County Offaly, between the Shannon District hurlers and the home club. Branches of the association were formed in Piltown and Callan in County Kilkenny. The Cork Athletic Club and Blarney joined the GAA. During 1885 clubs were also formed in many other counties.

One of the great strengths of the early association was the Parish Rule. The parish was a unit its inhabitants could identify with. This territorial identification, as well as being a great bonding force for club teams in those early years, was to be strengthened when neighbouring parishes and counties were pitted against each other. Dr Kevin Whelan has drawn attention to this phenomenon by quoting the painter Tony O'Malley, who contrasted the tribal-territorial element in Irish sport with English attitudes. 'If neighbours were playing, like New Ross and Tullogher, there would be a real needle in it. When Carrichshock were playing I once heard an old man shouting, "Come on the men that bate the proctors," and there was a tremor and a real fervour in his voice. It was a battle cry, with the hurleys as the swords, but with the same intensity.' Whelan continues: 'Similar forces of territoriality have been identified behind the success of cricket in the West Indies and rugby in the Welsh valleys.'[11]

This territorial allegiance was reinforced by the adoption of club colours, often drawn from the old faction favours. Clubs and counties have become so identified with their colours that one could not imagine Cork without their red jerseys or Kilkenny not in the black and amber. The colours seem to tell one something about the team and give a shape and an attitude to the players in them. The same colours, while giving a feeling of identification to followers of the team, can also excite feelings of fear, antagonism and even hate in the minds of their opponents.

As well as some of the colours being inherited from the days of the faction fights, an occasional faction slogan has been carried over too. 'If any man can, an Alley man can.' 'Squeeze 'em up, Moycarkey, and hang 'em out to dry.' Lingering animosities can sometimes surface in surprising ways: it is not unknown for an irate Wexford supporter to hurl abuse at Kilkenny, recalling an incident that occurred in Castlecomer to indignant United Irishmen: 'Sure what good are they anyway? Didn't they piss on the powder in '98?'[12]

Local rivalries between parishes gradually evolved into county identifications. During 1886 the GAA developed by leaps and bounds, and most of the country became organised as clubs sprang up in almost every parish. But not everything in the garden was rosy. Rivalries often spilled over into unpleasant happenings. Grounds were sometimes invaded during matches as intense feelings gave way to emotional outbursts. The referee could become the object of hostilities, and the teams sometimes left the field of play in protest before the match was finished. Lack of punctuality in starting the matches was also a cause for general complaint. Teams tended to be governed by their own consider-ations, and the public sometimes had to wait for hours after the advertised time for the matches to start.

Not until 1886 did inter-county fixtures take place, whether between clubs or counties. One of the first such contests was played in the Phoenix Park between North Tipperary and South Galway on 16 February. The Tipperary team travelled up the previous day and met their opponents at Broadstone Station at ten o'clock that evening. The two teams marched out to the venue the following day.

> The Galwagians, active and sinewy, did not appear to be equal to the Tipps, in strength and weight, but they nevertheless showed unmistakeable symptoms that whoever defeated them would not be indulged in a walkover. The Tipperary men looked as fit as if to fight an empire. In fact the appearance of both teams drew forth warm expressions of admiration from the multitude assembled that eventful morning to witness the match in the Phoenix Park.[13]

To begin the match an arch of hurleys was formed by the teams facing each other. The Tipperary ball was rolled between the lines, and the great hurling match had begun. For full forty minutes the game waxed fast and furious, during which the Tipperary men drove twenty-six wides and resisted every attempt by Galway to transfer the sphere of operations to the other end. In the second half the Galway ball, which was a smaller version, was introduced. The play was less one-sided, but the Galway men failed to make an impression on Tipperary. After about twenty minutes a great Tipperary attack, spearheaded by Charlie McSorley of Silvermines, resulted in a goal and deafening cheers from the crowd. During the remaining twenty minutes the Galway men made some brilliant dashes but without avail, and the final score left Tipperary victorious by a solitary goal. The victorious team was given a torchlight procession on their return to Nenagh, and about four thousand people turned up in front of the Castle Hotel to be addressed by Frank Moloney, umpire of the team. The match was refereed by Michael Cusack, and it gave a great stimulus to hurling in Dublin.

More inter-county contests followed. Tournaments were held in Thurles and Athlone at Easter and attracted thousands of people. For the contest in Thurles,

> thousands attended and enthusiasm ran riot during the many tussles for supremacy. Point posts were erected for the first time and the teams presented themselves in gay and gorgeous costumes. Beaten but unsubdued, was the verdict of the hurling clash between the Dublin Metropolitans and Holycross. Holycross won by a goal dashed in by Pat Ryan. 'I hit in the first goal scored in Tipperary under Davin's rules,' Pat would say to the day of his death … The undertaking was—everything considered—a huge success; it brought lasting credit to its promoters, and was the forerunner for coming events. Spontaneously, the crowds forgetting home, headed by Maurice Davin, Tom Condon, the dauntless John O'Leary, and the Dublin bands, marched through the streets and to the Palace, to get the blessing and encouragement of the Archbishop. Visibly affected as he surveyed the sea of faces before him, Most Rev. Dr Croke said, amongst other things: 'You have today safely planted the G.A.A. and your magnificent tournament will ever constitute the premier page of Irish Gaelic history.'[14]

Other inter-county tournaments during the summer of 1886 were organised in Kilkenny, Dublin, and Cork. Smaller contests between clubs from different counties took place in Birdhill and Portumna. There were also contests between clubs from the Dublin region and various parts of

Wicklow. The Cork tournament took place on 29 August between clubs from that county and Tipperary. It attracted a huge attendance to Cork Park. The visiting teams were met at the railway station by four bands and marched through the city as far as the park. The route was crowded with welcoming citizens. Four of the five scheduled contests took place, after which the visitors were entertained at the Gymnasium Club on the South Mall and then the teams were played back to the station, where there were many cheers 'for the gallant Tipps' as the train steamed out.

The first inter-county championship was inaugurated in 1887. For different reasons, such as disagreement over venues, difficulties within counties, and inability to field teams, only five counties took part. The following rules governed the championship:

1. It would be open to all affiliated clubs of the G.A.A. All entries to be made on or before the 1st of January each year. Each team to pay an entrance fee of 2/6 [12½p].
2. Clubs in the county had to play the ties out first and the winner of the final tie would be entitled to play for the championship.
3. The first ties were to be played on such days and venues as County Committee appointed, but no sooner than February 1st or later than March 17th, and the final ties at such times and places as the Executive appointed.
4. The final match was to be played on the last week of April or the first week of May. The winning team and the second were to receive championship medals of the G.A.A. A player was not allowed to play for more than one club in the championship.
5. The number of players a side in each of the matches was to be 21.[15]

Originally twelve teams had entered, and the draws were made, but Wicklow, Louth, Waterford, Cork, Dublin, Meath and Limerick did not play. Wicklow had been drawn to play Clare at Athlone on Tuesday 19 July, but the county committee objected: 'That we are of opinion that it would be most unreasonable to expect any team to play against Clare in the first tie in the inter-county championship while Galway, Waterford, Louth, Meath, Wexford and Limerick are accorded the privilege of playing at Elm Park, Merrion, and while Wicklow is prepared at any time to meet Clare or any other county on reasonable terms, we must decline to ask a team to go to Athlone at this season for a match.'[16] The counties, accordingly, did not meet.

Galway, represented by Meelick, beat Wexford, represented by Castlebridge, by 2-8 to 1-0. At that time hurling was the very poor relation of football in Wexford, and in order to field a team against Galway at Elm

Park, Dublin, Castlebridge had to gather up every kind of stick they could find. More than ten thousand people turned up for the match on 24 July. A reporter wrote:

> There was a good deal of heated temper on both sides. The conduct of the Wexford men was severely censured by most of those present. One incident of the day's proceedings cannot be too highly valued. Lord French, when he heard of the great victory of Galway, directed his steward, Mr. Balfe, to go to the Midland Hotel and hand from him £3 to treat the team and also £2 to one of the team that had lost two teeth by a blow of the hurl.

To cover the expenses of the trip to Dublin the parish priest, Father Kirwan, gave £14 to the team.

Tipperary, represented by Thurles, got a walkover from Dublin, whose application for a postponement on the grounds that some of their players were on holidays was refused, and beat Clare at Nenagh by 1-7 to 0-2. Afterwards they beat Kilkenny, represented by Tullaroan, at Urlingford by 4-7 to 0-0. Earlier the teams had travelled to Clonmel for the match but found that the South Tipperary Board, then in dispute with the Central Council, had other games in progress in the venue, and the visitors could not play the match. They returned home and agreed to play the following Thursday in Urlingford. Tullaroan objected to some of the Thurles players before the start of the game, on the grounds that they were not from the Thurles parish. However, Thurles had no difficulty in getting replacements from among their supporters and won the match easily.

The final was not played until 1 April 1888. The venue was Hoare's field in Birr, quite close to the present hurling field, and the referee was Patrick White from Toomevara, who was then working in Birr. The Meelick team consisted of twelve men from Meelick and nine from Killimor. The two parishes joined up as a result of three games they had played against each other the year before the championship. The games ended in a draw, and as the teams couldn't beat one another they decided to combine. The Meelick men on the team were Pat Madden, who was the captain and one of the famous O'Maddens of the area, Patrick Cullen, Mike Manning, John Colohan, John Scally, Willie Madden, Tom Hanley, James Kelly, Pat Manning, Jim Connolly, John Cosgrave, and Arthur Cosgrave. The Killimor men were John Lowry, John Callinan, Pat Haverty, Tom Foley, Owen Griffin, Patrick Larkin, John Manning, Charlie Melody, and John Sanders. According to local tradition, only Fenians could get on the team. One fine player in the area, named Burke, failed to get selected for this reason. The hurleys for the final were made on the kitchen floor of Patrick Cullen's house.

Cullen was a carpenter who was to escape to America in 1891 as a result of land trouble in the locality. He was never to return.

The team went by McIntyre's brake to the final, with the exception of John Lowry, who walked all the way from Killimor to Birr. When they arrived they heard that Tipperary were not going to appear. Some say that this was a rumour put out by the Tipperary men to get Meelick off guard, but it may have been because of a disagreement in the Tipperary camp. Whatever the cause, the Galway men went for a drink and while imbibing heard that Tipperary were ready.

There was a dispute in the Tipperary camp that day, and it was about expenses. The captain, Denis Maher, and six of the Killinan players did not travel to the match. They had requested the committee to pay their expenses to Birr, because of the cost incurred in travelling to Nenagh, Clonmel and Urlingford for the earlier rounds. The committee did not agree and, in the words of the aggrieved captain, 'there were men from Gortnahoe, Drombane and Moyne called in and their expenses paid and seven of the old hurlers left standing on the platform, namely D. Maher, Jack Maher, Con Callanan, Pat Ryan, Matty Maher, Ned Maher and myself.'[17] The actual selection was as follows: Jim Stapleton (captain), Matty Maher, Andy Maher, Tom Bourke, Ned Murphy, Tom Stapleton, Ger Dwyer, Mick Carroll, Tom Carroll, Tom Maher, John Leamy, Ned Lambe, Martin McNamara, John Mockler, Ger Ryan, Danny Ryan, Tom Dwyer, Ned Bowe, Tommy Healy, Jim Leahy, and Johnny Dunne.

Both teams togged out in Cunningham's Hotel and then marched to the field. Togging out is probably a misnomer, as it is generally accepted that the Galway men played in their shirts and trousers; each player wore a green knitted cap with a tassel on it. Meelick were led by their non-playing captain, James Lynam, who had held the military rank of captain in the American Civil War. Although a noted pugilist he was counted a quiet man. His family came from Rahan, County Offaly, and he had a farm in Eyrecourt. Later, in the nineties, he was to contest unsuccessfully the East Galway seat in the Parnellite interest against John Roche MP.

The game was fought at a fierce pace. One of the Thurles players got a blow to the nose and had to be carried off. As a result John Lowry, the man who had walked from Killimor to Birr and who played at full-back, was taken off by Captain Lynam. He was none too pleased with the decision, because for some time thereafter, until he was warned by the referee, he would dart onto the field and take part in the play. Thurles won by a goal and a point and one forfeit point to nil.

Meelick have not since been listed as Galway senior hurling champions; but because of their participation in the historic first All-Ireland, the name

This photograph, taken in June 1910, shows the members of the Thurles side who were the first All-Ireland champions in 1887. **TOP ROW** (LEFT TO RIGHT): D. MAHER, J. SULLIVAN, E. MURPHY, J. RYAN, M. MAHER, E. LEAMY, T. BURKE, C. CALLANAN, D. DAVOREN, M. MAHER. **SECOND ROW** (LEFT TO RIGHT): P. RYAN, D. MAHER, J. STAPLETON, T. MAHER, J. LEAMY, J. RYAN, J. DWYER. **FRONT ROW** (LEFT TO RIGHT): M. CARROLL, M. McNAMARA, T. BUTLER.

This photograph, taken on Friday 14 September 1888, shows the 'Invasion Team' before its departure for the United States. The photograph was taken at St Patrick's, Thurles. Maurice Davin, first president of the GAA, stands on the left holding a hammer.

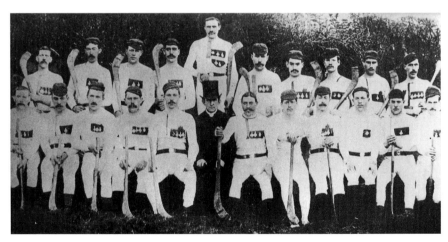

Cork, 1890. **BACK** (LEFT TO RIGHT): J. BUCKLEY, D. LINEHAN, D. LOONEY, D. DREW, D. LANE (CAPT.), J. HENCHION, J. O'CONNOR, T. TWOMEY, T. HORGAN, P. BUCKLEY. **FRONT** (LEFT TO RIGHT): P. O'RIORDAN, J. O'REILLY, T. KELLEHER, D. O'SULLIVAN, T. GOOD, FR A. O'RIORDAN, D. HORGAN, E. O'REILLY, J. LINEHAN, J. KELLEHER, J. O'SULLIVAN, P. O'RIORDAN.

Michael Hennessy, Ballyduff, Co. Kerry, captained Kerry in winning the All-Ireland junior final of 1961. He is seen here with Paddy Carroll of the Ballyduff team that captured All-Ireland senior honours in 1891. As the lone survivor of that team, he marched around the field with the Ballyduff team in the 1955 county senior final, won by Ballyduff. It was their first county senior success since 1891.

The 'Barrs in 1894. The players pictured are: **BACK ROW:** MICK SEXTON, JACK (BAWN) MURPHY, BILLY WALSH, TOM HORGAN, 'BILLEX' MOLONEY, ARTHUR CALLANAN (SEC.), WILLIE JOHN O'CONNELL, DINNY HIGGINS, MORTY DOWNEY, JACK YOUNG, 'COCKER' FOLEY, JOSIE KELLEHER. **FRONT ROW**: CHRISTY YOUNG, TIM O'KEEFFE, DONAL MURPHY, TIM MURPHY, CONNIE LEARY, JIM HARRINGTON, 'LUCAS' LEARY.

Tubberadora, 1898 All-Ireland champions. **BACK ROW** (LEFT TO RIGHT): WATTY DUNNE, WILL DEVANE, NED BRENNAN, MIKEY MAHER (CAPT.), E. D. RYAN, JOHN RYAN, TIM CONDON. **SEATED** (LEFT TO RIGHT): THOMAS LEAHY, PHIL BYRNE, JOHN CONNOLLY, JACK MAHER, DENIS WALSH, JIM O'KEEFFE, DICK O'KEEFFE, MICHAEL CONLON. **FRONT ROW** (LEFT TO RIGHT): TOMMY RYAN, JACK MAHER, NED MAHER, JOHNNY WALSH.

Kilkenny's first All-Ireland team, who defeated Cork in 1904 in the All-Ireland final at Carrick-on-Suir and again in 1906 in the Railway Shield. THE TEAM WAS: R. BRENNAN, R. WALSH, E. DOYLE, P. LANIGAN, J. J. BRENNAN, D. GRACE, J. HOYNE, S. WALTON, P. FIELDING, D. STAPLETON, J. DOHENY (CAPT.), J. LAWLOR, J. ROCHFORD, R. DOYLE, P. SAUNDERS, J. ANTHONY, AND THE FAMOUS GOALIE R. 'FOX' MAHER, EXTREME RIGHT SECOND ROW.

The Thurles selection who brought the 1908 All-Ireland championship to Tipperary. The game was played in Athy in 1909, and this photograph was taken on the day of the match. **FRONT ROW**: DENIS O'KEEFFE, P. BROLAN, JACK MOONEY, H. SHELLY, J. McLOUGHNEY, A. CAREW. **CENTRE ROW**: JER HAYES, J. KAVANAGH, PAT FITZGERALD, J. MOCKLER, T. SEMPLE (CAPT.), FR M. K. RYAN, J. FITZGERALD, T. 'GAFFER' KENNA, MIKEY MAHER. **BACK ROW**: M. MULCAIRE, M. RYAN, J. 'HAWK' O'BRIEN, M. O'DWYER, P. BURKE, TIM GLEESON, M. O'BRIEN, TOM KERWICK, JIMMY BURKE, J. M. KENNEDY.

A young hurler, taken at the Glens Feis, circa 1906. The hurl is of the old style and the footwear also. The photograph was taken by F. J. Bigger, a well-known historian of the time and also a talented amateur photographer.

WILLIAM BULFIN

William Bulfin (1864 – 1910), from Derinloch, near Birr, Co. Offaly, is best remembered as the author of the classic *Rambles in Eirinn*. But he was also one of the pioneers of hurling in Argentina, where the game still survives and where Bulfin spent much of his adult life.

Ned Barrett, a native of Ballyduff, Co. Kerry, won an All-Ireland senior medal with London in 1901. Seven years later, in the London Olympics, he won a gold medal in wrestling.

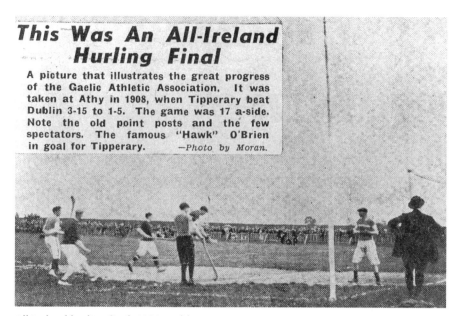

This Was An All-Ireland Hurling Final

A picture that illustrates the great progress of the Gaelic Athletic Association. It was taken at Athy in 1908, when Tipperary beat Dublin 3-15 to 1-5. The game was 17 a-side. Note the old point posts and the few spectators. The famous "Hawk" O'Brien in goal for Tipperary. —*Photo by Moran.*

All-Ireland hurling final, 1908, Dublin v. Tipperary.

Confederates Hurling Club, Dublin. This photograph dates from about 1910.

Cork's first 15-a-side team, photographed before their Munster championship match with Limerick in July 1913. **BACK ROW** (LEFT TO RIGHT): J. J. WALSH, L. FLAHERTY, W. 'BOWLER' WALSH, M. DORNEY, A. FITZGERALD, DAN KENNEFICK, TOM IRWIN. **SECOND ROW** (LEFT TO RIGHT): M. BYRNE, CONNIE SHEEHAN, DICK O'GORMAN, BARRY MURPHY, PADDY MAHONY. **FRONT ROW** (LEFT TO RIGHT): JAMESY KELLEHER, T. O'LEARY, W. P. AHERNE, J. 'MAJOR' KENNEDY, JIM 'SPUD' MURPHY.

Clare's All-Ireland winning side of 1914. Little did the Banner County imagine that they would have to wait eighty-one long years to repeat this triumph. **BACK ROW** (LEFT TO RIGHT): THOMAS McGRATH, JOHN FOX, ROBERT DOHERTY, MICHAEL FLANAGAN, JAMES CLANCY, JOE POWER. **MIDDLE ROW** (LEFT TO RIGHT): J. GUERIN, PATRICK McINERNEY, W. CONSIDINE, AMBY POWER (CAPT.), M. MOLONY, ED GRACE, J. SHALLOO. **FRONT ROW** (LEFT TO RIGHT): BRENDAN CONSIDINE, SHAM SPELLISSY. THE TRAINER OF THE TEAM WAS JIM HEHIR, FATHER OF THE FAMOUS BROADCASTER MICHEÁL.

The Laois team of 1915, the only side from the county ever to win the All-Ireland championship. PLAYERS ONLY: **TOP ROW** (LEFT TO RIGHT): JOE CARROLL, J. DEEGAN, J. LOUGHMAN, P. RYAN, J. DUNPHY, JOHN PHELAN, P. CAMPION. **MIDDLE ROW**: JOE PHELAN, T. FINLAY, J. WALSH, J. FINLAY (CAPT.), R. O'KEEFFE, E. McEVOY, JIM CARROLL. **BOTTOM ROW**: J. HINEY, J. DALY, JACK CARROLL.

The Cork side of 1919 that beat Dublin in the All-Ireland hurling final. **INSET:** J. J. WALSH.
BACK ROW (LEFT TO RIGHT): S. McCARTHY, E. GREY, C. LUCEY, C. SHEEHAN, R. O'GORMAN, SEÁN ÓG MURPHY, J. HASSET, JOHN BARRY MURPHY, J. O'KEEFFE, T. IRWIN. **MIDDLE ROW** (LEFT TO RIGHT): BARRY MURPHY, P. HEALY, J. KENNEDY (CAPT.), FR E. FITZGERALD, J. 'SPUD' MURPHY, D. RING, F. KELLEHER, J. O'CALLAGHAN. **FRONT ROW** (LEFT TO RIGHT): P. O'HALLORAN, T. NAGLE, EUDIE COUGHLAN, MICK MURPHY, P. AHERNE, F. BARRY.

Kilkenny All-Ireland senior hurling champions, 1922. **BACK ROW** (LEFT TO RIGHT): PETER DUNNE (MASCOT), JACK ROCHFORD, MICK HEFFERNAN (HAT). THE REST ARE HURLERS ONLY: TOM TIERNEY, BILL BRENNAN, NED PURCELL, EDDIE DUNPHY, DICK GRACE, MATTY POWER, BILL KENNY, MICK BRENNAN. **MIDDLE ROW** (LEFT TO RIGHT): SEÁN F. GIBBONS, MARTIN 'ROUNDY' LALOR, JIMMY TOBIN, PADDY O'DONOGHUE, WATTY DUNPHY, MARK McDONALD, JOHN HOLOHAN, PADDY GLENDON, TIM SCOTT. **FRONT ROW** (LEFT TO RIGHT, PLAYERS ONLY): TOMMY CARROLL, DICK TOBIN, JOHN ROBERTS, PAT 'DEXTER' AYLWARD.

An Antrim team of 1925 or 1926 before an All-Ireland junior semi-final. Seated on extreme right is county chairman, Liam Harvey, after whom the cup for the Ulster senior hurling championship is named.

The Galway side that won the county's first All-Ireland title in the 1923 championship. Galway would not win again until 1980.

The Dublin side that won the 1924 championship. **BACK ROW** (LEFT TO RIGHT): (KICKHAMS UNLESS OTHERWISE STATED): E. FLEMING, P. DONNELLY, R. DOHERTY (FAUGHS), J. BANNON (FAUGHS), T. KELLY, P. KENEFICK, J. RYAN. **SECOND ROW** (LEFT TO RIGHT): R. McCOWEN (HON. SEC.), M. DROMGOOLE, P. KAVANAGH (TRAINER), M. DARCY (UCD), P. AYLWARD, J. WALSH (FAUGHS), M. HOLLAND, J. CONROY (GARDA), R. MOCKLER (FAUGHS), A. HARTY (CHAIRMAN, DUBLIN COUNTY BOARD), J. O'NEILL (TREASURER). **FRONT ROW** (LEFT TO RIGHT): T. FINLAY, T. BARRY (FAUGHS), T. WALL (CAPT.), P. J. WALSH (PRESIDENT), D. O'NEILL, W. SMALL (UCD), G. HOWARD (GARDA), M. GILL (GARDA). **SITTING** (LEFT TO RIGHT): W. BANIM, T. DALY (UCD).

The Ireland team that competed at the Tailteann Games in 1924: **BACK ROW** (LEFT TO RIGHT): M. DERVIN (GALWAY), J. J. HAYES (TIPPERARY), M. KELLY (LAOIS), R. NEALON (TIPPERARY), M. RYAN (TIPPERARY). **SECOND ROW** (LEFT TO RIGHT): J. KAVANAGH (TRAINER), D. MARNANE (LIMERICK), J. KENNEDY (CORK), W. RYAN (LIMERICK), B. GIBBS (GALWAY), J. DARCY (TIPPERARY). **SEATED** (LEFT TO RIGHT): M. DARCY (TIPPERARY), J. WALSH (DUBLIN), J. HUMPHREYS (LIMERICK), G. HOWARD (DUBLIN), D. RING (CORK). **FRONT** (LEFT TO RIGHT): J. MAHON (GALWAY), I. HARNEY (GALWAY), W. GLEESON (LIMERICK).

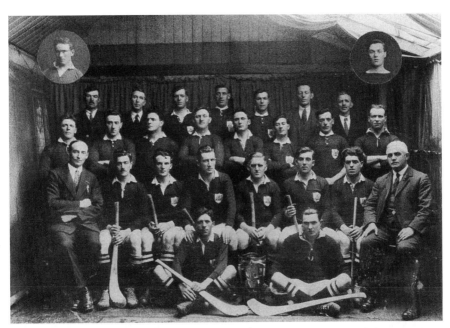

The Cork team that won the championship in 1926, beginning one of Cork's greatest eras. **INSET** (LEFT): J. COUGHLAN (BLACKROCK). **INSET** (RIGHT): P. AHERNE (BLACKROCK). **BACK ROW** (LEFT TO RIGHT): M. DORNEY (CHAIRMAN, BLACKROCK), M. LEAHY (SEC., BLACKROCK), M. AHERNE (BLACKROCK), M. MURPHY (COLLINS), E. O'CONNELL (BLACKROCK), P. J. O'KEEFFE (SEC., COUNTY BOARD), T. LONG (HON. TREASURER, COUNTY BOARD). **MIDDLE ROW** (LEFT TO RIGHT): W. HIGGINS (COLLINS), DR J. KEARNEY (ST FINBARR'S), M. MURPHY (BLACKROCK), J. KENNEDY (CARRIGTOHILL), M. O'CONNELL (ST FINBARR'S), B. MULLINS (REDMONDS), M. SCANNELL (BLACKROCK), M. MURPHY (BLACKROCK). **SEATED** (LEFT TO RIGHT): SEÁN McCARTHY (CHAIRMAN, COUNTY BOARD), E. O'CONNELL (BLACKROCK), J. O'REGAN (KINSALE), J. HURLEY (BLACKROCK), SEÁN ÓG MURPHY (CAPT.) (BLACKROCK), EUDIE COUGHLAN (BLACKROCK), P. DELEA (BLACKROCK), E. FITZGERALD (BLACKROCK). **FRONT** (LEFT TO RIGHT): D. B. MURPHY (CLOUGHDUV), J. EGAN (GLEN ROVERS).

Despite a vigorous hurling tradition in south Offaly, the county had little national success until the 1980s. This team, however, were All-Ireland junior hurling champions in 1929, repeating their first success of six years earlier. **BACK ROW** (LEFT TO RIGHT): TONY HANNON, MICK DIGAN, JOE KING, DICK CONWAY, MICK BRIEN, P. J. GROGAN (CAPT.), TOM CARROLL, JIM DOOLEY, BILL GUINAN, JIM O'DONNELL. **FRONT ROW** (LEFT TO RIGHT): MICK DOOLEY, MICK CARROLL, JOHN VERNEY, JIM BRIEN, MICK CORRIGAN, JIM HOLLIGAN, 'SKULL' BRIEN, JACK KINNARNEY, SONNIE WRAFTER, TED DOWNEY.

of the village on the west bank of the Shannon and the tradition it represented in south Galway will live for ever in the annals of the GAA.

What kind of hurling game was played that day in Birr? It was based principally on the *iomáin* version that was common in the south and that Cusack had known as a child growing up in Clare. But it was a synthetic version, incorporating some of the elements of 'commons'. 'Not surprisingly, this new game never caught on in the old "commons" area, with the Glens of Antrim being the only major exception.'[18] There were twenty-one players a side, divided, according to one source,[19] between ten backs and eleven forwards.

The development of the rules, the spread of the games and the organisation of hurling were not a unique phenomenon. It was part of a wider movement in the final decades of the nineteenth century. Other sports were being codified and organised for the first time: soccer, rugby and tennis immediately come to mind. 'All these were linked to rising spending power, a shortened working week (and the associated development of the "weekend"), improved and cheaper mass transport facilities which made spectator sports viable, expanded leisure time, the desire for organised sport among the working classes, and the commercialisation of leisure itself. The really distinctive feature of the GAA's success was that it occurred in what was still a predominantly agrarian society.'[20]

Early Rivalries

From the modest beginnings of the 1887 championship, hurling was to grow and develop. There were a number of hiccups. The so-called 'American invasion' interfered in 1888; the idea was to give Irish athletes an opportunity to compete internationally and exhibit the distinctive Irish game of hurling in prominent centres in America and Canada. An attempt by the IRB to take over the GAA at the 1887 convention led to a split, which resulted in the resignation of Maurice Davin as president. A 'reconstruction' convention took place later in the year and Davin was reinstated; however, the IRB fought back and another row developed at the 1889 convention, resulting in a second and permanent walk-out by Davin. The association was further divided by the Parnell split in 1891.

All these developments were bad for the progress of hurling. They led to fewer clubs being affiliated and fewer counties participating in the championship. It was intended to run off the championship in 1888, and the draws were made. No less than eighteen counties were affiliated, and inter-provincial draws were made for the first time. A number of games were played, but the championship was not completed.

Because a number of counties refused to recognise the Central Council, the number of entries for the 1889 inter-county championship was not very representative. Three Leinster and five Munster counties participated, and Dublin beat Clare in the final. One of the winning side, W. J. Spain from Nenagh, who scored three goals, had already won an All-Ireland football medal with Limerick Commercials in 1887. The Clare captain was John Considine, who, however, did not play with his team. According to one historian there are a number of instances of matches played in the early years of the association where the captains were not playing members but were selected because of their influence in keeping the teams together and in making them practise.[1]

In the 1890 championship eight teams played, four in Munster and four in Leinster. Cork and Wexford came through to the final at Clonturk Park on 16 November. It was a rough contest. The Castlebridge men played a reckless game, which resulted in several Aghabullogue players being knocked out of action. The Cork men appeared to have the better side, and they played in their bare feet! They were faster and more skilful hurlers. During the second half, with the Cork team leading by 1-6 to 2-2, the Aghabullogue captain withdrew his team from the field. On the recommendation of the referee the match was awarded to Cork.

Only five counties entered the 1891 championship, with Kerry and Wexford contesting the final and the Munster champions winning by a point. Wexford might have won with a point from a free puck at the end of normal time. However, the score was not awarded, as the referee blew his whistle before the ball crossed over the bar, to leave the sides level; he said he had no power to extend the time beyond the hour. Extra time was played for the first and only time in an All-Ireland final and Kerry won by 2-3 to 1-5.

Three teams contested the 1892 championship. Dublin, represented by Davitt-Faughs, got a walkover in the Leinster championship. Cork, represented by Redmonds, defeated Kerry, represented by Kilmoyley, for the Munster decider. The final, the first to be played with seventeen players a side, was played at Clonturk Park on 26 November 1893 and was won by Cork.

The same number of counties played in the 1893 championship, with the final contested between Cork and Kilkenny, who were making their first appearance. Originally scheduled for the Ashtown Trotting Grounds, the teams refused to play there, as the place was entirely unsuitable. The game and the goalposts were then removed to the Phoenix Park, where Cork won easily by 6-8 to 0-2.

Although the GAA showed definite signs of revival in 1894, only four teams contested the championship. Blackrock, representing Cork for the second time, had an easy victory over the Dublin Rapparees, who had got through to the final without having played a game.

The following year was to see the advent of one of the great teams of the early years of the GAA, Tubberadora. The team was picked from a small area of the parish of Boherlahan-Dualla, which had two other affiliated teams in Suir View Rangers and Boherlahan. Its advent and progress may have been inspired by an editorial in the *Cashel Sentinel* on 9

March 1895, which was critical of the performance of Tipperary (Drombane) against Cork (Blackrock) in the 1894 Munster final, played at Charleville on 3 March 1895.

> Our representatives had not the life nor the energy of the Cork men, nor did they display any science whatever, not so when the spirited Boherlahan and Clonoulty men used meet for championship honours ... Then you would recognise you were looking at a hurling match in a proper sense.

The words are significant and reflect a great pride in the hurling prowess of the county and the importance of upholding that pride in contests outside the county, especially against Cork. Many would be of the opinion that this Cork-Tipperary rivalry was the result of the many encounters in the decades following the foundation of the GAA. Jim Cronin, the Cork GAA historian, believes this rivalry predates the GAA. He cites the first meeting between the teams to substantiate his belief. This took place in Cork in August 1886, when five Tipperary teams travelled by train to Glanmire station to take on the best in Cork.

What is significant about these encounters is not so much the result— Tipperary won—as the tumultuous welcome given the visitors. Canon Fogarty describes it thus:

> Amid a hurricane of cheering the train entered Glanmire station. Cork was out in force to welcome the visitors and, preliminaries over, a vast procession headed by four bands set out for the field. Side by side marched the opposing teams, ten in all, hand and heart united, to uphold the ancient civilisation of the country.

And after the matches were over, he adds, 'Cork Gaels, though defeated, entertained their conquerors in a manner calculated to kill them with kindness.'[2] Jim Cronin has remarked that what sticks in his mind from the contemporary Cork newspaper reports is the enormous respect Cork had for Tipperary hurling at the time. They held the county in awe. His point is that such respect and awe were not born overnight but must have developed over time—in other words, long before the GAA was founded, and the corollary of this is that Tipperary had equal respect for Cork or they wouldn't have travelled in such numbers to Glanmire.

The strength of hurling in the parish of Boherlahan-Dualla can be seen in the fact that two teams from the parish contested the 1895 county final, Suir View and Tubberadora. After the latter defeated Drombane, the *Cashel Sentinel* did not conceal its admiration.

The Tubberadora men when lined out in the centre of the field seemed to be much younger than their opponents. They were, however, more of an athletic build and betrayed all the qualities necessary for speed, endurance and a facility for using the camán. Their big pucks elicited the applause of the spectators, and strikingly suggested that they were worthy of their successors of 20 years ago, who were undoubtedly the best hurlers in Tipperary and perhaps in all of Ireland.[3]

The final was played at the Rock Athletic Grounds in Cashel before an estimated four thousand people. This was the first time a charge for admission was made, two pence for adults and six pence for vehicles. The game was a cracker and had to go to extra time before Tubberadora triumphed.

One of the outstanding performances on the day was by the winning captain, Mikey Maher, who was to go on to lead Tipperary to three All-Ireland successes in 1895, 1896 and 1898 and to win two further champion-ships himself with Horse and Jockey in 1899 and with Two-Mile Borris in 1900. Of him Carbery was later to write:

Of the 100 odd All-Ireland captains I have seen … for inspired leadership and dynamic force in a crisis, I'd give the palm to big Mikey Maher of Tubberadora—a thundering man—6 feet 2 and 15 stone hard-trained.[4]

Seven teams played in the 1895 championship, and the final between Tipperary (Tubberadora) and Kilkenny (Tullaroan) was the first All-Ireland to be played at Jones's Road, Dublin, later to become Croke Park. It took place on 15 March 1896 and was to be the first of five All-Irelands at which medals were won by Denis Walsh. The last of these was not to be until January 1917, when Tipperary (Boherlahan) defeated another Tullaroan selection under the famous Sim Walton. One of the stars of the Tubberadora success was Paddy Riordan, who had the distinction of scoring the whole of Tubberadora's score of 6-8. (This has not been recognised as the highest for an All-Ireland final; the record is held officially by Nicky English for his 2-12 in the 1989 All-Ireland.) All that Tullaroan could muster on the day was a solitary goal scored early in the game.

Tubberadora repeated their success in the 1896 championship, defeating Ballyhea of Cork in the Munster final and beating Commercials (Dublin) by 8-13 to 0-4 in the All-Ireland, which wasn't played until 28 March 1898. The reason for the long delay was the introduction of a second inter-county competition in 1896. In the previous year Archbishop Croke presented two valuable silver cups to the association, and it was decided to run competitions distinct from the championship. In the first Croke Cup hurling competition, Tubberadora defeated Cork in style, which gave great satisfaction, as it had been mooted abroad that had Cork played in the 1895 championship Tubberadora would never have won. Clare were the opponents in the Munster final of the Croke Cup and caused consternation by beating the Tipperary men. The reason is reported in Canon Fogarty's book: 'Mikey Maher took only a reconnoitring party. The men who blazed the trail against Ballyhea were absent.'[5]

The defeat by Clare was the only one inflicted on this famous Tubberadora team in inter-county hurling. They tried to reverse it by objecting to the result. The captain, Mikey Maher, and one of the players, Will Devane, gave evidence that at one period of the game they counted an extra player on the Tulla (Clare) team, and when they informed the referee a Tulla player was seen disappearing into the crowd. The objection, however, did not succeed.

Tubberadora did not participate in the 1897 county championship after defeating Killenaule 8-15 to nil in the first round. They were drawn to play Suir View in the county semi-final. While practising for this game, John Maher broke his leg in a clash with Phil Scanlon. So upset were the team that Mikey Maher requested and was granted permission by the county board to withdraw from the championship. Their opponents went on to win the county final but were beaten in the All-Ireland championship.

It is fair to say that had Tubberadora continued on they would have made it the three in a row. This belief is borne out by the experience of the team in the 1898 championship. They defeated Cork in a replayed Munster final before fifteen thousand people at Kilmallock, accounted for Peterswell (Galway) in the All-Ireland semi-final at Athenry, and defeated Tullaroan (Kilkenny) in the final by 7-13 to 3-10. The game was played at Jones's Road on 25 March 1900, and the team had prepared by practising in Walsh's kiln field in Tubberadora, playing backs and forwards, and the latter improved their shooting prowess through the band of a cartwheel. The successful outfit was Mikey Maher, Ned Maher, Ned Brennan, Johnny Walsh, Denis Walsh, John Connolly, Tommy Ryan, John Ryan, Will Devane, E. D. Ryan, Thady Flanagan, Phil Byrne, Watty Dunne, Jack Maher (N), Tim Condon, Jim O'Keeffe, and Dick O'Keeffe. During its existence this master combination of hurlers had played fourteen championship matches without defeat and scored 71 goals and 108 points to 17-46 against. Having won three championships and a Croke Cup,[6] the champions had established a permanent place in the history of hurling and decided to call it a day. But although they went out of existence as a club, many of the players continued to win honours with neighbouring clubs.

The arrival of the twentieth century saw new developments, keener rivalries, and a successful challenge by Kilkenny for hurling supremacy. One development in 1900 was the admission of English clubs to the All-Ireland championship. Having been declared for GAA purposes a province of Ireland, England availed of its right to compete and was to do so for the first four years of the century. The first representatives were London Desmonds, and they played Tipperary (Two-Mile Borris) in the 1900 final, played at Jones's Road on 26 October 1902. About ten thousand supporters saw a well-contested game, described by *Sport* as 'the best, the cleverest and the fastest we have ever seen in an All-Ireland final.' At half time the score stood at 0-5 to 0-3 in Tipperary's favour. In the second half London scored three more points and were leading with three minutes to go. Then Tipperary got a free that resulted in a goal and, on the puck-out, rushed a second to win by 2-5 to 0-6.

The English entrants were to go one better in 1901, when they were represented by London Emmets. The team included nine players from Cork (including Tom Barry of Glanworth, who played with London Irish against Scotland in the famous game at Stamford Bridge in 1896), four from Clare, two from Limerick, and one each from Tipperary and Kerry. They met Cork at Jones's Road on 2 August 1903. According to Jim Cronin, nobody considered the visitors a match for the Cork team but a surprise was in store. Cork took the game too casually and had had little sleep the night before. The wet ground helped the well-equipped visitors, and despite the fact that Cork were the better hurlers, they had to concede victory to a powerful exiles seventeen after a great game. The match finished 1-5 to 0-4 in London's favour.[7]

That was to be London's finest hour and the only time the championship crossed the water. In 1902 Cork, who were again the 'home' champions, easily wiped out their previous year's defeat. On this occasion they came up against London's Brian Bórú, who had Paddy Mehigan (better known as 'Carbery') on their team, and the Cork men won well on a score of 3-13 to nil. The game was played in the new Athletic Grounds in Cork on 11 September 1904 and marked the official opening of the venue.

Cork played London Irish in the 1903 decider and once again had an easy victory, by 3-16 to 1-1. The game was played at Jones's Road on 12 November 1905, and it was to be the last year for some time that representatives of the English province participated in the All-Ireland senior championship. The following year they played instead in the Croke Cup competition.

Dr Croke's silver cup was played for in 1896 and 1897; afterwards the competition was amalgamated with the championship. In accordance with a resolution passed at the 1902 Convention, the cup was put up for competition between the provinces. Because of the delay in getting possession of the cup, it was not until 1904 that the Central Council was in a position to arrange the competition. In the final, Cork, representing Munster, defeated London Irish by 5-10 to 0-3 before seven thousand spectators at Jones's Road on 19 February 1905. It was to be London's only participation in this competition.

Cork dominated hurling in the early years of the decade. They took five Munster finals in a row between 1901 and 1905. Significantly, Tipperary provided the opposition in only one of the finals, in 1904, when they were beaten by 3-10 to 3-4. This was the Semple era and the time of the famed Thurles Blues. Dan Fraher's field in Dungarvan had been opened some years previously and it became the venue for numerous Munster finals and many encounters between Tipperary and Cork.

When the two teams qualified for the 1906 final, Tipperary were determined to put an end to the Cork gallop. 'Since 1901,' according to Canon Fogarty, 'Cork hurlers had built a wall around the Munster championship and held it intact.'[8] The game turned out as well as it promised. When the final whistle sounded, Semple's vow was fulfilled: he had changed the line of succession to the throne, and his team had written the first epic event in their history, Tipperary 3-4, Cork 0-9.

While Cork reversed the decision the following year, Tipperary were to succeed again in 1908 and 1909 and go some way towards restoring the county's honour. The Cork victory in 1907 was by two points, and the game was a thriller. The following year Tipperary won by a point, with the teams matching score for score before the Premier County triumphed. These games attracted throngs of people because of the element of uncertainty in their outcome.

The excitement in the county the following year, when the Blues made it a double, was intense. During the interval, with Cork ahead by 1-6 to 1-2, Semple said to his team: 'Now, lads, listen! Cork can't play without the ball, so don't let them have it. Do you hear?' 'We do!' they resolutely replied.

> Play resumed; the captain's words were taken to heart and had effect but not before Dungourney had gone another goal ahead. Then the homesters began to assert themselves and the enemy was up against difficulty in earnest. There was first a point, and next a green flag to herald the change. Excitement was now at fever heat and roofs of sheds collapsed in the pandemonium. With 20 minutes to play the figures were 2-6 to 2-3. Come weal! Come woe!

The Blues were determined to hold their prestige. A hurricane greeted their unparalleled courage, obstinacy and endurance. The Cork forwards were completely blotted out but the team as a whole held out to the bitter end, unwilling to yield but unable to rise. The whistle sounded; Tipperary 2-10 Cork 2-6.[9]

The Blues were to fall to Kilkenny at the final hurdle, played in Cork in cold, wintry conditions. It was a day of misfortune for the Thurles men. They lacked all their usual fire and dash, failed to score a goal, and were beaten by 4-6 to 0-12.

When one writes about this period two teams, the Thurles Blues and Dungourney, dominate. The Thurles Blues are synonymous with Tom Semple. As a leader of men and a wielder of the camán he had few equals. A commanding figure, his magnificent physique and easy manner earned him the respect of many. Carbery described him thus in the *Cork Examiner* in December 1908:

Few men playing the game in Ireland today have achieved the fame that the Thurles captain—Tom Semple—has known. As an organiser and a player he deserves a high place in any story of the progress of hurling during the infancy of the 20th century. Tom is a conspicuous man—there is no chance of mistaking another player for Semple … In build Semple is one of the tall, sinewy type, more of a thoroughbred than a hunter, if I may so express myself. He is well over six feet in his 'vamps', and, like most Tipperary men, square cut and as hard as nails. Considering his great height, he is light all over him, particularly at the waist and limbs. A grand ball player he is a most dangerous wing scorer. On ground he has a fine 'slog' off left or right and always sends the ball where his centre can't help scoring. But his favourite stroke is a lift, catch with left, turn to deceive an opponent and shoot low and long. It is as quick and spectacular a movement as one could wish to see, and countless scores have come off those efforts. He doesn't throw up the ball when he handles it—it simply drops to his swinging stick. When a rival is too close for him to catch, he trusts to the drop-puck … and a most deceptive ball it is to save. He doesn't love close work and generally makes room for himself by dribbling before he strikes. It generally pays a team to set a man specially to watch Semple for his backs feed him invariably.

Semple's career as a player stretched from 1897 to 1911, and its height coincided with the success of the Thurles Blues. He led his club to county championship victories in 1904, 1906, 1907, 1908, 1909, and 1911. He was a regular on the county team for many years and led the Blues to All-Ireland victories in 1906 and 1908. In 1906 also he won the All-Ireland long puck championship, sending the nine-ounce ball 96 yards. He was also captain of the Tipperary team that travelled to the Continent in 1910 and played exhibition games at Brussels and Fontenoy.

No greater tribute could have been paid to Semple's memory than the naming of the Thurles stadium after him in 1968. Years earlier he was the leader of a gallant band who were instrumental in acquiring Thurles Sports Field from the Thurles Show Committee, and he played a leading part in the raising of funds for its early development.

By his example and enthusiasm Tom Semple inspired the players around him with a burning desire for victory. Among these players were Jack Mooney and Jack Mockler, who made a powerful midfield partnership. There was James 'the Hawk' O'Brien, renowned for the quickness of his eye and the speed of his reactions between the posts. Tom Kerwick and Martin O'Brien were outstanding defenders and Paddy 'Daddy' Brolan, who owed his sobriquet to the superlative quality of his hurling, and Hughie Shelly forwards of rare skill and talent. Others to be mentioned included Tom 'Gaffer' Kenna, Joe Mouloughney, and Mick O'Dwyer.

Raymond Smith relates that Paddy Leahy confided to him the opinion that the Blues were the most perfect machine that ever graced a hurling field. The breakthrough came in the 1904 county final against De Wets, one of the most formidable forces in hurling at the time. However, they were defeated in the Munster final at Dungarvan by a Cork (St Finbarr's) selection. Two-Mile Borris proved too good for Thurles in the 1905 county championship.

In 1906 a great victory over Moycarkey-Borris and a county final success over De Wets brought the Blues into Munster and a march to victory. Limerick and Clare were overcome, and Cork were taken in the Munster final. Galway provided derisory opposition in the All-Ireland semi-final, and Dublin were handily overcome in the final.

However, the team to beat at that time was Dungourney. They had arrived in 1902 and with them one of the greatest hurlers ever to come out of the Rebel County, the peerless Jim Kelleher, regarded as one of the best backs in the game. Not a tall man by any means—he was 5 feet 9 inches—but he was stockily built and commanded the whole defensive scene from the full-back position. Carbery waxed eloquent on him in the *Cork Examiner* on 16 February 1909:

Kelleher first made his debut as a goalkeeper and as such was a great success—very sure to stop and quick to strike. But he soon discovered that his exceeding speed of foot, as well as of hand and eye, were wasted under the bar, so he came out to play back and to make name and fame for himself and his team. Today for all-round merit among backs, he can beat them all—Tipperary men, Kilkenny men, Wexford or Dublin men, followers of Rockies, Reds or 'Barrs, alike give him pride of place—king of them all. As good a dribbler as Mackessy, as clever to catch and as quick to deliver as Nolan, as graceful a striker as Keeffe of the Reds, as strong a pucker as Tom Coughlan, as sticky a fighter as Dave McGrath—the combination was never before equalled in Gaeldom. Beyond all this Kelleher has a peculiar instinctive grasp of the right thing to do in every conceivable emergency. With a wonderful variety of strokes, it is a pleasure to any ardent student of the game to watch him ... His judgment is extraordinary—he has rarely been known to miss a ball, for he never strikes unless he is sure of getting his puck in. A lifelong teetotaller and non-smoker, he is never out of form and the end of the hour always sees him smiling. His perpetual equanimity is superb as he sends back attack after attack with admirable ease ... On ground or overhead, out of his hand or a flying drop, a doubler or an incoming ball—he commands them all with equal skill. He has one distinctive faculty that I have never seen with another player. He races at full speed after a ball, then with his opponents coming up, he digs his heel into the sod, turns like a hare and, in the same movement, is speeding back with the leather in full command, whilst his opponents knock against empty air. Quiet to a fault, manly and honest in his hurling, energetic in organisation, an ideal captain, the hero of this note occupies an enviable position of popularity amongst the Gaels of Ireland today.

Kelleher led Cork to an overwhelming 3-13 to nil victory over London's Brian Bórú in the 1902 championship. He was also a member of the victorious Blackrock selection the following year, and in the succeeding seasons his fame and skill grew.

In 1907 the Blues went down to Dungarvan to face Dungourney in the Munster final before a wildly cheering crowd of twenty thousand. It was a contest of champions. Jim Kelleher's men led by 1-2 to 0-2 at the interval. In the second half Tipperary were still baffled by the Cork defence, but by the final quarter the score stood at 1-5 to 1-4 in Cork's favour. Then a free was awarded to Tipperary, and only the veteran Jim Kelleher stood between Semple and the winning score. All Semple's efforts were in vain as the ball was stopped by Kelleher and the Cork men got a further point to win by 1-6 to 1-4.

The Blues were back in 1908 with a victory over Cork (Blackrock). The sides were level at half time, and a titanic second-half struggle for supremacy developed before a late Tipperary goal gave victory to the Blues on a score of 2-11 to 3-7. The All-Ireland, against Dublin (Kickhams), was won in a replay by 3-15 to 1-5.

Probably the greatest contest between the two great sides came in the 1909 Munster final. Although the Blues were champions and had two All-Irelands to their credit, Dungourney were firm favourites to win. Their record that season had been impressive. A powerful Blackrock side had failed to halt them at home, and it appeared that they had the overall strength to repeat their 1907 success. This expectation was confirmed in the first half, at the end of which they led by 1-6 to 1-2.

In the Dungourney camp there was such confidence that the supporters were already letting off the pigeons carrying the news of the victory to the banks of the Lee. This confidence appeared justified when Cork increased their lead to 2-6 to 1-2 early in the second half to take a seven-point lead. But Semple's words had put new life into the Blues. Their dying flame became a raging fire, and Cork's resistance began to wilt against its force and intensity. Gradually Cork were overcome, the sides drew level, and the Tipperary men went on to win by four points, 2-10 to 2-6, a magnificent victory.

Alas, it turned out to be the Blues' greatest game that year. They were poor against Galway in the All-Ireland semi-final and lacked all their old fire and dash against Kilkenny in the final. They were ten points in arrears after the first half, and although they improved their performance after the interval they could never reach the glorious heights they had scaled in the Munster final and went down 4-6 to 0-12.

The last fling for the Blues was in 1911, when they gave a mighty display to humble Toomevara in the county final. But it was a last flickering light, and though Cork were overcome in the Munster championship, the Blues were defeated by Limerick in the Munster final. Dungourney also disappeared from the scene; they were beaten by Blackrock in the 1910 county final, and this was to mark their passing and the advent of the Rockies' dominance for a number of years to come.

Cork and Tipperary provided stirring encounters in those years; but the team that dominated the scene was undoubtedly Kilkenny. They may have been late in winning All-Ireland honours, but once they had made their mark they went on to win seven titles in ten years.

They made their first All-Ireland appearance in 1894, but it wasn't an auspicious beginning, and they were beaten by 24 points. One of the linesmen that day was James Nowlan, later president of the GAA. In the following year they were beaten by an almost similar amount, this time by Tipperary. They made a better attempt in 1897 but were defeated by Limerick in Tipperary on the score 3-4 to 2-4. Although they had the better of the first half of the 1898 final against Tipperary, the latter had 12 points to spare at the end. The county were not to qualify for another final for five more years. In Leinster they were awarded the 1903 final against Dublin, who had been credited with a disputed goal, they destroyed Antrim in the All-Ireland semi-final but were themselves overcome by Cork in the 'home' final at Dungarvan by 8-9 to 0-8. In one report of the game Andy Buckley of Cork is credited with scoring six goals, which, if correct, was the second-best score for an All-Ireland final, equalled by Nicky English, who scored 2-12 in the 1989 final.[10]

This record of defeat was to be transformed into a glorious decade of success, beginning in 1904. Although they subsequently won the Leinster final, Kilkenny were a nominated team in the All-Ireland semi-final against Galway at Athlone.

Having accounted for the westerners before a crowd of ten thousand, they came up against Cork in the final at Carrick-on-Suir, which was, as usual at the time, nearly two years behind time and was not played until 24 June 1906. The game was a very tight struggle and in total contrast to the previous year's encounter. Kilkenny led at half time by 1-5 to 0-5. Cork levelled soon after the interval and then went a point ahead. Kilkenny fought back and went two points in front. Cork tried hard in the closing minutes and scored a point, but Kilkenny held out to win their first All-Ireland and dramatically reverse the previous year's defeat with a score of 1-9 to 1-8. The winners, a Tullaroan selection, included players who became household names, not only in Kilkenny but well beyond the county. The team was: Dick Brennan, 'Drug' Walsh, Eddie Doyle, Paddy 'Icy' Lanigan, Martin Lalor, Jack Hoyne, Sim Walton, Pat Fielding, Dan Stapleton, Jer Doheny (captain), Jim Lalor, Jack Rochford, 'Fox' Maher, Dick Doyle, Pat Saunders, Dan Grace, and Jack Anthony.

Kilkenny and Cork again contested the 1905 final, which was played in Tipperary. The Nore men lined out in variously coloured jerseys, in contrast to Cork, who had an all-blue rig-out. 'Fox' Maher, who had stated after the 1904 All-Ireland that it was his last game, was sorely missed, and Cork got three early goals. Kilkenny recovered and were behind by 3-7 to 2-6 at half time. They got a goal after the resumption, to come within a point of Cork, but despite a brilliant performance by Sim Walton the Leesiders won by 5-10 to 3-13. Kilkenny objected to the result, on the grounds that Daniel McCarthy, the Cork goalkeeper, was illegal because he was a reservist with the British army. Cork raised a counter-objection that the Kilkenny player Matt Gargan had played with Waterford in the Munster championship. After a Central Council meeting it was decided to replay the game.

There was a change of venue to Dungarvan, and close on ten thousand attended. Kilkenny lined out in black-and-amber jerseys and were to win their first All-Ireland in the famous colours. Cork scored 2-3 before Kilkenny opened their account with a goal by Jim Kelly, who was to have a second before half time, when Cork led by 2-6 to 2-2. Kelly ran riot in the second half and is credited with 5-2, which was not equalled until Eddie Keher scored 2-11 in the 1971 All-Ireland. At the final whistle Kilkenny were in front by 7-7 to 2-9. For the game, which was played on 30 June 1907, Cork were short a number of their best players, but their line-out did include Paddy Mehigan.

Kilkenny had played three matches in the 1906 championship before they won the 1905 All-Ireland. The third of these was against Antrim in the All-Ireland semi-final. They had to be nominated for the game, as the Leinster championship wasn't complete. But after winning the game they lost the Leinster final to Dublin, who went on to play Tipperary in the All-Ireland.

The Noresiders were back with a bang in 1907 to claim their third All-Ireland. Again their opponents were the Dungourney selection from Cork under their famous captain Jamesy Kelleher. The venue was Dan Fraher's field in Dungarvan, and an estimated fifteen thousand people attended. Father J. B. Dollard, the poet-priest from Mooncoin, threw in the ball. There was a belief among the Kilkenny players that if one of their priests threw in the ball they would win. The game was a classic, regarded as the best final played till then. Kilkenny won by a point, 3-12 to 4-8, having been behind by two goals at the interval. It was a titanic struggle in the closing stages, and Jack Anthony earned undying fame when he scored what proved to be the winning point. Describing the match in *Sport*, Father Dollard said:

> In such a tremendous struggle the almost entire absence of any exhibitions of ill-temper among the hurlers was truly marvellous.

Hurling as played by these premier teams is truly a national game to be proud of, a national heritage, a national glory … If the young men of Ireland could only be made see the fact as it really is, namely, that one grand day like that at Dungarvan (no matter who wins) gives pure enjoyment and more genuine satisfaction than a thousand years of America or other foreign lands, they would know how privileged they are and would choose the better part of staying in the old country working for her weal, living and dying within the four walls of her holy hills …"

When the team was photographed a fortnight after the match in St James's Park, the players wore Mooncoin jerseys as a gesture to Father Dollard, who was given pride of place in the centre of the middle row. In the match itself the team played in Tullaroan jerseys, because Mooncoin had supplied the captain. This agreement was to lead two more Kilkenny teams to All-Ireland winning sides.

Kilkenny lost their first match in the 1908 championship to Wexford but got it on an objection. They refused to contest the Leinster final against Dublin, because of a dispute about the Railway Shield, which had been won by Leinster, and this probably cost them the 1908 All-Ireland.

They were back on their winning streak in the 1909 championship, when they defeated Tipperary in the All-Ireland final at Cork Athletic Grounds by 4-6 to 0-12. Kilkenny were short-handed on the day. The team included eight from Mooncoin, five from Tullaroan, three from Erin's Own, and one from Three Castles. Newcomers to the All-Ireland final included Jim Ryan, who was to play a marvellous game against Tom Semple, Jim Dunphy, who kept a clean sheet in goal, Joe Delahunty and Bill Hennebry of Mooncoin, and Mick Shortall from Erin's Own.

Kilkenny had the better of the first half and led by 3-4 to 0-3 at half time. After the interval Tipperary came more into the game and scored eight points without reply to come within two of Kilkenny. When it seemed that Tipperary might make it, Kilkenny struck back with a point and then a goal to win by 4-6 to 0-12. It was the first time Tipperary had failed to score a goal in a major final.

Another dispute robbed Kilkenny of a further All-Ireland in 1910. Nominated to represent Leinster in the All-Ireland series, they defeated London Irish but then went under to Dublin in the Leinster championship. They were without the Doyles, Eddie, Dick, and Mick, who refused to play the 1909 county final against Erin's Own, because the match was played at Waterford Sports Field, which the owners wanted to use for other sports.

As the final had gone ahead they withdrew from the county team, and Kilkenny were beaten by Dublin 4-1 to 2-1. It can be argued that, as with the disputes in 1906 and 1908, the county might have won the All-Ireland.

Another dispute in 1914 left the county without Jack Rochford, Sim Walton, and Dick Doherty, and Laois went on to beat Kilkenny by a point. So, the argument goes, Kilkenny might have won eleven instead of seven All-Irelands in that marvellous era from 1904 to 1914.

The 1911 All-Ireland never took place. Having avenged their previous year's defeat by Dublin in the Leinster final, Kilkenny beat Antrim in the All-Ireland semi-final and qualified to play Limerick in the final, which was scheduled for Cork Athletic Grounds. Before the game John F. Drennan of Conway Hall presented a set of black-and-amber jerseys to the county board to be worn by the county team; thereafter these were the colours worn by the county.

When the teams arrived in Cork they found the pitch in an unplayable condition. Heavy rain on the preceding days had made it impossible to mark out the pitch. Limerick, who had beaten Tipperary in similar conditions some weeks previously, wanted to play at all costs. Captained by the redoubtable 'Tyler' Mackey, the team was the most formidable that had come out of Limerick for some time. Limerick togged out and pucked around. The referee, Tom Kenny of Galway, and some officials from the Central Council took a look at the pitch and declared it unplayable; the game would be held later in Thurles. Limerick dug their heels in and declared 'for Cork or nowhere.' The result was that Kilkenny were awarded the All-Ireland title and the Limerick County Board were suspended. To compensate for the loss of revenue the Central Council organised a game between Tipperary and Kilkenny in lieu of the All-Ireland final. It was played in Dungarvan for a special set of medals and was won by Kilkenny by 3-3 to 2-1.

Kilkenny had to fight hard to defeat Wexford in the first round of the 1912 Leinster championship, snatching a winning goal just before time to win by 4-4 to 4-3. On their way to the All-Ireland final they defeated Laois and Galway.

Cork were their opponents in the final, played at Jones's Road, and the match was the lowest-scoring up to that time, with Kilkenny winning by 2-1 to 1-3. Almost eighteen thousand spectators turned up; the charge at the gate varied from six pence and a shilling to half a crown (12½p) for sideline seats. Sim Walton was captain. The Kilkenny team was led onto the field by their own pipe band.

Cork were on top for most of the match but found it difficult to breach the Kilkenny defence. They led by 1-2 to 0-1 at the interval and would have been ahead by more but for the brilliance of John T. Power in the Kilkenny goal. They seemed to be on their way to victory until they conceded a soft goal ten minutes from time. Matt Gargan sent a long drive into the Cork goal. With all the time in the world, Andy Fitzgerald ran out to meet it and pulled on it when he had time to stop it. Unbelievably, he missed, and the ball hopped over the goal-line. Cork made several attempts to retrieve the situation, but the stewards had lost control and the crowd spilled out onto the pitch.

This was the first All-Ireland won by the county in what was later to be known as Croke Park. Kilkenny made it three in a row when they won the 1913 All-Ireland, which was the first with fifteen men a side. Their opponents were Tipperary, who were known as the 'Toomevara Greyhounds' because the team was anchored by nine players from the famous club and captained by Wedger Meagher. Tipperary were strong favourites, having routed Kilkenny 5-4 to 1-1 in the Croke Cup final a few months previously. As Tipperary were noted for their speed, Kilkenny trained as never before, and on the day they were well able to stay with their opponents. It was a wonderful game, played at a hectic pace. Kilkenny revealed a sharpness from the start; in contrast, Tipperary were stale and lifeless, showing none of the zest they had displayed in the Croke Memorial Tournament final. At half time Kilkenny led by 1-4 to 1-1. Tipperary did not show much change in the second half, and at the final whistle the Noresiders were champions on a score of 2-4 to 1-2.

Sim Walton played one of his greatest games. Mick Doyle and 'Drug' Walsh, who was the captain, also showed up well, while John T. Power was brilliant in goal. Others to stand out were Matt Gargan and Jack Lannon. The result of the match was flashed to the *Kilkenny People* office by telegraph at 4:45 p.m. Crowds had congregated outside to hear the news, and when it came through there was prolonged cheering.

This was to remain Kilkenny's only hat-trick of titles. The Kilkenny County Board believed the presentation of the black-and-amber jerseys had something to do with the success; to show how grateful they were they presented John F. Drennan with a gold medal and a large photograph of the 1913 team.

It is difficult to mention all the heroes from this era. One of the least-known must be Danny O'Connell, the coach of the seven All-Ireland winning teams. Four players figured in all the teams: Sim Walton of Tullaroan, Jack Rochford of Three Castles, and Dick Doyle and Dick Walsh of Mooncoin. The Doyles of Mooncoin created a record that is unlikely to be surpassed: they won eighteen senior medals between them (Dick seven, Eddie six, and Mick five). Paddy 'Icy' Lanigan was part of the seven winning teams but was only a sub in 1913. Another great family were the Graces of Tullaroan, where three brothers won fifteen All-Ireland medals, seven in hurling and eight in football. Dick won five hurling medals, the first in 1909 when only eighteen years old. Jack, who died at the age of thirty-one, won five All-Ireland football medals with Dublin. Pierce is one of the few players to have won medals in both codes: he won two football medals with Dublin and three hurling medals with Kilkenny. Finally, mention must be made of Pat 'Fox' Maher, who was known as the father of hurling and was one of Tullaroan's and Kilkenny's most outstanding hurling personalities. Wherever he went he had crowds of admirers. Though winning only one All-Ireland title, in 1904, his name stands out more than any other of his generation.[12]

Kilkenny's victims in the 1913 All-Ireland were the Toomevara Greyhounds. This band of players created an image in the mind of the sporting public as distinctive as that created by the men of Tubberadora, Dungourney, the Thurles Blues, Tullaroan, and Mooncoin. Their arrival on the hurling scene at the end of the first decade of the new century saw the dawning of a new era in the history of the Toomevara club. 'It ushered in a period of fame and glory for the hurlers of the parish making their name a household word throughout the length and breadth of Ireland.'[13] Led by Pat 'Wedger' Meagher, the Greyhounds burst on the horizon, giving new life to hurling in Tipperary. Their greatest year was 1913, and the highlight was their victory over Kilkenny in the Croke Memorial Tournament final at Dungarvan. Lithe, agile and sinewy but above all fleet of foot, they pushed Kilkenny aside in a brilliant display of hurling.

But, alas, it was the pride of Toomevara that fell to Kilkenny in the 1913 All-Ireland. The Greyhounds never won an All-Ireland, but it speaks volumes for their magnificent exploits that their fame has lived on in the annals of hurling, and in any roll-call of the greats the names of 'Wedger' Meagher, Jack 'Skinny' O'Meara, Stephen Hackett, Jack Harty, Mick Ryan, Ned Guilmartin, Jim O'Meara and Frank McGrath still hold pride of place.

6

——————— A *Period of Flux*, 1914–27 ———————

For the next decade or more after 1913, no team was to dominate the All-Ireland championship. Cork, Kilkenny and Tipperary were to take one championship each. Three new teams—Clare, Laois, and Galway—made the breakthrough. Limerick won twice, and Dublin took three titles.

Clare came good in 1914 after showing promising form in the previous couple of years. Having given Limerick a drubbing, they came up against Cork in the Munster final in Thurles, with Tom Semple in charge of the whistle. A huge crowd turned up, and Clare more than justified the confidence of their supporters with a thrilling hour's hurling. Both sides maintained a fast pace to the game right up to the final whistle, when Clare were ahead by 3-2 to 3-1.

Because the Munster final had been delayed, Cork were nominated to represent the province in the All-Ireland series, and they defeated Galway in the semi-final. Clare went through to the All-Ireland, where they defeated Laois by 5-1 to 1-0, having led by 3-1 to 0-0 at the interval. Drawn from seven clubs, the Clare team included as captain Amby Power of Quin, a man 6 feet 4 inches in height. In goal was the famous Pat 'Fowler' McInerney, later to become better known as a full-back with Dublin as well as his native county. Brendan Considine of Ennis was then only at the beginning of a career that would include football as well as hurling. At half-back was a clubmate, Martin Moloney; and another Ennis player was 'Sham' Spellisey, who was also a sprinter of note. Others deserving of mention were Paddy McDermott of Whitegate and two good and strong hurlers from O'Callaghan's Mills, Jack Shaloo and Ned Grace. The trainer of the team was Jim (Andy) O'Hehir, father of the famous Micheál.

Laois were to make amends in 1915. They beat Offaly, Kilkenny and Dublin to take the Leinster title and faced Cork in the All-Ireland, which was played in Croke Park on 24 October. One of the newcomers on the Cork team was Seán Óg Murphy. Rain fell throughout the second half, which suited the heavier Laois men, who added four goals to Cork's goal and a point, and this gave them victory by 6-2 to 4-1. The result was a great surprise.

Laois were helped to prepare for the final by the legendary Dick 'Drug' Walsh of Mooncoin. He used his influence to bring the Kilkenny team to Port Laoise on three consecutive Sundays before the final to give Laois the practice they so badly needed. The players travelled by sidecar to Port Laoise every Sunday; the panel and mentors went up to Dublin by train on the Saturday night and stayed in a hotel in Gardiner Street. There was close surveillance on all the players so that nothing amiss would be done by them or to them. On the Sunday they stripped in the hotel and walked to the grounds and a little later hurled themselves into the list of illustrious teams that have won All-Ireland titles. They didn't realise on the day that their victory was to be unique for so long. The medals were presented in early 1916 in Abbeyleix; it was a rousing all-night party, which fitted the famous victory.

Tipperary had one victory during this period of flux. Eight years had passed since they last won an All-Ireland. The new revival began in the parish of Boherlahan, in fact in the small townland of Tubberadora that had won such glory in the eighteen-nineties. Three teams of note had come out of the parish: Tubberadora, Suir View, and Ballytarsna. Now an attempt was made to form a new team out of the remnants of the three. The great Mikey Maher of the three All-Irelands and Johnny Leahy of one of the greatest hurling families in the country were the guiding lights in building the new team. Out of their efforts Boherlahan was born, and the first chairman of the new club in 1912 was Tommy Dwyer, who had played in his time with all three of the component teams.

The arrival of Boherlahan coincided with the famous Toomevara Greyhounds, and Boherlahan had to play second fiddle to Toom for a number of years until 1916, when the breakthrough was made. The teams met in the county final in Thurles, and in a cracker of a game the reign of Toomevara came to an end in very definite fashion: Boherlahan 2-2, Toomevara 0-0.

When the Boherlahan men took the field in the Munster championship they did so in the blue jersey with gold sash of their invincible predecessors from Tubberadora. This was the first time Tipp wore these colours, which they have done ever since. They impressed in overcoming

Limerick, Kerry and Cork in Munster and Galway on their way to the All-Ireland final. They scored the equivalent of seventy points and conceded only sixteen. Kilkenny, a Tullaroan selection captained by Sim Walton, provided the ultimate opposition. Not since 1898 had Kilkenny been defeated in an All-Ireland final.

The game was delayed until 21 January 1917 and took place in the atmosphere of tension and imprisonments that followed the Rising. Tipperary held their own in the first half and led by 1-2 to 0-1 at the break. Kilkenny came out transformed in the second half and led by five points with ten minutes to go. Victory seemed to be within their grasp, but Tipperary rallied and turned apparent defeat into a glorious victory by 5-4 to 3-2. The champions had put together a team of talented players, such as Johnny and Paddy Leahy, Arthur O'Donnell, Denis Walsh, who was winning his fifth All-Ireland, Jack Power, Willie Dwyer, and Jack Doherty, and seemed set for a successful run. They qualified for the final again in 1917 but were sensationally beaten by Dublin on the score of 5-4 to 4-2. Played on 28 October, this was the Premier County's second All-Ireland in the same year, and they were beaten probably because of over-confidence. The county had to wait for seven more years before victory was to be theirs again.

The Leahys were synonymous with Boherlahan and Tipperary hurling. Johnny, who captained in 1916 and was to do so again in 1925, led Tipperary to five Munster championships, two All-Irelands, and one National League; he also led Tipperary on their American trip in 1926. Paddy won All-Irelands in 1916 and 1926 and was the chief architect of the county's dazzling success between 1949 and 1966. Mick won All-Ireland medals with Tipperary in 1916 and with Cork in 1928 and 1931, while the youngest, Tommy, won the highest honour in the game in 1930.

Dublin's victory over Tipperary in the 1917 All-Ireland was to usher in the greatest period of hurling in Dublin. Over a period of eleven years the county was to dominate the All-Ireland championship, playing in six finals and winning four. Dublin had won their first All-Ireland in 1889, when they were represented by Kickhams. They defeated Clare, represented by Tulla, in the final at Inchicore on 3 November by 5-1 to 1-6. The Kickhams club had been formed on Easter Monday 1886 but didn't play hurling at first, as the game was considered too dangerous.[1] One of the victorious side was W. J. Spain, the first man to win All-Irelands in both codes. Born in Nenagh, he was on the Commercials team that won the first All-Ireland football final for Limerick in 1887 and in the 1889 final scored no less than three goals for Kickhams. Another member of the side was Frank Coughlan, who had been a member of the 'Invasion' hurling team in 1888.

Dublin (Flag-Davitts) next played in the 1892 final against Cork. The match was played on 26 March 1893 at Clonturk Park. Dublin led by 1-1 to 0-0 at half time but left the venue after fifty minutes' play, on the grounds that their opponents were not entitled to a second goal awarded to them by the referee, Dan Fraher of Dungarvan. The match was awarded to Cork, and the official score was Cork 2-4, Dublin 1-1. This was the first All-Ireland with seventeen players a side.

In 1894 the Dublin Rapparees became champions of the province without having played a single match and met Blackrock, the Cork representatives, in Clonturk Park on 24 March 1895, when the Cork side had an easy victory by 5-20 to 2-0. In 1896 Dublin (Commercials) were beaten 4-1 to 0-1 by Tipperary (Tubberadora). In the 1902 final, played in Tipperary, Dublin (Faughs) drew with Cork in the 'home' final but were beaten 2-6 to 0-1 in the replay. The Dublin Faughs lost the 1906 final to Tipperary by 3-16 to 3-8. Defeat was again their lot (this time Kickhams) in the 1908 decider against the same opposition. The teams drew the first day at Jones's Road, but Tipperary won easily, 3-15 to 1-5, in the replay in Athy.

This losing sequence of six defeats was to be halted in 1917. Dublin were strengthened by the influx of hurlers from the country. When a noted player took up employment in the city he could not declare for his own county but could play only for Dublin. As a result Dublin had a choice pick in those years of players of the calibre of Tom Daly, Dr Tom Finlay, Mick Gill, Garrett Howard, Matty Power, and Brendan Considine. There was not one Dublin-born player on the 1917 team, which included Tommy Daly and Brendan Considine of Clare, Seán Hyde of Cork, Joe Phelan of Kilkenny, Bob Mockler of Tipperary, and Dr John Ryan of Wexford. Tipperary may have suffered from over-confidence, but Dublin deserved to win by 5-4 to 4-2.

Dublin were beaten by Wexford in the 1918 Leinster final but were back in the All-Ireland the following year and were in fact to contest three consecutive finals. For the 1919 final, against Cork, Dublin had most of the players who had performed so well in the 1917 final but they slumped on the day and were beaten by 6-4 to 2-4. Charlie Stuart, brother of the later GAA President, Dr J. J. Stuart, was captain.

Dublin were to have revenge against the same opposition the following year. Faughs had the selection and were captained by Bob Mockler, who had missed the previous year's final because of flu. Another Tipperary man in the side, who would later lead his native county to victory in 1930, was John Joe Callanan. Also in the side was Bob Doherty, who had won an All-Ireland with Clare in 1914. In a fine display Dublin had six points to spare at the end on the score 4-9 to 4-3.

The Dublin Faughs were back for the final in 1921 but were heavily beaten by a Limerick side captained by the famous Bob McConkey. It was a very disappointing final, with Limerick substantial winners by 8-5 to 3-2. Part of the blame for the disappointing performance was the postponement of the game, which wasn't played until 4 March 1923.

Dublin made their next appearance in the 1924 final. Their opponents, Galway, were favourites as defending champions and as a result of having defeated Tipperary in the semi-final. Dublin, facing wind and sun, were only a goal behind at the interval, 2-6 to 3-0. Galway failed to score in the second half, while Dublin added 2-3 to win by 5-3 to 2-6. One of the key players for Dublin was Mick Gill of Ballindereen, County Galway. He had figured prominently on the Galway team that had beaten Limerick convincingly in the 1923 final, played exactly three months previously on 14 September 1924. A few days after the game Gill was approached by Dublin, as he was no longer eligible to play for his native county, having taken up residence in the capital.

With the setting up of the Free State and the formation of the new army and Garda, the flow of players to Dublin increased. This added strength was seen in the Dublin team of 1927. It was a powerful Garda-dominated side and was described by one commentator as 'probably the greatest Dublin team ever.'[2] And it had to be a good team to beat Cork in the final and do so comprehensively by 4-8 to 1-3. That Cork team was starting out on one of the greatest eras for the county, champions in 1926 and winners of the National League, Ulster Cup and Thomond Feis as well. However, the Dublin side pushed them aside with ease. The line-out is interesting, as it reveals the origin of the fifteen: Tommy Daly (Clare), Joe Bannon (Tipperary), 'Fowler' McInerney (Clare), Bill Phelan (Laois), Ned Tobin (Laois), Martin Hayes (Limerick), 'Builder' Walsh (Kilkenny), Mick Gill (Galway), captain, Jack Gleeson (Clare), Tom O'Rourke (Clare), Dinny O'Neill (Laois), Garrett Howard (Limerick), Tommy Barry (Tipperary), Ned Fahy (Clare), and Matty Power (Kilkenny).

The sides were to meet again in the 1928 All-Ireland semi-final, when the result was reversed in emphatic fashion, Cork winning by 5-3 to 0-2. The game was played in Kilkenny and marked the official opening of Nowlan Park by Seán Ryan, president of the GAA. The 'Declaration Rule', which allowed a player living away to declare for his native county, came into operation in the same year and greatly depleted Dublin as a hurling force.

Limerick won two All-Irelands during the period and were the first county to receive the famous McCarthy Cup. Limerick's first victory had come as early as 1897. Having beaten Blackrock of Cork in the Munster final, they went on to win their first All-Ireland championship in Tipperary on 26 November 1898. Represented by Kilfinnane, they beat Tullaroan for Kilkenny by 3-4 to 2-4 and later added the Croke Cup to their trophies.

In 1910 a Limerick (Castleconnell) selection created a surprise by defeating Cork in the Munster final in Tralee. The famous 'Tyler' Mackey was their captain, and the result was most unexpected. Cork were cocksure of victory, and one of their players, Willie Mackessy, stated afterwards: 'We let the All-Ireland fall off our hurleys.'[3] Limerick's opponents in the All-Ireland, Wexford, were also unexpected. Showing splendid teamwork in the first half, they led at the interval, 6-0 to 0-1. In the second half Limerick came into their own and were only a point in arrears with seven minutes to play. They had a goal disallowed and in a frenzied finish could not get the equaliser and were beaten 7-0 to 6-2. Limerick lodged an objection on the basis of the disallowed goal and an earlier disputed goal that was awarded to Wexford, but the Central Council refused to entertain it.

It was the first time that sideline seats were introduced at Jones's Road. The captain of the Wexford team was Seán Kennedy of New Ross, and he had the distinction of adding three All-Ireland football medals to his hurling medal, leading Wexford to the first three of their four All-Irelands in a row from 1915 to 1918. He missed out on the 1918 encounter through having to go into hospital for an operation.

Another member of the team, Paddy Mackey, also of New Ross, went one better. As well as winning the hurling in 1910 he took part in all four of the football triumphs. A native of Kylemore, the Rower, and therefore a Kilkenny man, Mackey lived in Rosbercon. He had to sleep on the Wexford side of the Barrow to qualify to play for Wexford; Seán Kennedy was the man who provided that bed in his house in Quay Street, New Ross.[4]

Limerick succeeded in qualifying for the All-Ireland again in 1911 and hoped to go one better. They had an impressive victory over Tipperary in the Munster final, dismissed Galway in the All-Ireland semi-final, and were scheduled to play Kilkenny in the final in Cork. When the game was called off, because the Athletic Grounds were unplayable, and rescheduled for Thurles, Limerick refused to play, believing that their best chance was in Cork. They were suspended, and Kilkenny were awarded the title.

Seven years were to elapse before Limerick got another chance. Two games were required to dismiss Tipperary in the Munster semi-final. For the replay there was collective training at Foynes. Part of the schedule for the weightier members of the panel was an early morning climb of Knockpatrick, a nearby peak. They had an easy victory over Clare in the Munster final and went into training for their All-Ireland tilt against

Wexford. Near the date they were notified that because of a virulent form of flu Wexford were unable to field a team. Limerick were offered a walkover but refused. The match was ultimately rescheduled for 26 January 1919, and twelve thousand people turned up to see a very disappointing game in which Limerick cantered home on the score of 9-5 to 1-3. Willie Hough of Newcastle West was the captain, and that year saw the arrival of two new stars, Bob McConkey of Young Ireland and Paddy Barry of Boher.

Limerick upset the odds in the 1921 Munster final when they defeated Cork by 5-2 to 1-2 at Thurles on 28 May 1922. Such was the unsettled state of the country that the final was not played for nine months, during which time Limerick beat Galway in the semi-final by 6-0 to 2-2. The final was most disappointing, with Dublin very much snowed under on the day by a Limerick side that gave a great all-round display to win by 8-5 to 3-2.

One of the highlights of the game was the presentation of the Liam McCarthy Cup for the first time. It was announced at the GAA Congress that McCarthy, who was active in the London GAA and in national circles, intended to present a cup for the All-Ireland hurling championship, for which no trophy had existed up to then. McCarthy had invested in the Dáil Loan some years previously. As the money was now being redeemed, he sought a further means of supporting a worthy cause; his friend Dan Fraher of Dungarvan suggested that it be used for an All-Ireland trophy.

The McCarthy Cup was presented by the president of the GAA, Dan McCarthy, to the Limerick captain, Bob McConkey, amid scenes of great excitement. The other members of the successful side were Mick Murphy (Young Ireland), Ter Mangan (Croom), Dave Marnane (Fedamore), Willie Hough (Newcastle West), Denny Lanigan (Young Ireland), Willie Gleeson (Fedamore), Jimmie Humphries (Cappamore), Willie Ryan (Cappamore), Garrett Howard (Croom), Mick Mullane (Croom), Chris Ryan (Pallas), and Tom McGrath (Claughan). Another Limerick man, Mick Neville of Kilfinnane, played with Dublin that day.

In the 1923 championship Limerick qualified for their seventh successive Munster decider, in which they beat Tipperary by 2-3 to 1-0 after a hard, dour struggle. In the All-Ireland semi-final they beat the unlikely Ulster champions, Donegal, by 7-4 to 0-1. This was the first championship game in which the players wore numbered jerseys. Fifteen thousand spectators came to Croke Park for the decider, in which Galway's speed, dash and robust tactics completely upset Limerick, who never showed their expected form and were defeated 7-3 to 4-5. Paddy McInerney was the captain, and among Limerick's stars at the period were Garrett Howard, Willie Gleeson, and Jimmie Humphries, as well as the newcomers John Joe Kinnane and Micky Cross of Claughan. An indication of the strength of Limerick at this time is the fact that five of the county— Jimmie Humphries, Dave Marnane, Willie Ryan, Willie Gleeson, and Garrett Howard—were included in the 1924 Tailteann team that beat America by 4-3 to 1-3. Jimmie Humphries, as captain of the Irish side, had the honour of receiving the New Ireland Assurance Company Cup from John Devoy.[5] It was to be a decade before Limerick appeared in a final again, and their arrival then was to herald the greatest period in their hurling history.

Three other counties won All-Irelands during this period of flux: Cork, Kilkenny, and Galway. Cork's victory came in 1919. Their Munster final victory over Limerick in the Markets Field attracted a crowd of over twenty thousand, despite the fact that no trains were allowed to run because of the War of Independence. For the All-Ireland final Cork were given a training grant by the Munster Council, and it paid dividends. It was sixteen years since the county had won an All-Ireland, having been on the losing side in 1904, 1905, 1907, 1912, and 1915. Cork won easily on a score of 6-4 to 2-4. The captain of the side was Jimmy Kennedy of Carrigtohill. There was great excitement at the victory, and a banquet was given for the All-Ireland champions at the Imperial Hotel.

This was the first Cork team to wear the red and white in the All-Ireland final. When the GAA Congress decided in 1913 that county teams must choose distinctive colours, Cork adopted royal blue and saffron; but in 1918, during a raid by the British army on the county board offices, the jerseys were taken. O'Leary's Hall team amalgamated with St Finbarr's in 1919 and so no longer required their own jerseys, which were red and white. The county board borrowed the jerseys for the senior hurlers, and they wore them right through that victorious campaign; and so it was decided that their achievement in being the first Leeside team to win the All-Ireland in sixteen years should be marked by retaining permanently the red and white.[6]

Kilkenny's lone victory came in 1922. Having beaten Dublin for the first time since 1916 in the Leinster final, Kilkenny went into collective training under Paddy 'Icy' Clarke and Mick Dalton for the All-Ireland against Tipperary. The game was excellent, with speed, dash, close tackling and accurate striking in generous measure. In the end it was remembered for the daring way that Kilkenny snatched victory from the jaws of defeat. With ten minutes remaining they were seven points in arrears. But, in the briefest time, they flashed two goals into the Tipperary net and then another to take the lead. Tipperary retaliated with a point that might have been a goal, but Kilkenny got the final score and won by 4-2 to 2-6.

It was their first victory since 1913, and after staying overnight in Dublin they returned to a heroes' welcome on Monday night. The team was captained by Wattie Dunphy, who became the first Kilkenny man to bring home the McCarthy Cup. Dick Grace, who won his fifth medal on that day, was man of the match; others who were prominent were Mark McDonald, John Holohan, Martin Lalor, Bill Kenny, Matty Power, and John Roberts. For Tipperary their defeat was a nasty rebuff. John Cleary, a clerical student, who played centrefield for Tipperary that day, was so disappointed that he threw his hurley into the Liffey as he walked to Kingsbridge (Heuston) Station to catch the train.

After thirty-six years of effort Galway finally won their first All-Ireland in 1923. They had contested their very first in 1887; they next appeared in the 'home' final of 1900 and, represented by Ardrahan, were badly beaten by Tipperary. According to one contemporary account,

> what told against them yesterday was their quietness on the field. They seemed to be very wanting in dash. They appeared like a lot of little schoolboys, who were afraid to stir lest doing so would bring punishment on them.[7]

Galway's next appearance was in the 1923 final. They reached this by beating Kilkenny 5-4 to 2-0 in the semi-final. It was the first year there were two semi-finals. Galway's victory was a surprise, as they were playing the All-Ireland champions, who had shocked Tipperary in the 1922 decider. Galway, playing with the dash and determination they were lacking in 1900, led by 3-2 to 0-0 at half time. Leonard McGrath scored 4-1 for the winners.

The final against Limerick was played at Croke Park on 24 September 1924. The team was: Junior Mahoney (Ardrahan), Mick Dervan (Tynagh), Jim Power (Tynagh), Tom Fleming (Galway City), Ned Gilmartin (Gort), Mick Kenny (Tynagh), Staff Garvey (Cappataggle), Mick Gill (Ballinadereen), Jimmy Morris (Gort), Ignatius Harvey (Tynagh), Dick Morrissey (Craughwell), Martin King (Galway), Leonard McGrath (Ballinasloe), Andy Kelly (Tynagh), and Bernie Gibbs (Gort); subs: Jack Dervan (Tynagh), Tom Cogavin (Gurteen), Michael Hurney (Galway), Jack Keogh (Kilconeiron), and Mick King (Galway). Bernie Gibbs and Ignatius Harvey played on the Tailteann Games team.

> In the centre of the field Gill and Morris were marvels. It was a treat to see Gill's masterly tactics. He was clearly the most effective player on the field. Gilmartin was like a cyclone amidst the forwards. O'Mahoney effected many fine saves. Among the

forwards McGrath was the star. One of the finest goals of the game was scored by Gibbs. It was a robust dashing encounter.[8]

Jim Power played for Tynagh, a small village in south Galway, and in 1995, at the age of a hundred, he was interviewed by Denis Walsh in the *Sunday Tribune*. The team had organised collective training in order to improve their chances.

> We stayed in this place between Athenry and Craughwell, a lovely place. There was a big gentleman's place in the estate, a big, vast house, and there was every accommodation for a team to train. There were grand fields and a lovely ball alley. For nearly three weeks we trained there.
>
> We met Kilkenny in the semi-final. Kilkenny were champions, and Galway—well, it was just that we were there. I remember we were up in the hotel on the night before the match and myself and another player overheard a couple of Kilkenny players talking. One of them was the captain, Dick Grace, who said he was going to retire after the All-Ireland. My friend turned to me and said: 'He should have said which All-Ireland, because it won't be this one.' We went out and beat them, 5-4 to 2-0. Wasn't that a fair old beating?
>
> The final against Limerick wasn't played until the autumn of 1924, sixteen months later, and we won handy.[9]

Jim was a full-back, in his seventh season on the team and at the height of his powers. In those days full-back was a thorny place:

> It was the awfullest place on the field; all the tough going was there. The only thing for it was first-time pulling. When I trained I had a man thirty yards away from me and he banged in balls, left and right, overhead, this side, that side. I never tried to stop that ball or catch it: I was all the time pulling first time. In the end very few balls passed me.

In the 1924 All-Ireland semi-final Galway created a sensation by beating Tipperary by 3-1 to 2-3. According to Ó Laoi, one could have got odds of 5 to 1 against Galway. 'The media and know-alls considered Galway's display in winning the 1923 All-Ireland as a fluke.'[10] An appeal was launched to help train the team to play Dublin in the final. The game was played on 14 December, three months after Galway had won the All-Ireland. They had practically the same team, with the exception of Mick Gill, who was now with their opponents. They played reasonably well in the first half and led by 2-6 to 3-0 at the interval; but they failed to raise a flag in the second half and were beaten 5-3 to 2-6. So, in the space of three months, Galway had won and lost the All-Ireland crown.

The strength of Galway hurling at this time is revealed by their success over Kilkenny again in the 1925 All-Ireland semi-final. Though beaten in the Leinster final, Kilkenny went on to represent the province as a result of a successful objection to the winners, Dublin. For the semi-final against Galway the selectors recalled John T. Power as goalkeeper, even though the Piltown man was now forty-three and had not played since he went on as a substitute in the 1920 Leinster final. The first half was fairly close, and Galway led by 4-3 to 4-0 at the interval, but the Tribesmen piled on the pressure in the second half and banged in the goals on the hapless Power. The final score was 9-4 to 6-0 in their favour.

Tipperary were their opponents in the final, and it was a very different outfit from the one that had gone down to Galway the previous year. An innovation in the game was the scoreboard on the Railway wall. Before the game the Artane Boys' Band gave a splendid display of gymnastics accompanied by a selection of music.

Tipperary outclassed Galway at every stage of the game. They led at the break by 3-2 to 0-3 and were comfortably in front by 5-6 to 1-5 at the end. It was the first time for Tipperary to receive the McCarthy Cup and the second time that Johnny Leahy captained an All-Ireland winning team.

This brought to an end a most interesting period in the history of hurling. Between 1914 and 1927 no team dominated the All-Ireland championship. Over the period of fourteen years, eight teams took the title, with Dublin getting the lion's share of four; Limerick, Cork and Tipperary had two each, and three new teams—Galway, Clare, and Laois—won the championship for the first time. The period is not remembered with the same fervour as the previous years of Kilkenny dominance or the period of Cork supremacy that was to follow, yet it was a time when more counties had a chance of winning an All-Ireland than any time before or since.

7

Cork's Era, 1926–31

The period from 1926 to 1931 undoubtedly belongs to Cork. During these six years the county won four All-Irelands and two National Leagues.

The era was ushered in by three exciting games against Tipperary in 1926 and was to be climaxed by three thrilling encounters with Kilkenny five years later. The second match against Tipperary was one of the first games to be broadcast, and the voice of P. D. Mehigan ('Carbery') brought news of the game to many who were not or could not be present. These games mark the beginning of a new development in the history of hurling. Many of the things we associate with the game today were taking shape: the glamour, the excitement, the record crowds. Also beginning was the growth in rivalries between teams: Cork and Kilkenny, Cork and Tipperary, Kilkenny and Limerick, to name a few.

The increased publicity in the daily and weekly newspapers contributed to these developments. When the Irish Press came into existence in 1932 it recognised the importance of sports coverage for its circulation and increased it accordingly; the appointment of Joe Sherwood, a north of England man, as sports editor ensured this. He decided that there was a readership waiting to be tapped.

> Coverage of the games was expanded and brightened up. Although the Irish Press had, in the view of the founder, very important other fish to fry, Sherwood was given his head. Coverage of sport in general and Gaelic games in particular expanded both in Burgh Quay and inevitably in the pages of the competing papers of the day. Sherwood realised that the Irish people had a passion for sport which could be harnessed to sell his newspaper and he set about it with typical dedication and enthusiasm.[1]

These developments were aided by the arrival of relative political peace following a period of national turmoil. The Rising in 1916 had ushered in a time of political and social unrest, evolving into the War of Independence and culminating in the Civil War. Although this came to an official end in May 1923, it was to continue to cause unrest until Fianna Fáil was founded in 1926 and the majority of republicans decided to give up the gun for politics. A period of peace arrived, during which people could concentrate on more leisurely pursuits.

Another development about this time increased the popularity of hurling: the inauguration of two new competitions, the National League in 1926 and the Railway Cup inter-provincial competition. These competitions generated a new interest and increased attendances at championship games. The first National League got off to an auspicious start, with twelve teams participating and a splendid display of hurling in the final, played at the Cork Athletic Grounds on 16 May. Cork and Dublin were the contestants; and while the game was close in the second half, Cork came out comfortable winners by 3-7 to 1-5. The Cork team on that occasion is worth mentioning, because it contained many of those who were to become household names in the coming years: Seán Óg Murphy (captain), John Coughlan (goal), Matt Murphy, Paddy 'Balty' Aherne, Eudie Coughlan, Michael 'Gah' Aherne, Jim Hurley, Mick Murphy, John 'Marie' O'Connell (Blackrock), Bill 'Love' Higgins (Cóbh), Maurice Murphy (Collins), Dinny Barry Murphy (Cloughduv), Jim O'Regan (Kinsale), and D. 'Fox' Aherne (St Finbarr's).

The first Railway Cup final on St Patrick's Day 1927 was another great advertisement for the game; it was rated one of the best exhibitions of hurling ever seen in Croke Park. The sides were level at half time: Munster 1-1, Leinster 0-4. As the game reached its climax only a point, in favour of Leinster, stood between the teams, and it was Lory Meagher who scored the deciding one to give Leinster a two-point victory on the score 1-11 to 2-6.

Two weeks after winning the first National League, Cork set off on the championship trail and beat Waterford by seven goals at Dungarvan. They followed with an easy victory against Kerry. In the meantime Tipperary, having returned from their tour of the United States as 'world champions', defeated Limerick in the other semi-final.

The final attracted a large crowd to the Athletic Grounds, and the venue was unable to accommodate them. The home side was captained by Seán Óg Murphy and the visitors by Johnny Leahy. Tipperary took an early lead and after sixteen minutes were 1-2 to 0-0 in front. In the meantime the crowd control fences had given way, and the crowd began to edge further and further onto the playing area and soon were well inside both sidelines. The referee, Dinny Lanigan of Limerick, believed the situation was impossible and abandoned the match.

A week later the sides met again, this time in Thurles, and the game attracted a record crowd of twenty-seven thousand. Cork went into an early lead, and two goals from 'Gah' Aherne gave them a lead of 2-3 to 1-0 at the interval. Just before half time 'Gah' and Martin Mockler of Tipperary got their marching orders. In the second half, Jim O'Regan of Cork and Jack Power of Tipperary retired injured. As the game progressed the home side began to establish itself, and the supporters went wild with delight when Martin Kennedy put Tipperary in front for the first time with a great goal. As the minutes ticked away 'Balty' Aherne came to Cork's rescue with the equalising goal.

Two weeks later, on 3 October, the second replay took place, again in Thurles and with a new record crowd of thirty thousand. There were a few changes from the previous game but essentially the sides were the same. Tipperary suffered a shattering blow after ten minutes when Martin Mockler was sent to the line. Despite this the team fought with great tenacity and were only a goal behind at the interval. Gradually the greater youth and exuberance of the Cork team won through, and they were ahead by 3-6 to 2-4 at the final whistle.

After the excitement of these games the All-Ireland final was an anti-climax. Snow fell on the morning of the game, but about twenty-five thousand supporters turned up to see Kilkenny play Cork. Kilkenny were at a disadvantage, having had such a long delay between the Leinster final and the All-Ireland. Led by Dick Grace, their challenge faltered a long time before the end of the game, and Cork were easy winners by 4-6 to 2-0. Ten of the Cork team came from the Blackrock club.

There was a sensation in the Cork county final later in the year when St Finbarr's beat the all-star 'Rockies'. The 'Barrs had just one player, Dr Jim Kearney, on the county side at the time.

After their great success in 1926, Cork seemed destined for victory in the years ahead. As well as the All-Ireland championship they had collared the National League, the Ulster Cup, and the Thomond Feis. Eight of the team—Seán Óg Murphy, Eudie Coughlan, E. O'Connell, M. Murphy, Jim O'Regan, Jim Hurley, 'Balty' Aherne, and 'Gah' Aherne—were selected to play for Munster in the first Railway Cup competition. In June 1927 the team embarked on a tour to Liverpool and London to promote hurling among Irish emigrants in England. They played two games against Tipperary. On their return they started their preparations for the championship and seemed to confirm their rating as the best team in the country by waltzing through the opposition. In three games they scored

16-23 and conceded 6-8, and they were definitely favourites to beat Dublin in the All-Ireland final. They had a long winning run behind them, which culminated in their defeat of Galway in the All-Ireland semi-final.

The result was to be totally different. It was a fast, close and robust game, and it was Dublin who showed their superiority right through the game. The Cork men were outpaced and outplayed and never looked like retaining their championship. As one commentator said of them, 'they were struggling, yet struggling like champions.'[2] The final score of 4-8 to 1-3 in favour of Dublin was a tremendous blow to Cork's expectations.

The defeat, however, was only a temporary setback. Five of the team— Seán Óg Murphy, E. O'Connell, Dinny Barry Murphy, Jim Hurley, and Eudie Coughlan—helped Munster to its first Railway Cup triumph on St Patrick's Day. Three other players—Mick Leahy (one of the famous Leahy family of Tipperary), Jim O'Regan, and 'Balty' Aherne—were selected but were unable to line out. Three of the team—Seán Óg, Eudie Coughlan, and Jim O'Regan—were chosen to represent Ireland in the Tailteann Games.

Having ousted Waterford in the first round, Cork drew with Clare in the 1928 Munster final. The selectors moved Eudie Coughlan back to centre-back to mark Brendan Considine, but all the move did was weaken the Cork attack; they were lucky to draw 2-2. The replay drew a crowd of thirty-seven thousand to Thurles, where Cork gave a faultless exhibition of hurling to win easily by 6-4 to 2-2.

Their opponents in the All-Ireland semi-final were their conquerors of the previous year, Dublin, who fielded only six of their winning side from the previous game. They proved no match for Cork, who won 5-3 to 0-2, and qualified to play Galway in the final. Galway received a bye to the final, and as Cork had overcome Dublin so easily in the semi-final, few people expected the westerners to provide much opposition, and only fifteen thousand turned up to see the game. From the throw-in Cork's superiority was all too evident, and they led by 3-5 to 1-0 at the break. The Galway team were upset by a serious injury to Mick King early in the game and never really functioned as a unit. In the second half the trend continued, and Cork ran out the easiest of winners on the record score of 6-12 to 1-0. The record winning margin was to be equalled in the 1943 All-Ireland, also by Cork, but it was never surpassed. Nine of the team had already won All-Irelands in 1926, the newcomers being Miah Burke, Mick Leahy, Morgan Madden, Tom Barry, Peter O'Grady, and Mick O'Connell.

Injury brought Seán Óg Murphy's career to an early end in 1929, and the man who assumed the captaincy was Dinny Barry Murphy from the new club Éire Óg, which came into existence in the twenties through the amalgamation of two junior clubs, Cloughduv and Bride Valley. The merger proved a success, and the club won its first county championship in 1928, beating Mallow in the final. Lightly built and fast, Dinny Barry Murphy played at right-half-back and was regarded as one of the greatest hurlers of all time. A piece of doggerel from the period captures something of the man:

Dinny Barry Murphy, boy,
Great hurler, boy!
He'd take the ball out of your eye, boy,
And he wouldn't hurt a fly, boy!

Chosen on the Munster selection in 1928, he was to remain on the team for seven consecutive seasons at a time when there was severe competition for places on the provincial side. He had the distinction of captaining the team to victory in the 1930 inter-provincial series.

Cork defeated Tipperary in the Munster semi-final in 1929. The game was played in Cork, and the home side won by 3-4 to 2-1. One writer at the time described the action thus:

The hurling was fierce but not foul—a struggle without poisoned gas. Men crashing into one another: one, two, three, four men went down in sequence. Virile manhood was manifested in all its power and glory. Willie Gleeson, the referee, knew his men and let them flake away. It was grand to see Cork and Tipperary hurlers engage in friendly conversation on their way back to the dressing-room when the fray was over.[3]

The passage is most revealing of the feeling between the sides and also of the high level of sportsmanship.

Cork defeated Waterford in a splendid Munster final in Dungarvan and then accounted for Galway rather easily in the All-Ireland. Galway made a wonderful comeback to beat Kilkenny by 7-7 to 7-1 in the semi-final in Birr. In the final the Galway backs and midfield were equal to the task, but their forwards were weak. The team was still without its best forward, who had his leg broken in the 1928 All-Ireland. To motivate the players, the Galway mentors had written on the hurleys the inscription *Remember Mick King!* but it was to no avail, as the final score was 4-9 to 1-3 in favour of the Munster champions.

Cork suffered a setback in 1930 when they were beaten by a goal by Clare in the Munster semi-final. The Banner County went into the Munster final as slight favourites as a result of this victory and justified expectations with a fine display in the first half that saw them just a point behind Tipperary at the interval, 2-3 to 1-5. In the second half an outstanding performance by the Premier County and the superb goalkeeping of Tommy O'Meara guaranteed them victory, 6-4 to 2-8.

Galway were Tipperary's opponents in the All-Ireland semi-final. As a result of Cork's easy victory over Galway in the 1929 All-Ireland the Central Council decided that Galway would play the Munster and Leinster champions in alternate years for the right to appear in the All-Ireland. The semi-final was played at Birr, with Mick King back as the Galway captain. The game was an exciting contest until the last quarter, when Tipperary pulled away for an easy victory by 6-8 to 2-4.

Dublin were next up in the All-Ireland final, with a team captained by the famous 'Builder' Walsh from Kilkenny and with five Tipperary players: Tom O'Meara, Tom Teehan, John Dwyer, Tom Quinlan, and Tom Burke. Tipp led by a point at half time and played with great courage and dash in the second half, epitomised by the blood-stained bandage around the head of Tommy Treacy, to win by 2-7 to 1-3. As well as Treacy the other legends on the team included Phil Cahill of Holycross-Ballycahill, who initiated the move away from ground hurling and to the more spectacular catching and striking from the hand, Phil Purcell of Moycarkey-Borris, and Martin Kennedy of Toomevara, about whom innumerable stories are told. Tipperary were to crown their hurling achievement that year by winning the junior and minor All-Irelands as well as becoming the first county to win all three in the same year—the 'Triple Crown Year'.

Cork may have failed to win the 1930 championship but there were consolations. Early in the year Dinny Barry Murphy, Jim O'Regan, Jim Hurley and Mick O'Connell had helped Munster to their third Railway Cup success. At the end of the year, in the Athletic Grounds, they had the satisfaction of winning their second National League when they defeated Dublin 3-5 to 3-0. For the 1931 championship Eudie Coughlan was captain, and his brother John returned to the side as goalkeeper. A newcomer to the side was Willie Clancy of Mallow. Most of the old squad were still there, more mature and more experienced; they included Jim Hurley at midfield, 'Marie' O'Connell at full-back, Jim O'Regan at centre-back, the Aherne brothers, Dinny Barry Murphy, and Paddy Delea, an effective forward. In addition there were 'Fox' Collins, Morgan Madden, 'Hawker' Grady, Mick O'Connell, Tom Barry, Georgie Garrett, John Kenneally, and Paddy Donaghue. Between them they would win Cork's fourth All-Ireland in six years and, surprisingly, their only success in the thirties.

Five of the side helped Munster to a Railway Cup success over Leinster and prepared for their first game against Clare in the Munster champion-ship. A four-point margin of victory qualified them for a semi-final meeting with Tipperary in Thurles. Two goals by Eudie Coughlan and another by

'Balty' Aherne helped them to a 3-5 to 2-3 victory over the All-Ireland champions; they showed by their display that they were still a force to be reckoned with. They played Waterford in the Munster final in Clonmel and were lucky to escape with a draw. However, they made no mistake in the replay, and goals by 'Gah' Aherne, Willie Clancy and 'Hawker' Grady enabled them to win easily by 5-4 to 1-2.

The clash with Kilkenny in the All-Ireland final on the first Sunday in September was a rousing match that enthralled the spectators. The first half was closely contested, with a goal from 'Gah' Aherne helping Cork to a half-time lead of 1-3 to 0-2. Cork stretched their advantage to six points in the second half, but Kilkenny came storming back with a goal and then four points on the trot to take the lead by one point. In the dying moments Eudie Coughlan got possession and made his way towards the goal. As he did so he slipped and fell but struck the ball while he was down on his knees, and it went over the bar for the equalising point.

The replay five weeks later was a superb game and was voted by many the greatest hurling exhibition of all time. The radio broadcast of the drawn game by P. D. Mehigan had increased interest and swelled the attendance. Cork got off to a great start and led by 2-4 to 1-3 at the break. The Cork goals came from Eudie Coughlan and Paddy Delea, and Kilkenny's from Johnny Dunne. In the second half Kilkenny drew level and went ahead, and again the Leesiders had to get the final score, as on the first day, to level the match 2-5 each, the equaliser being their only score in the second half.

Even greater interest was generated by the second replay, which become a talking-point throughout the length and breadth of the country. At a meeting of the Central Council it had been suggested that the two counties be declared joint champions, but this proposal was defeated by ten votes to six, and 1 November was fixed for the replay. Seán Robbins of Offaly, who had refereed the two games so far, was replaced by Willie Walsh.

As it was now November, the crowd was somewhat down on the second game, to thirty-two thousand. Kilkenny were severely handicapped. Their captain, Lory Meagher, was a non-starter because of injured ribs, while Paddy Larkin was also absent because of injury. Kilkenny kept pace with Cork in the first half and two minutes before the interval were level, but the Munster men got two goals before the break and led by 2-5 to 1-2 going in. In the second half the Black and Amber came storming back and came within a point of Cork. The crowd were in a frenzy of excitement, and the expectation was of another close finish. But as if the effort were too great, Kilkenny collapsed at this stage and Cork ran out easy winners, 5-8 to 3-4. Eudie Coughlan, whose contribution on the days was enormous, later stated: 'Kilkenny were a young team coming along that year. We were old and experienced, nearing the end of our tether, if you like. I think that was one of the main reasons that Cork won.'[4] How right he was! During the next decade Kilkenny went on to win four All-Irelands, while Cork's name would not appear once on the roll of champions.

The year 1931 marked the end of the Cork era. During the years of success the county had been backboned by Blackrock players. The end of the era was signalled by the retirement of one of the most legendary of these players, Eudie Coughlan. This was precipitated by the decision of the county board to withdraw the selection of the Cork team from Blackrock and nominate a panel of selectors instead. Eudie maintained that under Blackrock's guidance Cork had done well enough to allow the status quo to continue; but the county board did not relent. They nominated Eudie as captain of the team in 1932 but he declined the invitation, stating his intention of retiring from inter-county games though continuing to play for his club. Though only thirty-one years old, he had played inter-county hurling since 1919, when he was a sub on Cork's All-Ireland winning team. He retired at the height of his brilliance, and his retirement provoked the retirement of other Blackrock hurlers.

When Cork won the first of their All-Irelands of the period in 1926 there were ten Blackrock players on the team, and there was to be a predominance of 'Rockies' men right through to 1931. As Tim Horgan described it,

> those were the great days of Blackrock and Cork. The sun would never shine so brightly for that club and county partnership again ...[5]

8

-------------------- *Limerick versus Kilkenny* --------------------

When we think about the thirties we remember the period as Limerick's greatest hurling era; but during the same decade Kilkenny wrote one of the finest chapters in its hurling history. A look at the record puts the decade in perspective. In the ten years from 1931 to 1940 Kilkenny played in eight All-Irelands, winning four. After the marathon against Cork in 1931 they won three in the following four years and then lost two on the trot. They came back to win in 1939 and lose in 1940 to finish a glorious period. During the same time Limerick played in five All-Irelands, winning three. Two of these victories were over Kilkenny, and their two defeats were by the same team.

It was in the National League that Limerick reigned supreme. In fact the great Kilkenny-Limerick rivalry may be said to have started with the National League final of 1932/33, which the Noresiders won decisively by 3-8 to 1-3. Following that defeat Limerick were to record five consecutive victories, while Kilkenny had no further success.

There is no doubt about the dominance of the two teams. Dublin was the only other Leinster team to appear in the All-Ireland, losing in 1934 and winning in 1938. Cork won in 1931 but lost in 1939. Three other Munster teams made it to All-Ireland day: Tipperary did so successfully in 1937, but Clare in 1932 and Waterford in 1938 fell at the final hurdle.

Limerick's dominance in the National League left meagre pickings for other teams. Cork won twice, and Galway and Dublin each had victories. Tipperary were on the losing end on four occasions.

Cork's run of success between 1926 and 1931 was followed by a lean period. However, they started 1932 in style, defeating Waterford and Limerick to qualify for the final against Clare. The game, played at Thurles before thirty thousand spectators, turned out to be a thrilling contest. In spite of the departure of a number of star players, Cork were favourites to take the title. Clare had been showing promise for a number of years and were beaten in the 1927, 1928 and 1930 finals. They had seasoned players in the goalie, Tommy Daly, the full-back J. J. 'Goggles' Doyle (he wore them), 'Fowler' McInerney, Larry Blake, Mick Falvey, Jim Mullane, and the renowned Tull Considine. After a terrific first half Clare led by 3-2 to 1-0 at the interval. The second half saw a superb performance from the Clare backs, who resisted tremendous Cork pressure, and a late Tull Considine goal gave them victory by 5-2 to 4-1.

If the Munster final proved an epic contest, the All-Ireland semi-final was to have a dramatic ending. Over ten thousand spectators came to Limerick to see Clare play Galway. In an extraordinary game Galway led by 4-7 to 2-0 at the interval and added two points soon after the resumption to go fifteen points in front. Then something magical happened to Clare: their game was transformed and they scored goal after goal, so that at the final whistle they had five points to spare on a score of 9-4 to 4-14. Galway supporters were to suggest three novel explanations for the Clare transformation: (*a*) the bottle that supplied mouthwash to the Clare players was dosed with poitín; (*b*) the Munster champions changed the sliotar at half-time and played with a brilliant white ball in the second half; (*c*) Biddy Early, the noted Clare witch of the eighteen-eighties, had cast a spell over the Galway team.[1]

But Clare must have used up their luck, because they could have done with some against Kilkenny in the All-Ireland. Two minutes from the end of that final Kilkenny were leading by two points and Tull Considine was in possession near the goal. 'I steadied myself to make sure,' he recalled. 'There must be no mistake. I knew this was my last chance. And so I swung—but before my hurley had even connected with the ball I was pushed in the back and thrown forward. It must be a twenty-one yards free, I thought; but we got no free.'[2]

The Kilkenny version is different. 'With only two points between the sides Clare made a last desperate effort and their star forward, Tull Considine, gained possession and got past Peter O'Reilly. It looked all over for Kilkenny. Then out of nowhere came Podge Byrne and his tackle put Considine off and his shot went wide. It was a save in a million and probably won the All-Ireland for Kilkenny.'[3] At any rate, the Noresiders recovered and clinched the title with a point from Matty Power in the last minute. The final score was 3-3 to 2-3. The winners were captained by Jimmy Walsh, who played in his first senior final. Lory Meagher played his best game of the year. Clare took their defeat sportingly and invited the

Kilkenny team and officials to their banquet in Barry's Hotel, where the players mingled in a friendly atmosphere. It was Clare's last appearance in an All-Ireland final until 1995.

In contrast, Kilkenny were to go on to great and glorious achievements. Just as Tullaroan had brought the first All-Ireland to the county, the same club, under the inspiration of Lory Meagher, was responsible for the revival of the county's fortunes in the thirties. As we have seen, it nearly made the breakthrough in 1931 but had to give way to Cork's experience in the second replay. These games marked a new departure in the history of hurling. They almost doubled the patronage at hurling finals—a record 34,372 people saw the 1932 final—and they broadcast the appeal of the game to a wider audience than ever before, placing hurling in an unassailable position as a vital force in the sporting life of the country.

Kilkenny were clear favourites for the 1933 All-Ireland, following their decisive win over Limerick in the National League final. They won a sensational Leinster final against Dublin. Behind 5-4 to 2-1 at half time, they made a Lazarus-like recovery in the second half and won by 7-5 to 5-5. Lory Meagher was at his brilliant best, as he was again before he retired injured in the All-Ireland semi-final against Galway in Birr. Kilkenny won by 5-10 to 3-8 and qualified to play Limerick in the final.

In the meantime an up-and-coming Limerick side beat the reigning champions, Clare, in the first round in Thurles. An unusual feature of this game was the chartering of a special train to bring two players, Jim Houlihan of Clare and Christy O'Brien of Limerick, from Dublin, where they were playing an important championship game in the morning. Thirty thousand people packed the same venue for the semi-final against Cork, in which Limerick had a six-point margin of victory.

The Munster final against Waterford in the Cork Athletic Grounds was unfinished. With Limerick leading 3-7 to 1-2 eight minutes from the end the field was invaded. When the pitch could not be cleared the game was abandoned and was awarded to Limerick in the council chamber.

There were huge expectations for the All-Ireland, and the interest was unprecedented. The attendance of forty-five thousand, with another five thousand unable to gain admission, smashed all existing records for a sporting event in Ireland. And the game fulfilled in every way the expectations of the most fervent supporter. It was played at a breathless pace, and the grimness and determination of both sides is reflected in the half-time score of four points each. The game continued close after the interval and remained so until a dazzling Johnny Dunne goal gave Kilkenny the edge and eventual victory by 1-7 to 0-6. Although the Kilkenny forwards Johnny Dunne and the Powers gave sparkling displays, it was the superb play by the back line that made the greater contribution to victory. Limerick forwards got plenty of the ball but weren't allowed to do much with it.

Because both teams figure so prominently in the thirties, their names deserve mention. Eddie Doyle was the captain of the Kilkenny side, and his team-mates were Johnny Dunne, J. Dermody, Lory Meagher, Paddy Phelan, Paddy Larkin, Martin White, Peter O'Reilly, Podge Byrne, Jimmy Walsh, J. Fitzpatrick, Eddie Byrne, Tommy Leahy, Martin Power, and Matty Power. Micky Fitzgibbon captained the Limerick stalwarts, and the other members of the team were Paddy Scanlan, Timmy Ryan, John Mackey, Mick Mackey, Micky Cross, T. McCarthy, Paddy Clohessy, Dave Clohessy, E. Cregan, M. Ryan, P. Ryan, Jim Roche, Garrett Howard, and Christy O'Brien.

Limerick's dashed hopes in 1933 were revived the following year. The first round of the championship was against Clare. For the first twenty minutes they outclassed the Limerick men, but gradually the men in green assumed control and came out deserving winners.

The semi-final against Cork in Thurles attracted twenty-five thousand spectators, who were treated to as fine a game as was ever played in a Munster championship. Limerick started off in rampant fashion but were soon reined in and the sides drew level. Fortunes fluctuated in the second half, and excitement reached fever pitch. Garrett Howard retired injured. Paddy Scanlan made a great save, and eventually Limerick advanced to the final on the score of 3-4 to 2-2.

There was incredible excitement along Shannonside. In the euphoria of success it was almost forgotten that nothing had been won yet: Waterford had to be beaten to win the Munster final. Played in Cork, it saw Limerick come through by 4-8 to 2-5. The next stop was the All-Ireland semi-final against Galway at Roscrea. Galway proved strong challengers and, though playing with fourteen men for most of the game, were within a point of Limerick with ten minutes to go. But the Munster champions put in a final spurt and scored a goal and two points to win comfortably.

Limerick's opponents in the final were Dublin, who had beaten Kilkenny in a Leinster final replay. In the drawn game Dublin were in front by 2-5 to 1-2 at the interval and with five minutes to go had increased their lead to eight points. Then the Noresiders staged one of their finest rallies, which netted three goals and put them in front by a point. With time almost up, Dublin levelled with a point from a free by Tommy Treacy. The final score was 2-8 to 4-2.

About twenty thousand people crammed O'Moore Park, Port Laoise, for the replay. The incredible half-time score was Dublin 3-3, Kilkenny 0-0. Admittedly Dublin had a strong breeze in their favour, and with memories of the drawn game still fresh in their minds they were expecting a Kilkenny rally in the second half. It never materialised, and Dublin were ahead by 3-5 to 2-2 at the final whistle.

The final exceeded all expectations and was packed with thrills from beginning to end. Limerick trained as they had never trained before and came to Croke Park in the peak of condition. The game was played at a tremendous pace. Dublin took an early lead, but the Limerick men came back to draw level and go a point in front at half time. Dublin equalised after the restart, but Limerick, playing with impressive verve, went into a five-point lead. Dublin came back with two points and, with a minute to go, scored the levelling goal.

The replay excelled the drawn game. Limerick invited Jim Barry, the Cork trainer, to help them in their preparation. Paddy Scanlan had to cry off through illness and was replaced by Tom Shinny of Fedamore. Over thirty thousand came to see a brilliant game. The sides were level at half time. In the second half Dublin went into a three-point lead. Great play by John Mackey turned the tide in favour of Limerick, and great goals by Dave Clohessy—four in all—ensured a Limerick victory by 5-2 to 2-6. On the Dublin side there were also notable performances, in particular from Andy Murphy, Joe Bannon, John Walsh and Dan Caniffe in defence. In attack Dinny O'Neill, who had scored the equalising goal in the drawn game and who was bidding for his third All-Ireland medal, to add to those won in 1924 and 1927, and Tommy Treacy, who had been a member of Tipperary's victorious side in 1930, excelled.

Scenes of wild excitement greeted the captain, Timmy Ryan, as he received the cup from Dr Harty, the patron of the GAA. The victory was Limerick's first since 1921, when they became the first team to receive the Liam McCarthy Cup, and there was a great feeling of satisfaction in having won again in the jubilee year of the GAA. Never was a demonstration of such size seen in Limerick as the one that greeted the hurling heroes on their return to the city the following evening, when an estimated thirty thousand people crowded the route from the railway station to the Imperial Hotel in Catherine Street.

Limerick swept through the 1935 Munster championship. In a twelve-point victory over Cork in the semi-final, Mick Mackey gave what was regarded as the finest individual display of hurling ever seen. This was followed by a thirteen-point victory over Tipperary to take a third successive Munster title. Paddy Scanlon gave an outstanding performance. In the meantime Kilkenny had overcome Laois in the Leinster final and Galway by 6-10 to 1-8 in the All-Ireland semi-final. Paddy Phelan at right-half-back and Jimmy O'Connell in goal gave outstanding performances for Kilkenny.

All was in readiness for the showdown between the two teams that had been vying for hurling supremacy over a number of years. Kilkenny had mastered Limerick in the National League and All-Ireland in 1933. Then in 1935 Limerick travelled to Nowlan Park and defeated the home side by 1-6 to 1-4 in a thrilling National League tie. Limerick had gone thirty-five games without defeat, and the experts reckoned that Kilkenny were too old.

A record number of 45,591 spectators turned up for the game, which was played in a steady downpour. In spite of the difficult conditions the players served up a magnificent exhibition of hurling, and the match stands out as one of the greatest finals ever played. Limerick took an early lead, but Kilkenny came back and were a point in front at the interval, 1-3 to 1-2. Early in the second half Limerick levelled, but then Kilkenny went in front and had a five-point advantage with fifteen minutes to go. The last quarter was breathtaking as Limerick sought to reduce the lead with admirable grit and determination. A Mick Mackey free was rushed to the net; another point followed, and in a welter of excitement during the dying minutes Limerick fought for another score and Kilkenny defended doggedly. In the end the Noresiders got the verdict by the smallest of margins, 2-5 to 2-4. Lory Meagher received the cup, and Tommy Leahy was man of the match, ably assisted by Jimmy O'Connell in goal and Paddy Larkin, Peter O'Reilly, Paddy Phelan, Jimmy Walsh, Matty Power, and Locky Byrne.

The intensity of the rivalry between the sides can be gleaned from the newspaper coverage at the time. One of the best examples is the report of the game in the Kilkenny *Post*. There is a triumphalism in the headline: 'Limerick forced to acknowledge defeat'. The report states:

> Kilkenny's hurling idols have carried the day. The very laws of nature have been defied. The veterans, the stale champions of 1933, have rocked the Gaelic world to its foundations with an amazing comeback, a glorious and memorable victory. Tradition has been upheld, nay, enriched, a thousandfold and the children of Clann na nGaedheal worship at the shrine of Kilkenny—the nation's greatest hurlers.[4]

The Limerick hurlers were well received in their city the following Monday night. The players were carried shoulder-high to their hotel, and the mayor in his address assured them that their prestige was in no way diminished by this setback.

The setback was only temporary. Limerick went on a tour to the United States early in 1936 and got a bye to the Munster final because of it. When they played Tipperary in Thurles on 2 August they were in superb form, winning easily by 8-5 to 4-6. This game was Mick Mackey's first as captain and it inspired him to a leader's role in which he scored 5-3, some of the goals being gems of the rarest kind. Mackey had injured one of his knees on the American tour and expected it to be a target for some of the Tipperary players. To mislead his opponents, he put a bandage on the good knee before taking the field.

The All-Ireland semi-final at Roscrea was unfinished. With fifteen minutes to go and Limerick leading by 4-9 to 2-4, Galway left the field because of a disagreement with the referee, Séamus Wrafter of Birr, who refused a request by the Galway captain to put off a Limerick player alleged to have caused deliberate injury to one of the team. Limerick were awarded the game, Galway were suspended for six months, and the scene was set for another showdown with Kilkenny.

A crowd of over fifty thousand, more than was to attend the football All-Ireland, packed into Croke Park on 6 September. Limerick determination was at a height. The first half produced a game in keeping with previous clashes, and Limerick had a two-point advantage at half time. In the second half Limerick took over and their superiority was unquestioned. They swept aside the Kilkenny challenge, which could muster only a point in the half, and were in front by 5-6 to 1-5 at the final whistle. Jackie Power of Ahane made his debut for Limerick that day and scored two goals. Another to shine was Paddy Clohessy at wing-back.

Five of the team—John and Mick Mackey, Timmy Ryan, Paddy Scanlan, and Jackie Power—came from Ahane, one of the greatest forces in club hurling at the time. Between 1931 and 1948 the club won fifteen county senior hurling championship titles, and to this must be added five football championships from 1935 to 1939. The Mackey brothers figured in all of them, giving them a grand total of twenty championship medals each. The club participated in many tournaments also; it was said that they built more churches than any club in history. Critics have claimed that this involvement in tournament hurling was detrimental to their inter-county record and that but for it they would have won more All-Irelands.

The big upset of 1937 was the defeat of Limerick in the Munster final. Having beaten Clare in the opening round, Limerick played a very determined and effective Waterford team in Clonmel. With seconds remaining, Waterford led by 3-2 to 2-4, but Dave Clohessy scored the winning goal for Limerick. In the meantime Tipperary beat Cork by a point in a Thurles thriller, and the final was scheduled for Cork.

Tipperary were given only an outside chance, and Limerick were red-hot favourites. However, Tipperary planned their game well and closed down the Limerick machine. Their defence gave a superb display, and in spite of a great personal performance by Mick Mackey and the inspired rallying of his side they had a six-point margin at the end of the hour in a score of 6-3 to 4-3. One of Limerick's greatest defenders, Micky Cross, played under considerable stress that day, for on the previous night a fire destroyed his stables and some of his best working horses, and he retired from hurling following the final.

Tipperary had a free passage to the All-Ireland, while their opponents, Kilkenny, accounted for Galway in the semi-final. This game was played in Birr, which was celebrating the golden jubilee of the first All-Ireland played in the town. Both teams were presented with hurling boots made in the town to mark the occasion. For the day the old-style goal-posts with the point post to the side and no crossbars were erected in the field where the first All-Ireland was played; this field bounded the existing field on one side.

The game was poor, with low scoring, and Kilkenny were ahead by 0-8 to 0-6 at the final whistle. A feature of the day was great goalkeeping by both goalkeepers, Jimmy O'Connell of Kilkenny and P. J. Hughes of Galway. Earlier, in the Leinster final, Kilkenny's opponents were Westmeath, who were making their first and last appearance in a Leinster senior hurling final.

The All-Ireland was played in Killarney, as Croke Park was not ready. Work had begun in February 1936 on a development that involved the terracing of Hill 16 and the erection of a new double-decker stand to be named in memory of Michael Cusack, but a two-month strike prevented the work being completed by the contract date of August 1937. Kilkenny were a veteran side, but nobody expected that their performance would be so poor on the day. For the forty-three thousand who attended, the game could hardly have been worse. It was too one-sided to draw even a decent cheer. From the start Kilkenny were beaten all over the place, and the final score was 3-11 to 0-3. Lory Meagher came in as a sub, and his appearance was to be the last in the black and amber, in which colours he had performed so well since 1924. It also marked the end of an era for Podge Byrne, Eddie Byrne, Tommy Leahy, Jack Duggan, Martin White, and Matty Power. The Tipperary team, which included Tommy Treacy, Tommy Doyle, Jimmy Cooney, 'Sweeper' Ryan, Jim Lanigan, and Willie Wall, seemed fully capable of capturing the 1938 All-Ireland.

That was until the 'Cooney Case' intervened. This stemmed from the attendance by Jimmy Cooney at a rugby international in Dublin on 12 February. He was seen, reported, and automatically suspended for three months. In due course he applied for reinstatement, and his suspension was removed on 14 May.

At this time, if a player lived outside his county, as Cooney did in Dublin, he had to make a declaration to play for his county every year. Ten days before he attended the rugby international he sent a signed declaration form to the Tipperary County Board, but for some reason it was not forwarded to the Central Council for ratification until shortly before Easter. The president, P. McNamee, ruled that the declaration was invalid, since at the time of making it Cooney was debarred from all GAA activities, even making a declaration. He would therefore be ineligible to play for the county. The Tipperary County Board responded by stating that Cooney's declaration was made on 2 February, ten days before he suspended himself by attending the rugby match; the Central Council replied by stating that it was the date on which they received the declaration that mattered.

Tipperary ignored the decision of the Central Council and decided to play Cooney against Clare in the Munster semi-final. Clare let it be known that they would object if the occasion arose. Within the county there were voices against playing Cooney, but the county board persisted in their decision. Tipperary beat Clare by 3-10 to 2-3, and would have done so without Cooney. The inevitable Clare objection followed and was upheld by the Munster Council. Tipperary counter-objected that a member of the Clare team, Michael Griffin, had attended the same rugby match—but the only evidence of this was that of Cooney, and it was inadmissible because of his status as a suspended player! Tipperary then appealed to the Central Council and were again defeated. Jimmy Cooney was suspended for six months.

If there was to be no joy for Tipperary, 1938 was to bring Waterford their first Munster senior hurling title. The Waterford side had made their first appearance in a Munster final as far back as 1903 but were annihilated by Cork. They had to wait twenty-two years for their next appearance, only to be beaten by Tipperary. Playing with them that day was Brendan Considine, who had previously played with Clare, Dublin, and Cork. Waterford's best show was in the 1929 final, played at Dungarvan, when they gave Cork a splendid game before going under by 4-6 to 2-3. Two years later they held Cork to a draw in Clonmel but had no answer to Cork's experience in the replay. They lost the 1933 final to Limerick in the boardroom after the pitch was invaded; the following year the sides met again, with Limerick winning by 4-8 to 2-5 and going on to win the All-Ireland. Although they failed to qualify for the next three finals, they were showing promise, particularly in 1937, when they almost dethroned the champions, Limerick, who survived by a last-gasp goal from Dave Clohessy. John Keane established a reputation for himself that day by containing Mick Mackey.

It didn't come as a great surprise then in 1938 when Waterford made the breakthrough. Having beaten Cork in the semi-final, they played Clare in the Munster final and won by 3-5 to 2-5 and went on to defeat Galway in the All-Ireland semi-final. However, they fell to Dublin in a low-scoring final by 2-5 to 1-6. Dublin had beaten Kilkenny in a replayed Leinster final that saw Jim Langton make his first appearance at senior level. Dublin had some fine players at the time in Charlie McMahon, Mick Daniels, Mick Butler, Mick Gill, and Harry Gray, who would play with Laois in the 1949 All-Ireland. Mick Hickey captained Waterford, and the side included such stalwarts as Charlie Ware, Willie Barron, John Fanning, Declan Goode, Tom Greaney, Jack Feeney, who had played with Dublin against Limerick in the 1934 All-Ireland, and John Keane, who played a brilliant game in stockinged feet and did everything a man could do to swing victory in Waterford's way. But Dublin were ahead by two points at the final whistle and won their sixth, and last, All-Ireland.

The Munster final of 1939 in Thurles has been classed as one of the greatest games of all times. It attracted a crowd of forty-one thousand, thousands more than the previous best. The contestants were Cork and Limerick. Level scoring and fluctuating fortunes ensured a glorious, thrilling, all-exciting game. Up to the last second it was anybody's victory. Limerick, holding a one-point lead, were being hailed as victors as the game entered its last moments, but a final Cork rally that produced a great goal dashed the cup of success from their lips and gave victory to Cork, captained by Jack Lynch, by 4-3 to 3-4. It was the Rebel County's first Munster final in eight years. For Limerick, captained by Mick Mackey, there were words of consolation:

> Truly, they were as great in defeat as they have so often been magnificent in victory. Each and every man gave of his best and they were beaten by a bit of ill-luck in those dazzling closing moments.[5]

Cork were to be the recipients of the consolatory words after their defeat by Kilkenny in the All-Ireland final. Kilkenny met Dublin, who were All-Ireland and National League champions, in the Leinster final. Kilkenny went into the game as underdogs, and the contest turned out to be exciting and memorable. Fortunes fluctuated, with Kilkenny going ahead only to be brought back with Dublin scores. Eventually the Noresiders won out with a score of 2-12 to 4-3. Paddy Phelan starred in defence, while Jimmy Walsh kept the great Dublin star Harry Gray under control. In the All-Ireland semi-final at Roscrea, Kilkenny had a nine-point margin over Galway.

Because the All-Ireland was a repeat of the 1931 final, interest in the game was intense. It was played two days after the Second World War broke out, and it can be said with certainty that the interest of the forty thousand spectators was firmly focused on the events in Croke Park rather than the invasion of Poland. To add to the drama was the atrocious weather that prevailed for most of the game. After heavy rain in the morning the sun shone brightly in the first half, but early in the second half a clap of thunder gave a warning of things to come, and the last twenty minutes were played in a downpour punctuated by thunder and lightning. In spite of the conditions the players served up a magnificent spectacle. Kilkenny had Paddy Phelan and Paddy Larkin from the 1931 side, with rising stars like Jim Langton, Terry Leahy, Jack Gargan, Jack Mulcahy, Paddy Grace, and Jimmy Kelly.

Cork were nervous at the start, and before they had settled down Kilkenny had scored two quick goals and at half time led by 2-4 to 1-1. Cork rallied in the second half, and Willie Campbell scored an equalising goal with two minutes to go. Kilkenny forced a seventy. Paddy Phelan's shot landed about twenty-five yards from the Cork goal; Jimmy Kelly got possession and sent the ball between the posts for the winning point by 2-7 to 3-3. The rain was so bad that the spectators couldn't make out immediately who had scored the winning point.

Jimmy Walsh captained his second All-Ireland winning team on that day. When the team returned to an enthusiastic reception in Kilkenny on Monday night the darkened town was lit by bonfires and Very lights.

The year 1940 was a glorious one for Limerick, which saw them win a minor and senior All-Ireland double. It brought to an end a period of ten years during which the Shannonsiders were the most exciting team in hurling. During this period they enjoyed more hurling success than before or since, and their achievements will rank with the greatest. The year was also to see them defeat their old rivals, Kilkenny, who had vied with them for hurling supremacy during the preceding years. Although Kilkenny won more All-Irelands during the period, Mick Mackey and his men left a more indelible mark on the memory.

Limerick's campaign opened in Killarney with a draw against Waterford. Matters were going badly for Limerick when Mick Mackey was switched to centre-back; then two great solo runs by Jackie Power led to goals and a draw. The replay was at Clonmel, and again Limerick snatched victory with a late score to win by 3-5 to 3-3.

The Munster final against Cork took place in Thurles and ended in a draw: Cork 3-6, Limerick 4-3. Carbery was ecstatic about the game:

Thurles was no place for weak hearts in Sunday's broiling heat and excitement. Every match between Cork and Limerick in recent years has its own individuality—fiercely earnest and packed with pulsating passages. Many of us thought the 1939 Munster final had reached hurling meridian. Yet this year's memories switched 1939 to the limbo of forgotten things and battles long ago ... So overwhelming was that closing delirium of surging scores like a crescendo of brass music—that all spectators were hushed and awestruck. Good men and true, all in action to that stirring finish. And there is more to come for they finished all square.

The replay lived up to the brilliance of the drawn game. The first half delivered thirty minutes of intense excitement, at the end of which Cork, who had more of the play, had scored a mere point. Limerick had failed to raise a flag. The sides resumed their terrific struggle, and in the middle of the half Limerick produced a glorious passage that resulted in ten points in as many minutes and gave them a seven-point lead. But Cork were not finished, and when Jack Lynch goaled and a point followed and attack after attack was mounted on the Limerick defence it appeared as if Limerick could not possibly hold out. But a superb defence by Paddy Scanlan, Timmy Ryan, John Mackey and Mick Kennedy saw them through and worthy winners by 3-3 to 2-4.

Galway were overcome in the semi-final at Ennis, and the team prepared for their encounter with Kilkenny in the final. Kilkenny had beaten Dublin in an uneventful final at Nowlan Park. Despite wartime conditions, nearly fifty thousand people turned up for the final. It was a repeat of the 1936 final, with Kilkenny, as then, the defending champions. They opened the game at a blistering pace and scored the opening goal and point; Limerick then took a point lead, but Kilkenny were in front by 1-4 to 1-2 at the interval. The Noresiders went a further two points in front on the resumption and appeared to have the initiative. Mick Mackey was moved to centrefield and began to dominate the game. Limerick got on top in the final quarter and, although Kilkenny remained a menace to the end, were clear winners by 3-7 to 1-7.

Jim Langton captained the Kilkenny side. One Kilkenny point of view on the defeat is interesting, from the pen of 'An Liathróid', a hurling commentator in the Post:

It was not the want of skill or speed that beat Kilkenny. They were out-generalled. They failed to adapt their play to the changing tactics of the Limerick men. They allowed Limerick to take the initiative and dictate the terms of play. Above all they failed to react in the proper spirit to the rough stuff when it came. They did what Limerick wanted; they tried to reply in kind.[6]

The Limerick side took possession of the pitch after their memorable victory, and Mick Mackey received the cup amid unbounded enthusiasm. His fellow Ahane men included Paddy Scanlan, Mick Hickey, Timmy Ryan, John Mackey, Paddy McMahon, and Jackie Power; the remaining members were Jim McCarthy (Feenagh), Mick Kennedy (Young Ireland), Tommie Cooke (Knockaney), Paddy Clohessy (Fedamore), Peter Cregan (Croom), Jim Roche (Croom), Dick Stokes (Pallas), and Ned Chawke (Granagh).

The team returned to Limerick on Monday. The army placed lorries at their disposal; suitably bedecked in green and white, the team made its way to Cruise's Hotel in one triumphant procession. The exuberance of the occasion was due to the feeling that the unexpected had happened. Many had thought that Limerick had gone over the top as a result of their defeats in 1937, 1938, and 1939, and this made the victory all the sweeter. It may have come unexpectedly, but it was no more than a magnificent team of skill and excitement deserved.

9

--------------------- *Another Cork Era* ---------------------

The forties belong to Cork. Between 1941 and 1947 Cork contested six out of seven All-Irelands, winning five. It was a period of success after a very lean decade.

When the team started out on its bid to win the championship in 1941 it was seeking to bring the McCarthy Cup back to the county for the first time in ten years. The five victories that followed over the next seven years were to make that decade a distant memory. These victories included a four-in-a-row from 1941 to 1944, the first time this feat was achieved and also the last. Begrudgers have attempted to downgrade the victories by claiming that the opposition was poor. In three of the four finals Cork played Dublin, and in the other they overcame Antrim. Neither of these teams would be regarded as a force in hurling today; but Dublin in particular were to be reckoned with at the time and had won the All-Ireland in 1938. Cork's victories were comprehensive and impressive. In the 1946 final their opponents were Kilkenny, and they won by 7-5 to 3-8. Their only defeat was in the 1947 final, when they were beaten by a mere point by Kilkenny, 0-14 to 2-7. So, whatever the opposition, Cork were the dominant team of the period, failing only to reach the 1945 final.

When the Munster championship draws were made, Tipperary were drawn to play Waterford in Thurles on 1 June. But with the disruption caused by the outbreak of foot-and-mouth disease in 1941, leading to the cancellation not only of animal fairs but also of many sporting events, the fixture list was thrown into disarray. Aggravating these problems was the wartime fuel shortage, which prevented trains from travelling to Thurles with supporters. During May the foot-and-mouth epidemic worsened. The Thurles game was postponed and was eventually played on the last

Sunday in July. Tipperary won and were scheduled to play Cork in the Munster semi-final in Limerick on 17 August, but six days beforehand the match was called off on the instructions of the Department of Agriculture.

Not only Tipperary inter-county fixtures were banned but all county championship games as well. Tipperary, and the other counties affected by the disease, wanted the Central Council to postpone the All-Ireland final. The Central Council disagreed and ruled that teams were to be nominated, and if such a team won the All-Ireland that team would be awarded the 1941 championship.

The Munster Council then decided that Cork and Limerick should play for the right to represent the province. Limerick had already qualified for the final, having beaten Clare; later in the year the winners of the Cork-Limerick game would play Tipperary for the Munster championship.

Cork played Limerick on 14 September in Cork and had an easy victory by 8-10 to 3-2. The All-Ireland champions, without the Mackeys and Paddy Clohessy, were a listless side on the day. Paddy Scanlan had a most unhappy day between the posts and conceded three goals within ten minutes of play. All efforts by Limerick to rouse their players in the second half were of no avail, and Cork ran out the easiest of winners.

Dublin were Cork's opponents in the All-Ireland final. At the beginning of the year Kilkenny, after their victory in the 1939 All-Ireland and defeat in 1940, looked good for the championship. But foot-and-mouth disease took its toll in Kilkenny too. Given a bye into the Leinster final, Kilkenny were prevented from playing by a directive from the Department of Agriculture forbidding the team to participate unless the county was three weeks clear of the disease. Dublin were therefore nominated to represent Leinster in the semi-final; they beat Galway by two points in Roscrea and qualified to meet Cork on the last Sunday in September.

Restricted rail services and a shortage of petrol kept the attendance down to twenty-six thousand. All sorts of means were used to get to Dublin, including bicycles and tandems. In the game Dublin provided no opposition. At half time Cork led by 2-8 to 0-3, and they completed the rout in the second half to win by 5-11 to 0-6.

Having won the All-Ireland, Cork still had to play the Munster final, and this took place in Limerick on 26 October. They found it difficult to muster enthusiasm for the game. In contrast, Tipperary were determined to prove a point. They scored a convincing victory, winning by 5-4 to 2-5 after leading 4-1 to 1-5 at the interval.

On the following Sunday, Dublin, the nominated Leinster representatives in the All-Ireland, played Kilkenny in the Leinster final and won by 2-8 to 1-8.

Cork may have suffered a setback in the delayed Munster final but it was only temporary, and they were back to their winning ways the following year. They played Limerick in a thrilling exhibition of hurling at the Gaelic Grounds in the semi-final and won by two points. Tipperary proved no match for them in the Munster final. They kept with Cork until the last quarter, when Cork went on the rampage to win by 4-15 to 4-1. Jack Lynch and Paddy O'Donovan totally outclassed the Tipperary pairing of Bill O'Donnell and Jimmy Cooney at centrefield, and but for the superb goalkeeping of Jimmy Maher the losers would have suffered an even greater defeat. Cork followed this with a sixteen-point victory over Galway in the semi-final.

Dublin had qualified for the All-Ireland by defeating Kilkenny in the Leinster final. Kilkenny gave one of their poorest displays ever and were beaten by 4-8 to 1-4. The game marked the final appearance in the black and amber of Paddy Phelan, who had made his debut against the same opposition in a tournament game in 1929. On both occasions he played in goal. Although Dublin were well beaten in the All-Ireland of 1941, they put up a better performance in this match. They trailed Cork by 1-7 to 2-1 at the interval and were in contention until the fiftieth minute; in fact they got within a point of the champions when they achieved their third goal. They missed a further goal during a hectic final quarter during which Cork established their superiority to win by 2-14 to 3-4. One of the stalwarts of the Dublin team was Harry Gray, who played on Jack Lynch that day. Harry played on the successful side against Waterford in 1938, lost in 1941, and was to lose again in 1944. Returning to his native Laois, he was to taste defeat once more in the 1949 final.

On the Cork side the team showed a number of changes from the successful 1941 outfit. Three teenagers—Seán Condon, Con Murphy, and Mick Kenefick—were drafted in. Ned Porter replaced Jim Buttimer in goal. Charlie Tobin in the backs and Derry Beckett in the forwards were two more newcomers, and Paddy O'Donovan, who had come on as a sub in the 1941 final, had established himself at midfield.

Cork continued their winning ways in 1943. Their opponents in the Munster final were Waterford, who had beaten Limerick in the semi-final. This victory did not come as a great surprise, as Waterford had been showing promise for a number of years and had suffered a couple of narrow defeats. Their victory on this occasion was due to some great goals from John Keane and inspired goalkeeping by Charlie Ware. The final was played in the Cork Athletic Grounds, and after a fine game Cork had five points to spare on the score 3-13 to 3-8.

Cork's opponents in the All-Ireland were a most unlikely team: Antrim. Their participation in the senior hurling championship was a result of the suspension of the junior championship because of the war. As Ulster junior champions they were given the opportunity to play Galway in the All-Ireland quarter-final. Their defeat of Galway by a point as a result of a Noel Campbell sideline puck in the closing minutes created some surprise; but it was the result of the match with Kilkenny that was really to make the headlines. The game was played at Corrigan Park, Belfast, on 1 August. Antrim's success over Galway was regarded as a fluke, and Kilkenny were expected to achieve victory. When the result of the game, 3-3 to 1-6, came over the radio on Sunday night it created a sensation and qualified the Northerners for their first All-Ireland. They had led at half time by 2-2 to 1-3 and their defence never wilted, despite frenzied attempts by the Noresiders to get the equalising goal.

Kilkenny's followers found the defeat hard to take, and when the team returned home on Monday evening—having left on the first stage of their journey on the Friday evening—they were accused of being drunk during the game. In any event it was the greatest upset in the history of Kilkenny hurling, although in retrospect it was shown that Antrim were a very difficult team to beat, as Leinster found to their regret in the 1945 Railway Cup semi-final.

On 5 September the Antrim team included such men as Jackie Bateson, Noel Campbell, Kevin Armstrong, Sammy Mulholland, Danny McAllistair, who had scored four goals against Galway, and the captain, Jimmy Walsh, who was given a rousing cheer when they took the field. Before the game the rival captains exchanged suitable wartime gifts: Jimmy Walsh presented tea to his Cork counterpart, Mick Kenefick, who in turn offered butter from Cork.

Unfortunately the fairy-tale didn't last. Men who had played great games against Galway and Kilkenny appeared to freeze in Croke Park. Cork, on the other hand, were an experienced side and were determined not to be ambushed in the way that Galway and Kilkenny had been. They took their opponents seriously and played as well as they could in the first half with the aid of the breeze. They led by 3-11 to 0-2 at the interval and gave Antrim no opportunity of coming back. In the end Cork were in front by 5-16 to 0-4, and the victory gave the county their second three-in-a-row.

Among the reasons given for Antrim's poor performance were their misfortune in running into a Cork team of all the talents, and the Ulster men's inexperience of centre stage on All-Ireland day. Another reason was the difference in hurling surfaces between Croke Park and pitches such as Corrigan Park, on which Antrim normally played.

According to Kevin Armstrong, the defeat was not all gloom, because from the defeat sprang the origins of the present Casement Park. Corrigan Park had been purchased in 1927 for £1,600. It had an uneven surface and indeed was partly to blame for the heavy defeat to Cork, and it was resolved that Corrigan Park should get a surface like a billiard-table to improve Antrim hurling. This led to the setting up of a committee to raise funds, and eventually ground was bought at Andersonstown and the building of Casement Park began. When it was opened, on 1 June 1953 by Cardinal d'Alton, it was free of debt, having cost £101,000.[1]

Cork made history when they won their fourth All-Ireland in a row on 3 September 1944. On that day the McCarthy Cup was received by 21-year-old Seán Condon from St Finbarr's club, who was winning his third senior hurling medal and his fourth in all, having won a minor in 1941. Although the victory over Dublin had been an easy one, there were times earlier in the championship when it appeared that Cork would fail to make the unique breakthrough.

Cork beat Tipperary in the Munster semi-final and met a great Limerick team in the final on 16 July. The Mackey brothers were back at their brilliant best when Limerick beat Clare in the semi-final. From the beginning of the year Limerick had been showing outstanding form, and their defeat of Cork in the final of the Thomond Cup gave added interest to the Munster final. Seldom has a hurling match, or any such contest for that matter, gripped the imagination of the public to such an extent.

There was another aspect to the final to make it one of the most memorable ever. Because of the wartime restrictions there was a complete absence of mechanically propelled vehicles, with the exception of rail and bus services. From dawn on Sunday the roads radiating from Thurles were black with bicycles—a veritable procession stretching forty and more miles in all directions. It was estimated that eighty per cent of the twenty thousand came by bicycle to what became known as the 'Great Bicycle Final'. In addition there were pony-traps, common carts, sidecars, and brakes, as well as a great many foot-sloggers to complete the colourful scene, with Thurles providing the old-world atmosphere that will never be recaptured. It was like a page out of the past and a day that will go down in memory as much for its unusual setting as for the great fare that the old rivals served to the enthusiastic crowd.[2]

The day was glorious, and the match was a cracker. Cork seemed all set to win for three-quarters of an hour, but a great Limerick rally spearheaded by Mick Mackey and Tommy Ryan brought a draw for Limerick, 6-7 to 4-13. Five minutes into the second half Cork led by 5-4 to 1-6, and things looked hopeless for Limerick. But a great rally brought them two points ahead with two minutes to go. In a frenzy of excitement Johnny Quirke scored a goal to give Cork the lead by a point; but in the dying seconds Dick Stokes flashed over a point to earn a draw.

Two weeks later the replay was held at the same venue, and eighteen thousand spectators turned up, ninety per cent of them on bicycles. The replay was as brilliant as the drawn game. Con Murphy was brought in to mark Mick Mackey. At one point it looked as if victory was within Limerick's grasp. They held a five-point lead going into the last quarter. Then Mick Mackey had a goal disallowed, and the resultant free wasn't scored. After this Cork staged a tremendous rally to draw level. They were now playing very well. Mackey made one trojan effort, but the ball went outside the post and wide. Then, with seconds remaining, Christy Ring collected the ball on his own half-back line, soloed to within forty yards of the Limerick goal, and unleashed a shot that went all the way to the net to give Cork victory by 4-6 to 3-6. Ring had snatched the last chance to record a victory that will be remembered as long as hurling is played.

A fortnight later Cork faced Galway in the All-Ireland semi-final in Ennis. Jack Lynch and John Quirke cried off because of injury. The match proved to be a much more gruelling affair than Cork had expected, but thanks to the superb marksmanship of their captain, Seán Condon, they pulled through by a point. He scored no less than eight points in the 1-10 to 3-3 victory. In fact Condon's last point was disputed by Galway, who claimed that he was fouled on the way when a hurley was thrown. Galway lodged an appeal at a special Central Council meeting, but the referee, Mick Hennessy of Clare, reported that he had given Cork the benefit of the advantage rule, and the result was allowed to stand.

Over twenty-six thousand people turned up for the final in Croke Park on 3 September. Dublin had qualified by beating Wexford in the Leinster final. Wexford had created a sensation by beating Kilkenny in the semi-final, for the first time since 1908. Dublin had to travel to Belfast to play Antrim, who were only a shadow of the previous year's team, and Dublin won easily by 6-12 to 3-1. Antrim had got directly into the semi-final and were to do so up to 1949.

For the first ten minutes of the final Dublin held Cork scoreless. The big names on their side were Ned Wade, Charlie Downes, Jim Byrne, Frank White, Harry Gray, Mick Butler, and the goalkeeper, Jim Donegan. Cork gradually settled down and led by 0-8 to 0-2 at the interval. There was a brief Dublin revival after the resumption, which resulted in a goal, but Cork took over, and great displays by Tom Mulcahy in goal and Joe Kelly in the forwards gave them a comfortable victory, 2-13 to 1-2. Kelly had played minor in 1941 but his duties as a priest prevented him from playing for a number of years until he was thrown in at the deep end in 1944. He was a great addition in that year and became the darling of the Cork supporters. After playing in two more All-Irelands his hurling career came to a premature end with his departure for New Zealand.

Nine players won all four All-Irelands on the field of play. Eight of them—Willie Murphy (Ballincollig), Batt Thornhill (Buttevant), Alan Lotty (Sarsfields), John Quirke (Blackrock), and Christy Ring, Jack Lynch, D. J. Buckley and Jim Young (Glen Rovers)—lined out in the first fifteen. A ninth player, Paddy O'Donovan of Glen Rovers, lined out in the 1941 and 1944 finals and came on as a sub in the other two. Glen Rovers provided the captain for the first two years in the persons of Connie Buckley and Jack Lynch. Buckley had the distinction of captaining Glen Rovers to victory in the 1941 county final, and this brought to an end the club's run of eight titles in a row. Buckley had the added distinction of being the only man to win all eight of them. St Finbarr's had the captaincy in 1943 and 1944, when Mick Kenefick and Seán Condon had the honours.

The following day the team returned to Cork by train to a heroes' welcome. The train stopped at Thurles and Mallow to be greeted by large crowds. The players broke their journey at Blarney and continued to Cork by horse-drawn coaches. A huge crowd met them at Blackpool bridge, and the Volunteers Pipe Band paraded them into the city, where over twenty thousand supporters had gathered to welcome the four-in-a-row champions.

If Cork had aspirations for a fifth All-Ireland in a row in 1945, other counties had plans to frustrate them. One of these was Tipperary, who played Cork in the Munster semi-final in Thurles on 1 June. The Premier County had many reservations about their forward line, but it came up trumps on the day. They played against the wind in the first half, and at half time they had scored 1-4 to Cork's 2-1. In the second half they were outstanding and were ahead of Cork by 2-13 to 3-2 when the final whistle sounded. One of the highlights of the game was the performance of Tommy Purcell, who held Christy Ring scoreless.

The victory strengthened Tipperary's confidence for their tilt with Limerick in the final. Two new forwards were introduced, and the big talking-point was how the back line would cope with the two Mackeys. For the greater part of the first half Limerick dominated the play, but they did not translate their superiority into scores and led by 0-5 to 1-1 at the interval. They got a goal soon after the resumption to put them four points in the lead. But then Mutt Ryan came into his own with a goal and a point to give Tipperary the lead. A further goal by O'Keeffe brought the wind of victory to Tipperary's nostrils. Limerick rallied with a goal, but Tipperary retaliated with another, and eventually the ding-dong struggle came to an end with Tipperary in front by 4-3 to 2-6.

Tipperary cleared the last hurdle to the All-Ireland final when they defeated Antrim by 5-9 to 1-6 at Croke Park on 5 August. However, the display was unimpressive, especially from their inner line of forwards. Noel Campbell put on a virtuoso display for Antrim.

Meanwhile 1945 saw a reawakening in Kilkenny. They came through Leinster in an impressive manner, defeating Wexford, Offaly and Dublin along the way. The All-Ireland semi-final against Galway was played in Birr. Galway had some fine players at this time, players of the quality of Seánie Duggan, John Killeen, 'Inky' Flaherty, Peadar Gantly, and Josie Gallagher. The team was on the verge of making the breakthrough, and they did when they won the Railway Cup in 1947 and the National League in 1950. With a bit of luck they might have beaten Kilkenny in this game and again in 1947. As it was they were completely on top of Kilkenny in the first half and led by 2-9 to 2-1 at half time. They were still ahead by seven points going into the last quarter. A great Kilkenny rally brought them two goals and then two points, the last by Jim Langton, and this put the Noresiders into the All-Ireland final.

A record crowd of over sixty-nine thousand turned up to see the teams meet in the final for the first time since 1937. The attendance was eighteen thousand higher than the previous record set in 1936, and another five thousand were locked out. Kilkenny played poorly in the first half and as a result of a number of soft goals trailed by 4-3 to 0-3 at half time. They staged a great rally in the second half and reduced the deficit to four points, but Tony Brennan got through for a Tipperary goal, and the Munster champions ran out winners by 5-6 to 3-6. The victorious captain, John Maher, who had won All-Irelands in 1930 and 1937, belied his years with a superb display against the great Jim Langton. There was jubilation in the county at the victory; there was also a huge sigh of relief that the elusive thirteenth title had been won and that the eight years of frustration had finally come to an end.

Cork had taken a sabbatical in 1945 and returned to the fray renewed and refreshed in 1946. Newcomers to the team included Con Murphy and the brothers Mossie and Gerry O'Riordan. With victories over Clare and Waterford they qualified to meet Limerick in the Munster final. Limerick had been impressive when beating Tipperary in the other semi-final, and expectations were high for another classic final. It turned out to be a huge disappointment for the thirty-nine thousand people who travelled to Thurles for the match. Limerick failed to reproduce their form, mainly because of the eclipse of Mick Mackey by the speedy Din Joe Buckley of

Cork. Time had at last caught up with him, and without his inspiration Limerick's challenge collapsed and Cork ran out easy winners by 3-8 to 1-3.

It was Mackey's last big game, although he did come on for the closing stages of the 1947 championship game against Tipperary, which Limerick won by 6-8 to 2-3. One newspaper described Limerick's eclipse thus:

> If Sunday's game proved one thing more than another, it was that the experience and guile of 'old hands' cannot stand up to the youthful speed and dash. After a great career when his name was a household one for his dazzling runs and great sportsmanship, Mick Mackey faced the inevitable on this occasion when he was but a shadow of his former self.[3]

Cork qualified for the final against Kilkenny as a result of an easy victory over Galway in the semi-final in Birr. Kilkenny qualified by beating Dublin in a closely fought Leinster final. Dublin led by two points at the interval, but Jack Mulcahy and Jimmy Langton proved to be the heroes for Kilkenny. The Leinster champions had no difficulty qualifying for the All-Ireland by beating Antrim 7-11 to 0-7 in Croke Park.

The final attracted a crowd of sixty-four thousand, who saw some fine hurling in the first half. Just on half time Kilkenny led by 0-5 to 0-3, but Cork scored two goals in as many minutes through Christy Ring and Gerry O'Riordan to lead by 2-3 to 0-5 at the break. Soon after the resumption they added a goal and a point. Kilkenny rallied to bring the deficit to five points, but Con Murphy got through for another Cork goal. Terry Leahy scored two goals to reduce the lead to two points, but Cork ran riot in the last ten minutes to win by 7-5 to 3-8. By his display on the day Ring had established himself as one of the great players of the game.

Cork's great run came to an end in 1947, the only year of the decade that did not have a Munster team as All-Ireland champions. They had the same team as the previous year, with one exception: Seán Condon was back in place of Paddy Healy. They beat Clare and Waterford and again met Limerick in the Munster final. Limerick, with John Mackey in irrepressible form, pushed aside Tipperary in the semi-final.

Despite the previous year's disappointment a crowd of over thirty-four thousand turned up for the final, and they got their money's worth. A contemporary report describes the game well:

> If ever a better team lost it was Limerick who were dogged throughout with ill-luck. Twelve months ago Limerick were completely blotted out by the same Cork fifteen but the boot was on the other foot last Sunday and it was a chastened Cork fifteen who left the arena winners on the score of 2-6 to 2-3.

But Cork had won, and they had an easy victory over Antrim to qualify for another All-Ireland final against Kilkenny. The Noresiders came through Leinster in style, beating Wexford and Dublin.

In the final they were without two of their stars, Jimmy Langton and Jack Mulcahy. The game was even in the first half, with Kilkenny leading by a point at the interval. In the second half it was a different matter, with Kilkenny pulling ahead of Dublin and winning in the end by 7-10 to 3-8. Tom Walton and Terry Leahy were the stars in attack, while Jimmy Purcell and Mark Marnell were best in defence.

The All-Ireland semi-final, played at Birr, was a thriller, and it had a controversial ending. Over twenty-five thousand turned up for the encounter, twice as many as the previous year. Galway were hopeful, having won the Railway Cup for the first time some months earlier, with a team of talented players who were lacking nothing except a winning tradition. The game lived up to expectations, and Galway led by a point at the break. They were still in front going into injury time. At this stage the referee, Dinny Costello of Tipperary, whistled for a free. The Galway supporters interpreted the whistle as full time and swarmed onto the pitch. When order was restored and the game resumed, Kilkenny scored two points, by Terry Leahy and Jimmy Langton, in the closing minutes to win by 2-9 to 1-11. It was a gallant result for Galway. Pat 'Diamond' Hayden at full-back for Kilkenny was the outstanding player on the field, and he got good support from Paddy Grace and Jim Kelly in defence, Jim Donegan in goal, and Tom Walton and Liam Reidy in the attack.

The 1947 All-Ireland is generally regarded as the greatest ever played, both in the quality of the play and the excitement of the exchanges. The game was watched by a crowd of more than sixty-one thousand and produced hurling that will live for ever in the memory of those who were privileged to see it. It was a game that saw the pride of Irish manhood represented by Kilkenny and Cork stand shoulder to shoulder, exerting every ounce of strength, speed and endurance to secure the distinction of being champions. Kilkenny were the better team and fully deserved to win, although they came from behind twice in the closing minutes.[4]

There was some drama in the Kilkenny dressing-room before the game. Bill Walsh was forced to cry off at the last minute, and this meant adjusting the line-out. Mark Marnell went to left-back. Jack Mulcahy moved to the left wing, and Jimmy Heffernan came in to partner Dan Kennedy, the captain, at midfield. Paddy Grace declined to walk around the field with the team, because of a knee injury, and did not make his appearance until the defenders were taking their places.

The first half was an even struggle, with Kilkenny going into an early lead, only to be pegged back by Cork. With the backs dominant, the scores came slowly, and at half time Kilkenny were ahead by 0-7 to 0-5. As Kilkenny had the wind and the sun in their backs in the second half, things did not look so good for Cork. Also, Jim Donegan was playing well in the Kilkenny goal, and Christy Ring was out of sorts on the forty-yard line.

The Cork effort was revitalised by a couple of changes made ten minutes into the half. Jack Lynch swapped places with Seán Condon, and Ring moved out to the wing. Cork soon goaled, but Kilkenny surged back to equalise. Points were exchanged, and with minutes to go Cork continued to lead by a point. Kilkenny strove harder to get the equaliser and were awarded a thirty-yard free from the Cork goal. Terry Leahy, who went to take it, did not like the way the ball was placed and moved it with his hurley. The referee, Phil Purcell of Tipperary, replaced it in its original position, although the Cork supporters claimed it should have been a free out. Ignoring the controversy, Leahy lifted the ball and sent it over the bar for the equaliser. From the puck-out Cork went after the winner, but Paddy Grace cleared and Kilkenny attacked. A Cork clearance came out to the unmarked Terry Leahy, who, from about sixty-five yards, sent over the winning point. The final score was Kilkenny 0-14, Cork 2-7.

Terry Leahy's name will forever be linked with this thrilling victory. He scored six points, but it was his coolness in sending over the equalising point, as well as his winning point, that revealed his greatness. Walter McGrath wrote in the *Cork Examiner* the following day:

> It would be difficult to over-emphasise the part that Langton and Leahy played in the team's success. Seldom does a puck from either of them go wide of the posts. The Cork forwards were way behind in their ability to turn opportunities to advantage and chance after chance, especially in the first half, was lost.

In an interview with Brendan Fullam, Leahy himself had this to say of the game:

> Our policy was to go for points, because we knew the great backs of Cork—Alan Lotty, Paddy Donovan, Dr Jim Young, Con Murphy, and the great goalie Tom Mulcahy—were like the Rock of Cashel. There was a terrible temptation to go for goals when Cork were leading by two points. But we didn't fall into the trap.[5]

It was Kilkenny's fourth attempt to win their thirteenth title. After the failures of 1940, 1945 and 1946 it was the sweetest of victories. For Cork it was the end of a brilliant era. Detractors of their achievements mention the quality of the opposition and the problems caused by the foot-and-mouth epidemic, but none can explain away the fact that Cork achieved more success during the period than any other team in the history of hurling. This achievement went a long way towards enhancing the standing of the game in the country and establishing hurling as a most attractive spectator sport.

10

Cork-Tipp Rivalry

When one focuses on the period 1949–54 one automatically thinks of the rivalry between Cork and Tipperary. These were epic days, when men were larger than life and hurling games were unforgettable experiences.

For Mickey Byrne, the draw and the replay in the 1949 Munster championship were the toughest and most memorable of all he played against Cork. After that he puts the 1950 Munster final at Killarney, which was 'dog-rough'. For Pat Stakelum the atmosphere was 'electric'. He reckons that 1949 was a 'steal'. Cork were a goal ahead in the fourth minute of injury time when Jimmy Kennedy and his golden goal gave Tipperary the chance of extra time, in which they gained a two-point victory.

Some who remember these games, with the results so close and uncertain, would suggest that they were dangerous encounters, and many of them were bruising, to say the least. But Jimmy Kennedy reckons Cork were very fair: 'When the ball came between you and a Cork man, the ball was his priority, not your head or your arm, as it was with some players.' The games, the stories, the excitement, the expectation, the ecstasy of success and the sadness of failure made one proud to be a Tipperary or a Cork supporter.

GAA coverage in the national papers took off in the thirties with the advent of the *Irish Press*. It became muted during the war, with the shortage of newsprint, but began to explode again in the late forties, coinciding with the Tipp-Cork clashes between 1949 and 1954. The attention paid to the games drove the attendances up from the twenty thousands of the mid-twenties to the fifty thousands. Matches were analysed, incidents highlighted, and personalities profiled, and it all made one love or hate

Christy Ring or John Doyle, depending on one's allegiance. The appeal of the Cork-Tipp clashes spread far beyond the province of Munster.

In 1948 it was ten years since Waterford had appeared in the All-Ireland final. In fact there were three survivors of that team in John Keane, Mick Hickey, and Christy Moylan. Keane is one of the great heroes of Waterford hurling. His career started in 1934 with a junior All-Ireland medal and was to continue until 1952; during that time he was one of the greatest of centre-backs, and when he moved to centre-forward in 1948 he brought a kind of decisiveness to the Waterford attack that it had lacked up to then and that was vital in achieving victory that year.

The Munster championship provided plenty of drama. The Limerick-Tipperary first-round game at the Cork Athletic Grounds had to be abandoned thirty minutes before the start because of a waterlogged pitch. The game was rescheduled for the following Sunday at the same venue, but Tipperary and Limerick agreed to toss for a home venue, and Limerick won. The chairman of the Munster Council refused to go along with the decision and confirmed Cork as the venue. A special meeting of the council overruled the chairman and fixed the venue for Limerick; Cork then appealed to the Central Council and won, and the match was finally played on 27 June.

If the background to the game was extraordinary so too was the game itself. Tipperary were being led by 7-3 to 2-1 at the interval but they made a remarkable recovery that almost forced a draw. They came within two goals of Limerick with seven minutes to play but failed to score again. The outstanding player on the field was Jim Devitt of Tipperary, who hurled the game of his life and scored three goals and a point from seventies. Limerick survived and were ahead by 8-4 to 6-4 at the end.

Limerick and Cork attracted a crowd of forty thousand to Thurles. In a hard, close encounter, Limerick were stymied by a close-marking Cork defence and were behind by 5-3 to 2-5 at the final whistle. This was John Mackey's last game for Limerick.

In the meantime Waterford beat Clare by two points in the other semi-final, played at Thurles. While Waterford were going for their first final in ten years, Cork were going for their sixth. After a shaky start Waterford settled down and led by a point at half time. They stretched their lead in the second half and went eight points in front, but Cork rallied and had the lead reduced to the minimum at the final whistle. Jim Ware in goal and John Keane at centre-forward played starring roles in the victory.

Two weeks later the winners accounted for Galway in the All-Ireland semi-final at Croke Park and qualified to meet Dublin in the final.

Treble crown victory. In 1930, Tipperary achieved a feat never previously known in the history of the GAA when they won the All-Ireland hurling championships in the senior, junior and minor grades. This remarkable photograph of the three teams was taken at Thurles sports field.

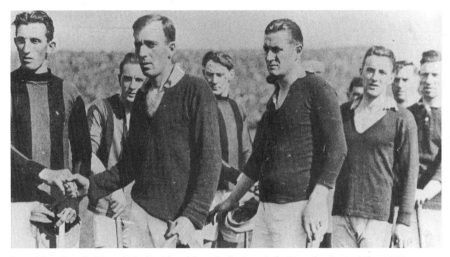

Lory Meagher (left) and Eudie Coughlan shake hands before the first of the 1931 games between Cork and Kilkenny at Croke Park. Behind Eudie stand Jim Hurley, Willie Clancy, 'Balty' Aherne and 'Hawker' Grady.

The Cork team that eventually won the 1931 championship after two thrilling final replays against Kilkenny. **BACK ROW** (LEFT TO RIGHT): E. O'CONNELL, J. HURLEY, P. AHERNE, P. O'GRADY, J. COUGHLAN, M. O'COUGHLAN, W. CLANCY, W. DORNEY (SELECTOR), P. DELEA. **FRONT ROW** (LEFT TO RIGHT): J. O'REGAN, M. AHERNE, D. BARRY MURPHY, T. BARRY, E. COUGHLAN (CAPT.), P. COLLINS, MORGAN MADDEN.

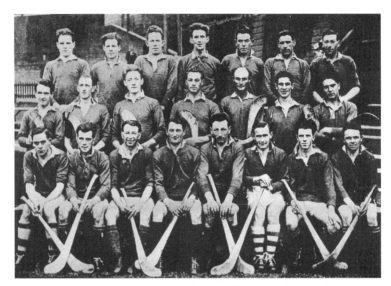

The Waterford team that won the All-Ireland junior championship in 1931. **BACK ROW** (LEFT TO RIGHT): TOM GREANEY, BILL SHEEHAN, VIN DONOGHUE, JOHN MORRISSEY, JOHN FITZGERALD, JOSH HANNIGAN, GEORGE KEHOE. **SECOND ROW** (LEFT TO RIGHT): ANDREW SANDFORD, JACKIE O'DONNELL, BILL CONDON, NOEL CONDON, JIM HUNT, SIMON WHELAN, JOHN HARTIGAN. **FRONT ROW** (LEFT TO RIGHT): PADDY GOFF, JIM FLYNN, TOM BURKE, MICK CURLEY, PAT CONDON, DECLAN GOODE, PA SHEEHAN, JACKIE ORMOND.

Hurling was played wherever there were Irish emigrants. This photograph shows the arrival at Dún Laoghaire of the South African hurling team for the 1932 Tailteann Games.

The Clare team that won the Munster senior title in 1932. **BACK ROW** (LEFT TO RIGHT): ART McCANN 'FEAR CIÚN' (RUAN), FR HAMILTON (CHAIRMAN, COUNTY BOARD), P. McNAMARA (NEWMARKET), ROBBIE LAWLOR, (TRAINER) (LIMERICK), MICK FALVEY (KILMALEY), DR J. HOGAN (BODYKE), JIMMY FLANAGAN (NEWMARKET), TULL CONSIDINE (ENNIS), TOM BURNELL (TUBBER), JOHN JOE DOYLE (CAPT.) (NEWMARKET), PA 'FOWLER' McINERNEY (O'CALLAGHAN'S MILLS), JACK GLEESON (KILKISHEN), SEÁN HURLEY (O'CALLAGHAN'S MILLS), MARTIN 'BOCKY' CONROY (NEWMARKET), ROM ROURKE (NEWMARKET), JIM HIGGINS (NEWMARKET), GEORGIE O'DEA (NEWMARKET), STEPHEN CLUNE (MANAGER) (QUIN), PADDY McNAMARA (ENNIS UDC). **KNEELING** (LEFT TO RIGHT): JIM HOULIHAN (TULLA), MICK ROURKE (NEWMARKET), DR TOMMY DALY (TULLA), JIM MULLANE (CLONLARA), LARRY BLAKE (ENNIS), TOM 'FOWLER' McINERNEY (O'CALLAGHAN'S MILLS). **FRONT ROW**: ART McCANN JR (RUAN).

The Kilkenny side that won the senior championship in 1933. **BACK ROW** (LEFT TO RIGHT):
SEÁN McCARTHY, J. WALSH, P. BYRNE, J. FARRELL, J. O'CONNELL, L. MEAGHER, REV. W. BRENNAN. **MIDDLE
ROW** (LEFT TO RIGHT): J. KEOGHAN, DICK SULLIVAN, E. BYRNE, MARTIN POWER, J. DARMODY,
P. O'REILLY, PADDY PHELAN, TOM LEAHY, S. GIBBONS, M. DALTON. **FRONT ROW** (LEFT TO RIGHT):
J. FITZPATRICK, JOHN DUGGAN, P. LARKIN, E. DOYLE (CAPT.), MARTIN WHITE, T. GRACE, MATT POWER,
JOHNNIE DUNNE.

The opening of the Tailteann Games at Croke Park in 1934.

The Limerick side that captured the All-Ireland title of 1934 against Dublin, following a replay. **FRONT ROW** (LEFT TO RIGHT): MICK HICKEY, MICKEY CONDON, DAN FLANAGAN, PETER BROWNE (TRAINER). **CENTRE ROW** (LEFT TO RIGHT): MICK NEVILLE, DENNY LANIGAN, MICKEY CROSS, JOHN MACKEY, BOB McCONKEY, MICK KENNEDY, JIMMY CLOSE, DAVE CLOHESSY, LIAM SCANLON. **BACK ROW** (LEFT TO RIGHT): DAVE CONWAY, JACK KEANE, PADDY MACKEY, PAT O'REILLY, MICK RYAN, JIM ROCHE, JACKIE O'CONNELL, PADDY SCANLON, ANTHONY MACKEY, GARRETT HOWARD, TIMMY RYAN, PAT RYAN, TOMMY McCARTHY, WILLIE HANNON, NED CREGAN, CHRISTY O'BRIEN, MICK MACKEY, PADDY CLOHESSY, W. P. CLIFFORD.

Limerick hurlers on board the *Manhattan*, returning from the 1936 tour of the United States. **BACK ROW** (LEFT TO RIGHT): TIM HUMPHRIES, NED CREGAN, MICKEY CROSS, PADDY McMAHON, MICK HICKEY, MICK KENNEDY, TOMMY McCARTHY, GARRETT HOWARD, PADDY CLOHESSY, DENNY LANIGAN. **FRONT ROW** (LEFT TO RIGHT): JACKIE POWER, JIMMY CLOSE, TON SHINNEY, JOHN MACKEY, MICK MACKEY, TIMMY RYAN, PADDY SCANLAN, MICKY CONDON.

The only Westmeath side to qualify for the Leinster senior hurling final did so in 1937, only to be beaten by Kilkenny.

The 1937 All-Ireland final was played at Killarney and saw Tipperary achieve one of their easiest victories over Kilkenny, by 3-11 to 0-3.

Fr Meagher, Tipperary County Board chairman, pinning the 'Blue Riband' on the Tipperary captain, Jim Lanigan, in 1937, with Johnny Leahy looking on.

Waterford made the breakthrough in Munster in 1938 but lost to Dublin in the All-Ireland final. The side that won the provincial title was: **BACK ROW** (LEFT TO RIGHT): CHARLIE WARE, DECLAN GOODE, DOYLE WALSH, JOHN KEANE, LOCKY BYRNE, JACK HALPIN, CHRISTY MOYLAN, MICK CURLEY, TOM GREANEY. **FRONT ROW** (LEFT TO RIGHT): JOHN BASTON, DAVY POWER, TOM FITZGERALD, SONNY WYSE, JOHN FANNING, JIMMY MOUNTAIN, WILLIE BARRON, SEÁN FEENEY, CON CURLEY, PADDY GREENE.

Jack Lynch (right) and the Kilkenny captain, Jimmy Walsh, await the toss of the coin before the first round of the National League at the Athletic Grounds in October 1939. Looking on apprehensively (behind Billy Campbell) is a youthful Christy Ring, about to play his first league game for Cork.

Limerick won their third championship in seven years in 1940 but were to wait a further thirty-three years before their next victory. **FRONT ROW** (LEFT TO RIGHT): PADDY CLOHESSY, MICK MACKEY, MICK KENNEDY, NED CHAWKE, DICK STOKES, PETER CREGAN. **BACK ROW** (LEFT TO RIGHT): MICK HICKEY, JIM McCARTHY, TOMMY COOKE, PADDY SCANLON, TONY HERBERT, JIM ROCHE, PADDY McMAHON, JOHN MACKEY, PADDY MACKEY, TIMMY RYAN, DAVE HURLEY, JACKIE POWER, MARTIN 'ROBBIE' LAWLOR.

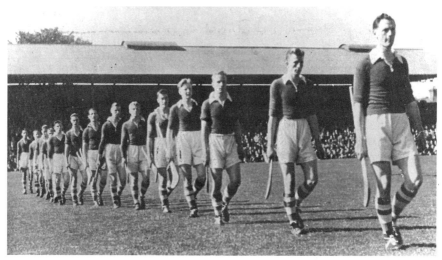

Jack Lynch leads Cork in the pre-match parade before the 1942 All-Ireland final against Dublin.

The team of the Seventh Brigade that won the All-Army final of 1943 in the Phoenix Park. Missing from the photograph is Charlie Tobin of Cork, who had returned to the mess before the picture was taken. **BACK ROW** (LEFT TO RIGHT): MAJ.-GEN. M. J. COSTELLO, JERRY RIORDAN (CORK), JIM DEVITT (TIPPERARY), JIMMY COONEY (TIPPERARY), PHIL BYRNES (AHANE), PADDY O'SHEA (LIMERICK), ALFIE O'BRIEN (CLARE), GERRY O'SULLIVAN (CORK), MICK O'GRADY (CLARE). **FRONT ROW** (LEFT TO RIGHT): JACK O'MAHONY (CORK), PADDY TUOHY (TIPPERARY), SEÁN O'HALLORAN (LIMERICK), MICK MACKEY (CAPT.) (LIMERICK), PADDY O'REILLY (WEXFORD), TIM MURPHY (LIMERICK).

The Cork side of 1944 that completed four-in-a-row and was to win another championship two years later. **BACK ROW** (LEFT TO RIGHT): W. WALSH (CHAIRMAN), J. QUIRKE, C. MURPHY, A. LOTTY, W. MURPHY, J. KELLY, T. MULCAHY, P. O'DONOVAN, B. THORNHILL, J. BARRY (TRAINER). **FRONT ROW** (LEFT TO RIGHT): J. YOUNG, J. LYNCH, S. CONDON, J. MORRISON, C. COTTRELL, C. RING, D.J. BUCKLEY.

The great Lory Meagher talking to the Kilkenny goalkeeper, Jimmy Walsh, in the 1945 Leinster senior final against Dublin.

Half time in the Munster final of 1946 in Thurles between Cork and Limerick. Cork's famous trainer, Jim 'Tough' Barry (right), is giving his pep talk. The player seated on the left (minus shirt) is the Cork full-back Con Murphy, who became President of the GAA 1976 – 79.

In 1946, Cork won their fifth title in six years. Here the captain, Christy Ring, is shown after the match with the Cork trainer, Jim Barry.

The Limerick side that won the National League of 1947. **BACK ROW** (LEFT TO RIGHT): CANON PUNCH (SELECTOR), PADDY FITZGERALD, JIM SADLIER, THOMAS O'BRIEN, JOHN BARRY, PADDY CLOHESSY, MICK HERBERT, JACKIE POWER, PAT O'REILLY. **FRONT ROW** (LEFT TO RIGHT): DENIS FLANAGAN, MICK DOOLEY, JOHN MULCAHY, PADDY COLLOPY, SEÁN HERBERT, PADDY FITZGERALD, TOM CREGAN.

Kilkenny were All-Ireland champions in 1947 for the first time in eight years. **BACK ROW** (LEFT TO RIGHT): NICK O'DONNELL, TOMMY MURPHY, SHEM DOWNEY, JACK MULCAHY, JIM LANGTON, FR NED KAVANAGH, TERRY LEAHY, TOM WALTON, JIM HEFFERNAN, JIMMY KELLY, BILL WALSH. **MIDDLE ROW** (LEFT TO RIGHT): TOM WALSH, MICK DALTON, LIAM REIDY, MARK MARNELL, PAT HAYDEN, DAN KENNEDY (CAPT.), PETER PRENDERGAST, WILLIE CAHILL, PADDY GRACE, SYD BLUETT. **FRONT ROW** (LEFT TO RIGHT): MICK JOYCE, JACK EGAN, JIM DONEGAN, PADDY LENNON, PADDY O'BRIEN.

Waterford finally achieved championship glory in 1948, winning the first of their two titles. **BACK ROW** (LEFT TO RIGHT): MICK HAYES, MICK HEALY, MICK HICKEY, EDDIE CAREW, ANDY FLEMING, JIM ALLEN, VIN BASTON, JOHN KEANE, DAVY POWER, TOM CURRAN, JOSIE MURPHY, PAT NEVILLE, WILLY GALVIN, JIMMY GALVIN. **FRONT ROW** (LEFT TO RIGHT): JOHN CUSACK, JACKIE GOODE, NED DALY, KEVIN O'CONNOR, JIM WARE, CHRISTY MOYLAN, MICK FEENEY, JOHN BASTON, JOHNNY O'CONNOR, LARRY FANNING.

Group taken on board the *Ryndam* en route to New York with the Tipperary team in 1950. **LEFT TO RIGHT:** DR MICHAEL RUSSELL, JIM RYAN, PHIL PURCELL, WILL HOUGH, JOHN D. HICKEY, PADDY LEAHY.

The St Mary's (City) Club, Sydney, Australia, 1952. Not all the players can be identified, but the photograph includes M. O'BRIEN, TIPPERARY (BACK ROW, LEFT), M. WOULFE, LIMERICK (BACK ROW, RIGHT), P. EGAN, GALWAY (FRONT ROW, LEFT) AND J. WOULFE, LIMERICK (FRONT ROW, THIRD FROM LEFT). Fortunately, all the middle row can be identified. THEY ARE (LEFT TO RIGHT): J. MURPHY (KILKENNY), T. WOULFE (LIMERICK), P. WOULFE (LIMERICK), P. HOLDEN (KILKENNY).

Waterford were favourites to win the final, and the opposition was the same as had beaten them ten years previously. On that occasion Croke Park inexperience probably cost Waterford the title; this time they played with confidence, with Mick Hickey, who had captained the 1938 side, at wing-back, Christy Moylan at wing-forward, and John Keane beside him in the centre. And there were other veterans to support them in Jim Ware, Andy Fleming, Vin Baston, and Mick Hayes. Although playing against the breeze, they led by 2-5 to 0-2 at the interval. They continued to dominate in the second half and, despite a late rally by Dublin, were comfortable winners in the end on the score 6-7 to 4-2. Playing wing-forward for Dublin was Seán Óg Ó Ceallacháin of broadcasting fame, and on the other wing was Jimmy Kennedy, who was to make his name for Tipperary the following year.

Waterford's players were given a tumultuous welcome when they returned home with the McCarthy Cup for the first time. Twenty-five thousand people and six bands formed a welcoming party, and they had a double victory to celebrate, as the minors had also been successful. It was the first time a new team had won the All-Ireland championship since Galway had done so in 1923. For Christy Moylan the victory was particularly sweet. His hurling career had started in 1935, and as the forties wore on his hopes of an All-Ireland became slimmer. He went to England in 1945, returning three years later to see his mother, who was unwell; he went back into training, was drafted into the team for the Munster final, and had the satisfaction of adding an All-Ireland medal to his Munster one when Waterford won their first All-Ireland.

When the Munster championship draws for 1949 were made, the one good thing from a Tipperary point of view was that they weren't drawn against Limerick. In the previous three years they had been defeated by the Shannonsiders, and a state of gloom had descended over the county. The draw pitted them against Cork, and, as they had played them twice in the previous eight months, they faced the championship with a new confidence. The two games in question were National League finals. The 1947/48 final wasn't played until October 1948, and even though Tipperary had been beaten by seven points there was a redeeming feature of a new goalkeeping find in Tony Reddin from the Lorrha club. Four months later the final of the 1948/49 league was played against the same opposition, and this time Tipperary had two points to spare to win their first league title since 1928. This victory lifted spirits in the county and made supporters look forward to the championship with greater hope. Another piece of good news was the decision of Jimmy Kennedy, who had played with Dublin the previous year, to declare for his native county.

The first round with Cork was played at Limerick on 29 May and ended in a draw. Jack Lynch made a major contribution for Cork, scoring 1-6 of his side's total of 3-10. There were a number of changes for the replay. John Doyle took over from Flor Coffey at left-full-back and began a distinguished career on the Tipperary team that would see him turn out for his county for no fewer than eighteen years, during which time he would win eight All-Ireland medals and eleven National Leagues. Seán Kenny of Borrisoleigh was brought in to partner Pat Stakelum at centrefield.

The game, played on one of the warmest days ever recorded, was one of the most dramatic ever played in the Munster championship. It was the first Munster game to be decided in extra time, and there was a dramatic finish to a contest in which Tipperary had been inferior for fifty-nine minutes. The Tipperary forwards had a poor game, and at half time the score stood at 1-2 to 0-2. But the game wasn't decided until after six o'clock, and those listening to Micheál O'Hehir's broadcast had their commentary cut off with only a few minutes of play left and had to wait until the end of the half six news to hear the result. Tipperary, their supporters almost resigned to defeat, earned the chance of extra time as a result of a spectacular goal by Jimmy Kennedy in the last minute of the game, bringing thousands of cheering supporters to their feet. Cork were still a goal in front four minutes into injury time when Kennedy scored his goal, and the final whistle followed a minute later.

One of the most important decisions taken by the Tipperary selectors at the end of normal time was to take the players off the field to the cool of the dressing-room before the final thirty minutes. The Cork players remained on the field, and their already exhausted energy was further sapped by the brilliant sunshine. Tipperary's freshness told in extra time, and they might have been ahead by more at the final whistle had it not been for poor forward play. The final score was 2-8 to 1-9.

An incident in the second half is still disputed. Cork claimed that Mossie O'Riordan scored a second goal that rebounded from the stanchion supporting the wire netting with such speed that the umpire failed to see it before it was cleared. The Tipperary view is that the ball struck the crossbar, bounced down, and rebounded outfield from the goalkeeper's boot. It was to be the first of a series of such incidents that were to be associated with Tipperary-Cork games. As a result of the episode, corded netting was introduced the following year.

The victory was Tipperary's first in the Munster championship since 1945. There was a tremendous new spirit abroad and a widespread interest in the team, which had no less than thirteen clubs represented on the panel.

Clare were overcome in the semi-final in a game that saw the arrival of a new star in Tommy Ryan of Sarsfields. Limerick, who had beaten the All-Ireland champions, Waterford, in a thrilling semi-final at Thurles, were Tipperary's opponents in the Munster final. They were dominant in the first half, but Tipperary gradually took over in the second half and were completely in control at the final whistle. The game was noteworthy for a wonderful ten points from the stick of Jimmy Kennedy and some superb goalkeeping from Tony Reddin. Kennedy's contribution to this Munster title was decisive, with a total of 2-27 to his credit from the four games. All Tipperary's points from frees—twenty in all—were scored by Kennedy.

Antrim proved no test for the Munster men in the semi-final; their unlikely opponents in the final were Laois. However, Laois had shown promise in 1948, when they sensationally defeated Kilkenny by four points at Port Laoise, only to suffer defeat at the hands of Dublin in the Leinster final. Laois reversed the decision in 1949 and qualified to play Kilkenny in the Leinster final. Kilkenny had been impressive in accounting for Wexford and Meath in the earlier rounds. The game was played at Nowlan Park, and Kilkenny were at sea in the first half as Laois built a half-time lead of 3-4 to 0-3. In the second half Kilkenny staged a great rally, but Laois held out for a two-point victory. They confirmed their form when they beat Galway in the All-Ireland semi-final in atrocious conditions at Croke Park.

The pairing of Tipperary and Laois in the final captured the public imagination and attracted a crowd of over sixty-seven thousand. Laois were appearing in their first All-Ireland in thirty-four years, and the team included Harry Gray, who had won an All-Ireland eleven years previously with Dublin, and Paddy Ruschitzko, of Polish descent, from the Clonad club, who was the captain of the side. After their performances so far the Laois men were expected to give a good account of themselves.

As it happened, Tipperary's victory was their easiest ever. From the time Pat Stakelum sent over the first point to the final whistle, when Tipperary led by 3-11 to 0-3, they were never in danger. It was a dull, monotonous hour, one of the poorest finals on record. Tipperary led by 1-5 to 0-3 at half time, and Laois failed to score in the second half. The victory was unique for Tony Brennan, who added a second All-Ireland at full-back to the one he had gained in 1945 at full-forward.

The Cork-Tipperary rivalry was resumed in the 1950 Munster final. Tipperary had a clear-cut victory over Limerick in the first round but made heavy weather of beating Clare in the semi-final. In the other semi-final Cork got the better of Waterford. The final was played in Killarney, and although the official attendance was thirty-nine thousand it was estimated that over fifty thousand got in as a result of gates being broken down and walls being scaled. As a consequence there were many incursions by spectators onto the field of play, and because the game was played in such a welter of excitement these became more frequent as the game progressed. Tipperary led by 1-13 to 1-6 at the interval. Forty-five minutes into the second half there was an encroachment onto the field that took a long time to clear; and after this Cork were a transformed side. They gradually reduced Tipperary's lead to three points and tried desperately for an equaliser. Cork supporters ran onto the field with every score, not realising that their enthusiasm was hindering rather than helping their side.

The scene around the Tipperary goals in the closing stages was even more remarkable. The Tipperary goalkeeper, Tony Reddin, found himself in the centre of a sea of spectators, while bottles, sods and other missiles were raining on his goal. Any time the ball came in he was teased, barracked, and even pushed. He remembers in particular one supporter catching him by the jersey as he ran out to clear a ball. Jack Lynch, playing his last game in the Cork jersey, appealed to the crowd, but they ignored him. The final attack on the goal caused the collapse of the net, from which Reddin escaped just in time.

None but the referee, Liam O'Donaghue of Limerick, could say exactly when full time had elapsed, but when he sounded the final whistle Tipperary had weathered the storm and retained their Munster title. The final score was 2-17 to 3-11. It was Tipperary's best display during the year and a tribute to every player, especially the three Ryans—Eddie, Mick, and Timmy—who made up the half-forward line. The remaining two games were something of an anti-climax. In the semi-final Tipperary beat Galway in Tuam by seven points. Star of the forwards was Paddy Kenny, who scored three goals.

Kilkenny were Tipperary's opponents in the All-Ireland final. The Leinster champions defeated Wexford in a great provincial final and became the first holders of the O'Keeffe Cup, named after Bob O'Keeffe of Kilkenny, a former president of the GAA. The game was played at Nowlan Park and attracted a record attendance of over thirty-six thousand. So great was the pressure on space that Micheál O'Hehir threatened to cut off his broadcast because the car he was working from was surrounded by people who were obstructing his view. He eventually did his job standing on the roof of the car. Wexford led at half time and mid-way through the second half, but Kilkenny made a few important switches to win by 3-11 to 2-11.

The All-Ireland was a disappointment. Tipperary went into the final with the record of not having won a second consecutive All-Ireland for fifty years. On the other hand their record against Kilkenny was impressive: in eleven finals between the sides, Tipperary had won on eight occasions, and their last defeat was in 1922. Prophecies of a record attendance were unfulfilled, and though very little separated the sides for most of the game, it lacked the usual atmosphere. Playing against the breeze in the first half, Kilkenny led by 0-7 to 0-5 at half time, Jim Langton scoring six of their points. At the start of the second half Kilkenny seemed to have the title for the taking but fell away. Not until the final moments did the goals come. Paddy Kenny crashed one home for Tipperary, only for Jimmy Kelly to reply almost immediately for the Noresiders, leaving the final score 1-9 to 1-8 in favour of Tipperary.

There was to be a further epic in the Cork-Tipperary series in the 1951 championship. In the opening round Waterford sprang a first-class surprise and put Tipperary to the pin of their collar, but they survived by a goal. However, they gave a great display when beating Limerick in the semi-final. In the other semi-final Cork got the better of Clare, and the stage was set for another encounter between the two teams.

The final was a memorable tussle and must rank as one of the greatest games of all time. Over forty-two thousand attended; many more could not get in and had to be content with the radio relay outside the gates. The game was a rattler from the beginning, with plenty of thrills and suspense. At half time Tipperary had a two-point lead. Cork put on a great rally in the third quarter and led by a goal, but a great goal for Tipperary by Ned Ryan revived their fortunes and inspired them to a storming finish that was too good for Cork's best efforts. At the final whistle Tipperary had two points to spare on the score 2-11 to 2-9.

Tipperary had a straight passage into the All-Ireland final, where their opponents were Wexford, who had beaten Laois in the Leinster final. Earlier the Laois men had inflicted on Kilkenny their most comprehensive defeat. In the final Laois were favourites, and they justified that billing in the first quarter, but Wexford came alive in the second quarter and led by 1-5 to 1-3 at the interval. In the second half Wexford dominated and would have won by a more comfortable margin but for an outstanding performance by the Laois veteran Harry Gray. In the end they had six points to spare. It was Wexford's first Leinster championship win in thirty-three years.

Wexford then had to play Galway in the All-Ireland semi-final. The Connacht men were tipped to win with something to spare, having beaten Wexford well in the League home final. The game was a very close encounter, with Wexford drawing level in the third quarter. With about five minutes of actual time remaining, Galway went ahead with a Josie Gallagher point. In response Nick O'Donnell hit a massive puck-out that went all the way to Nicky Rackard, who broke from his marker and buried the ball in the net. This score electrified Wexford, and they went on to win by 3-11 to 2-9.

For the All-Ireland, Jimmy Langton of Kilkenny fame came across to Enniscorthy to lend a hand at Wexford training sessions. The authorities decided that both sides should change their jerseys, with the Munster men wearing their provincial blue and Wexford donning the green of Leinster. Nearly seventy thousand spectators saw Wexford get off to a flying start. They tore through Tipperary's ranks and looked as if they would take their first title in forty-one years. They had five points to spare at the end of the first quarter, but Tipperary led by a goal at half time, and by the end of the third quarter Wexford were a spent force. They had to face tremendous goalkeeping from Tony Reddin, while their own Ray Brennan made numerous mistakes. In the end Tipperary were ahead by 7-7 to 3-9, a score that flattered the Munster men somewhat. The victory gave Tipperary their second three-in-a-row and their sixteenth All-Ireland title.

The GAA columnist in the *Tipperary Star*, 'Winter Green', best expressed the hopes and expectations for 1952 in his column of 5 January:

> Foremost is perhaps the all important one—can Tipperary, like Cork, make it four-in-a-row, and by doing so lead all others in the championship race with a grand total of seventeen All-Ireland championships? Of course we can. By that I mean that we have here in Tipperary a hurling fifteen capable of defeating the best that Cork, Wexford, Limerick or Kilkenny, or any of our famous rivals, can put on the field ... In these three years we have defeated, not once, but several times, counties that have been accepted as hurling's top notchers and there was no game which we won where the losers could have truthfully said that victory should have been theirs.

Cork might have had a different opinion on some of those encounters.

Tipperary began the year in an impressive manner. They won the National League and trounced Waterford in the Munster semi-final. They came into the final as seasoned veterans against a Cork team they had beaten in the three years previously. Cork had a number of new players in John Lyons, Tony O'Shaughnessy, Willie John Daly, Vince Twomey, Liam Dowling, and the captain, Paddy Barry. Tipperary confirmed pre-match opinions during the first half and led by two goals at the interval. However, they suffered a number of setbacks. John Hough was absent from centrefield and was sorely missed; Tommy Doyle retired injured after only ten minutes; while Jimmy Finn was a sick man before he went onto the field. With the wind in their backs in the second half, Cork were a transformed team. They played some brilliant hurling and went into a three-point lead. In the last ten minutes Tipperary tried desperately to get a goal, but a point was all they could manage, and Cork won by 1-11 to 2-6. An indication of Cork's performance was that Tipperary only scored one point in the second half.

Cork were jubilant. They had reversed the trend of the previous years and prevented Tipperary from going for a possible four-in-a-row. Spearheading a great display was Christy Ring, who was shouldered from the field with blood streaming down his face. He had given a heroic performance.

Cork failed to repeat the performance against Galway in the All-Ireland semi-final but won by two points after an unimpressive display. The selectors made a number of changes for the final, the most unusual of which was the introduction of a complete newcomer, Billy Abernethy, a former minor, at right-corner-forward. Josie Hartnett had to be omitted because of appendicitis.

Cork's opponents in the final were Dublin, who had beaten Wexford in the Leinster championship. At the start of the championship Wexford were hopeful, but then came an injury to Nicky Rackard's knee, and they had to turn out against Kilkenny without him. Despite his loss they had a very satisfactory three-point win, and the future looked bright. Dublin, although impressive in disposing of Meath and Laois, were not expected to cause much trouble, especially as Nicky Rackard would be fit for the final. Wexford led by four points at half time. In the second half they continued to dominate until Art Foley had to retire injured and the untried Paddy Kelly of St Fintan's replaced him in goal. Within a few minutes Dublin had scored two goals and a point and were two in front. Sensationally, they continued to score until they led by 7-2 to 2-6. In injury time Nicky Rackard got a goal. Wexford were shocked. Pádraig Puirséal wrote:

> I have never come away from a game and found such an air of gloom over the departing fans, which shows how predominant were the Wexford fans amongst the gathering and how remarkable had been the fall of their favourites. I came away from Kilkenny, happy in the knowledge that I had just witnessed the greatest upset in hurling history since Laois beat Cork in the All-Ireland final of 1915.

On the basis of this display some reporters tipped Dublin for the first title since 1938. The team included Jim Prior of Tipperary, who was captain and played at centre-back, Des Ferguson, who had a fine game on Christy

Ring, Kevin Matthews, Norman Allen, Seán Cronin, Roger McCarthy, Phil Ryan, Jimmy O'Callaghan, and Jack Finnan, playing at corner-forward, whose departure through injury completely upset what had been until then a competent Dublin performance. At half time Cork were a goal in front, chiefly through the brilliant goalkeeping of Dave Creedon. Dublin collapsed in the second half and could manage only two more points, while Cork scored 1-9 to win by thirteen points on a score of 2-14 to 0-7. Paddy Barry, who had helped Sarsfields win their first county title the previous year, received the cup for Cork's seventeenth title.

The Cork-Tipp rivalry was renewed in 1953 when the sides met in the league final in April, and seldom if ever have Tipperary supporters come away from a game so bitterly disappointed. For the greater part of the first half they had four-fifths of the possession, but the forward line missed score after score, and they were behind by a point at half time. In the second half Cork forged ahead, and only two late goals by Tipperary took the bad look off the score, 2-10 to 2-7 in favour of Cork.

As the championship approached, however, things began to look up for Tipperary. They defeated Cork in two tournaments and went on to account for Waterford in the Munster semi-final. Cork accounted for Clare, and the final was played in Limerick. Cork refused to play in Thurles, blaming the catering arrangements there the previous year; a more likely explanation was the heightening tension between the two sides.

In the final itself Cork had a relatively easy victory. Tipperary never looked like producing the fine team movement that had been the basis of victories on other occasions. Playing with the wind in the first half, they led by four points at the interval. In the second half, with Christy Ring playing especially well and being ably assisted by Josie Hartnett and Willie John Daly, Cork came into their own and were the stronger, fitter and better all-round combination and were deserving winners by five points. The victory was a personal triumph for Christy Ring, who showed unlimited skill and artistry as he roved far and wide around the field. On one occasion he was found in his own goal stopping and clearing a Paddy Kenny 21-yard free. He had the honour that day of captaining the side because the county champions, Avondhu, had no representative on the team and they invited Ring to accept the honour.

Cork played Galway in the All-Ireland. The Connacht champions surprised Kilkenny in the semi-final. The Noresiders, having beaten Wexford in what was regarded as the best Leinster final in twenty years, were favourites. They led by five points at the break and increased it to seven soon after the resumption; then two long-range goals by John Killeen brought Galway back into the game, and a point brought them level. Five minutes before the finish Hubert Gordon got another point to give Galway the lead for the first time, and they held on to their slender margin until the final whistle.

This was another great Galway team, almost on a par with the team that won the Railway Cup in 1947 and that might have won an All-Ireland. It was still backboned by some of the stars of 1947, such as Seánie Duggan, Jim Brophy, Hubert Gordon, John Killeen, Josie Gallagher, and Inky Flaherty. The team also included a new star, Joe Salmon, who had made his debut for the county at minor level in 1947.

The 1953 All-Ireland, played before a record crowd of over seventy-one thousand on a beautiful day, is remembered as one of the most unsporting finals ever. From early in the game the Galway players in general and Mick Burke, the captain, in particular were determined that the Cork captain and star was going to be marked out of the game. Added to this was the behaviour of a large section of the crowd, which booed Ring every time he went near the ball or took a free. Instead of a free-flowing game it was a tough, bruising encounter. Five points down after twenty minutes, Galway clawed their way back into the game and, as it entered injury time, were only a point behind. However, instead of getting an equaliser Tom O'Sullivan scored a goal, which gave Cork victory by 3-3 to 0-8. It is generally accepted that on the day Galway were the superior outfit but they made tactical errors. One of the crucial ones related to Mick Burke. Badly injured half way through the second half, Burke insisted on continuing and moved out centrefield to follow Christy Ring. This move upset the solidarity of the Galway half-back line and allowed Cork back into the game. In fact Burke should have retired, as he was clearly concussed and wasn't in a fit state to play the remainder of the match. Contributing enormously to Cork's victory was their last line of defence: Gerry O'Riordan, John Lyons, and Tony O'Shaughnessy.

Cork and Tipperary qualified for their fifth successive Munster final in 1954 by virtue of wins over Waterford and Clare, respectively. All attendance records were broken when the sides met in Limerick on 18 July. Tipperary had the aid of a stiff breeze in the first half but didn't make enough use of it and were behind by five points at the interval. It appeared at this point to be Cork's game, but the Tipperary performance improved in the second half and there was only a point between the sides, in Tipperary's favour, as the game entered lost time. Christy Ring got the ball on the wing and, faced with three defenders, hit a speculative towards the goal. The ball bounced off the chest of Tony Reddin in the Tipperary goal and fell to the onrushing Paddy Barry, who finished it to the net. Before the final whistle Ring added a point to give Cork a sensational victory. The match will be remembered for the brilliant display by Ring, who not only made the final goal but also scored one earlier from a fine 21-yard free.

In the All-Ireland semi-final Cork came face to face with Galway, and many were apprehensive in view of the 1953 struggle. But the match passed off quietly enough, and Ring gave one of his best performances, despite the close attentions of Billy Duffy. The Galway selectors reshuffled their side and had seven newcomers. It was hoped that the mixture of the new and the experienced would work out, but after the first quarter Cork completely took over and beat the westerners by 4-13 to 2-1.

For the first time the two semi-finals were played at Croke Park. Antrim, who hadn't participated at this level since 1949, decided to enter their side in the All-Ireland hurling series. Their opponents were Wexford, who had come through Leinster in style. They pushed Kilkenny aside with ease in the semi-final and trounced Dublin in the final. Nicky Rackard's personal tally was 5-4. After these impressive performances lowly Antrim didn't stand a chance; however, nobody could have expected the extent of their defeat. Wexford created inter-county hurling records that day, scoring 12-17 to Antrim's 2-3. Despite some courageous goalkeeping by the Antrim keeper, Mullen, Nicky Rackard scored an individual record of 7-7. Some spectators thought this kind of scoring indecent, but Rackard was probably remembering how he had been held for an hour by the Antrim full-back, Donnelly, in a league tie in Belfast the previous winter.

The 1954 All-Ireland, between Cork and Wexford, created greater interest than any other hurling final before or since. Certainly more people than ever—eighty-four thousand—came to see it. Each side had its colossus, be it Ring or Rackard. In spite of Wexford's impressive scoring record, 25-33 for and 3-14 against, Cork were slight favourites. As so very often happens, the game turned out totally different from expectations. The final score was Cork 1-9, Wexford 1-6, a derisory total considering the scoring potential of the two sides. Ultimately it was a game in which the defences were dominant. Each side curbed and controlled the other's forward strength, and this is vividly shown in the scoring contributions of the titans of each side, Ring and Rackard. Neither scored a goal nor had a hand in the two that were scored.

Yet despite the paucity of scores it was one of the greatest hurling battles ever seen. Wexford led by a point at half time and continued to dominate into the second half. Then disaster struck as the great Nick O'Donnell broke his collarbone in a collision with Ring. Bobbie Rackard, who was playing a superhuman game at centre-back, was moved back to fill O'Donnell's place in the resulting reorganisation. Wexford continued to control the game and were four points up with fifteen minutes to go. However, with five minutes to go Johnny Clifford caught Art Foley out of position and scored the winning goal. There was still some time left, in which Cork added two more points to give them a three-point margin.

In the post-mortems the loss of Nick O'Donnell was seen as a crucial factor in Wexford's defeat. Many believed that Bobbie Rackard should never have been moved back and that this change had led to Cork's resurgence in the final quarter. Although Rackard continued to hurl superbly at full-back he was sorely missed at centre-back.

For Christy Ring it was a unique occasion. He became the first player to win eight All-Irelands, and he joined another elite by being only the third man (along with Mikey Maher of Tubberadora and Dick Walsh of Mooncoin) to captain three All-Ireland winning teams. His contribution to the game in his general play and the five points he scored was a significant element in Cork's victory. Soon after the All-Ireland he helped Glen Rovers beat Blackrock in the county final, and in the following months he travelled with the Cork team to the United States, where he was greeted by massive publicity as the 'Babe Ruth of hurling'.

11

The Rise of Wexford

Wexford's claim to hurling fame is based on their appearance in two of the most famous All-Irelands, 1954 and 1956. Losing the first and winning the second, Wexford also entered the record books for the two highest attendances at hurling finals.

Both of these games ended dramatically. In 1954 indecision by the Wexford goalkeeper, Art Foley, gave Cork their winning goal, and it was the same goalkeeper who made one of the most famous saves ever in the 1956 final. With four minutes to go he stopped a point-blank shot from Christy Ring and cleared the ball, and within a minute Nicky Rackard had a goal at the other end. So great was the save that Ring ran in and congratulated the astounded Foley.

For a county noted for its hurling prowess, Wexford were late arrivals to the championship. Hurling was at a low ebb in the county, partly because of poor organisation and also because of intense local rivalries that led to endless disputes and unfinished finals.

In the 1949 championship Wexford were beaten 4-11 to 1-4 by Kilkenny, so expectations against Meath in the first round of the 1950 championship were not high. The match was won, however, in an impressive manner. Victory over Laois followed, and qualification to play Kilkenny in the Leinster final. The game was played at Nowlan Park and attracted a record crowd. The Wexford men gave an exhibition of hurling that was as unexpected as it was brilliant. With the wind in the first half, they were not very impressive and only led by two points at the interval. But they played a storming second half, and only a brilliant Kilkenny performance prevented victory. Wexford lost by three points, but some pride had been restored.

Matters improved in 1951. Wexford qualified for the league final but were surprisingly beaten by Galway on a day when Art Foley had a nightmare game. With a revamped team against Meath in the championship they could only manage a draw the first day but won the replay easily. They overcame Dublin in the semi-final and Laois, who had scuttled Kilkenny's chances, in the Leinster final. They reversed the league result by beating Galway in the All-Ireland semi-final but fell to Tipperary in the All-Ireland.

In the 1952 league final Wexford lost by a point to Tipperary in a majestic contest. Nicky Rackard scored three times from 21-yard frees. On the third occasion there was a recurrence of an old knee injury, and he had to retire with ten minutes to go. Wexford became a bit disorganised in the resulting reshuffle, and Pat Stakelum scored the winning point for Tipperary in the dying minutes.

Although they lost, Wexford felt they had gained a moral victory, and prospects for the championship looked good, even if they had to plan without Rackard. Having a bye to the semi-final, they met Kilkenny at Croke Park on 8 June. John Cummins of Horsewood was introduced at full-forward, and he played a magnificent game and helped Wexford to a thrilling 4-7 to 5-1 victory. It looked well for the Leinster final, with Rackard's knee responding to treatment and only Dublin to beat. Things didn't go all Wexford's way in the first half, but they had four points to spare at the interval and were expected to turn it on in the second half. The opening minutes seemed to confirm this expectation; then Art Foley was injured and had to retire. An unknown, Paddy Kelly of St Fintan's, was sent in to replace him. Within a short time his namesake of Dublin had two balls in the net and Dublin were ahead; soon afterwards he scored again. Panic crept into Wexford's play as attack after attack brought nothing but wides. The nightmare eventually came to an end with the scoreboard shouting Dublin 7-2, Wexford 3-6.

But they managed to put the debacle behind them and showed by a few fine displays in the Oireachtas tournament that the performance against Dublin was a temporary lapse. The team began 1953 in great style by annihilating Kilkenny in a league encounter at New Ross. A loss to Cork put them out of the league, but they approached the championship with resurgent hope. There was bad news with the absence of Bobbie Rackard, who, as a result of a nose injury that had complications, had been advised never to play hurling again. Despite this setback Wexford overcame Laois easily and qualified to play Kilkenny in the Leinster final. The selectors sprang a surprise when they announced the team by leaving out Padge and Paddy Kehoe and going for a blend of youth and experience. Ned Wheeler was transferred to centre-back to replace Rackard.

In one of the greatest hurling finals for a long time, Wexford were beaten by two points by a team they had beaten by twenty-six points six months earlier. A number of factors contributed. The loss of Rackard and the two Kehoes was just too much. The famous 'Diamond' Hayden kept Nicky Rackard under control. Leading by six points at the interval, Wexford relaxed in the second half and allowed Kilkenny nine scores on the trot. In the end some scoring failures doomed Wexford. Only two points in arrears, Rackard took a twenty-one for the lead; incredibly, he failed to lift the ball. Two later seventies were missed and the game was lost: 1-13 to 3-5.

As a consolation, Wexford went on to win the Oireachtas for the second time, with victories over Kilkenny and Clare. More importantly, the team had a new find in Tom Ryan of St Aidan's, who had come on as a sub in the Leinster final and had shown by his tally of six goals in two Oireachtas games that he was a force to be reckoned with.

Whether by accident or design, Wexford kept a low profile during the league and looked forward to their first championship outing on 6 June. The good news was that Bobbie Rackard, unable to accept the monotony of retirement, had decided to return to the game. Torrential rain made conditions deplorable. Wexford's tactics in the forwards were to bring Nicky Rackard out to the half-forward line and even as far as centrefield and give greater scope to Tom Ryan around the goal. By half time Hayden was thoroughly exhausted; however, Wexford had only a two-point lead, and the result was still in doubt at the interval. In the second half Wexford put in a performance that tore the Kilkenny resistance to shreds. In the end the score was 5-11 to 0-7 in Wexford's favour, but their superiority was so pronounced that Kilkenny only managed one point from play.

In the final against Dublin there was no repeat of the debacle of 1952 but a comprehensive victory by 8-5 to 1-4.

Wexford's progress in the All-Ireland semi-final and final has already been related. They savaged Antrim, not knowing that they had only played against a second string: the Antrim mentors knew there was no chance of winning at senior level, while success at junior level was quite on the cards, so they put out their first string in the junior championship and reached the 'home' final, only to be beaten by a very good Limerick side by three points. The second string played Wexford. The full-back, Donnelly, was a brother of the Brendan Donnelly of Ballycastle who had kept Nicky Rackard to a last-gasp goal in Belfast the previous winter. When Rackard went for the first ball in the semi-final with Donnelly he found himself on his backside, and this, with the memory of the previous winter, probably sparked him to the performance that was to result in seven goals and seven points.

Things went badly for Wexford in the final. According to Bobbie Rackard,

> the Wexford defence was outstanding. The Cork defence was tight, but outfield Wexford dominated the play and won an abundance of possession. They failed, however, to capitalise on this superiority and missed numerous scoring opportunities. Late in the game, when Cork got their only goal—which proved to be the winner—Wexford ought to have been well in front. It was a game that should never have been lost.[1]

A close follower of Wexford hurling looking back over the previous four years from the perspective of 1955 would have been tempted to believe that the team had let the opportunity of glory pass. Such great teams, so many outstanding players, such brilliant displays, and so little achievement. However, as if there had been no disappointments, the team swept all opposition aside and qualified for the league final against Tipperary on 1 May 1955. Then, a week before the match, disaster struck with the death of the father of the Rackards, which meant that Billy, Bobbie and Nicky were unavailable. Nevertheless the team put in a marvellous performance and did not deserve to lose by six points.

Wexford had a bye into the 1955 Leinster semi-final against the surprise packet, Westmeath, who had shocked everyone by dismissing Offaly and Laois through the inspirational hurling of 'Jobber' McGrath. Although Wexford won by eleven points, the result did not do justice to Westmeath's effort, and the crowd cheered them off the field, especially the goalkeeper, Casserly, who had saved a 21-yard free from Nicky Rackard.

For the third year in a row Wexford and Kilkenny, who had accounted for Dublin in the other semi-final, met in the Leinster final. Wexford had one newcomer on the side, in the shape of Mick Morrissey of New Ross, who was to play an important part in blotting out Kilkenny's danger man, Seán Clohessy. The game was a tough, close struggle, and it took a Padge Kehoe point near the end to bring Wexford level, at 2-7 each. The replay took place two weeks later on a scorching day, and the sides were level at the break. On the throw-in Nicky Rackard got possession and hit a speculative lob towards the goal. It hit the hard ground before the goal and bounced over the shoulder of the Kilkenny goalkeeper for an unlikely score, to give Wexford a three-point lead, and that was the margin they had to spare at the end. One feature of the game was the swapping of positions by Bobbie and Billy Rackard. They had done so in the drawn game but had reverted to their normal positions for the replay. Each of them played brilliantly in his new position and continued to play there afterwards.

Meanwhile, shock waves were upsetting Munster hurling. Clare, who had one of the finest teams ever to grace a hurling pitch, had given notice at the end of the previous year that other counties had better watch out. They qualified to play Wexford in the Oireachtas final and, after a marvellous display, drew level with a Jimmy Smyth point in the final seconds. The replay was as good, as exciting, and as brilliant, and at the end Clare had three points to spare. One of the stars of the victory was Mick Hayes in goal, who kept a clean sheet. Other players of renown on the team were Dan McInerney, Dónal O'Grady, Jimmy Smyth, Matt Nugent, Des Dillon, Paddy Russell, and Jackie Greene.

It shouldn't have come as a surprise when Clare caused upset in the 1955 Munster championship. In the first game, against Cork on 5 June, they led by 2-5 to 1-0 after twenty minutes. Admittedly Cork fought back under the inspiration of Ring, going for his ninth All-Ireland victory, but Jimmy Smyth had the last word when he shot the winning point. To prove this was no flash in the pan Clare went on to dismiss Tipperary, the National League champions, in the semi-final by 1-6 to 0-8. Having accounted for Wexford, Cork and Tipperary in the space of seven months, Clare were showing unmistakable All-Ireland potential.

Their opponents in the Munster Final were Limerick, who had defeated a highly rated Waterford team in the other semi-final. The Shannonsiders were a young team, trained like a pack of greyhounds by Mick Mackey and possessing a high level of skill. Despite this, Clare were odds on to win their first Munster title since 1932. The result was very different. The Limerick lads ran Clare off the field and overwhelmed them so much that they had ten points to spare at the final whistle. Whether through overconfidence or an inability to deal with the sweltering conditions, Clare were unable to cope. The majority of the Clare team played below themselves; but credit must also be given to the speed of Limerick. Their wing-forwards, Liam Ryan and Ralph Prendergast, split the Clare defence open and gave the opening to Dermot Kelly to go on a scoring spree. It was a sensational summer.

So it was on to the All-Ireland semi-final between Wexford and Limerick. The Ulster champions, perhaps as a result of the slaughter of 1954, didn't play. There was a record crowd of nearly fifty-one thousand, and they got a good first half, during which Limerick played some great hurling and led by 2-2 to 1-3 at the interval. In the second half Wexford's superior weight, stamina and experience told, and they closed down Limerick to such an extent that all they could manage was a Dermot Kelly point. In contrast, Wexford scored 1-9 and won by double scores, 2-12 to 2-3.

Wexford at last seemed on the verge of All-Ireland glory. As a result of the non-appearance of the Ulster champions, Galway were given a bye to the final, just as the senior champions of Munster and Leinster used to get before the advent of Ulster in 1943. Wexford went into the game as favourites as a result of their performance so far and of Galway's lack of competition. Both teams were looking for All-Ireland honours after long periods in the wilderness.

Wexford got off to a flying start with a goal and a point, but Galway, after a few replacements and some fine play by the teenager Paddy Egan and Joe Salmon, settled down and led by 2-5 to 2-3 at the interval. For about ten minutes of the second half the sides remained equal, but then, as if roused out of a lethargy, Wexford came alive and dominated the game, to win by 3-13 to 2-8.

The jubilation at Wexford's victory spread from the supporters at Croke Park to the lighters of bonfires in the county and on to other counties as well. The feeling was that if any team deserved an All-Ireland it was Wexford: they had suffered so many disappointments and endured so many near-misses that there was a great relief that they had finally come through. Above all, their splendid players, with such exciting dash and skill, deserved the reward. The homecoming of the heroes lasted a week. Micheál O'Hehir's radio commentary was played over and over again so that supporters could savour the long-delayed taste of victory.

Wexford followed up with victory in the Oireachtas. In the semi-final they easily dismissed Clare, who hadn't recovered from the debacle of the Munster final, and comprehensively beat their old rivals Kilkenny in the final on 23 October. Pádraig Puirséal summed it up well:

> The All-Ireland champions, Wexford, set the seal on their greatness by the grandeur of their victory over Kilkenny at Croke Park on Sunday last … From goal to full-forward, the champions looked all but the perfect team. They hurled with all the dash that has been for so long the characteristic of the camán-swingers from the Model County, but besides they displayed to tremendous effect the craft and cohesion that they have acquired in their past two All-Ireland campaigns. Their lengthy striking is still as notable as ever, but they are now placing the sliotar to far better effect than they did formerly, and their accuracy from frees and line-balls has improved out of all knowledge.[2]

Wexford's success continued impressively through the league, and they qualified for the final against Tipperary. In the meantime they backboned the Leinster Railway Cup team that comprehensively defeated the mighty Munster before forty-six thousand fans on St Patrick's Day. In fact it included no less than nine members of the Wexford team: Art Foley, Nick O'Donnell, Bobbie Rackard, Jim English, Billy Rackard, Ned Wheeler, Jim Morrissey, Tim Flood, and Nicky Rackard; one wag claimed that Wexford could have won on their own.

This was the background of the build-up to the meeting between Tipperary and Wexford on 6 May 1956. The Wexford captain, Jim English, won the toss and elected to play against a strong breeze. By half time the Tipperary men were in front by fifteen points on the score 2-10 to 0-1. Whatever happened in the dressing-room is not known, but Wexford came out a transformed side and in an incredible second half tore away at Tipperary's lead, reduced it, annihilated it, and eventually went on to win by 5-9 to 2-10, to the consternation of their opponents and the amazement of everyone.

The winners soon had to turn their attention to the championship. They easily overcame Laois in the semi-final and qualified to play Kilkenny in the final. Making his first appearance in the black and amber was Ollie Walsh. Wexford got off to a good start and seemed set for an easy victory. Kilkenny fought back to be a mere point behind, but Wexford accelerated again to lead by 3-5 to 2-3 at the break. The second half was a tremendous contest, in which two players particularly excelled, Ollie Walsh in the Kilkenny goal and the Wexford captain, Jim English. Eventually Wexford scraped home by 4-8 to 3-10 to win their first hat-trick of Leinster senior hurling titles.

Meanwhile in Munster, Christy Ring was giving plenty of proof of his hurling genius. In the championship semi-final Tipperary were leading by 11 points at the interval only to be thwarted by Ring and beaten by a point. In the final against Limerick the Shannonsiders looked good with ten minutes to go, holding on to a lead of 2-5 to 1-2, but in the final minutes Ring scored three goals and a point to snatch an amazing victory.

Cork had a bye to the final, while Wexford played Galway. This turned out to be no contest. Backed by a superb team, Nicky Rackard did what he liked and scored 5-3 out of his side's total of 5-13 to Galway's 1-8. So impressed was Joe Sherwood by Wexford's performance that he wrote in the Evening Press the following day:

> I expect for saying this I'll bring the wrath of all God-fearing Cork people down on my head, but I reckon that there is only one way that Cork can win the 1956 All-Ireland. It is to have Wexford's great combination, which like good wine appears to get better with age, either kidnapped or shanghaied, say a week before the final ...

The final was in fact postponed for three weeks, because of an outbreak of polio. It was to be one of the most exciting and memorable finals ever, a game of outstanding individual performances and magnificent sportsmanship. Full of tension, grandeur and drama, the final minutes are unlikely to be surpassed for sheer excitement. Wexford started in style and dominated the opening twenty-five minutes, after which they led by 1-6 to 0-2. Mick Morrissey made a memorable goal-line clearance, and Bobbie Rackard tapped the ball off Ring's hurley when a Cork goal seemed certain. Cork came into the game in the last five minutes of the half and scored three points, to be only four behind at the interval.

Early in the second half Cork drew level and then went ahead. Wexford levelled, and the game continued to hang in the balance. Then the champions went two points ahead, and time began to run out for Cork. However, Ring got through and raced towards the Wexford goal with only Art Foley between him and a ninth All-Ireland medal. He struck the ball for what seemed an inevitable goal, but Foley kept it covered, grabbed it safely, sidestepped the incoming Ring and another Cork forward, and cleared it up the field, where it was eventually delivered to Nicky Rackard. He sidestepped his marker, John Lyons, and gave the Cork goalie, Cashman, no chance. (Johnny Fogarty of Cashel, who was behind the Wexford goal, is definite that the shot was not hard and was not caught by Foley: instead he blocked it with his hurley and as it dropped hit it back out the field. The accepted version is that Foley caught the ball.) Tom Dixon added a point to leave the final score 2-14 to 2-8 in Wexford's favour.

If Ring shook Foley's hand after the brilliant save, Wexford were not to be outdone in their appreciation of their gallant opponents: immediately after the final whistle Ring was seized by Bobbie Rackard and Nick O'Donnell and carried shoulder-high from the field—a memorable event on a day of memories.

Although they didn't qualify for the league final in 1957, Wexford had the consolation of a trip to the United States in June. Over thirty thousand people turned up at the Polo Grounds in New York to see them defeat Cork by 7-15 to 5-5. On the following Sunday they defeated a New York selection and returned to Ireland in triumph to prepare for the championship. Soon afterwards they were hit with the news that Bobbie Rackard had torn some ligaments and tendons in his leg in a farm accident. For the Leinster semi-final against Offaly the team also had to do without Billy Rackard and Séamus Hearne, who had remained on in New York. Despite these setbacks, Wexford won easily enough.

The scene was now set for another Kilkenny-Wexford clash in the final. In expectation of another exciting contest, over fifty-two thousand attended. They were to be thoroughly disappointed. Ned Wheeler retired injured in the first minute. Kilkenny soon established themselves, and Wexford had no answer as Kilkenny sped to a 6-9 to 1-5 victory. It seemed to be the end of an era for Wexford hurling, and this feeling was confirmed when Nicky Rackard soon afterwards announced his retirement from inter-county hurling, bringing to an end a career that had spanned twenty years and had thrilled and delighted so many over that period.

In contrast, Kilkenny were euphoric. They hadn't won a Leinster title since 1953, and the victory was regarded as a great day for Kilkenny hurling. Their opponents in the All-Ireland were their near neighbours Waterford, who confirmed the form they had shown in the 1956 championship, when they were unlucky to go down to Cork. After a brilliant exhibition of hurling they defeated Limerick by 4-12 to 5-5 in the semi-final and qualified to play Cork in the Munster final.

In one of the best hurling matches for years Waterford came out on top and won by 1-11 to 1-6, mainly because of an excellent defence. Cork were without the services of Christy Ring, who had been injured in the semi-final against Tipperary. The Waterford men went on to defeat Galway by ten points in the All-Ireland semi-final.

The final produced brilliant hurling and top-class entertainment. Fifteen minutes from the end Waterford, playing outstanding hurling, were leading by six points, and the All-Ireland seemed to be going their way. But Kilkenny staged a last-quarter rally and snatched victory with a late point by Mickey Kelly, to win by 4-10 to 3-12.

Afterwards Waterford looked back at a lost opportunity and blamed it on inexperience. Kilkenny had struck at the right moment, when Waterford thought they had done enough to win. It was a welcome win for Kilkenny, who had gone ten years without entering the winners' enclosure. It was their seventh title to be won by one point, and it was Father Tommy Maher's first year as trainer.

Wexford's crushing defeat was attributed to a number of causes. The American trip was blamed. The loss of Bobbie Rackard was incalculable, and the early departure of Ned Wheeler aggravated that loss. There may have been an element of staleness in Wexford's performance. As a result of the defeat the prospects for the county looked less bright. As well as the retirement of Nicky Rackard—the country's leading scorer in 1956, with the incredible tally of 35 goals and 50 points—two other members of the team, Mick O'Hanlon and Paddy Kehoe, decided to call it a day. It certainly appeared as if it would take some time for the team to recover.

However, these forebodings were soon dispelled by the performance in the league. The biggest boost to Wexford's morale came with the defeat of the All-Ireland champions, Kilkenny, in the first round and with continued success right up to the final victory over Limerick the following May. The newcomers performed well. Pat Nolan of Lylegate successfully filled the shoes of Art Foley, who had emigrated to America. Oliver 'Hopper' McGrath, although dropped for the final, showed plenty of promise; others coming up the ranks were Oliver Gough and Martin Long. Though defeat at the hands of Kilkenny was to be their lot in 1958, supporters were not as depressed as they had been the previous year. The team had recovered from the serious loss of players in 1957, and the new blood gave hope that more success was possible in the future.

The names of the players who won the first All-Ireland for Wexford in 1910 are inscribed in stone in Castlebridge cemetery. It is a fitting way to remember the men who were carried shoulder-high from the field of victory to the strains of 'The Boys of Wexford' after beating Limerick by the narrowest of margins. The Wexford team was not to be victorious again until 1955 and 1956. Two further All-Irelands were won in 1960 and 1968; since then, in spite of much striving, victory has eluded the county.

It may not appear a great reward in comparison with the achievements of Cork, Tipperary, and Kilkenny, but Wexford's victories in the mid-fifties made a greater impact on the collective hurling mind than any comparable success in any other county. The popularity of Wexford can be seen in the drawing power of the team. In the 1955 final against Galway 72,854 turned up, the eighth-largest attendance at an All-Ireland. In the league final that May against Tipperary the attendance of 45,902 constitutes a record. The record for a hurling All-Ireland was set in 1954 at 84,856, when Cork beat Wexford, and the second-biggest crowd attended the 1956 final, when 83,096 saw Wexford beat Cork. The fourth and fifth-biggest crowds were in 1960, when Wexford beat Tipperary, and 1962, when Tipperary defeated Wexford.

It might be said that these were the days of record crowds. However, a study of the figures shows that attendances were in the sixty thousands until 1952. In fact the record up to then was 69,459 in 1945. The figure went over seventy thousand in the 1953 All-Ireland between Cork and Galway, partly as a result of the build-up to the game because of the incidents in the semi-final the previous year. We have seen the figures for 1954, 1955, and 1956, when Wexford were involved; in contrast, the attendance in 1957 was back to seventy thousand and the following year was down to forty-seven thousand. In 1959 the drawn game attracted 73,707 and the replay 77,285. In 1961 the attendance was back to 67,866.

Wexford had something special to offer. Physically they were big men, but allied to their size was a high level of skill. They were noted sportsmen, renowned for performances that sometimes approached chivalry. Many of them revealed qualities of leadership that set them apart from the rank and file of humanity: there was a romance, an energy and an excitement about them that made them larger than life; they appeared to step out of the pages of a heroic past of myths and legends. These men from Wexford, who thrilled so many through the fifties, will never need to have their names carved in stone, for they are indelibly etched in the memories of those who saw them.

12

Tipperary's Time, 1958–68

The years from 1958 to 1968 were dominated by Tipperary. In the eleven All-Irelands during that period Tipperary contested eight, winning five and losing three. In the eyes of their more ardent supporters they could have won six in a row, since they should have beaten Wexford in 1960 and were surprisingly ambushed by Waterford in the 1963 Munster championship.

Six other teams—Galway, Waterford, Kilkenny, Dublin, Wexford, and Cork—also contested finals. Of these, Kilkenny and Wexford each had two victories, while Waterford and Cork each had one. Cork's victory came as a welcome relief after twelve years in the doldrums. Galway and Dublin had no luck, although Dublin, making its last appearance in an All-Ireland senior final, nearly created a sensation and could have beaten Tipperary on the day.

Tipperary became Munster champions in 1958, for the first time in seven years. They defeated their old rivals, Cork, in a semi-final that failed to generate any excitement, and qualified to play Waterford in the final. This was one of the poorest finals for years, with Tipperary much too good for their rivals and winning by 4-12 to 1-5. From a Tipperary perspective Larry Keane impressed at corner-forward, and John Doyle, playing at wing-back, gave an outstanding display.

Kilkenny opposed Tipperary in the All-Ireland semi-finals. The Black and Amber were lucky to be there, having nearly been caught by Dublin in the Leinster semi-final. They survived a replay and went on to beat Wexford by six points in the final. Ollie Walsh was outstanding, especially in his clearances, and Wexford contributed to their own downfall by hitting twelve wides, to Kilkenny's four.

The All-Ireland semi-final will be remembered as the game of the 'two Doyles'. The 'dynamic' John and the 'deadly' Jimmy made a huge contribution to Tipperary's 1-13 to 1-8 victory. Played in incessant rain, the first half was as tense and exciting as anything seen in Croke Park for years, ending with Tipperary leading by one point. The second half was an anti-climax, with a big deterioration in the standard of play. In the end Tipperary were convincing winners.

The All-Ireland attracted a smaller crowd than the semi-final, a mere forty-seven thousand, the lowest attendance since the Cork-Dublin final of 1944; nor has there been as small an attendance since. Tipperary started the warmest of favourites. They won the toss, and Tony Wall decided to play against the wind.

Whatever hopes Galway had were shattered in the first ten minutes, when Tipperary scored two goals, and they went into the dressing-room with a lead of 4-4 to 1-3. It appeared as if they were set to win by a cricket score, but Galway changed goalies at the interval and put up a good rally in the second half, so that the final score in Tipperary's favour was 4-9 to 2-5. The game may have been a poor one but it was a proud day for the Tipperary corner-back Mickey Byrne, who won his fifth All-Ireland medal, his first having been as a sub in the 1945 final against Kilkenny.

The All-Ireland champions went into the 1959 Munster championship with reasonable confidence, having defeated a much-improved Waterford team in the league final. The advent of Galway into the Munster championship (given approval at the GAA Congress) gave an extra dimension of interest to the association's diamond jubilee year. However, the entry was not an auspicious one, and the new arrivals were routed by Waterford in the first round. In the other first-round game Tipperary had a five-point margin over Limerick.

The two winners met in the semi-final in Cork. Even though they were missing Jimmy Finn through injury, Tipperary were expected to beat Waterford. The Waterford men had other ideas. Tipperary won the toss and decided to play against a strong end-to-end breeze. From the throw-in Waterford got a grip on the proceedings and, playing their own unbeatable brand of first-time hurling, soon stretched the Tipperary defence to breaking point. Spectators watched in disbelief as Waterford's precision striking netted them eight goals and two points without reply. With Tipperary forced to go for goals in the second half, Waterford were able to contain their efforts and finish winners by 9-3 to 3-4.

Many reasons were advanced for the rout. The decision to play against the breeze in the first half was criticised. Speed was a vital factor in Waterford's triumph: the bewildering pace they set in the first twenty minutes and the drive and enthusiasm of their attacking play swept Tipperary out of the championship. However, poor goalkeeping, allied to poor covering by the full-back line and the almost total collapse at centrefield, also contributed to the concession of so many goals in the first half. The selectors were blamed for not replacing the Tipperary goalkeeper, Terry Moloney, sooner.

Waterford's opponents in the Munster final were Cork, and they came to the game with impressive credentials, having scored no fewer than sixteen goals in their two qualifying rounds. The Cork team contained no fewer than eight players who were making their championship debut. A record crowd of over fifty-five thousand came to the match and were treated to a game worthy of the occasion. The star of Waterford's win was the right-full-back, Joe Harney, who got the better of the duel with Christy Ring. Others to star were his partners in the full-back line, Austin Flynn and John Barron. Further outfield Martin Óg Morrissey, Séamus Power and Phil Grimes played a significant part in Waterford's 3-9 to 2-9 victory.

Having beaten Galway, Tipperary, and Cork, Waterford looked good for the All-Ireland, in which Kilkenny would be their opponents. Kilkenny had beaten Dublin in the Leinster final, after a semi-final victory over Laois. Dublin had a fine team and had shown their mettle in defeating Wexford in the other semi-final. In the final they led Kilkenny all through, and the game was in lost time when a Johnny McGovern line ball into the Dublin goal-mouth was flashed to the net by Seán Clohessy for a one-point Kilkenny victory.

The All-Ireland was a repeat of the 1957 decider, and it attracted a crowd of 73,707. It was rated one of the greatest finals ever, a tense and thrilling contest played at a furious pace. For a long time it appeared to be going Waterford's way, and they led by five points at the interval. They increased the lead to six on the turnover with a great Tom Cheasty point. Then a Kilkenny rally brought two goals from Tommy O'Connell. The Waterford men went ahead again, but Kilkenny hauled them back and a minute from time were a goal in front. Then in one final effort Waterford attacked. Séamus Power raced up the right wing and sent in a shot. Ollie Walsh, who had played one of the finest games of his career, had it covered, but Jim Walsh had the misfortune to put his hurley to the ball and deflect it past the goalkeeper for the equalising goal. It was the first drawn All-Ireland since Limerick and Dublin drew in 1934.

The replay attracted a bigger attendance, 77,825, the greatest number to see either a Kilkenny or Waterford team play. In contrast to the drawn game, Kilkenny were in front early on and led by 1-4 to 0-1 after twelve minutes. Then a goal by Mick Flannelly set Waterford on their way, and they were in front by 3-5 to 1-8. Kilkenny scored only two points in the second half, both by Eddie Keher, who went on as a substitute. He had been added to the panel for the replay following his displays in the minor All-Ireland championship and some senior games. In contrast, Waterford were on song, especially in the final quarter, when they outpaced Kilkenny with their turn of speed and general fitness. The captain, Frankie Walsh, had a superb game and inspired his men to victory. Another difference was the display of the full-back line. In the drawn game they had fallen back on Ned Power, and this contributed to Kilkenny scoring five goals.

Entering the final quarter, John Barron of Waterford and Dick Carroll of Kilkenny were sent to the line. One of the most dramatic players on the Waterford team was Tom Cheasty at centre-forward. A big, strong player and a most unorthodox striker of the ball, his forte was cutting through the centre, making straight for the goal, and palming the ball over the bar. On occasions he would flash passes to his wingers, Mick Flannelly and Frankie Walsh.

The final score was Waterford 3-12, Kilkenny 1-10. The victory gave Waterford their second All-Ireland and was a great achievement for the team. Not that they didn't deserve it: they were without doubt the best team in 1959.

A feature of the first rounds of the Munster championship in 1960 was the very high scoring. Waterford beat Galway by 9-8 to 4-8, and Tipperary did better, beating Limerick by 10-9 to 2-1. The victors met in the semi-final at Limerick on 17 July, and Tipperary had sweet revenge for their overwhelming defeat the previous year. Before a crowd of thirty-five thousand they were on top from the beginning and were in front by 6-9 to 2-7 at the final whistle. It was a great Tipperary performance, in which every player made a contribution, especially the two Doyles, who shone above all the rest.

The Munster final was rated the toughest ever played, contested by the old rivals Cork and Tipperary in Thurles before nearly fifty thousand people. When the teams met in the league final the previous May, Tipperary had a four-point margin. Cork were in the throes of team-building and were still dependent on veterans like Christy Ring, Liam Dowling, and Paddy Barry. Tipperary were expected to win, but in a game in which no quarter was given or asked the verdict might have gone either way. Cork had the better of the play in the first half, but Tipperary made better use of their opportunities and led by a goal at half time. By the final quarter Tipperary had established their dominance, but Cork remained a threat to the end, and their last-minute goal left only two points between the sides in a score of 4-13 to 4-11. The gruelling contest was to take its toll on the winners in the All-Ireland.

Tipperary were hot favourites for the final against Wexford. In the Leinster championship Wexford had beaten Dublin in a semi-final replay and Kilkenny in the final. In the latter game the Slaneysiders gave a performance that brought back hope and expectation to their supporters. With the aid of a breeze in the first half they led by 2-8 to 0-4 at the interval. However, in a glorious five-minute spell after the break Kilkenny scored 1-4 and seemed likely to take the title. One of the stars of the game was Eddie Keher, who scored 1-8. But Kilkenny squandered chances and in the next twenty-five minutes shot no less than twelve wides to one for Wexford. With a couple of minutes to go and five points in arrears the Kilkenny goalie, Ollie Walsh, came outfield and was replaced by Séamus Cleere. Amid fierce excitement, Walsh joined the Kilkenny attack and passed the ball to Tommy O'Connell, who palmed it to the net. But it was too late, and the final whistle sounded to a 3-10 to 2-11 Wexford victory.

In spite of this performance against Kilkenny the pundits did not give Wexford much hope against Tipperary: it was believed that they weren't in Tipperary's league. The focus of much of the pre-match publicity was Jimmy Doyle, who had excelled when scoring 1-8 against Cork. The Tipperary trainer, Phil Purcell, was rash enough to say in one interview that 'there is not a man in the game capable of holding Jimmy Doyle for the full hour.' Perhaps the biggest morale-depressant for Wexford was a pre-match assessment of their chances in the same newspaper, which predicted that their defence, 'skilled, seasoned but no longer in the full flush of youth, would be exposed to a merciless pounding by the searing, searching persistency of this most talented of all attacking machines.'[1]

The reality on the day could not have been more different. Tipperary were only a shadow of what had been expected. They played far below par in every section, but the failure of their centrefield and the virtual eclipse of the highly rated half-forward line were the most glaring disasters. The only time they looked like rising to the occasion was a spell before the interval when they sent over four points, to leave Wexford with a lead of two points at the break. However, it was Wexford and not the Premier County that came out revitalised in the second half, and the Leinster men went on to win all too easily by 2-15 to 0-11.

Although a one-sided contest, the game was sheer delight for Wexford followers. They savoured the brilliance of Pat Nolan in goal, the magnificence of Nick O'Donnell at full-back, the way Billy Rackard outplayed Liam Devaney, the powerful performance of Jim Morrissey, the skilful efforts of Padge Kehoe, and the manner in which John Doyle was outclassed by Jimmy O'Brien. Above all they rose to John Nolan at wing-back, who was making his senior inter-county debut on All-Ireland final day and who outplayed Tipperary's most brilliant prospect, Jimmy Doyle. It was the sweetest of Wexford's victories.

Appetites for the 1961 Munster championship were whetted by the clash of Waterford and Tipperary in the league final. Although Tipperary were ahead by ten points entering the final quarter, a Waterford rally reduced the lead to three points at the final whistle. The winners had a new goalie for the occasion, Donie O'Brien of Kickhams, who was to have the distinction of adding two All-Ireland medals to his league one during a very short career on the team. Another newcomer on the day was J. 'Mackey' McKenna of Borrisokane.

In the championship Tipperary had a bye to the semi-final and played Galway, who had their first and, as it turned out, only success in the Munster championship when they beat Clare in the first round. Tipperary played with the wind in the first half and were 6-9 to 1-4 in front mid-way into the second half. Then Galway rallied and scored 4-2, but Tipperary weathered the storm and were in front by 7-12 to 5-6 at the final whistle.

The second semi-final attracted a record crowd of 42,824 to Thurles. Waterford were favourites to beat Cork because of some fine performances in the league. In a tremendous contest the decision remained on a knife edge until Waterford's full-back, Austin Flynn, retired injured. His departure left the back line unsteady, and Christy Ring capitalised, scoring 3-4 to give Cork victory by 5-7 to 2-7.

There was unprecedented interest in the Munster final at Limerick. The game attracted an official attendance of 62,175, the biggest crowd to witness a sporting event outside Croke Park. However, as the gates had to be thrown open half way through the minor game to avoid panic as the crowd swayed dangerously, it is estimated that the attendance exceeded seventy thousand. The day was overcast but very warm. The Cork team, which togged out as usual in the Railway Hotel, had to leave their cars half way up the Ennis Road and force their way through the throng of spectators to get to the ground. With their concentration broken, they arrived at the pitch in twos and threes. Under these circumstances it is not surprising that they made a hesitant start. They had gone into the game as favourites because of their great performance against Waterford. The return of Paddy Barry to the fold was also expected to give an impetus to the attack. It seemed to many supporters that the time of victory had arrived and that they would be returning victorious to the Lee.

This hope was not fulfilled in the first half, at the end of which Tipperary led by 3-3 to Cork's lone point. Cork improved somewhat in the second half but were too dependent on Ring, who was approaching his fifty-first birthday. Tipperary players gave fine displays, especially Jimmy Doyle,

Donie Nealon, Liam Devaney, Theo English, and Donie O'Brien, who, by a brilliant display on goals, silenced any criticism that had surfaced after the semi-final. In the end Tipperary were clear winners by 3-6 to 0-7.

This was Christy Ring's seventeenth and last appearance in a Munster final, although he continued to wear the county jersey for another two years. It was also his seventeenth championship game against Tipperary. His record stands alone. He is accepted as the greatest hurler ever, and it is improbable that his likes will ever be seen again. During the height of his career no-one was more feared by opposing players and supporters. He seemed to be the embodiment of skill and cunning. Nothing seemed impossible to him; no game against him was won until the final whistle had blown. He was a colossus in an era of great men, fierce rivalries, and epic struggles. Allied to his incredible ability was his emphasis on preparation, his great guts and a terrific will to win.

Christy Ring's career stretched over four decades, from 1939, when he took his place on the Cork senior team, until 1963 (though he continued with Glen Rovers until 1967). During that great span he won eight All-Ireland senior hurling medals and captained the winning team on three occasions: in 1946, 1953, and 1954. In the first of those years he was also a selector, as he was for Cork's three-in-a-row in 1976–78. Between 1941 and 1963 he never failed to be selected for the Munster Railway Cup team and won medals on eighteen occasions. He was selected eight times for the Rest of Ireland team. He won four National League medals and an All-Ireland minor hurling medal. Incredibly, he never won an Oireachtas medal. Within the county his record is equally brilliant, with minor, junior and senior medals. In the senior grade he won no less than fourteen, and also a county senior football medal. He won a Munster club championship in 1965, a Texaco award in 1959, and the Texaco Hall of Fame award in 1971.

Tipperary were expected to beat Dublin in the All-Ireland final on 3 September. And, because of Dublin's record since 1938, many expected the victory to be easy. The result—in the first hurling game to be televised—was different. Dublin had created their own sensation in qualifying for the All-Ireland; they beat a fancied Wexford side by 7-5 to 4-8 in the Leinster final, a result that shocked not only the losers but hurling followers at large.

The team had traditionally contained a majority of outside players who had taken up residence in Dublin, but there was a change during the fifties, when the hurling authorities decided on native players, with a few exceptions. The policy began to pay off, as evidenced in the team's draw with Kilkenny in the first round of the 1957 championship. Kilkenny went on to win the All-Ireland. In 1958 Dublin almost dethroned the champions, losing a replay by a single point. The following year they reached the Leinster final and were beaten by Kilkenny in the last puck of the game, which was deflected to the net. In 1960 they were beaten by Wexford, who went on to win the All-Ireland. But in spite of this record of improvement Dublin found themselves rank outsiders in the 1961 All-Ireland.

The team was captained by Noel Drumgoole of St Vincent's and included four other players from the club: Des 'Snitchie' Ferguson, Lar and Des Foley, and Shay Lynch. Drumgoole was a sub on the 1952 side beaten by Cork and continued to play until 1962, when cartilage problems brought about his retirement. The Boothman brothers came from the Crumlin club. Billy Jackson and Christy Hayes were from New Ireland, Mick Bohan and Larry Shannon from Scoil Uí Chonaill, Fran Whelan from Eoghan Rua, and Jimmy Grey from Na Fianna, while the only non-native, Paddy Croke from Rahealty, Co. Tipperary, played with Young Ireland. The trainer of the team was Mick Ryan, a teacher in North Strand Vocational School, and the team did some indoor training over the winter in the school.

Tipperary went into the game with a number of injuries, to Kieran Carey, Tony Wall, and Jimmy Doyle. During the game Wall retired and Liam Devaney went to centre-back. It was to be an important move, as he was to play the game of his life repelling Dublin attacks in the second half. At half time Tipperary had an advantage of ten points to six, and this barely reflected their first-half superiority. In the second half the game remained stalemated for a few minutes until Dublin got a goal that set the spectators buzzing. In the next few minutes they equalised, then went ahead. Things began to look bad for Tipperary, who lost Matt O'Gara, who had been playing inspirational hurling through the half. Two events then halted Dublin's gallop. The first was the sending off of Lar Foley and Tom Ryan, who had replaced 'Mackey' McKenna at half time. Foley's departure was a great loss, because it left a gap in the corner-back position, where he had been playing a storming game. The second event was the saving of a certain goal by O'Brien, who deflected a Jackson shot over the bar. Had Dublin got that score they would have wrapped up the game; instead, inspired by Devaney's hurling, Tipperary came right back into the game and scored four points without reply. In the dying minutes Achill Boothman got a point, to leave the minimum between the sides in a score of 0-16 to 1-12.

Tipperary were much relieved at the final whistle, and in the post-mortems the contribution of Jimmy Doyle was regarded as vital. Though injured, he succeeded in scoring nine points and was the difference between victory and defeat.

For Dublin the defeat was a misfortune from which they never recovered. In the following year's championship they were to be badly beaten by Kilkenny. They reached the Leinster final in 1963 and 1964, only to be beaten by the same opposition. Since then they never reached the final stage of the provincial championship until 1991, losing by two points to Kilkenny. There is still speculation about what might have happened to hurling in Dublin had the 1961 team been victorious.

In preparation for the 1962 championship Tipperary played a number of games, one of which was a repeat of the All-Ireland, this time at Wembley Stadium in London in the annual Whit tournament. On this occasion they confirmed their All-Ireland superiority before a crowd of forty thousand by 3-11 to 2-10. They drew with Limerick in the Munster semi-final, a thrilling encounter with a dramatic ending. Tipperary dominated the first half and led by nine points at the interval. Limerick came back with a bang in the second half and forced a draw. The referee, Jimmy Smyth of Clare, blew up the game four minutes early, with Tipperary a point in front. After some hurried consultations the game was restarted, and during the remaining minutes P. J. Keane equalised for Limerick. In the replay three weeks later Tipperary were a rejuvenated team and swept Limerick aside by 5-13 to 2-4. In fact Limerick didn't get a score from play until twelve minutes into the second half.

In the second semi-final Waterford defeated Cork in what was to be Christy Ring's last championship outing with Cork. In the Munster final at Limerick on 5 August, Waterford were a complete disappointment, and Tipperary supremacy was as pronounced as against Limerick in the semi-final. They won by 5-14 to 2-3.

The All-Ireland against Wexford was a thrilling encounter. Wexford had upset the odds by winning the Leinster final. By virtue of winning the National League and beating Dublin by five goals in the semi-final, Kilkenny were favourites for the title. But the Noresiders got off on the wrong foot and were seven points behind after eight minutes. Wexford still had a seven-point advantage at the interval. Kilkenny had the better of the exchanges in the second half, but Wexford were ahead by 3-9 to 2-10 at the final whistle and never really looked like losing.

Tom McLoughney goaled for Tipperary in the first minute of the game. Nick O'Donnell, the hero of so many games, mis-hit the puck-out, which travelled twenty-five yards to the waiting Seán McLoughlin, who buried it in the net to give Tipperary a dream start. But Wexford fought back and drew level before half time. Tipperary then got three points, to lead by that margin at the turn. Wexford continued to make an impression after the resumption and were two points in front with thirteen minutes to go. A Tipperary goal followed from Tom Ryan, and Wexford levelled with seven minutes remaining. During that period Donie Nealon and Seán McLoughlin pointed to give Tipperary the lead and victory by 3-10 to 2-11.

It was the superior freshness of Tipperary in the closing stages that brought them victory before a crowd of over seventy-five thousand. Best Tipperary displays came from the goalie, Dónal O'Brien, Jimmy and John Doyle, Tony Wall, Tom Ryan of Killenaule, and 'Mackey' McKenna. For Wexford, Tom Neville gave an outstanding display, helped by Pat Nolan in goal, Nick O'Donnell after his nightmare start, Martin Long and Phil Wilson at centrefield, and Ned Wheeler and Paul Lynch in the forwards. Liam Connolly and Tom Ryan of Toomevara replaced Matt O'Gara and the captain, Jimmy Doyle, in the second half and contributed to Tipperary's victory. There was to be some questioning why the Wexford mentors had not done something similar.

Tipperary set their sights on their third in a row when they went into the 1963 championship. With a bye to the semi-final they played Cork, with Christy Ring a sub for the first time in his career, in a game Cork expected to lose and Tipperary expected to win. It finished accordingly but lacked the clear-cut character expected in the circumstances. Although Tipperary won by five points, their display left a lot to be desired.

Their opponents in the Munster final at Limerick on 28 July were Waterford. The two sides had met in the league final in May, with victory going to Waterford by two points. Tipperary looked a bit stale on the day and Waterford the faster and fitter team. It was one of the most thrilling games seen for a long time, particularly in the second half. Waterford played sparkling hurling and came back several times to equalise and eventually win.

Tipperary were determined to reverse the result in the championship. Their effort would have been successful but for the inaccurate and ill-judged shooting of a well-supplied forward line, together with the concession of costly frees in defence. Tipperary conceded no goal, nor did they score any, but confined Waterford to a mere three points from play. The efforts of Waterford's key men—Cheasty, Condon, and Morrissey— were well countered by Wall, English, and Larry Kiely. At half time Tipperary led by five points to three, despite enjoying a vast superiority through the field. During that period they hit no less than ten wides. In the second half they were punished severely for fouls by the sharp-shooting of

Phil Grimes. A Seán McLoughlin goal was disallowed, and a McKenna effort went just wide. In the end they were three points adrift of Waterford in a score of 0-11 to 0-8, and Tipperary supporters went home with the bitter memory of the most galling defeat since the match against Cork in 1957.

Kilkenny were Waterford's opponents in the All-Ireland. They had come through Leinster beating Wexford and Dublin. The encounter with Wexford attracted a crowd of thirty-five thousand, one of the biggest for a Leinster semi-final. They got real value for money in a furious game that was fought fairly and sportingly. In the end Kilkenny had a four-point margin in a game that produced some spectacular individual displays, none more so than that of Eddie Keher, who scored 2-5 during the hour.

In the Leinster final Dublin had the edge in the first half and led by a point at the interval, but the Noresiders pulled away in the second half to win by 2-10 to 0-9.

It was the third time in seven years that Kilkenny and Waterford were to meet in an All-Ireland. Each side had a victory to its credit, Kilkenny in 1957 and Waterford in 1959. The game was a record-breaker in that the combined scores created new figures for a sixty-minute final: Kilkenny 4-17, Waterford 6-8. Waterford had the better start and were soon in front by 1-4 to 0-2; then Kilkenny struck and were in front by 3-6 to 1-5 at the interval. Ned Power was replaced by Percy Flynn in the Waterford goal, but Kilkenny kept scoring with a Tom Walsh goal and an Eddie Keher point. Waterford came back with two goals from Séamus Power and Mick Flannelly. Three points for Kilkenny followed, then another Waterford goal from Flannelly. With minutes to go Waterford were two points behind and were prevented from winning by two great saves by Ollie Walsh from Séamus Power and John Meany.

Kilkenny attributed their victory to a few outstanding displays, none better than Eddie Keher's, who scored fourteen points in the game, ten from frees. Vying with him for honours was the captain, Séamus Cleere, who was later to receive the Hurler of the Year award when he took the Caltex trophy. Seán Clohessy and Paddy Moran dominated at centrefield. It was Clohessy's final display for Kilkenny and one of his best ever. Others to shine were 'Fan' Larkin, Ted Carroll, Tom Walsh, and Ollie Walsh (even though he let six past him on the day). For Waterford, Martin Óg Morrissey, Larry Guinan, Séamus Power and Phil Grimes were the stars.

The year 1964 started in fine style for Tipperary. They were impressive in the league, nowhere more so than in the final, when they overwhelmed Wexford by 5-12 to 1-4. This was followed by victory over Kilkenny in London in the middle of May and over New York in Gaelic Park at the end of the same month. On their return from America the team had a month to prepare for the Munster semi-final against Clare. Tipperary won easily and qualified to play Cork, who had defeated Waterford in a thrilling clash. The semi-final turned out to be a complete anti-climax for the forty-four thousand who turned up in Limerick. The Cork team failed to rise to expectations, and but for the performance of Paddy Barry in goal Tipperary's victory of 3-13 to 1-5 might have been greater.

Tipperary's victory in the All-Ireland on 5 September was equally facile. Their opponents, Kilkenny, were the favourites and had played some fine hurling when beating Wexford in the Leinster semi-final. In the semi-final against Dublin the sides were fairly evenly matched in the first half, but the introduction of Denis Heaslip at the break transformed Kilkenny, and Dublin were completely out of their depth after that. In the end Kilkenny won by 4-11 to 1-8 and were established as favourites for the All-Ireland title.

In fact they went down by 5-13 to 2-8 and suffered their greatest defeat since the 1937 final at Killarney. Over seventy-one thousand spectators attended. Although Kilkenny conceded some soft goals, they were beaten by a great Tipperary team that gave an exhibition of power-packed hurling to which there was no answer. The gulf between the sides lay in the fact that Tipperary were expertly served in almost every position. They led by 1-8 to 0-6 at half time; a goal by John Teehan three minutes after the interval put the losers in a great position, but the forwards could make little headway against a tight Tipperary defence, and in the last quarter the Noresiders were overrun.

Every Tipperary player contributed handsomely to the victory; there was no man of the match but a great team effort. Highlights of a great display were the performance of John O'Donoghue between the posts, Jimmy Doyle's ten points, the goals Seán McLoughlin laid on and the three Donie Nealon scored. The two sides met in the Oireachtas final in October, and although Tipperary confirmed their superiority they had only two points to spare.

The Tipperary team of 1964/65 is generally regarded as one of the greatest hurling forces that ever took the field. Teams from the Premier County were traditionally noted for sterling defences rather than fluent attacks. This team continued to defend heroically, none more so than John Doyle, who was to win his eighth All-Ireland senior hurling medal in 1965 and equal Christy Ring's record set up in 1954. But it was by its forwards it was better known. Every one of them was a match-winner in his own right. With Jimmy Doyle and Babs Keating on the wings, Donie Nealon and Seán McLoughlin in the corners, and Larry Kiely and 'Mackey' McKenna providing the backbone, Tipperary had a forward line that was unrivalled in its brilliance. John O'Donoghue between the posts received magnificent coverage from John Doyle, Michael Maher, and Kieran Carey. Further out Mick Burns, Tony Wall, Michael Murphy in 1964 and Len Gaynor in 1965 were outstanding, and the team was completed by Theo English and Mick Roche in the centre of the field.

Tipperary repeated their All-Ireland and Oireachtas wins by beating Kilkenny in the 1965 league final at Croke Park on 23 May. The game was a gruelling one, and forty-one thousand spectators saw Tipperary take their twelfth title and John Doyle his eleventh. All through, the game was played with reckless ardour and was noted for some very uncompromising tackling. In the end Tipperary were in front by 3-14 to 2-8 and qualified for a trip to America in September, when they beat New York in a two-leg National League final.

Before that came about the championship had to be played. Tipperary overcame Clare in the Munster semi-final and were strong favourites to beat Cork in the final. Nearly forty thousand spectators saw the pre-match forecasts proved only too right as Tipperary inflicted a crushing defeat on the Leesiders by 4-11 to 0-5. An indication of the Premier County's superiority was the fact that the victory was achieved without the services of Babs Keating or Larry Kiely, absent through illness and injury. The winners were in front by 2-4 to 0-4 at the interval and held Cork to a point in the second half. It was Tipperary's twenty-ninth Munster title and brought them level with Cork.

Tipperary's opponents in the All-Ireland were Wexford. They beat Kilkenny in a tightly fought Leinster final; in fact the Noresiders looked good at the interval, when they led by 2-3 to 0-6 after playing against the breeze. But Wexford got on top at centrefield in the second period and, helped by two goals from Martin Byrne, levelled with seven minutes remaining. The sides exchanged points later, and four minutes from time Martin Codd scored the winning point for Wexford, 2-11 to 3-7. Kilkenny were handicapped by the absence through injury of two of the half-back line, Séamus Cleere and Ted Carroll.

In contrast to the Tipperary team, Wexford was relatively inexperienced, with nine newcomers. Tipperary won the toss and played against a slight breeze. From the beginning they were in command, and the foundation of their success was an impregnable inner line of defence and two goals by Seán McLoughlin in the first quarter. Tipperary led by 2-5 to 0-6 at half time. Some positional changes by Wexford in the second half failed to make much improvement, and for most of the half they were fighting to stay in the game. At the final whistle they were behind by 2-16 to 0-10.

Two weeks after the victory the winners travelled to New York and on their return had to play Kilkenny once again in the Oireachtas final. A little tired and spent, they were outhurled for half an hour and trailed by seven points at the interval but came back with magnificent resilience in the second half to win by five points. It was their third Oireachtas in a row and their second successive League-Championship-Oireachtas treble. Were it not for the disastrous defeat by Waterford in the 1963 championship they might have been the winners of five in a row in 1965.

When 1966 dawned, the question in the minds of hurling followers was: could Tipperary be beaten? The team won its two remaining league games to qualify for the semi-final against Clare. In a game that saw the forwards hit twenty-two wides, Tipperary were hard pressed to win by four points. In the final against Kilkenny their unbroken run of success in important games came to an end when they were beaten by 0-9 to 0-7. In as dour a struggle as one could imagine, the Leinster men recorded their first league final success over Tipperary and their first defeat of the All-Ireland champions in the final of a major competition since the 1922 All-Ireland.

Tipperary's opponents in the Munster championship were Limerick, who were young and unrated and not expected to give the champions much trouble. There were a number of changes on the Tipperary team. Tony Wall was out, having been posted to Cyprus with the army. Mick Roche, Larry Kiely and Jimmy Doyle were out because of injury. It was expected that Tipperary would be forewarned by the league defeat, but they didn't learn anything in either physical or mental readiness. Limerick showed themselves a team of fire and dash, and Tipperary just couldn't cope with their super-fitness. Outstanding among them was 21-year-old Éamon Cregan, who devastated the Tipperary rearguard and scored three goals and five points. Further outfield Bernie Hartigan dominated. The final score was 4-12 to 2-9 in favour of Limerick, and the result seemed the end of an era and the end of the road for some long-established Tipperary players.

Clare and Cork played in the other first-round game, and the match ended in a draw. The Banner men appeared to have won until they conceded a shock equalising goal late in the game. Cork were a transformed side in the replay, which they won easily by 5-11 to 1-7. The semi-final between Cork and Limerick attracted a record crowd to Killarney. Two goals in the space of a minute in the final quarter gave Cork a fortunate victory by 2-6 to 1-7. Meanwhile Waterford had an easy victory over Galway in the other semi-final.

The Munster final was a dour, closely contested affair that never rose to any great heights. It will be remembered for the two goals scored by the Cork veteran John Bennett and the goal scored by Waterford's Larry

Guinan, who travelled almost a hundred yards with the ball on his hurley before smashing it past Paddy Byrne. The final score was 4-9 to 2-9 in Cork's favour.

Kilkenny were Cork's opponents in the All-Ireland. In the Leinster final the Noresiders defeated their old rivals, Wexford. In a game of sharply contrasting halves Wexford led at half time by 2-5 to 0-7. Kilkenny introduced Claus Dunne at the interval, who played a leading part in transforming Kilkenny's challenge. In the second half they took control, so much so that they scored 1-8 to Wexford's solitary point and won by 1-15 to 2-6.

Kilkenny entered the All-Ireland the hottest of favourites, having beaten Tipperary in the league final and Cork by no less than twelve points in the semi-final. Cork had struggled through the Munster championship and hadn't won an All-Ireland in twelve years. In addition they were short their centre-back, Denis O'Riordan. Kilkenny had such experienced players as Ollie Walsh, Ted Carroll, Martin Coogan, Séamus Cleere, Pat Henderson, Eddie Keher, Pa Dillon, and Tommy Walsh. The one advantage Cork had was a fierce determination to win and to put an end to the frustrations and disappointments that had dogged them for twelve years. They also believed they were better than they were being painted. Although beaten well by Kilkenny in the league semi-final, they had shot fifteen wides. They had also beaten Wexford in the Wembley tournament. This was the first thing they won, and as the championship progressed, however precariously, they concluded that they were getting things together, gaining momentum and confidence.

If Cork performed above themselves on the day, Kilkenny gave one of their worst displays. In a very disappointing game the Kilkenny forward line proved totally inadequate. Cork played against a stiff breeze in the first half and trailed by 0-7 to 1-2 at the interval. They took the lead in the forty-first minute with a Colm Sheehan goal and were in the driving seat for the rest of the game, to win by 3-9 to 1-10. The team was helped by a quartet of splendid players from the under-21 side: Gerald and Charlie McCarthy, Justin McCarthy, and Seánie Barry. The tactics adopted by the side were important. The players were great at keeping the ball moving and in doing so never let Kilkenny settle down and hurl.

There were unprecedented scenes of joy when the final whistle sounded. It took nearly ten minutes for the cheering to die down and allow Gerald McCarthy receive the cup. Next evening in Cork the scenes were equally jubilant as a crowd estimated at thirty thousand thronged around the returning heroes, bearing witness to the intense desire for success after so many years of failure.

The euphoria carried over into 1967, and some of the more sanguine supporters were inclined to see a successful vista stretching into the years ahead. A more realistic assessment was that until the team beat Tipperary its true worth would not be known.

Before facing that challenge, however, Cork had to play Waterford in the first round, and the Waterford men relieved them of their Munster and All-Ireland crowns by a substantial margin of eight points in Walsh Park. Tipperary, who hadn't done very well since the 1966 championship, in turn swept Waterford out of the championship with a convincing semi-final win. One of the highlights of the game was the display of Tony Wall, who showed himself as masterful as ever. On the other side of the draw Clare qualified for the final with impressive victories over Limerick and Galway. The game was played in Limerick, and for forty minutes Clare appeared to have a good chance of victory. Then Mick Roche began to dominate at midfield, and a Babs Keating goal at the end of the third quarter was the beginning of the end for Clare. During the final quarter Tipperary swept the challenge aside and won by 4-12 to 2-6. For Tipperary the victory was a great boost to morale after a period of uncertainty. For a man of the calibre of Jimmy Smyth it was his last chance.

Tipperary's opponents in the All-Ireland were Kilkenny, and their victory was to be a milestone in the history of the wearers of the black and amber. Not since 1922 had Kilkenny beaten the Premier County in an All-Ireland; defeat had been their lot in 1937, 1945, 1950, and 1964, as well as in the semi-final of 1958. The Munster men had also been successful in league finals in 1950, 1954 and 1957 and in the Oireachtas finals of 1964 and 1965. The one victory in a major competition during that period was the league 'home' final of 1966.

Kilkenny started the 1967 championship with an easy win of 6-10 to 1-5 over Dublin and qualified to play Wexford in the Leinster final. Wexford had the breeze in the first half but were only four points in front at the interval; however, within ten minutes they had increased their lead to eight points, and Kilkenny seemed to be heading for defeat. Then, within a space of ten minutes, the Noresiders scored three goals and a point to take the lead. Wexford settled again and drew level, but in the closing ten minutes Kilkenny scored a goal and four points without reply from Wexford and won by 4-10 to 1-12.

All-Ireland day was a blustery one, and Tipperary had the use of the breeze in the first half. They led by 2-6 to 1-3 at the interval, a lead that would have been much greater but for the fantastic display of goalkeeping by Ollie Walsh, who had one of his greatest games in the Wexford jersey. His display was all the more meritorious when it is realised that he entered the game with seven stitches in his wrist, the result of an accident on the train on his way to the game.

The story of the second half is simply told. Kilkenny got on top at centrefield, where John Teehan and Paddy Moran outhurled Mick Roche and Theo English. Eclipsed in this vital sector, Tipperary's forwards were deprived of the ball and succeeded in scoring only one goal during the period. Any ball that did get in was pounced on by an extremely effective back line that included Ted Carroll, Pa Dillon, Jim Treacy, and Pat Henderson. Added to this were severe problems in the Tipperary full-back line, where Kieran Carey and Noel O'Gorman had a most unhappy hour. The strong wind prevented good hurling. The only Tipperary line that made any impression was the half-back line, where Len Gaynor in particular was outstanding. Under all these circumstances, it is surprising that Kilkenny did not win by more.

There was also a sad note to the game. Tom Walsh, the Kilkenny centre-forward, had to have his left eye removed as a result of an injury received in the second half, and what was shaping up as an illustrious career was abruptly halted.

Many reasons were put forward for Tipperary's defeat. Dermot Gilleese in the Daily Mail had this to say: 'Kilkenny proved beyond all doubt that hurling is a young man's game. The bitter truth which Tipperary must now face is that they had little chance of taking their 22nd title with eight players over thirty in the side; and the result was that their oldest player, John Doyle, was deprived of a record ninth all-Ireland.'[2]

John Doyle did not turn out for Tipperary in 1968. For nineteen seasons between 1949 and 1967 he had played senior hurling during a period when Tipperary was in the forefront of the hurling counties and when it was possible to cut good backs in any ditch from Lorrha to Carrick-on-Suir. During these years Doyle never failed to turn out in a championship game and never retired injured. Starting at right-corner-back, his career got a new lease of life in 1958 when he lined out at left-wing-back, and he finished his hurling days at left-corner-back. He played in eleven senior All-Irelands and won eight of them. His ability and his longevity at the top were recognised when he received a decisive vote for the left-corner-back position in the 1984 Team of the Century. When his record eleven National League medals, six Oireachtas medals and eight Railway Cup medals are added, his record stands second only to that of Christy Ring.

Kieran Carey, Tony Wall and Theo English, as well as John Doyle, had disappeared from the hurling scene when Tipperary faced into the 1968 championship. They had a successful league campaign, beating Wexford, Cork and Kilkenny in their final three games. The last of these had all the expected tension, the residue from the 1967 All-Ireland. Sandwiched between a superb first quarter and a desperately close second half was a black spell in which Croke Park saw some of the most unrestrained trouble for years. Following a lengthy investigation, Ollie Walsh and John Flanagan were both suspended for six months. Tipperary won by three points and headed off to New York for the final proper at the end of May. The first leg was fixed for 2 June but was postponed for a week because of torrential rain. The postponed game was again called off because of the assassination of Robert Kennedy, and the two legs were played on successive days, 15 and 16 June. Tipperary won both. The team had little time to recover from their American trip before they met Clare in the Munster semi-final. In a tough, full-blooded game with the occasional outburst of bad temper, Clare got off to a great start, scoring three goals in the first nineteen minutes and leading by a point at the interval. Tipperary moved John Flanagan to midfield to curtail a rampant Liam Danaher, and they had a four-goal blitz between the second and sixteenth minute of the second half. This put paid to Clare's chances, who were behind by 5-11 to 5-6 at the final whistle.

Much was expected of the Munster final, but it proved bad value for money. Tipperary opened well, with a goal and a point in the opening minutes. These scores seemed to unsettle Cork, who struggled afterwards. The Tipperary half-back line of Mick Burns, Mick Roche and Len Gaynor was in outstanding form, as was Babs Keating in the forward line. Tipperary led by 1-7 to 0-5 at the interval and were in front by 2-13 to 1-7 at the final whistle; but for the resilience of the Cork defence their defeat would have been greater.

In the Leinster championship, Kilkenny—minus Ollie Walsh, who was in hospital with a stomach complaint—made heavy weather of beating Offaly in the semi-final. They won by three points, and Offaly had to play with fourteen men for fifty minutes. The suspension of Ollie Walsh as a result of the incidents in the league final was announced shortly afterwards, and Kilkenny County Board held a special meeting to decide whether they would play the Leinster final or not; after much discussion, it was decided to play.

The first half was a pedestrian affair, with hardly a cheer from the crowd of twenty-five thousand, and Wexford took the lead with 1-8 to 1-4. The second half was transformed into a fine game, with plenty of championship fervour. Kilkenny put in a storming finish, and Eddie Keher almost snatched a draw in the dying seconds. The final score was 3-13 to 4-9 in Wexford's favour.

Wexford's success in the All-Ireland is especially remembered not only because it was the county's first success since 1960 but also because of the way it was achieved. Trailing ten points after twenty-six minutes, the team stormed back like men inspired, to draw level entering the third quarter and to go eight points in front with three minutes to play. Of vital importance to this revival was the pep talk delivered in the dressing-room at half time as Wexford trailed by 1-11 to 1-3; another motivation must have been the memory of the almost impossible comeback against the same opposition in the 1956 league final. Whatever the reasons, the great rally was a marvellous team effort, and of particular satisfaction were the displays of newcomers like Tony Doran, Teddy O'Connor, and John Quigley. In inspired form was the entire half-back line of Vinny Staples, Dan Quigley, and Willie Murphy. Tipperary got two last-minute goals, to leave the final score 5-8 to 3-12. Nobody played as well for Tipperary as Mick Roche, who was unfortunate to be captain of a defeated team for the second time. Tipperary missed John Flanagan and needed the services of a fully fit Jimmy Doyle, who was injured early in the game and had to retire at half time.

Tipperary's greatest period of hurling dominance was to come to an end with the defeat in the 1968 final. There was to be one brief flash of brilliance in 1971 before the county settled down to a long spell in the hurling wilderness. After the riches of the fifties and sixties, the famine of the seventies and eighties was difficult for the county's supporters to bear; and when it came to an end at the close of the eighties there were unprecedented scenes of joy and euphoria throughout Tipperary.

13

Kilkenny and Cork Vie for Supremacy

The period 1969–79, following the era of Tipperary dominance and preceding the decade that saw the breakthrough of Galway and Offaly, may not seem at first sight to have a thread of unity running through it. But it contains a certain unifying theme: a struggle for supremacy between Kilkenny and Cork. With Tipperary out of the way and other counties offering only sporadic resistance, the field was left very much to these two counties.

A look at the statistics will support this claim. Twenty-two teams contested the eleven All-Irelands. Kilkenny appeared eight times, five times as winners and three times as losers. Cork had six appearances, four in victory and two in defeat. Wexford made three appearances and lost all three, as did Galway in their two appearances. Limerick had one success and one failure, and Tipperary made one successful appearance.

So Kilkenny and Cork won nine of these eleven All-Irelands. Another feature of these two counties' supremacy is the way they dominated their respective provincial championships. Kilkenny won the Leinster championship eight times during the period, including five in a row from 1971 to 1975. Cork also won eight Munster championships at the same time, and their successes included five in a row from 1975 to 1979.

Cork defeated Tipperary in three major competitions during 1969, a year that probably marks the turning point in Munster hurling from the Tipperary dominance of the sixties to the Cork supremacy of the seventies. Cork's first victory was in the league semi-final at Thurles, their first major win over the Premier County since 1957. It was followed by victory in the Munster final. Tipperary had beaten Waterford and Limerick to reach the final, while Cork had overcome Clare in a replay, and Galway.

It was to be the westerners' last game in a disappointing sojourn in Munster, during which they won only one game in ten years.

In the final, three first-half goals with the wind, two of them by the centre-forward Willie Walsh, laid the foundation for victory. Tipperary made a spirited come-back in the second half but could never penetrate the Cork defence or get past a sharp Paddy Barry. The victory, 4-6 to 0-9, was Cork's first championship success over Tipperary in twelve years. The final encounter between the sides was in the Oireachtas final in October, when Cork gained their third victory by five points.

Cork's opponents in the All-Ireland were Kilkenny, who were lucky to get out of Leinster. Their opponents in the provincial final were the unlikely Offaly, who had surprised the All-Ireland champions, Wexford, in the semi-final. Offaly showed amazing dash and enthusiasm, and Kilkenny had to fight tooth and nail to avoid defeat. With seven minutes to go the Faithful County led by two points, but Pat Delaney struck for the third time in the game to score a great goal. This was a crushing blow to Offaly, and Kilkenny eventually won by two points.

Kilkenny had to play an All-Ireland semi-final against London, who were competing in the senior championship for the first time since 1903. London's entry came about as a result of defeating Dublin in the All-Ireland intermediate final the previous year. But they provided little opposition for the Noresiders, who won by 3-22 to 1-10.

The All-Ireland between Kilkenny and Cork was entertaining if not brilliant. Justin McCarthy, who had been having a great season at centre-back, fractured his leg in a motorcycle accident on the way to training. Con Roche was also unavailable. The selectors moved Willie Walsh to centre-back to mark Pat Delaney, brought Charlie Cullinane to the forty, and introduced Ray Cummins for his first full championship game.

The changes upset the forwards. Cork got a dream start with a Charlie McCarthy goal and led by six points approaching half time, when Kilkenny got a goal. The exchanges remained even for the first ten minutes after the resumption; then Pat Delaney received a blow to the head and had to be stretchered off. This seemed to spark off a response in Kilkenny, who ended up easy winners by 2-15 to 2-9. It was a tremendous turn-about, to be repeated even more dramatically in the 1972 final. Credit must go to the whole team but particularly to Ted Carroll, who was to win the Texaco Hurler of the Year award, Pat Henderson and Martin Coogan in the backs, Mick Lawlor in the centre of the field, and the captain, Eddie Keher, whose contribution was outstanding, especially when he moved to centre-forward at the end of the third quarter.

The playing time for provincial finals and All-Ireland semi-finals and finals was increased to eighty minutes in 1970. Kilkenny set out in defence of their title in the Leinster semi-final against Offaly. They won by two goals, but the turning point in the game was a save half way through the second half by Ollie Walsh at one end, followed by a rather soft goal from the clearance at the other end for Kilkenny. In the Leinster final Kilkenny had to line out without Eddie Keher, who was suffering from the flu. He came on in the second half, but by that stage Wexford were ahead by 3-12 to 1-4. Two other Kilkenny players, Mick Lawlor and Ollie Walsh, retired injured during the game. Kilkenny made a late rally and, but for some excellent saves by the Wexford goalie, Pat Nolan, might have been closer than five points behind at the final whistle.

Galway had been given permission to opt out of the Munster senior hurling championship, with the result that there were two All-Ireland semi-finals, both played on 16 August. In Athlone, Galway put up a good performance before going down to Wexford by 3-17 to 5-9. The second game was played in Limerick, and Cork scored a comprehensive victory over London by 4-20 to 2-9.

Cork had succeeded in retaining the Munster championship when they defeated Tipperary in the third final in a row between the sides. Cork had qualified by a victory over Limerick, while Tipperary had accounted for Waterford. The final was a close, tough encounter that saw Liam King of Tipperary get his walking papers with twenty minutes remaining. The goalkeeper, John O'Donoghue, conceded two soft goals and was replaced by Peter O'Sullivan. The second half was memorable because of the closeness of the encounter and the cliffhanger of a finish. Tipperary enjoyed an eight-point lead at one stage, but as a result of the softish goals and the extra man, Cork forged a two-point lead with the final whistle approaching. In the final minute John Flanagan burst through but his attempt at a winning goal was narrowly wide.

The All-Ireland was disappointing. Wexford were dogged by injury and had to line out without a number of key players, including Eddie Kelly, Willie Murphy, Ned Buggy, and Phil Wilson. Despite the tonic of an early goal and some spirited play in the opening ten minutes, Wexford faded away badly. By the second minute after the interval Cork led by thirteen points; in all there were forty-two scores, with a final result of 6-21 to 5-10. Eddie O'Brien, at left-full, probably had his best game in the Cork jersey, scoring 3-1; but he was outdone by Charlie McCarthy, who scored 1-9. It was a bad-tempered final, marked by some rough play. The only memorable aspect of the game from a Wexford perspective was the tremendous display of Michael Jacob and Dave Bernie at centrefield.

Another unusual feature was the inclusion of four brothers on the Wexford team: Dan Quigley played at centre-back, and his brothers Martin, Pat and John formed the half-forward line. It was a significant win for Cork, as it brought them level with Tipperary, with twenty-one titles each. The team was captained by the goalie, Paddy Barry.

Cork were National League 'home' champions as well as All-Ireland champions, and on the Thursday after their victory over Wexford they headed for the United States to play New York in the final proper. There were two games in the series, the winner to be decided on aggregate scores. The two games were hectic and close. In the first, Cork won by 4-11 to 4-8, while New York were successful in the second by 2-8 to 1-10. The result left Cork league champions by two points on aggregate. The referee, Clem Foley, was assaulted as he was leaving the grounds. Relations between the New York Board and the Central Council, which had been deteriorating for some time, reached breaking point. All tours were suspended for a period.

When the 1971 Munster championship came around Limerick were the form team, having beaten Tipperary in the league final. They had five points to spare over Waterford in the opening round and came up against Cork in the Munster semi-final. Cork were only a shadow of the previous year's team, and Limerick recorded their first championship win over the Leesiders in thirty-one years. It was the first championship clash of Ray Cummins, who scored two goals, and Pat Hartigan. The final score was 2-16 to 2-14, in Limerick's favour. Meanwhile Tipperary had qualified by virtue of a five-point victory over Clare.

The Munster final was played at Killarney, an eighty-minute thriller in showery conditions. Limerick had a six-point lead at the interval; but Tipperary reappeared transformed in personnel and in attitude. Liam King and Roger Ryan replaced Noel Lane and Jimmy Doyle, and with fifteen minutes remaining they had turned their deficit into a five-point lead. At this point Limerick rallied and, with five minutes remaining, had drawn level. Points were exchanged, and just before the finish John Flanagan got possession about sixty yards out and, though closely marked, sent the ball sailing between the posts for the winning point with a score of 4-16 to 3-18.

Meanwhile in Leinster, Kilkenny were adding another title to their record. They had great difficulty in beating Dublin in the first round, however, and did not clinch victory until a last-minute goal by Kieran Purcell. The Leinster final against Wexford produced forty-one scores, but it was anything but a memorable game. Wexford led at half time by 1-9 to 1-8. Kilkenny had a goal by Mossie Murphy immediately after resuming, and never looked back. At the final whistle they had a three-goal margin, 6-16 to 3-16.

Kilkenny played London in the All-Ireland semi-final. They failed to impress in the first half, and the sides were level at 1-7 each at the interval. Kilkenny were a much different team in the second half and won by 2-23 to 2-8. A notable feature of the game was the superb goalkeeping of the London goalie, Mick Butler. In the other semi-final Tipperary did not impress against Galway. The backs were suspect, and the team played in fits and starts; altogether they conceded six goals. Tipperary led by 3-14 to 3-4 at the interval and were in front by 3-26 to 6-8 at the final whistle. The best performances came from Len Gaynor and Babs Keating, the latter scoring 2-12.

The smallest crowd at an All-Ireland since 1958 turned up in Croke Park on 5 September 1971—perhaps because the match was being televised in colour for the first time. It produced the second-highest number of scores in a final, 5-17 to 5-14 (the highest having been the previous year's final). Tipperary had the breeze in the first half but didn't make enough use of it and were ahead by only six points at the break. Half way during the second half Kieran Purcell got a great goal, to level the scores at Tipperary 3-14, Kilkenny 4-11. A few minutes later Kilkenny went into the lead. With twelve minutes to go Roger Ryan got a goal for Tipperary, and they were never headed after that. They probably deserved their victory, because whenever Kilkenny threatened their superiority they were able to fight back, and they dominated in the last eight minutes. Eddie Keher scored 2-11 for Kilkenny, of which 2-8 came from frees, and this remained the highest individual score in a final until Nicky English bettered it in 1989.

Before Tipperary set out to defend their All-Ireland crown in 1972 they made a historic trip to San Francisco to play the All-Stars. The All-Stars scheme came into existence in 1971 with the sponsorship of P. J. Carroll and Company of Dundalk. A number of schemes had existed during the sixties to give recognition and reward to players for such things as skill, ability, fair play, and loyalty to club and county, including the Cú Chulainn Awards in 1963 and the selections for the Cardinal Cushing games, which began in 1965. Carroll's All-Stars were picked by journalists, and in the early years the rewards included a trip to the United States to play against the All-Ireland champions. Two games were played in San Francisco, each side winning one, but the All-Stars won on aggregate and received the Thomas Cahill Trophy, presented by the former San Francisco chief of police and president of the United Irish Society.

Tipperary were beaten by Cork in the league semi-final, and the two sides met again in the Munster semi-final at Limerick. At half time it appeared as if Tipperary, leading by 3-7 to 2-1, would win. Noel O'Dwyer added another point on the resumption but it was to be Tipperary's last score, and for the remainder of the half Cork whittled away at the lead, and at the final whistle the sides were level at 3-8 all. Babs Keating was the Tipperary captain, because Moyne-Templetuohy, the 1971 county champions, had nobody on the team. It was his only time to lead Tipperary in the championship: in the replay Mick Coen was selected and assumed the captaincy. Neither game was a happy occasion for Keating, who was held scoreless on both days by Tony Maher. Admittedly a broken toe didn't help his efforts. In the replay Cork had a slight edge all the way through and won by 3-10 to 2-7.

Meanwhile Clare had shattered Limerick's hopes by recording a surprise win at Ennis. The Munster final was played at Thurles, and Clare failed completely to reproduce the form they had shown against Limerick, with Cork winning in a canter by 6-18 to 2-8.

In Leinster, Kilkenny got a fright in the first round against Laois but recovered in the end to win by seven points. The Leinster final against Wexford produced a draw, the first since 1955. Kilkenny started well and went into the lead, but Wexford suddenly came alight and were three points in front at the interval. With the breeze in their favour in the second half they quickly stretched their lead to ten points. Kilkenny pegged it back a bit to seven points, but then, with twenty-three minutes remaining, Mick Brennan was sent off and Kilkenny didn't appear to have a chance. But it had the opposite effect, and in a tremendous rally Kilkenny grabbed a draw on a score of 6-13 each.

With ten minutes left in the replay the sides were locked together. Then a Liam O'Brien free from the sideline was flicked to the net by Eddie Keher. Ned Byrne got through for another, and further points by Keher and Pat Delaney saw Kilkenny win comfortably by 3-16 to 1-14. Noel Skehan, who had been blamed for some of the goals in the drawn game, had an impressive display. Pat Delaney also excelled.

Kilkenny had the easiest of victories in the All-Ireland semi-final, beating Galway by 5-28 to 3-7. Eddie Keher set a record of point scoring in a championship game when he scored seventeen times, seven from frees. Cork had an equally facile win in their semi-final against London, winning by 7-20 to 1-12.

Kilkenny were rank outsiders against Cork in the All-Ireland. It was expected that the eighty-minute game would suit the younger Cork team, but it was the older and more experienced Kilkenny players who were the sprightliest at the finish. Closely contested in the first half, Cork led at half time by 2-8 to 0-12, the two goals coming from Ray Cummins. The second half was a brilliant game, played in tremendous heat. Cork stretched their lead to eight points with twenty-two minutes remaining. Eddie Keher was switched from the corner to left-forward, a move that changed the game. Another was the arrival of Martin Coogan, who replaced the injured Fan Larkin. Both these players rallied Kilkenny, and in the time remaining the team scored 2-9 without reply from Cork and changed the eight-point deficit to a seven-point lead with a score of 3-24 to 5-11. This dramatic transformation made it one of the most exciting and spectacular finals ever played. Individual performances stand out, such as Keher's and Coogan's, Pat Delaney's and Jim Treacy's, but everyone contributed to a stunning victory. This was the day when Pat Delaney introduced the solo-run style by hopping the ball off the ground with his hurley, used effectively in the second half. For Cork the game can best be forgotten, even though two players in particular, Con Roche and Ray Cummins, gave displays that could hold their own in any company.

Kilkenny started out impressively in the 1973 championship, beating Dublin by 2-9 to 2-11 in the Leinster semi-final. Mick Brennan at centrefield had a most impressive performance for the winners. In the final they faced Wexford and gave one of their greatest displays. Leading by eight points at half time, they increased their lead to fourteen points with fifteen minutes to go. During the last quarter they slackened somewhat, and Wexford came back to within seven points. However, Kilkenny finished the stronger with three points from Eddie Keher and won by 4-22 to 3-15. This display is often quoted as Kilkenny's best in the period 1972–75 but it is 'forgotten' in the context of their defeat by Limerick in the All-Ireland.

Kilkenny faced Limerick in the final. The Shannonsiders, who had been beaten by Wexford in the league final (in which Ned Rea played at full-back and was blamed for much of Wexford's 4-13 score), qualified for the Munster final through a two-point win over Clare. Their opponents were Tipperary, who, having beaten Waterford in the first round, played Cork in the semi-final. With six minutes remaining, Cork seemed likely winners with a five-point advantage; however, during the remaining time Tipperary's full-forward, Roger Ryan, went on a scoring rampage, getting two goals and setting up another. All Cork could register during the same period was a point, and the final score was 5-4 to 1-10 in Tipperary's favour.

This was to be Tipperary's last championship win until 29 May 1983. The Munster final in Thurles was a repeat of the 1971 encounter at Killarney. On a glorious day it turned out to be a seesaw contest between a Limerick side with good goal-scoring ability and a Tipperary fifteen in which the emphasis was on point-getting. John Flanagan, who had featured in the closing minutes of the Killarney encounter, shone again on this occasion, getting an equalising point from seventy yards with a minute remaining. In the dying moments Limerick forced a seventy, and the referee, Mick Slattery of Clare, informed Richie Bennis that he had to score direct. He did so, although some Tipperary supporters claimed the ball veered wide in the end. But the umpire had no doubt, and Limerick won by 6-7 to 2-18. They followed up with victory over London (who had, surprisingly, beaten Galway in the quarter-final) in the All-Ireland semi-final in Ennis. Richie Bennis scored their goal from a penalty in a 1-15 to 0-7 win.

It was the first time since 1940 that Limerick and Kilkenny met in an All-Ireland final. Kilkenny entered the game under a severe handicap. Missing from the side that had won the Leinster final were Éamon Morrissey, who had emigrated to Australia, Kieran Purcell, who was recovering from an appendix operation but went on at half time, and Jim Treacy and Eddie Keher, who were injured. It was an uphill struggle for Kilkenny, who also had to contend with an outstanding Limerick display. The Shannonsiders led by two points at the interval, but Kilkenny were level six minutes after the resumption. Then what seemed a certain goal for Kilkenny was deflected over the bar by Séamus Horgan, and soon afterwards Limerick got a scrambled goal, credited to Mossie Dowling following a short puck-out by Noel Skehan. Limerick went on to win by 1-21 to 1-14, their first win in thirty-three years. In the aftermath the Limerick selectors were given credit for one match-winning move: they took Éamon Cregan out of attack to play at centre-back on Pat Delaney. He succeeded in stymieing the Johnstown man, and this, together with the absence of Kieran Purcell and Eddie Keher, rendered the Kilkenny attack only a shadow of what it might have been.

Limerick were badly beaten by Cork in the 1974 league final, televised live from Limerick, and the Leesiders seemed hot favourites for the Munster championship. However, they were sensationally beaten by Waterford in the first round. There was a dramatic turn in this game just before half time when Cork's long-serving goalkeeper, Paddy Barry, was sent off following an incident with an umpire. At the interval Cork brought in the sub goalie, Martin Coleman, and took off the defender Pat Barry of Glen Rovers. In spite of a great effort by Cork in the second half, Waterford held out for a four-point victory. After a tremendous game in the semi-final Waterford went under to Limerick by a point. In the other semi-final Clare defeated Tipperary in a low-scoring game. It was Mick Roche's last championship match. The Munster final at Thurles was a one-sided affair, in which Clare failed to reproduce their semi-final form and Limerick had an easy victory by 6-14 to 3-9.

Kilkenny had a big victory over Offaly in the first round of the Leinster championship. The game saw Ger Henderson make his senior championship debut for the Noresiders. The Leinster final against Wexford produced one of the most fantastic matches seen at Croke Park. It was a game that had everything: excitement, drama, tension, and a nerve-racking finish. At the end of the first half Kilkenny led by 3-8 to 0-10. Just on the break Wexford were reduced to fourteen men when Phil Wilson was sent to the line. He was having a fine game, and it seemed that with the wind in their favour in the second half Kilkenny would have an easy victory. They were seven points ahead fourteen minutes into the second half; then Wexford struck it rich. Within fifteen minutes, despite conceding a goal, they had levelled; then, to the delight of their supporters, John Quigley sent them into the lead. Kilkenny levelled, the sides exchanged scores, and in the dying moments Eddie Keher got a free from an awkward angle under the Hogan Stand and sent the ball between the posts for a dramatic Kilkenny victory, 6-13 to 2-24.

The Kilkenny forwards gave an exhibition of scoring against Galway in the All-Ireland semi-final at Birr. Kilkenny led by 1-19 to 1-10 at half time and were in front by 2-32 to 3-17 at the final whistle.

The pairing of the All-Ireland was a repeat of the previous year's. Kilkenny had the services of Eddie Keher, Jim Treacy, and a fully fit Kieran Purcell. Despite their return it was Limerick who got off on the right foot and got the first four points. The first was scored by Frankie Nolan, who had done the same the previous year. Kilkenny settled, levelled, then pulled ahead to be in front by 3-7 to 1-9 at the interval. Kilkenny were completely on top in the second half. Their defence gave little away, the forwards picked off points in a fluent fashion, and at the final whistle they were in front, 3-19 to 1-13. Again Eddie Keher contributed handsomely to the victory with a personal tally of 1-11. However, the outstanding player on the field was Pat Henderson, who gave an inspired performance at centre-back, keeping the best attacking moves by Limerick at bay.

Kilkenny's opponents in the first round of the 1975 Leinster championship were Dublin. The sides were fairly close during the first half and for ten minutes after the resumption, but Kilkenny pulled away and won by 3-16 to 1-7. For the sixth year in succession Kilkenny and Wexford met in the Leinster final. It was another exciting game, with patches of brilliant hurling. The champions led by 1-12 to 1-8 at the interval, with Wexford guilty of much faulty shooting. The sides remained closely locked until the twentieth minute, when Eddie Keher blasted a penalty to the Wexford net. This established Kilkenny superiority at a vital stage of the game, and they held on to the end, when they were winners by 2-20 to 2-14.

The outstanding man of the match was Brian Cody, closely followed by Kieran Purcell.

Meanwhile in Munster, Cork qualified for the final by virtue of victories over Waterford and Clare. In the other semi-final Limerick and Tipperary played a thrilling draw in Thurles in a match that saw superb displays by Babs Keating and Pat Hartigan. Keating came out of retirement for the game, but the replay marked his last championship match with Tipperary. Limerick won the replay by four points. Nearly forty-seven thousand came to the Gaelic Grounds in Limerick for the final, and in a match in which Cork took their chances and Limerick didn't, the Leesiders won by 3-14 to 0-12 points. The Limerick challenge was severely dented by two Cork goals, from Charlie McCarthy and Willie Walsh, just before half time.

Cork were shocked in the All-Ireland semi-final against Galway. A three-goal burst by the westerners in the opening ten minutes left Cork struggling all the way through. They managed to reduce the arrears to a single point with four minutes to go, but Galway rallied to score another point before the finish and won by 4-15 to 2-19. In doing so they qualified for their first All-Ireland since 1958 and had the chance of winning their first title since 1923.

Galway's success against Cork had not been totally without warning. In May they had won the league after an interval of twenty-four years, beating Tipperary in the final and Kilkenny in the semi-final. They were expected to have a fair chance against the Leinster champions, but their performance was a big disappointment. They took the lead for the only time with a Frank Burke goal after nineteen minutes but didn't score again for twenty-two minutes. During that time Kilkenny clocked up 1-8 to ensure a successful defence of their title. The basis of their success was a great performance by Liam O'Brien and Frank Cummins at centrefield, with another outstanding performance by Eddie Keher, who scored 2-7. Others to excel were Fan Larkin and Brian Cody. It was the first seventy-minute final, and it was the first time since 1933 that Kilkenny had successfully defended their title. Looking back to 1973 and the loss of the final to Limerick, Kilkenny believed that had they the missing four in that game they would have won and would now be celebrating a four-in-a-row.

Kilkenny started 1976 in grand style, beating Clare in the league final. It had taken them two games to beat Cork in the semi-final and two more to win the final. In the replay of the final—after Kilkenny returned from the All-Stars tour to America—they gave a superb performance, eventually winning by 6-14 to 1-14. Their opponents in the Leinster championship were Westmeath, who stayed with the champions for the first twenty minutes but were eventually annihilated by a superb machine. Kilkenny were clear favourites to win the Leinster final against Wexford but were to suffer their biggest defeat in a provincial decider since 1896. They looked so bad and so lacking in appetite for the game that supporters attributed their staleness to the two draws in the closing stages of the league. So much were the All-Ireland and league champions out of it that they got just one point from play. Wexford led at half time by six points and were in front by 2-20 to 1-6 at the final whistle. The margin would have been greater but for the brilliance of Noel Skehan in the Kilkenny goal.

In Munster the final at Páirc Uí Chaoimh was a disappointing affair in which Cork had the measure of Limerick all through. Earlier Limerick had beaten Clare and Cork and had overcome Tipperary in the semi-finals. In the latter game Tipperary seemed likely winners, until Cork introduced Jimmy Barry Murphy after the interval. The Leesiders drew level with two minutes remaining, and Tipperary were unlucky in a last-minute attack when a Séamus Power shot struck the post. Had that goal been scored it is possible that the course of Munster hurling would have been changed. As stated above, Cork's victory in the Munster final by 3-15 to 4-5 was easy. One of the outstanding performances of the day was that of Éamon Cregan, who scored 4-1 of Limerick's total.

Cork had a bye to the All-Ireland final, while Wexford had to play Galway. This game was played at Páirc Uí Chaoimh and ended in a draw. Galway showed that their game was on a steadily rising graph and scored 2-23 to Wexford's 5-14. Wexford won the replay at the same venue by a goal, and Galway claimed that John Quigley was given a similar score after the referee had blown the whistle for a free.

Wexford appeared to benefit from the extra games to sharpen them up for the All-Ireland. They got off to a great start and had two goals and two points on the scoreboard before Cork registered a score. However, the Leesiders recovered their composure, and with Pat Moylan playing excellently at centrefield they came back to draw level at half time. It was Wexford who resumed in better form, with a Tony Doran goal within a minute; but Cork settled down again and in a brilliant second half came back into the game and eventually won by 2-21 to 4-11. Pat Moylan's contribution to Cork's victory was enormous. As well as dominating centrefield he scored ten points of his side's total. The decisive move by Cork was the change of Jimmy Barry Murphy from wing to centre-forward on a tiring Mick Jacob; he shot some late points after what had been till then a quiet game.

The Cork captain, Ray Cummins, was the first Blackrock man to collect the McCarthy Cup since Eudie Coughlan in 1931. The team got an enthusiastic reception in Cork the following evening and encouraging praise from the greatest Corkman of them all, Christy Ring, who was on the platform to greet them. 'My hurling days are over,' he said, 'but let no-one say that the best hurlers belong to the past. They are with us now, and better yet to come.'

Cork started their defence of the championship in the 1977 Munster semi-final against Waterford in Thurles. The Waterford men held the advantage at half time and were eight points in front ten minutes after the resumption. However, Cork made a strong rally and won by 4-13 to 3-11. Clare and Limerick contested the other semi-final, with the Banner County advancing to the final. Nearly forty-five thousand people came to Thurles for the game, during which armed thieves got away with over £24,000 of the day's takings. Clare were hopeful in the light of their recent performances and the fact that they had recently beaten Cork twice at under-21 level. Inexperience, however, proved their undoing, and they suffered the blow of having their full-back, John Power, sent off before half time after a scuffle with Ray Cummins. In the end the margin of five points, on a score of 4-15 to 4-10, did not do justice to Cork.

Wexford opened their defence of the Leinster title with a victory over Offaly and qualified to play Kilkenny in the final. Kilkenny were a much-improved team on the previous year, and the game turned out to be a thriller. Kilkenny missed the services of Pat Delaney and Mick Brennan, both of whom were injured. Wexford had a four-point advantage at half time and were eight points clear with seventeen minutes to play. But, as so often happens between the halves, Kilkenny staged a rally and reduced the deficit to three points with five minutes to go. During this time Eddie Keher burst through for what seemed like a certain goal, but the ball was deflected over the bar by the Wexford goalie, John Nolan. Martin Quigley then had a closing point, to leave Wexford winners by 3-17 to 3-14. Wexford had arrived in Dublin without their jerseys. They borrowed an unnumbered set from Clery's, which left Mick Dunne of RTE in serious difficulty for his commentary. Kilkenny missed the services of Pat Delaney and Mick Brennan, both of whom were injured.

It was Eddie Keher's last championship game for his county. In a distinguished hurling career he became one of the greatest scoring forwards of all time, and his name fits comfortably in the company of Christy Ring, Mick Mackey, Nicky Rackard, and Jimmy Doyle. It was also the last championship outing for Kieran Purcell and Pat Lalor.

Cork qualified for the All-Ireland, between the same opponents, but did not produce the excitement of the previous year. Wexford's display was extremely disappointing. They had trained and prepared hard, yet most of them failed to play to form on the day. Cork ran up a six-point lead early in the game and were in command for most of the time but had to withstand a great rally by Wexford towards the finish. An outstanding save by Martin Coleman prevented Christy Keogh getting the equaliser; the final score was 1-17 to 3-8 in favour of Cork. The Cork team gave a superb display, and none better than the oldest two on the team, Denis Coughlan and Gerald McCarthy. In a pre-match puck-around Seán O'Leary suffered a nose injury; however, he took his place on the team and contributed a goal (a controversial one because of the number of steps taken) and two points to his side's total. The captain was Martin O'Doherty of Glen Rovers, who was outstanding at full-back. Sadly for Wexford, it was to be their last appearance in an All-Ireland final.

In 1978 Cork made it three in a row when they beat Kilkenny by four points. They beat Waterford in the Munster semi-final and came up against Clare, who had beaten Limerick, in the provincial decider. Clare, who had retained their league title in May, were hopeful of their chances, and so were the crowd of fifty-four thousand who filled Thurles for the occasion. There was value for money as the sides fought out a close, dour contest. Cork, with the wind in the first half, led by five points to three at the interval, and the chances looked good for Clare in the second half. However, Cork rearranged their forces, got a grip at midfield, made good use of the wings, and generally prevented Clare from getting a grip on the game. In the end there were still two points between the sides on a score of 0-13 to 0-11. It was the last great effort by this particularly good Clare team, which, with two league titles to their credit, deserved a breakthrough in Munster. Their half-back line of Ger Loughnane, Seán Stack and Seán Hehir was the finest in the game. The full-back line had prevented Cork's talented full-forward line of Charlie McCarthy, Ray Cummins and Jimmy Barry Murphy from scoring even one goal. Clare's failure probably lay in the forward line, where they didn't have the talent required to penetrate Cork's defence.

Kilkenny were Cork's opponents in the All-Ireland. They had one of their easiest victories ever over Offaly in the Leinster semi-final and qualified to meet Wexford in the final. It was another thrilling encounter between these two sides, with never more than a goal separating them. Wexford led at half time by 1-7 to 0-9, thanks to a Ned Buggy penalty goal. The second half was equally close, and Wexford were in front by two points with five minutes to go. In the remaining time a great drive by Mick Crotty was blocked by the Wexford goalie, John Nolan, but the rebound was struck to the net by Matt Ruth. In the closing minutes Kilkenny got two more points, to finish winners by 2-16 to 1-16.

In the semi-final against Galway, Kilkenny had a comfortable lead at the interval. The second half proved to be an epic encounter as Galway fought back and brought the lead down to two points. In the final minutes Kilkenny rallied once again and had a seven-point victory, 4-20 to 4-13.

A classic was expected between Cork and Kilkenny, the first time the sides had met since Cork returned to the top in Munster in 1975. The game did not live up to expectations, and at half time the sides were level. They remained evenly balanced in the second half until a Cork switch of Tim Crowley from left-half-forward to midfield to mark Frank Cummins had the desired effect. Cork gradually went ahead and at the final whistle were in front by 1-15 to 2-8. Jimmy Barry Murphy got a goal that might have been stopped but for a deflection off Dick O'Hara. As well as Crowley, Martin O'Doherty had an outstanding game at full-back, while Charlie McCarthy and Jimmy Barry Murphy impressed in the forwards. As well as captaining the side, Charlie McCarthy had the satisfaction of scoring seven points, including the last.

Cork won their fifth Munster final in a row in 1979 when they beat a disappointing Limerick side in Thurles. Pat Hartigan had been injured at a Limerick training session, and his loss had a bad effect on the team. The Shannonsiders defeated Waterford and Clare to qualify for the decider. Cork defeated the league champions, Tipperary, by a point in the other semi-final in Páirc Uí Chaoimh. In an exciting encounter Tipperary had the chance of an equaliser in the final minute, but the Pat O'Neill shot trailed wide. In beating Limerick by 2-14 to 0-9 Cork were recording their second five-in-a-row, a feat they previously achieved in 1901–05. They looked good for their fourth All-Ireland in a row, but their plans came unstuck against Galway in the semi-final. Even though they did not strike top form they could have won had they taken a few simple chances in the second half. In the closing minutes the effect of all their games over the previous four years took its toll, and they did not have the final push to achieve victory. They also had to contend with a Galway team that had been showing signs of making a breakthrough for a number of years. In the previous year they had defeated Tipperary in a replayed under-21 final, which had given them a much-needed shot of confidence. The strength of their effort against Cork lay in a powerful half-back line of Joe McDonagh, Seán Silke, and Iggy Clarke. They defended brilliantly and by forward movement set up many attacks. In the end they had a four-point margin with a score of 2-14 to 1-13.

Kilkenny were Galway's opponents in the All-Ireland. In their first-round game against Dublin they seemed set for an easy victory when leading by eight points at the interval after playing against the breeze. Dublin introduced George Hayes at midfield during the break, and he turned the game around. In the end the Noresiders had to struggle for their 4-15 to 4-11 victory. In the Leinster final Kilkenny and Wexford met once again, and in a thrilling contest there was little between the sides. They were level on no less than seven occasions, including half time. During the second half Wexford hit a particularly good patch, which took them six points in front, but Kilkenny made a few changes, fought back, and eventually won by 2-21 to 2-17. Mick Brennan had one of his finest games for Kilkenny and scored eight points.

Galway faced Kilkenny in the All-Ireland final with considerable expectations. They felt they had gained in experience since the sides last met in 1975. The day was most unsuitable for hurling, with heavy rain and high winds, which Kilkenny chose to play against in the first half. Galway gained plenty of possession in the opening half but squandered it and shot eleven wides. Another blow to Galway was when a Liam O'Brien seventy went off the chest of the Galway goalkeeper, Séamus Shinnors, into the net. It gave Kilkenny a half-time lead of 1-4 to 0-5. Galway played well in the second half and looked good when taking the lead with a Noel Lane goal, which was to win Goal of the Year on RTE, in the twentieth minute. However, Kilkenny came back with four points, and when Noel Skehan blocked a John Connolly penalty Galway's chance of victory disappeared. Kilkenny got another goal and a point, to win by 2-12 to 1-8. It was not a good game of hurling, and the attendance of less than fifty-four thousand was the lowest since 1958. A railway strike, announced the day before the game, left thousands of supporters stranded, and the bad weather didn't help either. The team was trained by two players, Eddie Keher and Pat Henderson, who had starred on the field of play not so many years previously, and the victory gave Kilkenny their twenty-first title.

Kilkenny could look back on a successful decade, which had seen them contest seven out of ten finals, winning four of them. The side that won five Leinster finals in a row between 1971 and 1975 was one of the best teams to come out of the county. One indication of their quality is the number of players who received All-Star awards. In the inaugural year of 1971 they included four Kilkenny players: Jim Treacy, Martin Coogan, Frank Cummins, and Eddie Keher. In 1972 the representation increased to six with Treacy, Cummins and Keher as well as Noel Skehan, Pat Lalor, and Pat Delaney. Seven received the awards in 1973: as well as Keher, Skehan and Delaney there were Fan Larkin, Pat Henderson, Liam O'Brien, and Kieran Purcell. Seven were again picked in 1974: Skehan, Larkin, Henderson, O'Brien, Purcell and Keher retained their places, with Mick Crotty as the seventh. Six were honoured in 1975: Keher gained his fifth award, and in addition to Skehan, O'Brien and Purcell there were the newcomers Brian Cody and Mick Brennan.

Cork could also be well pleased with their spoils from the decade. They had won four All-Irelands and lost one. The three-in-a-row was an achievement to be proud of and, since it has not been emulated in the meantime, stands out as something special. Yet it was not regarded as a significant achievement at the time. To some it was easily achieved. Cork's detractors claim that it was achieved through a couple of easy successes in Munster; added to this is the claim that Tipperary were going through a valley period at the time. What is forgotten is that Cork beat a particularly good Clare team twice during the period. They also beat Tipperary, Wexford, Kilkenny, Limerick and Galway to be successful. The team included players of outstanding ability, such as Tom Cashman and Dermot McCurtain, Ray Cummins and Jimmy Barry Murphy, Martin O'Doherty and John Horgan, Gerald McCarthy and his namesake Charlie McCarthy, to name but a few. Regardless of how the opposition may have been limited, Cork achieved what no team has found possible since.

14

Breakthroughs

The nineteen-eighties saw the arrival of two more teams as successful contenders for All-Ireland honours. Galway, who had a lone All-Ireland senior championship to their credit, dating back to 1923, became a force in hurling and captured three titles. Offaly, whose previous achievement was confined to two junior titles, in 1923 and 1929, broke through the psychological and traditional barriers to win senior championships for the first time. The period also saw Antrim return to the All-Ireland championship for the first time since 1954 and qualify for the final in 1989.

During the period 1980–94 thirty teams qualified for the All-Ireland final. Galway head the list with eight, of which they won three and lost five. Put into context this compares more than favourably with the county's record up to 1980. Between 1923 and 1979 nine finals were contested without success. Kilkenny were next and a more successful team during the period, with two doubles separated by a decade out of six appearances. Cork qualified on six occasions, with three victories. Offaly's success rate was the best, winning three out of four. Tipperary won two out of three; Limerick lost in 1980 and 1994; and Antrim tasted defeat on their only appearance. Another interesting fact is Offaly's achievement in Leinster: during this period they contested twelve Leinster finals (including eleven in a row, from 1980 to 1990), winning eight.

Galway's victory in the 1980 All-Ireland was received with tremendous enthusiasm, not only in Galway but further afield. The estimated thirty thousand who greeted the team in Eyre Square were probably more enthusiastic and emotional than any crowd that came out anywhere in Ireland to welcome home an All-Ireland side. The wait had been so long and the disappointments so many that the crowd wallowed in the joy and pride of it all.

During the previous decade there were signs that Galway hurling was turning a corner. There were still upsets and disappointments, as in the 1975 and 1979 All-Irelands, but there were important straws in the wind. The first was in 1972, when the under-21 team, which included such future stars as Iggy Clarke, Frank Burke, and P. J. Molloy, defeated Dublin to win the All-Ireland. The following year Kilkenny pipped the minors by a point. The senior breakthrough came in 1975, when Galway took their first National League title since 1951 by beating Tipperary. They maintained the good work when beating Cork in the semi-final. The All-Ireland defeat by Kilkenny was a disappointment, as was defeat by Wexford in the replayed semi-final the following year. Senior success evaded the team in 1977 and 1978, but the under-21 team had a great victory over Tipperary in a replayed All-Ireland in 1978. There was to be more disappointment in 1979 before success finally came.

Galway hurling got a boost in 1980 when Castlegar won the All-Ireland club championship. Powered by Connollys, it was the first Galway team to achieve success. Earlier Galway, representing Connacht, won the Railway Cup competition by beating Munster in wintry conditions in Croke Park, the first victory since 1947. The team had been taken over by Cyril Farrell, and there was a new purpose in Galway hurling.

Galway had to play Kildare in the All-Ireland quarter-final to decide the opponents of the Leinster champions in the semi-final. The westerners had an easy victory and qualified to play Offaly, the unlikely Leinster winners. One of the reasons for Offaly's emergence was the successful proposition to the Leinster GAA convention that the championship be run on the basis of an open draw. This resulted in Kilkenny and Wexford meeting in the Leinster semi-final. Under the old 'seeding' system the sides had met in every Leinster final since 1970.

The second semi-final matched Offaly and Dublin, a game won by Offaly but not very impressively. The Kilkenny-Wexford game was an exciting affair, especially in the second half. Kilkenny led by twelve points, but Wexford suddenly caught fire and reduced the deficit to a point with seven minutes to go. During the final minutes the Wexford rally was contained, and Kilkenny survived by five points.

Kilkenny were such favourites for the Leinster final that a crowd of less than ten thousand turned up. Offaly got off to a good start to lead by six points after eight minutes. Kilkenny came right back into the game and led by two points at the interval and seemed set to overcome the opposition. However, Offaly were not to be pushed aside lightly: they stuck to their task, kept coming back when Kilkenny seemed to have it, and won by the minimum margin on a score of 3-17 to 5-10. Thus did Offaly make history in taking the Leinster senior hurling title for the first time. The role of Diarmuid Healy, who had become coach in the autumn of 1979, was another significant reason for the breakthrough.

In Munster, Cork seemed to be destined for victory going into the championship. Having won the league, they easily defeated a listless Tipperary side in the semi-final on a day that marked the opening of Ardán Uí Riain in Semple Stadium. In the other semi-final Limerick defeated Clare, who had promised well when beating Waterford in the first round. The final was played in Thurles, and Cork were going for their sixth successive Munster championship. In one of the best finals for years Limerick displayed determination, skill and fitness in upsetting the odds and winning by four points. It was a particularly sweet victory for Limerick, who had been defeated by nine points in the league final replay by the same opposition.

It was an unusual pairing of Galway and Offaly for the All-Ireland semi-final on 3 August. Both teams had everything to play for and believed that an All-Ireland title was a real possibility now that Limerick had beaten Cork. A crowd of about twenty-two thousand witnessed a poor game, with Galway getting the verdict by two points. The experience of the westerners told on the occasion. Since 1975 they had played in two All-Irelands and beaten Cork twice in semi-finals. But they struggled to win. The forwards shot seventeen wides. Iggy Clarke had to retire with a shoulder injury, and Sylvie Linnane got his marching orders in the middle of the second half. Mike Conneely, who had replaced Séamus Shinnors early in the year, had an unhappy time between the posts. When the final whistle was blown Galway were just hanging on. In fact the referee, J. J. Landers, didn't play the full period in the second half; this was a source of much annoyance to Offaly, who felt they were coming through at the end.

The pairing of Galway and Limerick in the final was also unique. Limerick were favourites on the basis of their league performance and their defeat of Cork in the Munster final. They also had one of the best lines of forwards in the game. Éamon Cregan, after a lifetime of hurling out the field, had made the corner-forward position his own. On the opposite side was the irrepressible Vincent 'Ollie' O'Connor and in the centre Joe McKenna, a colossus among full-forwards. The greatest strength out the field rested in the half-backs, Liam O'Donoghue and Seán Foley; but in every position there was a range of talent. Against them were pitted players of the quality of John Connolly, Seán Silke, Niall McInerney, Frank Burke, and P. J. Molloy. But ultimately it is form that counts, and Limerick failed to produce the form that had brought them their earlier victories. On a beautiful day Galway played against the wind, having lost the toss, and got off to the best possible start when Bernie Forde kicked a goal. Ten minutes later P. J. Molloy got a second, and the westerners led at the interval by five points. They increased their lead ten minutes after the restart and seemed set for victory. Limerick came back to reduce the deficit to two points after a Cregan penalty in the sixty-first minute. However, because of a brilliant display by Mike Conneely in the Galway goal they failed to make further headway, and Galway had a three-point margin at the final whistle, 2-15 to 3-9.

The scenes that greeted the victory in Croke Park were the most exciting and emotional ever seen, and the victory speech of the captain, Joe Connolly, and Joe McDonagh's rendering of 'The West's Awake', matched the occasion. The victorious side was: Mike Conneely, Conor Hayes, Niall McInerney, Joe Cooney, Sylvie Linnane, Seán Silke, S. Coen, M. Connolly, Steve Mahon, Frank Burke, Joe Connolly (captain), P. J. Molloy, Bernie Forde, John Connolly, and Noel Lane.

It was to be Offaly's turn in 1981. Kilkenny again met Wexford in the semi-final, and after a close tussle Wexford came out on top by three points and qualified to play Offaly in the final. There was a fine prize for the winners of a straight ticket to the All-Ireland. In contrast to the previous year, nearly thirty thousand came to see this game. Sixteen minutes after the start of a close, tough game Tony Doran was carried off injured. At one point Offaly were eight points in front, but, chiefly through a superb display by George O'Connor, Wexford cut the margin to a point two minutes from time. Johnny Flaherty increased it to two, and just on time Pat Delaney intercepted a Wexford pass that would have given them a goal and victory. Offaly had survived by two points.

They had just survived also in the semi-final, finding themselves two points behind Laois with four minutes to go. In these last minutes Offaly levelled, and in the final puck the left-half-back, Pat Kirwan, hit a mighty ball over the bar from ninety yards for the winning point. These close survivals were to stand to the Offaly men on All-Ireland day.

There was a most exciting championship in Munster. Clare showed sparkling form in defeating Waterford and the highly rated National League champions, Cork, to qualify for the final. It was their first championship defeat of Cork since 1955. In the other semi-final Limerick came back from fourteen points down to force a draw with Tipperary in Thurles. In the replay in Limerick the Shannonsiders had a comfortable margin of eight points. If Joe McKenna was the thorn in Tipperary's side he was to be the same in Clare's in the final in Semple Stadium. His three goals put paid to the Banner County's chances, and Limerick won by 3-12 to 2-9 to take their second Munster final in a row.

Limerick had to play Galway in the All-Ireland semi-final; and if any team were to be given the prize for misfortune and ill-luck it had to be Limerick. The match turned out to be a tough affair, in which Seán Foley was sent off for a foul against P. J. Molloy after only nine minutes. Instead of taking the advantage Galway failed to lift their game and had to depend on a late point by Finbarr Gantley to earn a draw, 1-8 to 0-11. It was an amazing game, in which four penalty attempts failed to get a goal. Towards the end John Connolly and Jimmy Carroll were sent off. In spite of the extra man Galway never led, and Limerick might have put the game beyond their reach had Éamon Cregan scored from his penalty ten minutes into the second half, when Limerick were leading by 0-9 to 1-3. Galway completely lacked firepower at the front and especially missed the services of Frank Burke, who was injured, and John Connolly, who had retired.

The selectors decided to bring Connolly back for the replay. The team also spent a lot of time in Fahy's Field practising their sharpshooting. Limerick had all sorts of problems in the second game. Foley was suspended. Dom Punch and Pat Herbert were out through injury, and Michael Grimes and Leo Enright were also lost because of injury during the game. So many setbacks meant that Limerick just ran out of talent and had to bow to defeat by 4-16 to 2-17. But despite their defeat they won many friends for the tremendous courage and tenacity shown in the face of misfortune. They might claim that with a full squad they could have won; but it was Galway's victory, and Joe Connolly's contribution of 2-7 to the winning score was an impressive tally.

Galway were undoubted favourites for the All-Ireland. They had the wind advantage in the first half and at half time had a comfortable lead of 0-13 to 1-4. Things hadn't gone Offaly's way, and the pattern continued into the second half, when Galway went a further point ahead. Gradually Offaly came into the game and, inspired by Pat Delaney and Ger Coughlan in the backs and Liam Currams and Joachim Kelly at midfield, slowly reduced the deficit. At the same time Galway were not scoring: in fact for some unexplained reason their much-lauded forward line scored only two points in the second half.

The game will mainly be remembered for Johnny Flaherty's goal about five minutes from time to put Offaly unexpectedly ahead. Pat Delaney caught the sliotar and went on a solo run. He transferred to Brendan Bermingham, who made a well-timed pass to O'Flaherty. Although the latter was surrounded by goalie and defenders, he succeeded in hand-passing it over his shoulder and into the net. Diarmuid Healy had practised this goal-scoring method in training! Two further points by

Danny Owens and Pádraig Horan gave Offaly a thrilling three-point victory on a score of 2-12 to 0-15. Johnny O'Flaherty's goal was the highlight of the victory, but the five points scored by Pat Delaney from long-distance frees when Galway were very much on top were a crucial contribution to Offaly's success.

Delaney was to feature equally prominently in the aftermath of the historic victory with his singing of 'The Offaly Rover'. Perhaps the reception wasn't as large or emotional as Galway's the previous year but it was widely savoured from Tullamore to Birr and in the small area of south Offaly that produced the All-Ireland champions. The first team from the county to win a senior hurling championship was Damien Martin, T. O'Donoghue (a native of Galway living in Offaly), Eugene Coughlan, P. Fleury, A. Fogarty, Pat Delaney, Ger Coughlan, Joachim Kelly, Liam Currams, Pat Kirwan, Brendan Bermingham, Mark Corrigan, Pat Carroll, Pádraig Horan (captain), and Johnny O'Flaherty.

Offaly made a satisfactory defence of their All-Ireland crown when they defeated Wexford in the first round of the 1982 Leinster championship and qualified for the Leinster final against Kilkenny after beating Laois in a semi-final replay. Kilkenny were league champions and had annihilated Westmeath in their first-round encounter. Offaly were in front by three points with six minutes remaining; then Damien Martin, the Offaly goalkeeper, was policing the ball wide when Liam Fennelly nipped in and flicked it across the square; the incoming Matt Ruth finished it to the net for the equaliser. Offaly claimed the ball was over the line, but the goal stood, and Kilkenny got two further points to win by that margin.

Kilkenny had to play Galway in the semi-final. The westerners were striving to qualify for their fourth All-Ireland in a row and were determined to compensate for the previous year's defeat. They beat Antrim handily in the quarter-final and came into the semi with a new-look team, caused by injuries and retirements. Frank Larkin had replaced Mike Conneely in goal; Conor Hayes was centre-back in place of Seán Silke; and Ollie Kilkenny, Pierce Piggott and Brendan Lynskey were in for Sylvie Linnane, Finbarr Gantley, and John Connolly. The team were hit by a hurricane in the opening half and found themselves behind by 2-11 to 1-3 at the interval. It was too much of a deficit to reduce in the second half, and Kilkenny ran out winners by 2-20 to 2-10.

In spite of this victory Kilkenny entered the final as underdogs to a Cork team who were firm favourites as a result of the ease with which they came through Munster. They easily won their opening games against Clare and Tipperary and qualified to play Waterford (who had beaten Limerick in a thrilling contest) in the final. The Waterford men, playing in their first

Munster final since 1966, completely flopped before a brilliant Cork display and were beaten by thirty-one points.

The opening quarter of the All-Ireland was even enough, with only a point between the sides after eighteen minutes; then came what is regarded as the turning point. A brilliant save by Noel Skehan in the Kilkenny goal seemed to spark off a tremendous display in his fellow-players. By half time the Noresiders were in front by 2-10 to 0-6. Ten minutes into the second half they were fourteen points to the good, and there was no way back for Cork, and at the final whistle the score was 3-18 to 1-13. Noel Skehan's save was the first of many in the game, and his display earned him the Man of the Match award. His performance was closely followed by Christy Heffernan, who scored 2-3. The difference in class between the forward lines is shown by the fact that Kilkenny scored 3-14 from play while Cork could manage only 1-6. The Noresiders neither made a switch nor introduced a sub throughout the game. The win put Kilkenny level with Tipperary, at twenty-two titles each, the first time since 1947 that Kilkenny had drawn level.

Kilkenny created a record for the county in 1983 when they won the league and the championship for the second year in a row. The championship success didn't appear likely early in the second half of their Leinster semi-final clash with Wexford. The Slaneysiders were nine points ahead, but Kilkenny suddenly caught fire in a glorious seven-minute spell and scored 2-3 to change the look of the scoreboard. Then Christy Heffernan and Tony Walsh were sent off; this opened up more space in front of the Wexford goal, which allowed Liam Fennelly to run riot. He scored 2-1 to put Kilkenny seven points in front. At the end of this incredible game the Noresiders had a four-point advantage, 5-13 to 3-15.

The Leinster final against Offaly drew one of the biggest attendances in years. In an exciting and memorable game in which the sides were level on six occasions, Kilkenny pulled away in the end to win comfortably by seven points.

Cork were Kilkenny's opponents in the All-Ireland for the second year running. The year had started off in Munster with Tipperary recording their first senior championship success in ten years. They beat Clare but came a cropper against Waterford in the semi-final. In the other semi-final Limerick came from seven points down against Cork in the closing stages to snatch a draw. However, they were beaten by two points in the replay in Páirc Uí Chaoimh when a brilliant goal by Jimmy Barry Murphy gave Cork victory in an exciting encounter.

The final was a repeat of the previous year, and expectations were reflected in the attendance of about twenty thousand, the lowest in years.

The Laois team of 1949, the last side from the county to reach an All-Ireland final. They are shown here after their semi-final victory. **FRONT ROW** (LEFT TO RIGHT): W. DARGAN, P. RUSCHITZKO (CAPT.), P. HOGAN, T. BYRNE, J. MURRAY, T. FITZPATRICK, P. LALOR, P. FITZPATRICK, A. DUNNE, J. CONROY (CHAIRMAN, LAOIS HURLING BOARD). **BACK ROW** (LEFT TO RIGHT): P. BRIEN, S. BARRETT (SECRETARY, COUNTY BOARD), L. WHITE, L. BRADY (CHAIRMAN, COUNTY BOARD), J. BERGIN, W. BOHANE, P. KELLY, P. McCORMACK, J. STYLES, P. FARRELL, D. FORDE, K. HYLAND, H. GREY, P. FARRELL (TRAINER), T. HIGGINS (TRUSTEE), P. CAMPION (VICE CHAIRMAN, COUNTY BOARD AND CENTRAL COUNCIL DELEGATE, MEMBER OF THE COUNTY'S ALL-IRELAND WINNING TEAM OF 1915).

This photograph, taken before the Churches Tournament game between Glen Rovers (Cork) and Rathnure (Wexford) in the early 1950s, shows Christy Ring kissing the ring of Dr Lucey, Bishop of Cork. Dinny Barry Murphy is on the left and Billy Rackard of Rathnure on the right.

Leinster Council chairman, Jack Fitzgerald, presenting the Bob O'Keeffe Trophy to the Dublin captain, Jim Prior, after a sensational victory over Wexford in the 1952 Leinster final.

The Westmeath team of 1953 that played Kilkenny at Tullamore in the Leinster championship.

The Galway side of 1953, beaten All-Ireland finalists.

Action from a Wexford county championship match on 5 July 1953. The Cloughbawn
backs are beaten by a Nicky Rackard 21-yard special.

Two great rivals! Bobby Rackard (left) and Christy Ring in the 1954 final, watched by Pat Barry and Eamonn Goulding.

Wexford were the glamour team of the 1950s, and the Rackard brothers (from left) Bobbie, Nicky and Billy were probably the greatest trio of brothers ever to play championship hurling.

The Cork side of 1954 that defeated Wexford in one of the greatest of all hurling finals.

Wexford finally came good in the 1955 final when they defeated Galway. This photograph shows the throw-in at the start of the game.

The entire Wexford back line facing up to a Christy Ring 21-yard free in the 1956 All-Ireland. Ring scored.

This famous photograph brought two of the greatest hurlers of all time into unusual contact. The occasion was the Munster semi-final between Cork and Tipperary at Limerick on 30 June 1957, which Cork won by 5-2 to 1-11. In the second half Christy Ring went off with a broken wrist. As he was leaving the field he met Mick Mackey, who was doing umpire for the referee, Mick Hayes of Clare. Mackey said something, as the photograph indicates, but what it was is a matter of endless speculation.

Period photograph. The Wexford District junior hurling final played on 2 March 1958 between St Benan's and Hollow Rangers.

Ned Power, Waterford goalkeeper, makes a dramatic catch against Christy Ring of Cork in the 1959 Munster championship game.

An incident in the Waterford goalmouth in the All-Ireland final of 1959 against Kilkenny.

Goalmouth action in the 1961 final between Dublin and Tipperary. Having lost to Wexford the previous year, Tipperary won this game by a point and repeated this margin of victory against Wexford the following year. In all, Tipperary dominated the first half of the sixties, winning the championship four times between 1961 and 1965.

A dramatic moment in the second half of the 1961 final, between Dublin and Tipperary, as the referee, Gerry Fitzgerald, orders Dublin's Lar Foley to the line. On the left is Noel Drumgoole, the Dublin captain.

Kilkenny's charismatic Ollie Walsh, one of the greatest of all goalkeepers.

The New York side that played Waterford in the final of the National League at Croke Park in September 1963. **BACK ROW** (LEFT TO RIGHT): B. HENNESSY (KERRY), D. O'BRIEN (TIPPERARY), S. LAKES (KILKENNY), R. KEATING (CORK), C. O'CONNELL (KERRY), J. J. NAUGHTON (CLARE), J. QUARRY (WATERFORD), B. McGANN (OFFALY), M. SWEENEY (GALWAY). **FRONT ROW** (LEFT TO RIGHT): P. DOWLING (CORK), P. HENNESSY (TIPPERARY), B. KELLEHER (LIMERICK), J. CAREY (TIPPERARY), S. REILLY (CORK), M. MORRISSEY (WEXFORD), J. MURPHY (TIPPERARY), P. KIRBY (CLARE), B. CAREY (TIPPERARY).

One of the game's greatest stylists, Eddie Keher, raises the McCarthy Cup after captaining Kilkenny to beat Cork in the All-Ireland final of 1969. On the right is the then president of the GAA, Séamus Ó Riain.

Was he the greatest ever? Christy Ring in retirement.

This time Waterford started off better and held their own for about twenty minutes but then fell away and suffered a nineteen-point defeat. Galway provided greater opposition in the semi-final, but Cork pulled away in the end to win by 5-14 to 1-6. The game is remembered for a great goal by Jimmy Barry Murphy when he pulled on a John Fenton shot.

And so the stage was set for a repeat of the 1982 final, with Cork determined to reverse the previous year's result and Kilkenny confident of confirming their superiority. The game was a disappointment, badly affected by a strong wind that blew from the Railway goal. The basis of Kilkenny's superiority was a brilliant display by Billy Fitzpatrick, who was a thorn in Cork's side throughout the game and scored ten points in all. He was greatly helped by a superb Frank Cummins at centrefield. Joe Hennessy was also excellent at right-half-back; A *little Hennessy beats your Murphy's* read one banner. Cork struggled to stave off defeat during the final quarter and did reduce their deficit to two points but failed to convert opportunities to scores.

For Noel Skehan the victory brought a record ninth All-Ireland senior medal; but although the number is greater than that won by Christy Ring or John Doyle it does not carry the same distinction, as three of them— 1963, 1967, and 1969—were won as a sub to Ollie Walsh. The remaining six were won in 1972, 1974, 1975, 1979, 1982, and 1983. Liam Fennelly joined his brother Ger as a winning captain, the first time that brothers had captained senior All-Ireland winning teams. The final score of 2-14 to 2-12 was exactly the same as when Kilkenny beat Limerick in the National League final earlier in the year.

The centenary year of the GAA brought greater than usual interest in the senior hurling championship. The All-Ireland champions, Kilkenny, started out with the ambition of making it three in a row but had their dream shattered by Wexford in the Leinster semi-final with a goal by Tony Doran two minutes from time. Brian Cody's absence from full-back was keenly felt.

Wexford's hopes of a first provincial victory since 1977 came to grief in the final against Offaly. Whether it was the heat or the effects of age (five of the Slaneysiders were in their thirties, including Tony Doran at thirty-eight), Wexford were dead for the first twenty-five minutes as Offaly went into a lead of eight points to nil; but they got going after that and were only three points in arrears at the interval. But they reverted to their earlier form in the second half and Offaly went into a five-point lead, which a late Wexford rally reduced to one point. But it was Offaly's victory and further disappointment for Wexford, who had earlier lost the league final to Limerick. Offaly's brilliant defensive play had won the day, particularly that of Eugene Coughlan at full-back, who held Tony Doran to a solitary point.

Cork came through in Munster. Earlier they had lost the league semi-final to Wexford but captured the Centenary Cup, organised on the 'open draw' system for 1984. In the Munster semi-final they beat Limerick by five points. In the second semi-final Tipperary beat Clare as a result of a penalty goal in the last minute and qualified for their first Munster final since 1973. The game was played in the renovated Semple Stadium, where over fifty thousand came to see Cork and Tipperary renew their ancient rivalry. And the game lived up to expectation, full of passion and excitement and with a dramatic ending. Cork were in the lead early, but a Nicky English goal gave Tipperary renewed hope. This was translated into a superb performance in the second half, and Tipperary seemed poised for success with seven minutes to go. Then the direction of the game changed completely. A hand-pass in the Tipperary forward line from Mick Doyle to Nicky English was intercepted by Denis Mulcahy, cleared, and picked up by Tony O'Sullivan for Cork. He sent a high ball towards the Tipperary goal, where it was brought down by John Sheedy, but the incoming Seánie O'Leary rushed it to the net for a goal. In the remaining minutes Cork scored a further 1-2 to transform a four-point deficit into a four-point victory by 4-15 to 3-14.

In one of the two All-Ireland semi-finals in 1984 Offaly had a comprehensive fifteen-point victory over Galway. It was a terrible defeat for the westerners, who had been serious contenders for All-Ireland honours a couple of years previously and who would defeat Cork at the same point of the competition the following year. In the second game Antrim, making their first appearance since 1954, were well beaten by Cork.

The All-Ireland was played in Thurles—the first time outside Croke Park since 1937—as the high point of the GAA centenary year. It did not live up to expectations, as Cork were so dominant: although slow to settle in the first half, they coasted to victory. Leading by two points at half time, Cork scored 1-6 without reply in the second half and were ahead by 3-16 to 1-12 at the final whistle. Beyond doubt the feature of the game was the performance of John Crowley at centre-back, one of the greatest ever seen. Not too far behind was the display of John Fenton, who captained the side in magnificent style and, as well as giving Cork a decisive edge at midfield, scored seven points.

Offaly were disappointed with their display in the Centenary final but put it behind them by winning the 1985 All-Ireland. Their prospects didn't look good early in the second half against Kilkenny in the Leinster semi-final, when they trailed by nine points; but they hauled themselves back into the game and forced a draw, going on later to win the replay. At the other side of the draw, unpredictable Wexford were defeated by Laois.

Offaly hadn't much problem in the final and beat their neighbours by 5-15 to 0-17.

In Munster, Cork and Tipperary qualified for the provincial final, and Tipperary agreed to travel to Páirc Uí Chaoimh for the game. Nearly fifty thousand turned up for a repetition of the 1984 epic. It wasn't as good but continued to be exciting and the verdict doubtful until the last quarter. At half time Cork were in front by two points, and Tipperary could bemoan the concession of soft goals during the opening period. The game remained poised until the final quarter, when Cork turned on the power and won by 4-17 to 4-11.

Cork looked good to qualify for the All-Ireland but were shocked by Galway in the semi-final. On a day totally unsuited to hurling less than nine thousand were in attendance. Hardly anybody from Cork travelled, and only the most loyal of Galway supporters turned up: they had too many memories of the previous year. Cork won the toss and chose to play against wind and rain and were probably quite happy to trail by a point at half time. They went further ahead before Galway suddenly came alive with goals by Lynskey, Cooney, and Lane, together with a number of points, and went ten points in front with ten minutes to go. Cork rallied and scored a couple of goals, but Galway were safely through and won by 4-12 to 5-5.

In the second semi-final, played at Armagh, Offaly had a fourteen-point victory over Antrim. This game marked the last appearance of Pat Carroll, one of Offaly's best forwards, who started the game but was unable to continue. He was to die in 1986.

Galway were favourites for the All-Ireland. They had a new-look team and a completely new half-back line in Peter Finnerty, Tony Keady, and Tony Kilkenny. Offaly had ten of the team that succeeded against the same opposition in 1981; although they had lost the 1984 final they had gained from the experience and had the satisfaction of having beaten Galway in the 1984 semi-final. It was not a great final, though keenly contested, with the verdict in doubt until the final whistle. The second half had barely started when Offaly increased their two-point lead by a goal from Pat Cleary, who was also responsible for the first-half goal. They went further ahead before Galway rallied and a P. J. Molloy goal followed by a few points brought the westerners back into the game. Paddy Corrigan steadied Offaly again with two points, and a great point by Pádraig Horan from the sideline put the seal of victory on Offaly's efforts. The score was 2-11 to 1-12, giving Offaly their second All-Ireland victory in five years. It was a fine performance, one of the best coming from the oldest player, Pádraig Horan.

Offaly failed to get out of Leinster in 1986. Six teams contested the provincial championships, with Westmeath and Wexford making their departures in the quarter-finals. Kilkenny and Offaly qualified for the final by victories over Dublin and Laois. The Noresiders had a comfortable eight-point victory over the champions and qualified to play Galway in the semi-final. In Munster, Cork came through as a result of victories over Waterford and Clare. The latter, who had put an end to Tipperary's hopes, gave the Leesiders a run for their money in the final at Killarney. Cork looked vulnerable in defence and had some anxious moments before winning by three points.

The semi-finals were played at separate venues. Cork, without Pat Hartnett and John Fenton, struggled to beat Antrim by five points in Croke Park. The Northerners, who were superbly fit, revealed some great point-scoring ability and notched up 1-24 to Cork's 7-11. Much of their effort was offset by the concession of soft goals. The second semi-final was played in Thurles, and Galway made the hurling world sit up by shattering Kilkenny's hopes with an eleven-point defeat. Galway baffled their opponents by playing a two-man full-forward line of Joe Cooney and Noel Lane. Outside they varied between a four-man half-forward line and a three-man centrefield. Kilkenny's backs were at sixes and sevens trying to find a forward to mark while Galway notched up the scores. It was Galway's first championship victory over the Black and Amber since 1953 and sweet revenge for their defeat by the same opponents in the league semi-final the previous May.

The tactics Galway employed to such effect against Kilkenny backfired against Cork in the All-Ireland. Galway were favourites, as Cork, unimpressive so far and suffering from injury problems, were not expected to contain the brilliant Galway attack. It was also recalled that Galway had beaten the same opposition in the 1985 All-Ireland semi-final. On the day, the underdogs had their revenge on the pundits, and Cork took control of the proceedings from an early stage. Although playing against the wind, they had two goals by John Fenton and Kevin Hennessy in the opening ten minutes. The Galway tactic of the two-man full-forward line was not working. John Crowley, left alone at corner-back, stayed in his position, catching and clearing the ball from Galway's attacks. This gave a boost to Cork and forced Galway to revert to the orthodox full-forward line. An injury to John Fenton upset Cork's rhythm, and Galway rallied to draw level by the interval. The game remained poised until about the thirteenth minute when Tomás Mulcahy scored a spectacular goal for Cork. He collected a puck-out from Ger Cunningham and soloed over fifty yards before planting the ball in the net. This set Cork on the road to victory, and their four-point win, by 4-13 to 2-15, did not flatter them.

As well as Galway's tactics in the full-forward line, the decision to play Sylvie Linnane at full-back and Conor Hayes at corner-back was blamed for their defeat. Galway were also critical of some refereeing decisions, particularly the failure to blow up Tomás Mulcahy for allegedly carrying the ball too far when he scored the vital goal in the second half. The victory, their twenty-sixth, gave Cork immense satisfaction, and all the players were acclaimed as heroes. It was Jimmy Barry Murphy's last championship game, as he was to retire the following spring.

It was a case of third time lucky for Galway in 1987. Having suffered the disappointment of two successive defeats in the 1985 and 1986 All-Irelands, they were to come good at the third attempt. Before that they had to overcome Tipperary in the semi-final. The Premier County had been occupying a back seat since 1971. They had made a brief impact in 1973, 1976, 1979, when they won the National League, and 1984; but the state of the senior hurling team had become a matter of general depression as year after year revealed further failures to get out of Munster.

In July 1986 it was decided to appoint Babs Keating as manager, and he chose as his two assistants Donie Nealon and Theo English. Their brief was to put Tipperary back on the hurling map. Some progress was made in the league, which came to an end in a semi-final defeat by Clare. In the championship Kerry and Clare, after a replay, were overcome to qualify for the Munster final against Cork. Semple Stadium was crowded for the occasion, and the sense of expectancy was overpowering. Tipperary proved they could outhurl Cork, but lapses in concentration at vital times nearly gave Cork the game; a draw was the result after two last-minute points by Pat Fox. The replay at Killarney ended in a draw, and in extra time Tipperary, shaking off at last the mantle of defeat, won by 4-22 to 1-22, and the magnificence of the victory was matched by Richard Stakelum's emotional acceptance speech.

In Leinster, Kilkenny came through after a brilliant contest with Offaly. Fielding fourteen of the players who had been outmanoeuvred by Galway in the previous year's semi-final, the Noresiders showed pace, precision and traditional skills in beating the Offaly men by 2-14 to 0-17. The winners travelled to Dundalk to play Antrim in the semi-final. The northerners, who had given a warning to Cork the previous year that they were no longer a push-over, made Kilkenny work hard for their seven-point victory. In fact they had to come back after a poor start that saw them conceding 1-5 in the first twelve minutes without registering a score; but, inspired by two goals from Harry Ryan in the second half, they found their form in the closing seven minutes and scored seven points without reply from Antrim to win by 2-18 to 2-11.

In the second semi-final at Croke Park one of the biggest crowds for years came to see Galway and Tipperary fight it out in an epic contest in which the experience of Galway triumphed over the newness and lack of experience of Tipperary. Galway were league champions and had been at or near the top for a good number of years. The speed and criss-crossing movements of their forwards baffled the Tipperary backs in the opening half, which saw the westerners leading by seven points. A goal from a penalty by Pat Fox before the interval evened matters a little. A Tipperary revival continued in the second half, and they reduced Galway's lead to a point; then a great Martin McGrath run for Tipperary went wide off the post. There was a second setback when a late tackle on the Galway goalkeeper, after Tipperary had got a point, resulted in a free out, which brought about a Galway goal. Both these developments were crucial, and Galway, who proved fresher and better on the day, went on to win by six points.

The All-Ireland final between Galway and Kilkenny was a tough game played in a tense atmosphere. In a low-scoring first half Galway had a point to spare at half time. Early in the second half Kilkenny took the lead for the first time, but Galway stormed back to regain it. A couple of fine saves by the Galway goalkeeper, John Commins, at one end with the only goal of the game by Noel Lane at the other finally put the game Galway's way, and they had six points to spare at the final whistle on a score of 1-12 to 0-9. Star of the winners was Gerry McInerney at wing-back, who had returned from New York for the final. He played a good first half and a storming second, during which he stymied many Kilkenny attacks and set up opportunities for his own forwards. Other architects of Galway's success were Steve Mahon at centrefield and John Commins in goal.

It was one of the lowest-scoring finals for years; Kilkenny hadn't scored as little in an All-Ireland since 1937, when they recorded a mere three points. In fact the defeat signalled the end of the Kilkenny team, and they were not to win another Leinster final until 1991. There was a great feeling of relief in Galway at the win. It was the first time the county had achieved the league-championship double. In October they added the Railway Cup to their list of trophies, and they won the Oireachtas trophy by beating Wexford the following year. The supremacy of Galway hurling was reflected in the All-Stars team, which included Conor Hayes, Ollie Kilkenny, Pete Finnerty, Steve Mahon, Michael McGrath, and Joe Cooney, with Cooney also taking the Texaco Hurler of the Year award.

Galway made it two in a row in 1988 by beating Tipperary in the final. The Premier County beat Cork comprehensively in the Munster final in Limerick. The Leesiders were a shadow of their best, and yet they could, with luck at the right time, have beaten Tipperary. An interval lead of eleven points was reduced to two during the second half, but Tipperary survived the fright and had nine points to spare at the final whistle. In Leinster, Offaly became champions once again after a lapse of two years, beating Wexford by four points in the final. The Slaneysiders, having beaten Kilkenny, fancied their chances against Offaly, who were less than promising in their opening match against Dublin. However, through grit and skill and some fine individual performances, Offaly came through.

The semi-finals were played in Croke Park on 7 August. Galway and Offaly were an intriguing pairing: they hadn't met in the championship since 1985, when Offaly were supreme. In the league quarter-final earlier in the year Offaly got the verdict by a solitary point. Offaly had lined out with Pat Delaney and Eugene Coughlan in the unusual positions of centre-forward and full-forward, respectively, but the team had an unbalanced look. Martin Naughton gave one of his best performances, causing the Offaly defence a lot of worries with his zigzag runs and scoring 1-5. Noel Lane also had a fine game. In the end Galway were in front by 3-18 to 3-11, after a late Offaly rally.

In the first semi-final Tipperary were not very convincing in beating Antrim by eight points. They went into the game as solid favourites, with the National League and the Munster final on their record, but came up against an Antrim team who had shown progress in the previous two years and had players like McFettridge, McAllister, McNaughton, and Barr. The final score was 3-15 to 2-10 in Tipperary's favour.

There was a great deal of hype and expectation about the All-Ireland final, much of it the product of the high-profile managers, Cyril Farrell and Babs Keating. The media had latched on to Tipperary in a big way, as it was the first time in seventeen years for the county to qualify for an All-Ireland. In his book *The Right to Win*, Cyril Farrell reveals his annoyance: 'Everywhere you turned it was Tipperary ... Tipperary ... Tipperary ... We were the defending champions but we seemed to be no more than bit-players to the great blue and gold show.' A talking-point when the side was announced was the dropping of the captain, Pa O'Neill, and his replacement with John Leahy and the captaincy going to the glamour figure Nicky English. (It was suggested by some of Keating's critics that as victory was assured, English was chosen because he could make a good acceptance speech.) Meanwhile in Athenry, Galway were training away, and the mentors—Cyril Farrell, Phelim Murphy, and Bernie O'Connor—were plotting the downfall of Tipperary.

Tipperary opted to play against the wind and felt in a strong position at half time though behind by 0-10 to 0-6. Thirteen minutes after the resumption they appeared to be on the road to victory, trailing by a mere point; but Galway clung on, and the defensive work of Peter Finnerty, Tony Keady and Gerry McInerney prevented Tipperary from getting on top. The introduction of Noel Lane in the second half was also to have a crucial influence on the outcome. Near the end he got clear of his marker and scored the only goal of the match to wrap up victory for Galway, 1-15 to 0-14, in a repeat of his performance the previous year. Just before he scored, John Commins had saved a blistering shot from Pat Fox. It was a historic occasion for Galway and for Conor Hayes, who was receiving the Liam McCarthy Cup for the second time. He also had the satisfaction of containing the best efforts of Nicky English. The winning goalkeeper, John Commins, had the distinction of keeping a clean sheet in consecutive finals.

Two things stand out in the 1989 final: Tipperary's first victory in eighteen years, and Antrim's first appearance since 1943. Tipperary came through Munster with an easy win over Waterford, who had put Cork out of the championship in a replay. Because of the expectation of a Cork-Tipperary final, RTE and the Munster Council made a decision to televise the match. What the viewers got was a poor game, a bad advertisement for hurling, and a runaway victory for Tipperary in the second half, after two Waterford players had got the sideline. In Leinster, Offaly had three points to spare over Kilkenny in a hard-fought final in which the Noresiders came out with a late surge. Mark Corrigan had a brilliant game at wing-forward. The final score was 3-15 to 4-9 in Offaly's favour.

The Ulster senior championship was revived after forty-three years. A new trophy, the Liam Harvey Cup (after a former Antrim County Board chairman), was presented. Antrim beat Down in the final, and this earned them a place in the quarter-final, in which they beat the B champions, Kildare.

Offaly and Antrim had met once previously in the All-Ireland championship, in 1985, when Offaly won comfortably. They were also expected to beat Antrim on this occasion. Although Antrim had troubled Kilkenny, Cork and Tipperary during the previous three years and had qualified for division 1 of the National Hurling League for the 1988/89 season, they were not expected to be good enough for the Leinster champions. What surprised most people was that Antrim not only won but had three goals to spare on a score of 4-15 to 1-15. The northerners, prepared for the game by Jim Nelson, put in such a storming finish that Offaly hadn't the legs to keep up with them.

The lead-up to the second semi-final was dominated by the Tony Keady affair: Keady had been suspended for playing in the United States without clearance. In addition, Galway had to line out without the injured Martin Naughton and Noel Lane. Éanna Ryan gave Galway a great start with a goal in the first minute, but, after scoring a point soon after, they failed to score for seventeen minutes, during which Tipperary played a blinder. Galway woke up again before half time, and another Ryan goal had them only two points in arrears before the interval. Tipperary pulled ahead in the second half with a brilliant Pat Fox goal and went six points in front. Then Galway suffered two body blows: Sylvie Linnane was sent off for a foul on Nicky English, and ten minutes from the end Hopper McGrath got his marching orders for a high tackle on Conor O'Donovan. Despite these setbacks Galway held on grimly until the final whistle. Galway were angry at the defeat. They were critical of some refereeing decisions, the dismissal of two of their players, and the failure of the referee, John Denton of Wexford, to punish two Tipperary players for serious infringements of the rules. The events during the game, together with the earlier suspension of Keady, soured relations with Croke Park.

Antrim were complete outsiders on All-Ireland day; nevertheless they brought a huge and colourful crowd of committed supporters to Croke Park. Never before had Antrim and Tipperary met in a final, and it was the first time in over fifty years that not one player on either panel was the holder of an All-Ireland senior medal. The opening fifteen minutes were keenly contested, with advantage going to neither side. Antrim squandered a number of good scoring chances. The match turned Tipperary's way after nineteen minutes when a lobbed shot from Declan Ryan deceived the Antrim goalkeeper, Niall Paterson, and went straight to the net. After this Tipperary never looked back and were in front by 1-13 to 0-5 at the interval. They continued to score in the second half and by the final whistle had notched up 4-24, of which 2-12, the official record for an individual score, came from Nicky English. Antrim scored three goals during the second half to give them a more respectable total of 3-9.

When Bobby Ryan received the McCarthy Cup, the first time it came to Tipperary since 1971, there was a great sense of delight and relief and a distinct feeling that the hurling famine in the county had come to an end. English got Man of the Match for his fine scoring performance, his second goal on a par with the best. He was closely followed in the honours list by Declan Carr, who had played an excellent game at midfield.

When Tipperary set out in defence of their championship in 1990 they were going for a fourth Munster final in a row, something they had never achieved up to then. Although Limerick were just about beaten in the semi-final, a game that saw the dismissal of the Limerick full-back Mick Barron, Tipperary's confidence was fairly high going into the final against

Cork, who hadn't impressed against Waterford. In fact in some areas there was a tendency to look beyond Munster to more important opposition on the horizon. An unwise remark by Babs Keating, in which he appeared to imply that Cork's chances of winning were as good as those of a donkey winning the Derby, turned out to be a marvellous spur to Cork and their motivation to beat Tipperary. On a day when Cork hurled out of their skins and many things—including some questionable selection decisions—went wrong for Tipperary, the Leesiders scored a glorious triumph by 4-16 to 2-12.

Offaly came through Leinster as a result of a victory over Dublin by 1-19 to 2-11. Dublin, who had reached the semi-final of the league, beat Wexford in a tight finish in the semi-final. Offaly hammered Kilkenny in the other semi-final: at one point they led by 3-7 to nil, and the final score was 4-15 to 1-8. In the final Offaly were in control all through, with Dublin's rally coming late in the game.

Galway were Offaly's opponents in the All-Ireland semi-final, but the Leinster champions put up a poor performance. They were behind by nine points at half time and didn't improve after the break. Galway won by 1-16 to 2-7, with 1-2 of Offaly's total coming in the last six minutes. In the second semi-final Cork played Antrim and were well held until the third quarter. The Leesiders found it difficult to come to terms with the hard-tackling northern side but eventually won by 2-20 to 1-13.

Perhaps because Cork didn't have matters all their own way against Antrim, and also because they hadn't been expected to be in the All-Ireland, Galway were the favourites. They had displayed their great power and experience against Offaly and revealed a fast-moving forward line—with Martin Naughton back in his first championship match in two years—an outstanding half-back line, and a new centrefield find in Michael Coleman. The tag of favourites seemed justified, as Galway led by seven points after ten minutes of the second half and appeared to be coasting to victory; then in the following nineteen minutes Cork scored 4-3 as Galway inexplicably collapsed.

Many explanations have been offered for the dramatic turn in fortunes. Cork had the breeze in the second half. Ger Cunningham began to rain his deliveries down on the Galway half-back line and create excellent opportunities for his forwards, and the transfer of Tomás Mulcahy to centre-forward in the second half helped Cork make greater use of these deliveries. On the Galway side Joe Cooney's excellent showing against Jim Cashman in the first half did not continue after half time. The supply dried up as it came to the Cork half-forward line in the second half. Galway were critical of a number of refereeing decisions. Éanna Ryan had the ball in the net in the first half, only to be whistled back for a free. A piledriver from Martin Naughton was brilliantly saved by Ger Cunningham and turned out for a sixty-five; incredibly, the referee gave a puck-out instead, which resulted in a point for Cork. But it was Cork's day and the end of an unbelievable championship for them. Twice they had upset the odds and carried off the laurels. The final score was 5-15 to 2-21 in a game that had plenty of excitement, fine individual performances, and an abundance of commitment, skill, and determination. When Tomás Mulcahy received the McCarthy Cup he became the last Cork captain to receive it, as it was replaced in 1992.

Cork seemed to be heading for a successful defence of their title eighteen minutes into the first half of the 1991 Munster final at Páirc Uí Chaoimh. They had three goals in the Tipperary net, and it didn't appear as if the Blue and Gold could rally. But they did, and they were only four points behind at half time, 3-5 to 1-7. Fitzgibbon got another goal for Cork soon after the resumption, but a couple of Tipperary replacements, Aidan Ryan and Michael Ryan, and some reshuffling of the pack brought about another rally. Tipperary levelled. Cork went ahead, and it took a Pat Fox point in the final minute to equalise: Cork 4-10, Tipperary 2-16. It was a marvellous match, and the replay was to be even more exciting.

Again Cork held the whip hand for long periods. They led by four points at the break and pushed that to nine in the middle of the second half. In a final quarter full of excitement and drama Tipperary clawed their way back and came through by a four-point margin, 4-19 to 4-15. It was sweet revenge for defeat at the same venue the previous year and ensured that the old rivalry was given renewed life. Nicky English didn't play, because of injury. Many things stand out in a memorable game; the brilliant performance of John Leahy, the superb goal by Aidan Ryan and the invasion by a crowd led by a man in a wheelchair are just some of them.

Meanwhile in Leinster, Kilkenny defeated Dublin in an unlikely final pairing. Earlier the Noresiders had two points to spare over their old rivals Wexford, while Offaly were stopped from going for a fourth in a row by Dublin. The latter proved difficult enough in the final, and Kilkenny eventually came through by two points, 1-13 to 1-11.

Croke Park was packed for the All-Ireland semi-finals. Tipperary renewed acquaintance with a Galway team that included five new players and was short Éanna Ryan through injury. In twenty-five minutes Tipperary built up the unimaginable lead of 2-5 to 0-2. Galway then hit their best spot and scored 1-3 in eight minutes, but the Munster champions struck back again to lead by six points at the interval. In an undistinguished second half Tipperary maintained their superiority and had ten points to spare at the final whistle with a score of 3-13 to 1-9. In the second semi-final Kilkenny escaped by a late goal to defeat a determined Antrim side by 2-18 to 1-19. Earlier Antrim had beaten Down to take the Ulster title and had an eight-point victory over Westmeath in the All-Ireland quarter-final.

Tipperary were favourites for the All-Ireland. The basic reason was Kilkenny's performance in their three championship games to the final, in which late goals helped them to escape apparent lost causes. In a performance that seemed to lack conviction Tipperary were given many anxious moments and were fortunate to be level at half time. Ten minutes into the second half they were a point in front when a mis-hit Michael Cleary free went all the way to the Kilkenny net. The score gave Tipperary more poise and confidence, but they were unable to pull away from Kilkenny. With seven minutes to go there was a goal between the sides, but try as they might, Kilkenny could not reduce the arrears, and it was Pat Fox who secured victory for Tipperary with a point near the call of time, with a final score of 1-16 to 0-15. Michael Cleary with 1-6 and D. J. Carey with 0-9 were the top scorers, and Declan Carr had the distinction of receiving the old Liam McCarthy Cup for the last time. For Tipperary fans it may not have been a spectacular performance, but the team had won the championship for the twenty-fourth time, beating most of the important hurling counties: Limerick, Cork, Galway, and Kilkenny.

Tipperary looked good enough at the start of the 1992 season to repeat their championship win of the previous year. Easily qualifying for the knock-out stages of the league, they beat Galway in the semi-final and looked good at half time in the final against Limerick, leading by eleven points to three. The second half saw a different Limerick, who upset all the half-time predictions and were a point in front for a sensational come-back. Tipperary supporters tried to put a gloss on the defeat by claiming prior interest in the championship, but this did not hold up, as the old rivals, Cork, preserved their unbeaten championship record in Páirc Uí Chaoimh and beat Tipperary by a goal. The Leesiders went on to beat Limerick by 1-22 to 3-11 in the final, extending their dominance over Limerick in provincial deciders and in doing so reversing the result of the league semi-final.

In Leinster, Wexford, seeking to reverse a trail of defeat that stretched back to 1977, had brought in Cyril Farrell in the summer. The team were lucky to get past Laois in the first round, having to do with fourteen men for most of the game after Jimmy Holohan was sent off. Dublin were overcome in the semi-final, and plenty of preparation and training was put in for the clash with Kilkenny, who beat Offaly in the other semi-final. Whatever kind of motivation stirred Kilkenny that day is not known, but it was enough to make them produce some brilliant hurling in the opening twenty minutes. They simply cleaned out Wexford, and by the time the latter had got to grips with the situation it was too late. When the final whistle sounded, Kilkenny had won by 3-16 to 2-9.

Down made history when they won the Ulster final for the first time since 1941, beating Antrim. Having lost five All-Ireland B finals between 1974 and 1988, they decided to appoint the former Antrim manager Seán McGuinness as coach in the wake of the revival of the Ulster senior hurling championship in 1989. McGuinness succeeded in breaking down the barriers that existed between the members of the three clubs that made up the team, Ballycran, Ballygalget, and Portaferry. A breakthrough came in the 1990/91 league campaign when they beat Offaly. In the reorganisation of the league the following year they found themselves in division 1 and in the way of top competition. They gave Antrim a good run in the 1991 Ulster final but suffered their third successive defeat. They were more determined and more confident in 1992 and scored a spectacular victory over a team that had always held the whip hand. In a historic win they scored 2-6 to Antrim's 0-11, and Noel Sands became the first Down man to receive the Harvey Cup. Before Down's All-Ireland semi-final, bookies in Cork were offering odds of fifty to one against a northern victory. While Down did indeed lose to the Leesiders, by 2-17 to 1-11, they were by no means disgraced on their first visit to Croke Park.

In the second semi-final Kilkenny beat Galway by 2-13 to 1-12. This was a touch-and-go game that may have been decided by some unusual switches by the Galway selectors. At half time it appeared to be Galway's game. However, Kilkenny won, though not impressively.

Kilkenny went into the final as outsiders and, having won the toss, decided to play against the wind. After a bright start that gave them a point it was Cork who settled down and scored five points without reply. Kilkenny came back into the game with a D. J. Carey penalty before half time, which left them only two points in arrears and the wind with them in the second half. They got a great uplift with the introduction of Christy Heffernan and a kicked goal by John Power. Another important move was changing Michael Phelan from centrefield to full-forward. All of this ensured that Kilkenny were in front by five points with about thirteen minutes remaining. Cork were revived with a Ger Manley goal, but it was to be Kilkenny's day, and they were in front by 3-10 to 1-12 at the end. Liam Fennelly had the honour of receiving the new Liam McCarthy Cup for the first time. It was Kilkenny's twenty-fourth All-Ireland win.

Kilkenny made it two in a row in 1993. They just survived the opening round against Offaly. John Power won a penalty for the Noresiders near the end, but Offaly claimed it should have been a free out for overcarrying the ball. Kilkenny went on to beat the B champions, Carlow, in the semi-final. On the other side of the draw, Wexford, after a marathon three-match league final, which they eventually lost to Cork, beat Dublin and Laois to qualify for the final. This was probably the best hurling match of 1993, and Kilkenny grabbed a dramatic draw with the final puck of the ball. Trailing by four points with about as many minutes to go, they scored four points in quick succession to earn a replay. Wexford rearranged their team for this game, but it didn't work out. The long league campaign had probably taken its toll, and an early Kilkenny goal from D. J. Carey didn't help. The final score was 2-12 to 0-11 in favour of the Noresiders.

In Munster, Kerry shocked the hurling world by beating Waterford in the first round but fell badly against Tipperary in the semi-final. The other sensation was the defeat of the league champions, Cork, by a Clare team who impressed greatly on the day. But the Banner men failed to reproduce the form in the Munster final, and Tipperary had the easiest of victories by 3-27 to 2-12.

Tipperary were favourites against Galway in the All-Ireland semi-final. A big talking-point before the game was the replacement of the centre-back Michael O'Meara by Bobby Ryan, the second occasion on which Babs Keating was to drop a captain. Tipperary started off well enough with two points, but then a soft goal by Hopper McGrath gave Galway a boost. Between that and half time Declan Ryan and Colm Bonnar were replaced by Pat Fox and Conor Stakelum. Galway were seven points ahead at the interval. Tipperary made a comeback to three points but somehow could never get on top of Galway. They had a third injury in the second half when Raymie Ryan had to be replaced after a collision with Paul Delaney. In the end Galway won by 1-16 to 1-14. They were deserving winners, and Tipperary were left to bemoan their injuries, some questionable selection decisions, and above all a performance that left a lot to be desired after the euphoria that followed the victory over Clare.

In the second semi-final Kilkenny beat Antrim by 4-18 to 1-9. Antrim put up a brave show in the first half and stayed with the champions until the interval, but Kilkenny proved unbeatable in the second half.

Kilkenny made it two in a row, as they had a decade earlier, when they defeated Galway by 2-17 to 1-15, a score that was a bit unfair to Galway. Adrian Ronan got Kilkenny off to the best possible start with a goal after two minutes, and the Noresiders dominated the first half. Galway were fortunate to be only two points behind at the interval as a result of a soft goal by Liam Burke following a fumble by the Kilkenny goalkeeper, Michael Walsh. The westerners played great hurling in the second half, with brilliant performances coming from Pádraig Kelly, Pat Malone and Joe Rabbitte in particular. They came within a point of Kilkenny, and Joe Cooney missed a reasonably easy free to level. A little later the same player, under pressure, hand-passed a ball to a colleague around midfield. The ball went over the side and from the sideline puck came to P. J. Delaney. He rounded Seán Treacy and Murt Killilea and put the ball past the goalkeeper, Richard Burke. Soon afterwards he scored a point, and another followed from D. J. Carey. Galway's only response was a point by Michael McGrath, and Kilkenny won their twenty-fifth title by a margin of five points. One of the outstanding performances was that of Pat O'Neill at centre-back, closely followed by Adrian Ronan and P. J. Delaney. Ronan, who was excluded from the starting fifteen in the previous two years, had the satisfaction of scoring 1-2. One of the best contests of the day was between Gerry McInerney at centre-back for Galway and his opposite, John Power of Kilkenny. Both very strong players, they cancelled each other out, with Power getting away from his marker for a glorious point towards the end of the game. For Galway there was nothing but a look back to wasted chances and to the unfortunate mislaid hand-pass, which provided Kilkenny with the chance to turn the game their way.

The question at the beginning of the 1994 championship was whether Kilkenny could make it three in a row. They had plenty of craft and experience, but there was a question mark over dedication and commitment. By the time the 1993 All-Ireland was over the players were already looking for the spoils of victory. In his acceptance speech the captain, Eddie O'Connor, put in his claim for a holiday in the sun. His request and the occasion of it caused controversy, and the whole episode did not augur well for 1994 and for the kind of effort that would be required to win another All-Ireland.

The team's position and state of preparedness was revealed somewhat in the quarter-final of the league when they played Tipperary in Croke Park. Their first game was against Meath on 5 June, when they had a comfortable eleven-point victory. Three weeks later they made their exit from the 1994 championship when they were beaten 2-16 to 3-9 by Offaly. At the other side of the draw Wexford took two games to beat Dublin before comprehensively defeating Laois to qualify for the Leinster final. Defeat was to be their lot once again. Having recovered from a shaky start, they drew level with Offaly at six points each. But the Offaly men struck almost immediately when a Billy Dooley shot gave Damien Fitzhenry no chance in the Wexford goal. The Wexford men found themselves six points behind at the interval and a further one soon after the restart. The Slaneysiders did their best, and the introduction of George O'Connor seemed to give hope; but poor shooting and a series of unforced errors ensured that at the final whistle they were behind Offaly by seven points, 1-18 to 0-14.

Meanwhile in Munster there were a number of unexpected results. Tipperary were brilliant in the league final and seemed set to sweep through Munster and certainly to beat Clare in the first-round game: they had waltzed through them in 1993. However, Tipperary had a number of injury problems. Out were Leahy, the star of the league final, Fox, Delaney, Hayes, and English. They also had to contend with a Clare team that had reason to avenge the humiliation of the 1993 final. On the positive side they had the memory of their victory over Cork at the same stage of the competition the previous year. The result, 2-11 to 0-13 in Clare's favour, rocked the hurling world and dramatically reversed Tipperary's eighteen-point margin in the 1993 Munster final. Having defeated Kerry in the semi-final, Clare's opponents in the final were Limerick, who had beaten Cork and Waterford. As Clare had beaten Limerick in the 1993 championship, their hopes and expectations were that they would win their first Munster final since 1932. Instead they were a sad disappointment, never really got going, and gave Limerick one of their easier Munster final victories on the score 0-25 to 2-10.

Limerick were impressive against Antrim in the All-Ireland semi-final. Admittedly the opposition were poor on the day and in no way on a par with the team that qualified for the 1989 All-Ireland. After fourteen minutes the Munster champions were leading by nine points; the winning margin was eventually 2-23 to 0-11. Galway had high hopes after their near miss in the 1993 final against Kilkenny, but they met an Offaly team that was better than them on the day. Galway had long periods of dominance and yet were beaten by 1-3. Offaly's success was aided by some Galway injuries and doubtful selection decisions. The absence of Pat Malone was a big loss; the placing of the brilliant wing-back Pádraig Kelly at centrefield and, later, corner-forward just didn't work; some of the finishing of the Galway forwards was bad. But none of this was to take from the worthiness of Offaly's success. When Galway threatened in the second half, the Offaly back line proved its mettle and the whole team turned their game up a gear, so much so that they had a six-point margin, 2-13 to 1-10. Billy Dooley's late goal proved decisive.

Offaly, with victories over Kilkenny, Wexford, and Galway, seemed to be the better chance for the All-Ireland. Limerick looked better in the first half and deserved their lead of six points—in fact but for some poor shooting they might have been further ahead. Offaly had a fortuitous goal from a rather doubtful penalty, giving a better look to the scoreboard than their play deserved. They scored four unanswered points soon after the resumption and threatened to take control; but Limerick pulled away again and were five points in front with five minutes remaining. Then Billy Dooley was fouled and a twenty-metre free awarded. Limerick were careless about guarding their goal; Johnny Dooley decided to chance the goal, and scored. The ball wasn't well pucked out when Offaly were back again and the substitute Pat O'Connor banged in another goal, to give Offaly the lead. During the remaining few minutes a rampant Offaly sent over five more points, to change their deficit of five points into a winning margin of six points, 3-16 to 2-13. It was an incredible victory for the Offaly men and an outstanding achievement for a team from such a small hurling area. When Martin Hanamy received the McCarthy Cup he became the second player from St Rynagh's club to have the honour.

For Limerick there was the unbelievable taste of defeat after victory had been so tantalisingly close. Ironically, it was a Limerick man, Éamon Cregan, who was in charge of the team that swiped the cup from his countymen's grasp.

15

Other Hurling Championships

I n the early days of the GAA the only unit recognised for games was the club, and there was only one grade. The clubs that won the county hurling championships represented the counties in the All-Ireland senior championship.

The first championship, in 1887, was run on the open draw system, but after that the provincial system came into operation. Under this system the All-Ireland championship couldn't begin until the local championships were completed. The annual convention of 1892 (which didn't take place until the following April) decreed that the county championships should be finished on the last Sunday in June. At an early stage permission was granted to the county championship club to pick players from other clubs in the county to help them in the inter-county championship. As early as the 1894 All-Ireland the Cork champions, Blackrock, included players from St Finbarr's and Evergreen National Club in the team that defeated the Dublin Rapparees in the final. The practice became common after that and gradually evolved into the present system, in which the county team is picked from the best in all the clubs in the county.

One vestige of the earlier system that continued for a long time was the selection of the county side by the county championship club; in Tipperary this remained the system up to 1948. The general practice now is for selection committees to be appointed independently of the county championship club, though there is a great diversity in the method used to make the selection.

With the increasing popularity of hurling and the growing number of players, it became apparent that grades other than senior were necessary. Dublin was the first county to establish a junior competition. A junior hurling league was formed in the county in 1901, and so successful was it that it was decided to set up a minor competition also. Limerick has the distinction of organising the first county junior championship. A junior board was formed at the convention held on 28 February 1901, which, as well as running junior championships, inaugurated the first juvenile competition. The next step was the organisation of inter-county games, and the first such games in junior and minor grades were contested by Limerick and Dublin at the Thatch Grounds, Drumcondra, Dublin, on 14 August 1904.[1]

The Junior Championships, 1903–94

The first national recognition of the junior grade was at the GAA annual convention in Thurles at the end of 1903. At the adjourned convention on 13 December, on the proposition of A. Murphy (Dublin), it was decided to establish a junior all-Ireland championship in hurling, the teams to consist of players who had not played in a senior county championship, provincial championship or All-Ireland championship since 1901.

It was to be nine years before this decision was implemented. The first province to make a start was Leinster, where a provincial championship was begun in 1905. The first winners were Kildare. Munster followed suit in 1910, when Tipperary took the first title. Ulster participated in 1913. The Congress that year graded Ulster counties as junior for hurling, and Antrim won the first provincial championship. Kilkenny beat them 7-3 to 3-1 in the All-Ireland semi-final. Connacht also fell into line in 1913, with Galway becoming the first winners in 1923.

The first All-Ireland junior hurling final was played at Jones's Road, Dublin, on 23 February 1913, the final of the 1912 championship. The finalists were Cork and Westmeath, and the Munster champions became the first winners of the competition, by 3-6 to 2-1.

Between 1912 and 1994 the competition was played on seventy-three occasions. It was suspended from 1917 to 1922 and from 1942 to 1945. The format changed during the period 1961–73. The championship was run in conjunction with the National League division 3, and a limited number of counties competed. The counties that opted out took part in a new intermediate championship. The original format was restored in 1983.

An important decision taken at the All-Ireland Congress in 1927 was to permit teams from Britain to participate in the championship.

Twenty-one counties have won the All-Ireland junior hurling championship. Six more—Carlow, Laois, Longford, Antrim, Monaghan, and Fermanagh—have unsuccessfully contested finals. Only five counties—Sligo, Leitrim, Donegal, Cavan, and Tyrone—have failed to reach a final. Two English counties, London and Warwickshire, have also won the championship; two other English counties, Lancashire and Hertfordshire, have contested without success. This success and participation rate compares more than favourably with the senior hurling championship, in which only twelve counties, together with London, were successful and one, Antrim, unsuccessful. Up to 1927 all the titles were won by second strings from the strong countries. In that year Meath made the first breakthrough for the weaker counties.

Although the success rate has been more widespread, it is the strong hurling counties who dominate the roll of honour. Cork are ahead, with eleven victories, followed by Tipperary with nine and Kilkenny with eight. Interestingly, London come next, with five victories; the same county leads the table for unsuccessful appearances, with twenty. It is followed by Galway with seven and Warwickshire and Kilkenny with five each. Tipperary and Cork follow with four each.

It may appear then that weaker hurling counties have a greater chance of success in this than in other hurling competitions. This is no longer so. A look at the winners since 1983 reveals that the competition is now dominated by the strong hurling counties. Cork, Kilkenny, Tipperary, Wexford and Clare have shared the honours since that date. Whereas the championship was originally envisaged for hurlers not up to senior standard and those no longer good enough for senior, this again is no longer so. The need to win has become so dominant that the stronger counties include in their teams good minors and under-21s and others not yet good enough for senior ranks; in this way the original purpose of the competition has been lost, and the players who should be catered for are not considered. The result is that the weaker counties have less and less chance of winning. These counties may consider their chances of success in the future to lie in the B championship.

The Intermediate Championship, 1961–73

A decision was taken at the 1960 Congress to inaugurate an intermediate championship, and it was first played in 1961. The decision was based on the recommendation of Coiste na hIomána, included in the secretary's report to the Congress in 1959. The first winners of the competition were Wexford, who beat London in the final by 3-15 to 4-4. In fact Wexford contested three of the first four finals, losing to Tipperary in 1963 but winning a second title in 1964. Tipperary were the most successful team in the competition, winning four finals in four appearances. London won twice but lost on six occasions. Carlow, Cork, Kildare, Antrim and Kilkenny won one final each. On the losing side as well as London were Dublin and Cork with two lost finals each and Warwickshire, Wicklow and Galway with one each.

All-Ireland B Championship, 1974–94

The All-Ireland B championship for weaker hurling counties was inaugurated in 1974. The winners of this competition enter the All-Ireland senior hurling championship at the quarter-final stage. No side has yet succeeded in winning at this stage.

Since its inauguration, nine teams have been successful, with Kildare winning the first championship. The final is played between the Irish winners and the winners of the English championship. The English champions have participated since 1975, and they have been, without exception, London. They have played in twenty finals, winning four: 1985, 1987, 1988, and 1990. London are followed by Kildare, Westmeath, Kerry, and Antrim, with three victories each. The other successful counties include Laois with two victories and Carlow, Meath and Roscommon with one each. An interesting development in the 1994 championship was the entry of New York into the competition. They were beaten by London in the semi-finals.

The National League, 1926–94

The decision to set up a National League was taken at the annual congress on 12 April 1925. The motion was proposed by S. McCarthy (Cork) and seconded by W. A. Clifford (Limerick) and was debated at length before the decision was reached, with a recommendation that the counties be graded. It was also decided that one of the Croke Cups—presented to the association by the Archbishop of Cashel in 1895—would be presented to the winners.

Twelve teams entered for the first National League, and they were graded into two groups. Cork, Dublin, Laois, Galway, Tipperary, Limerick and Kilkenny participated in the premier competition; the second division included Clare, Offaly, Kerry, Waterford, and Wexford. The first National League games were played on 4 October 1925. Cork, the eventual winners of the premier division, made a poor start, losing to Laois by 11-0 to 3-0 after being forced to call on the county secretary, Pádraig Ó Caoimh (after whom the Cork GAA stadium is named), to line out in goal. However, they overcame Galway, Dublin, Tipperary, Limerick and Kilkenny to qualify for the final against Dublin.

Dublin, who had won the All-Ireland in 1924 and were to win again in 1927, had players of the calibre of Dr Tommy Daly, Mick Gill, Jim 'Builder' Walsh, and Garrett Howard. The final was played at Cork Athletic Grounds on 17 May 1926 before a crowd of fourteen thousand, and Cork won by 3-7 to 1-5. Clare won the second division, with eight points from their four games.

The league was to become as much a fixture as the championship; in all it has been played on sixty-three occasions up to 1994. Whereas the championship has retained the same structure since 1888, the league format has been changed many times. In fact up to 1970, sixteen different formats have been used. It was not played in 1926/27, 1931/32, or during the war years from 1942/43 to 1945/46. Ten counties have won the competition: Tipperary, Cork, Limerick, Kilkenny, Galway, Wexford, Clare, Dublin, Offaly, and Waterford. All these counties have won All-Irelands, so it can be seen how National League success closely parallels championship success. Two teams that have won All-Irelands but have not been successful in the league are Kerry and Laois.

The second league, in 1927/28, was run on a straight points system. Tipperary, with fourteen points from eight games, headed the table and were declared winners. Dublin were runners-up. The original format was restored the following year and remained in place until the points system was reintroduced in 1934/35 for three years. This was in the middle of Limerick's period of great success, during which they won a record five leagues in a row. The original format was restored for the 1937/38 league. Tipperary's period of dominance began with their victory over Cork in the 1948/49 league. Between then and 1968 they were to contest fourteen league finals, winning twelve. John Doyle has the record of winning eleven league medals during this time.

This period saw the introduction of a new dimension to the league with the decision to allow New York to play the 'home' winners. From 1950 to 1952 the winners—Tipperary twice and Galway once—played New York. Two of the games were in New York and the third in Croke Park; the league winners were successful on the three occasions. This practice was discontinued for a number of years, until 1963, when New York visited Ireland and played the league winners, Waterford. The game ended in a draw at Croke Park, and Waterford won the replay at Kilkenny. Tipperary visited New York in the following two years, winning on both occasions. On the second visit there were two games, with the aggregate score counting. Kilkenny travelled to the United States in 1966 and won well on aggregate. Tipperary were back again in 1968, losing the first game but doing well enough in the second to win overall.

The final visit up to 1990 was by Cork, in 1970, and it turned out to be a stormy affair. They won the first leg but were defeated by New York in the second; however, they had a two-point advantage on aggregate. The referee, Clem Foley, was assaulted coming off the field, and as a result of this incident and other matters in the relations between the GAA and the New York Board, all tours were suspended. In fact the next was not to take place until 1990, when New York were allowed back into the league on a two-yearly basis. Kilkenny travelled to America that year and beat New York, but there have been no more visits since.

Between 1952 and 1962 there was an alternative competition, the St Brendan Cup. Following the visit of New York to Dublin in 1952 for the league final against Tipperary, friction developed between the New York Board and the Central Council, resulting in a decision to debar New York from further participation. During 1953 negotiations were reopened, and it was decided to inaugurate a new competition for the St Brendan Cup, which would be played between the league winners and New York. In 1955 New York came to Dublin and played the league champions, Tipperary. Harmony was not restored, however, as the New York Board issued invitations to individual county teams. Tipperary travelled to New York as league champions in 1957. The following year New York came to Dublin and recorded their first victory in the St Brendan Cup, over the league champions, Wexford. Tipperary travelled to New York in September 1959 to regain the cup. This was the last game in the series.

The National League got a new format in 1970/71, when the competition was rearranged into two groups, with promotion and relegation. There have been variations on that format in the intervening years, and it now contains three groups of eight teams and one of nine, which includes London. In the quarter-finals the top two teams in group 2 play the third and fourth in group 1 for semi-final places.

Success in the league continues to reflect success in the championship. In the period 1980–94 six teams have won the league. Kilkenny lead with four victories, followed by Cork and Limerick with three each. Tipperary and Galway had two victories each and Offaly had one. On the other side Wexford were unsuccessful in four finals, Galway, Tipperary, Offaly, Clare and Limerick in two, and Waterford in one. Cork held the distinction of being the only county to have won at least one National Hurling League title in every decade since the competition was inaugurated. Tipperary came closest to the Cork record, but the Premier County missed out in the thirties, when they lost the two finals they contested. There have been two goalless finals. One was in 1959, between Tipperary and Waterford at Nowlan Park, when Tipperary won by 0-15 to 0-7. The second, also involving Tipperary, was in 1992, when Limerick beat the Premier County by 0-14 to 0-13.

Attendances at league games, particularly finals, have never been as large as at championship games. The largest attendance was 45,902 in 1956, which saw Wexford win a remarkable game at Croke Park. They trailed Tipperary by a whopping fifteen points at the interval after playing against a gale-force wind but rallied superbly to grasp a 5-9 to 2-14 win and their first National League title. A year later Tipperary beat Kilkenny before 43,721 spectators at Croke Park.

There have been a number of drawn finals. The first was in 1946, when Clare, who had held Dublin to a draw at Limerick, beat them by five points at Croke Park, 2-10 to 2-5. A year later the Kilkenny-Limerick final, which was delayed until October 1947, was further delayed when the sides finished level at Croke Park, and it was well into March 1948 before the issue was decided, in Limerick's favour, 3-8 to 1-7. Waterford were held to a draw by New York in 1963 but made no mistake in the replay and won by 3-10 to 1-10. In 1976 Clare drew with Kilkenny, only to be humiliated in the replay by 6-14 to 1-14. The longest final saga was in 1993, when Cork and Wexford fought out a marathon over three weekends at Thurles. Cork came through by 3-11 to 1-12 in the second replay.

The National League comes in for its share of criticism. It is compared unfavourably with the championship, which has a glamour and excitement of its own. The problem for the league is that it is played during a time of the year unfavourable for hurling. In many instances counties cannot field their top fifteens as players take winter breaks. The unfinished club championship also makes players unavailable. And because the games are not knock-out until the later stages, the players don't give the same commitment as in the championship.

However, the league has its own importance. It gives counties the opportunity to try out new players and, while the exchanges are not as intense as in championship hurling, provides a more reliable yardstick than challenge games by which to measure a player's ability with a view to grooming him for the championship. It also gives the young player the opportunity to mature and adapt to the game at a higher level by bringing him into contact with more experienced players. Overall the league is an important competition, second only in importance to the championship. At a practical level it provides much-needed income to county boards.

Early inter-provincial competitions, 1786–1928

The earliest reference to an inter-provincial contest is in *Finn's Leinster Journal* of September 1786. According to this report the grandest match that was ever hurled in Ireland was played on Thursday 8 September between the provinces of Leinster and Munster for 68 guineas at the noted green of Lisduff near Urlingford.

The next inter-provincial competition took place outside Ireland. The venue was Stamford Bridge, London, and the date was 25 May 1896. The idea came from the London Irish, who put it to the Central Council that the promotion of hurling in London would be helped by an exhibition from some of the best hurlers in Ireland. The council agreed, and teams representing Leinster and Munster came to London for the occasion. The Munster men wore royal blue shirts with the three yellow crowns of the province, white caps, and navy-blue shorts. The Leinster men wore green shirts with a yellow harp, and white shorts and shoes. The Munster team had eight players from Tipperary, six from Limerick, and three from Cork; Leinster had seven from Wexford, six from Dublin, three from Kilkenny, and one from Meath. The Munster team included the well-known athletes John Flanagan and T. F. Kiely. Flanagan broke two world records with the hammer in the sports meeting that followed, while Kiely won the long jump. The game turned out to be a terrific struggle and aroused great enthusiasm. Munster put in a storming finish to win by 5-7 to 2-8.

In 1905 the Great Southern and Western Railway put up a shield to be played for by the pick of the hurlers in all four provinces. The shield became the property of the team that won two years in succession or three times in all. In 1908 Leinster and Munster clashed in the final, and whichever province won was going to keep the shield, as each side had recorded two previous victories. The game attracted an attendance of fifteen thousand to St James's Park, Kilkenny. After an exciting game Leinster—drawn almost entirely from Kilkenny—won by 0-14 to 2-5. The team was captained by 'Drug' Walsh of Mooncoin, and the players wore Mooncoin jerseys of green and white. Because there were so many players from the county the shield was awarded to Kilkenny, and it occupies a prominent place today in the Tholsel.

When the Tailteann Games were revived in 1924 an inter-provincial hurling competition was included in the programme, and Leinster beat Munster by 7-2 to 5-1. A further inter-provincial contest took place in the 1928 games. Both these games were in fact trial games to pick an Ireland team.

The Railway Cup, 1927–94

The Railway Cup, as the annual inter-provincial competition is more popularly called, was inaugurated in 1926 and was to have a longer history than any of the previous attempts. The first final, played on St Patrick's Day, 1927, drew a crowd of ten thousand to Croke Park and revealed an appetite for Gaelic games that could not be satisfied fully with inter-county competition.

At the annual congress on 4 April 1926 it was agreed 'that inter-provincial teams be selected annually and matches arranged at provincial venues.' The Central Council on 16 July decided that provincial councils would select the teams to represent the province and that the competition would be organised immediately after the completion of the All-Ireland championship. At the same meeting a letter was received from the Great Southern Railway confirming that 'the Company will present two silver cups and two sets of gold medals for competitions in hurling and football.' The council decided that one of the cups and one set of medals would be presented to the winners of the inter-provincial hurling competition.

Leinster, Connacht and Munster took part the first year. Leinster beat the westerners by 7-6 to 3-5 at Port Laoise on 21 November 1926, and the final was played the following St Patrick's Day in Croke Park. It was an exceptionally brilliant game, regarded by many as one of the great hurling games of all time. Leinster had a point to spare at the closing whistle on a score of 1-11 to 2-6.

Attendances broke the limit of thirty thousand for the first time in 1944 and climbed during the late forties and fifties, achieving the record in 1954 with forty-nine thousand when the final was played in June to coincide with the opening of the Hogan Stand. After that there was a gradual decline, which became steeper during the seventies and reached its lowest point in the 1985 final at Thurles between Munster and Connacht, when a mere 511 paid at the turnstiles—though perhaps a lower point was reached in 1990, when no competition took place.

The great era of Railway Cup hurling coincides with the playing career of the legendary Christy Ring. He was first chosen by Munster as a substitute in 1941. He made his debut as centre-forward in the 1942 final; between then and the 1963 final replay he made forty-four inter-provincial appearances, scoring a total of 42 goals and 105 points. He failed to score in only three games and collected a record eighteen medals.

Munster won the second Railway Cup in 1928, beating Connacht at Tuam by 7-3 to 2-4, and had a goal to spare over Leinster on a score of 2-2 to 1-2 in the final on St Patrick's Day. In all, Munster have won the Railway Cup on thirty-eight occasions. The province never failed to reach the final until 1979, when they were beaten in the semi-final by Connacht in Ballinasloe by 4-9 to 2-7. Since then they have failed to make the final on seven occasions. Munster have won the final in six successive years (1948–53), in five successive years twice (1942–46 and 1957–61), and in four successive years twice (1928–31 and 1937–40).

Connacht participated in the games from the start and have won the competition nine times. They won their first semi-final in 1944, when they beat Leinster in Birr by 4-5 to 1-5, only to lose to Munster in the final by six points. Their first success came in 1947. Having beaten Leinster by a point in the semi-final, they won their first Railway Cup by beating Munster 2-5 to 1-1 in the final. Connacht were not successful again until 1980, and they won the competition six times in that decade.

Ulster made their first appearance in 1944 and have never won the competition. They won the semi-final three times: in 1945, 1992, and 1993. They beat Leinster (who had Nicky Rackard at full-forward) by 3-1 to 2-3 in the semi-final in Belfast in 1945. Munster beat them 6-8 to 2-0 in the final. Ulster participated without fail from 1944 to 1958; they did not compete in 1959 but continued to play in the semi-final from 1960 to 1968. From 1969 to 1971 they played a preliminary round against Connacht and from 1972 to 1974 against the Combined Universities, who took part in the Railway Cup during these years. Ulster were not successful in the preliminary rounds, and when they entered the competition at the semi-final stage again in 1975 they were not to be successful until they beat Connacht at

Kilkenny in 1992, only to lose the final to Munster by 3-12 to 1-8. They were again successful against Munster in the semi-final at Casement Park in 1993 but lost to Leinster in the final.

Having won the inaugural competition, Leinster had to wait until 1932 for a second victory. They won three times in the thirties, only once in the forties, twice in the fifties, and four times in the sixties, and dominated the competition in the seventies with seven successes. Tony Doran (Wexford) played on all seven successful teams; these included five in a row between 1971 and 1975. They had only one success in the eighties and one (so far) in the nineties. One of the longest-serving players on the Leinster team was Paddy Phelan of Kilkenny. Although only a minor and never a goalie, he was selected in goal for Leinster in 1930 because a number of players were absent. From then until 1942 he played for Leinster, though never again in goal, and won four medals.

Varying reasons are put forward for the decline in interest in the Railway Cup. Television is often mentioned: the games were played in inclement March, and it was now possible to see them in the comfort of home. The domination of the competition by Munster and, to a lesser extent, Leinster meant that finals on St Patrick's Day became repetitive and predictable. Another reason was declining interest among players, who began to see the games as a chore, and this attitude was reflected in their performance. It took a while for an awareness of this attitude to seep down to the spectators, but when it did they stopped going, regarding the games as exhibitions rather than meaningful contests. Many attempts to halt the decline were of no avail. Moving the games out of Croke Park to provincial venues and playing them at a different time of year were two of the solutions tried, without success. The competition still exists, but an effort has to be made annually to squeeze it into the hurling calendar.

Everybody would agree that the competition served a substantial purpose. Until the advent of the All-Stars awards it was the only system under which great players could be given recognition beyond the borders of their counties. To be picked for one's province was an honour and a sign that one was a player above the ordinary. Players from strong hurling counties had the opportunity of achieving national recognition in winning All-Ireland honours, but players from weaker hurling areas had no such opportunity. One immediately recalls players of the calibre of Jimmy Smyth of Clare, Jobber McGrath of Westmeath, Pat Dunny of Kildare, and Christy O'Brien of Laois, who never won All-Irelands but who got the opportunity in the Railway Cup of winning the kind of national acclaim their talents deserved. Players from no less than fifteen counties have won Railway Cup hurling medals.

The Minor Championship, 1928–94

The decision to inaugurate a minor championship for players under the age of eighteen was taken at the 1927 Congress, held in Dublin on 17 April. Cork were the sponsors of the idea, and, appropriately enough, the county were to become the winners of the inaugural championship. An earlier attempt to set up such a competition, in 1904, was not successful.

The first championship was held in 1928. It didn't get the attention it deserved and wasn't finished until October 1929. Only Munster and Leinster participated in the first competition. Waterford had the distinction of winning the first minor game in Munster, when they defeated Limerick. Later Cork beat Waterford in the Munster final. In Leinster, Kilkenny beat Wexford in their first-round game and Laois in the second round. However, the Noresiders had not complied with the requirement to submit the names and ages of the players to the Leinster Council and so were disqualified. Dublin won the provincial final and qualified to play Cork in the All-Ireland. This game was played as a curtain-raiser to the 1929 senior final between Cork and Galway and ended in a draw: Dublin 1-8, Cork 3-2. The replay took place at UCC Grounds on 28 October, and Cork won by 7-6 to 4-0.

Thirteen counties have appeared in the sixty-four minor All-Irelands played so far. Kilkenny are out in front with most appearances: thirty-three in all, of which sixteen were successful. The Noresiders are followed by Cork and Tipperary, with the same number of appearances each, twenty-five, and the same number of successes each, fifteen. These three counties have dominated the competition, winning forty-six of the sixty-four finals, and the pattern of the other hurling competitions is repeated. Dublin come fourth, with eight appearances, four of which were successful. Four counties won the championship on three occasions: Galway won three out of fifteen appearances, Wexford three out of six, Limerick three out of five, and Offaly three out of three. The ninth county to win, Waterford, has two victories out of three appearances. Four counties played in finals without success: Laois twice and Antrim, Clare and Meath once each.

Whereas Tipperary dominated the competition in the fifties, Cork and Kilkenny reaped most of the honours in the sixties and seventies. Since then other counties have made their mark. While Tipperary haven't won since 1982 nor Cork since 1985, other counties have come to the fore. Kilkenny continue to make an impact, but they are now joined by Offaly and Galway. A sign of the shift in direction of the competition is the fact that no Munster team has been successful since 1985.

$$\text{\textsection} \quad \text{\textcircled{}} \quad \text{\textcircled{}}$$

The Under-21 Competition, 1964–94

The introduction of the under-21 competition in 1964 was a significant addition to the hurling calendar and the first addition since the minor championship in 1928. The decision resulted from a Kerry motion at the 1963 Congress to 'inaugurate an All-Ireland and provincial under-21 championship.' Among the arguments was the suggestion that such a competition was the way to build up games in the colleges and that it could act as a transition for the player moving from minor to senior ranks. The inaugural competition was won by Tipperary, who scored a very impressive 40 goals and 39 points in their five games. Having beaten Waterford in the Munster final, Tipperary qualified to play the Connacht representatives, Roscommon (Galway were then competing in the Munster championships, and continued to do so until 1969), in the All-Ireland semi-final at Roscommon. Tipperary won by 11-6 to 2-4. In the second semi-final Wexford travelled to Casement Park and defeated Antrim by 5-8 to 2-3. The Munster champions had an easy victory, 8-9 to 3-1, over Wexford in the final. Many of the winning team's players were to graduate to senior ranks in a short while. The Premier County won the competition seven times in all, including three in a row from 1979 to 1981. They lost five finals.

Wexford won in 1965, and this remains their only success. They were beaten in a second replay in 1966 and have been beaten five times in finals. Their victors in 1966 were Cork, and this county has been the most successful in the competition, with nine victories. The Rebel County dominated the competition between 1966 and 1977, winning eight and losing two finals. These successes included four in a row from 1968 to 1971. Apart from the record number of wins, Cork's performance is ahead of their rivals. The county lost only two finals, and their only semi-final loss in eleven appearances was against Galway in Cusack Park, Ennis, in 1991.

Galway were the fourth team to succeed in the competition, beating Dublin 2-9 to 1-10 in the 1972 final. They beat Tipperary in a replayed final in 1978 at Limerick by 3-15 to 2-8. They lost in 1979 and 1982, before winning for a third time in 1983. They won in 1986 and lost in 1987. Two more victories followed, in 1991 and 1993, and a defeat in 1994, giving the county six victories out of nine final appearances.

Kilkenny did not make their winning debut until 1974. They won the Leinster championship in 1968 but were beaten by Cork in the final. In 1974 they beat Galway in the semi-final and had a point to spare over Waterford in the final on a score of 3-8 to 3-7. They retained the title in 1975, beating Cork by 5-13 to 2-19. The following year Cork beat them in the final, but they were back again in 1977 to get their revenge on the Leesiders by 2-9 to 1-9. Their next victory was in the Centenary final in 1984, when they beat Tipperary by 1-12 to 0-11. Two more victories followed, in 1990 and 1994, bringing their total to six. The county lost seven finals.

Two other counties have won the under-21 championship. Limerick succeeded in 1987 at their first attempt and Waterford, after a replay in 1992, on their second attempt. Offaly have made three unsuccessful final appearances in recent years, in 1989, 1991, and 1992. The only other county to appear in the final was Dublin, with two unsuccessful appearances in 1967 and 1972. No Ulster team has won the competition; three Ulster counties—Antrim, Down, and Derry—have appeared at the semi-final stage over the years.

A good indication of the interest in the competition is the level of attendance. This has been consistently good from the early days, with crowds of ten to fifteen thousand being common. The biggest attendance was at the 1989 final at Port Laoise, when there was an estimated crowd of thirty thousand; many more were caught up in the traffic and didn't get to see the game at all, including Dr Clifford, patron of the GAA and successor to Dr Morris, who presented the trophy for the All-Ireland winners.

The trophy for the All-Ireland under-21 championship is unusual. It is in the form of a Cross of Cashel and is cast in bronze. It was presented by the GAA's patron, Dr Thomas Morris, Archbishop of Cashel and Emly, in 1969, and therefore the first three winning captains—Francis Loughnane in 1964, Willie O'Neill in 1965, and Gerald McCarthy in 1966—did not receive the trophy.

The All-Ireland Club Championship, 1970–94

The decision to inaugurate an All-Ireland club championship was taken at the Congress held in Galway in March 1970. The motion was proposed by Galway and Wexford. Among the arguments was the claim that the club was the most important unit of the association and that the proposed championship would give backing to that claim. It was also proposed that the competition would give the ordinary club player a chance to win an All-Ireland medal. It would also afford the player not of inter-county standard the opportunity to oppose players from outside his own county.

There were earlier attempts to introduce a club championship. In 1905 a Munster Cup in hurling was organised to raise funds for the provincial council. The teams taking part were to be winners of the previous year's county championships. This was the equivalent of a Munster club championship, but it made only a small profit and was discontinued after one year. In 1947 a Limerick motion to the GAA Congress, to start a club championship, failed to get a seconder. As a result of motions from Cork and Tipperary to the 1964 Munster Convention it was decided to inaugurate a provincial club championship. Although it took a long time to complete, it was rated a success. The final, between Glen Rovers of Cork and Mount Sion of Waterford, was played at Cashel on 5 December 1965 in atrocious weather. Nine minutes from the end, with Glen Rovers leading by 3-6 to 2-6, the referee abandoned the game because of deteriorating weather and the encroachment of spectators. The replay took place in Limerick on Easter Sunday, 1966, and was won by the Cork champions, 3-7 to 1-7. Included in the Glen Rovers line-out was Christy Ring, who had won his first Munster championship medal twenty-eight years previously, in 1938. The 1965 final was won by St Finbarr's (Cork). Carrick Davins (Tipperary) won in 1966; Newmarket-on-Fergus (Clare) brought the title to the Banner County in 1967 and 1968; and Roscrea (Tipperary) were successful in 1969.

The first All-Ireland championship took place in 1970 at the completion of the county championships. The final wasn't played until 19 December 1971, and it didn't attract much notice. It was played in Birr and saw Roscrea, the Tipperary champions, defeat St Rynagh's, the Offaly champions, by 4-5 to 2-5. It was Roscrea's only appearance in the final.

Thirty teams from ten counties have appeared in the twenty-four club All-Irelands played so far. Three teams have appeared on four occasions, Blackrock (Cork), with three successes and one failure, Rathnure (Wexford), with four failures, and Ballyhale Shamrocks (Kilkenny), with three successes and one failure. St Rynagh's (Offaly) made three unsuccessful appearances, and St Finbarr's had two successes out of three appearances. Glen Rovers (Cork), James Stephens (Kilkenny) and Sarsfields (Galway) had two successes each out of two appearances. Sarsfields have the added distinction of being the only club to win two titles back to back. Two more clubs, Castlegar (Galway) and Buffer's Alley (Wexford), had a fifty per cent success in their two appearances.

The club championship is the only senior club competition in which the winners have come from the four provinces. Munster provided the winners in the first five championships. The first Leinster winner was James Stephens (Kilkenny) in 1976. Castlegar (Galway) made the breakthrough for Connacht in 1980, and Loughguile Shamrocks (Antrim) made history in 1983 when they became the first Ulster team to win a major hurling title.

The club final had no fixed date in the hurling calendar in the early days. The first was played on 19 December 1971; the following finals were played in March, April, May, June, or December. In 1985 the final was played on St Patrick's Day, and, with a couple of slight variations (1 March in 1986 and 18 March in 1987), this date has been as firm a fixture as it was a Railway Cup fixture in the past.

The club final has ended in a draw on four occasions: 1974 and then, amazingly, three years in a row, 1983, 1984, and 1985. Another unusual fact is that on five occasions there were consecutive finals featuring different clubs from the same counties that contested the previous decider. In 1975 St Finbarr's (Cork) played the Fenians (Kilkenny), and the following year Blackrock (Cork) played James Stephens (Kilkenny). In 1984 Ballyhale Shamrocks (Kilkenny) played Gort (Galway), and the following year St Martin's (Kilkenny) played Castlegar (Galway). In 1986 Kilruane MacDonaghs (Tipperary) played Buffer's Alley (Wexford), and the following year Borrisoleigh (Tipperary) played Rathnure (Wexford). In 1990 Ballyhale Shamrocks (Kilkenny) played Ballybrown (Limerick), and the following year Glenmore (Kilkenny) played Patrickswell (Limerick). For the record, Cork and Kilkenny shared the honours in 1975/76, while Kilkenny had doubles in 1984/85 and 1990/91, and Tipperary achieved a double in 1986/87.

Attendances have not reached the size associated with the inter-provincial competitions, but they have been substantial, at ten to fifteen thousand. There is no doubt that the competition is keenly contested and generates tremendous local interest during the off season. The fact that the games are played most often on poor grounds does not detract in any way from the quality of the displays or the intensity of the exchanges. The competition got a boost in 1991 when Kiltomer (Galway) and Cashel King Cormac's (Tipperary) played two draws in the semi-finals and drew an aggregate attendance over the three games of nearly forty thousand, which says a lot for the drawing power of the clubs and the appeal of the championship. It can be said with reasonable certainty that the club championship is alive and well and here to stay.

Other hurling competitions

Mention should be made of a number of competitions that generated interest in their day and attracted large crowds of spectators. The first of these is the Croke Cup. In honour of his silver jubilee in 1895, the Archbishop of Cashel, Dr Thomas Croke, presented two silver cups to the GAA. The association decided to use one of the cups for a new hurling competition, separate from the championship, and it was first played for in 1896. The final, between Clare (Tulla) and Wexford (Crosstown), was played on 27 June 1897, and Clare won easily by 6-16 to 0-2. According to one report, the winners scored goals and points with machine-like regularity. The 1897 final wasn't played until 9 July 1899. Limerick (Kilfinnane) beat Kilkenny (Tullaroan) by 3-8 to 1-4. Because of the difficulty in getting it played, the competition did not take place for the next four years: instead the cup was handed over to the winners of the championship. Tipperary (Tubberadora) received it in 1898, Tipperary (Moycarkey) in 1899, Tipperary (Twomileborris) in 1900, and London in 1901.

At the GAA convention in 1902 it was decided, on the proposition of J. C. O'Brien (Dublin), that the Croke Cup be competed for as a separate competition from the All-Ireland championship, carried out as an inter-provincial contest under the Central Council. Because of a delay in getting possession of the cup it was not until 1904 that the Central Council was in a position to arrange contests. At Limerick on 2 October, Munster (Cork) beat Connacht (Galway) by 5-11 to 1-6. Two weeks later at Dundalk, Leinster (Dublin) got a walkover from Ulster (Derry). The home final was played 'at Thurles on 6 November, and Munster beat Leinster by 1-1 to 0-2. The final proper was played in Dublin on 19 February 1905, and Munster beat London Irish by 5-10 to 0-3. Three of the provinces played in the 1905 series. Munster (Cork) beat Connacht (Galway) by 1-9 to 0-7 in Tuam on 21 January 1906. In the final, played in Dungarvan on 27 May, Munster beat Leinster by 6-9 to 0-5.

At the 1905 Convention, held in January 1906, it was decided, on the proposal of F. M. Crowe (Dublin), 'that the Croke Cup be awarded to the winners of the All-Ireland championship and be held for not longer than twelve months under usual conditions.'

The Thomond Tournament, 1913–56

The Thomond Tournament in senior hurling began in 1913 and continued until 1956. It was confined to four counties, and at first the winners received the Thomond Shield. Tipperary won it outright in 1916 and the Thomond Cup, which replaced it, in 1931. The next trophy was the *Limerick Leader* Cup, which was won by Limerick in 1933, as was the Spillane Shield in 1935 and the *Limerick Leader* Shield in 1944. The last trophy competed for was the *Irish Independent* Perpetual Challenge Cup.

Limerick were the first winners of the competition, in 1913. The final was played in Limerick on 18 May, and after a hard game Limerick beat Tipperary by 4-0 to 3-2 before a crowd of ten thousand. Played every year with the exception of 1923, when the Civil War prevented it, the tournament was dominated by Limerick, who won it fourteen times in all. Tipperary won it eight times, Cork seven times, and Clare three times, including the last final, played in Limerick on 2 May 1957. They beat Limerick by 4-7 to 3-3 in what was the 1956 final. The hurling tournament formed part of a festival known as the Thomond Feis and was launched by Dr Douglas Hyde in May 1913.

The Oireachtas, 1947–94

An tOireachtas—later called Oireachtas na Gaeilge—is a cultural festival founded in 1897 but abandoned some time in the nineteen-twenties. When it was revived in 1939 the GAA gave permission for a game of either hurling or football to be played in Croke Park between selected teams on 'Oireachtas Sunday'. There was no set method by which the teams were chosen, and until 1946 only one game was played each year. In the first final, in November 1939, a handful of people saw Limerick hurlers beat the All-Ireland champions, Kilkenny, by 4-4 to 2-5. In the following year

Kilkenny beat Cork by 7-11 to 1-6. For the next three years it was football. Hurling returned in 1944, and Dublin beat Galway by 6-6 to 3-6. In 1945 Tipperary beat Galway by 4-6 to 4-3 after a hard-fought and exciting struggle. The competition was merged with another one organised by Conradh na Gaeilge in 1946, and it was decided to provide a perpetual cup for the winner. The cup, which takes the form of a bowl resting on standards shaped as hurleys, was named Corn Thomáis Ághas but is more commonly known as the Oireachtas Cup.

In 1946, the first year of the competition, football was played, and Antrim beat Laois in the final. The series did not arouse much interest and it was decided to change to hurling in 1947, and it has been a hurling competition since, usually with four teams participating. The competition went from strength to strength, eventually establishing itself as one of the most attractive in the hurling calendar. There were tremendously exciting finals between Clare and Wexford in 1953 and 1954. In fact Wexford's involvement enhanced the competition and helped their championship breakthrough in 1955. Its popularity reached its peak in 1956, when 37,277 spectators saw Wexford beat Kilkenny in an all-Leinster final. The next-biggest crowd was at the 1960 final, when 33,733 assembled to see Tipperary beat Cork in an all-Munster pairing.

By virtue of their win in 1993 Galway lead the table with eleven victories, followed by Tipperary with ten; they are followed by Wexford with nine wins and Kilkenny with seven. Cork, who didn't win until 1973 (a result being that Christy Ring never won an Oireachtas medal), have four victories, Clare three and Dublin, Waterford and Limerick one each.

In latter years the competition has fallen on lean times, no longer attracts the crowds, and finds it difficult to get a date in the hurling calendar.

❂ ❂ ❂

The Monaghan Cup Tournament, 1927–75

What came to be known as the Monaghan Cup tournament began at Whitsuntide 1927, when the Cork and Tipperary hurling teams travelled to England to play exhibition games in Liverpool and London. The teams were no doubt chosen because of their displays in the marathon Munster championship clash the previous year. They were accompanied by the Cork Volunteers Pipe Band, and they thrilled the crowds that turned up to see them in both cities. The London game was played at Herne Hill

Athletic Grounds, where nine thousand spectators saw Cork defeat Tipperary by 4-5 to 0-3. Liam McCarthy presented his own All-Ireland cup to the winners—Cork had won it in 1926—and sets of medals to both teams. The visit was an undoubted success and was repeated the following year by the All-Ireland champions, Dublin and Cork, with victory going to the Leesiders by 4-5 to 3-3. In 1929 a London businessman, Owen Ward, who originally came from Clontibret, County Monaghan, presented a cup for the annual competition, and it was named the Monaghan Cup. Cork won it for the first time when they beat Kilkenny by 3-2 to 1-2 during the 1929 visit to Herne Hill.

The competition continued to be played until 1975, when it was contested by Kilkenny and Limerick. From 1931 to 1935 the games were played at Woolwich. In 1936 they found a new home in Mitcham Stadium and continued to be played there until 1955, with the exception of 1940, when Tipperary and Kilkenny played in Carrick-on-Suir, and 1941–45, when there were no contests. In 1955 and 1956 the games were played in Woolwich again, and then in 1958 the move was made to Wembley Stadium and the event took on a much greater scale. The association with Wembley continued until the competition ceased to be played in 1975.

The move to Wembley increased the numbers attending. Previously the biggest recorded crowd, of twenty-two thousand, came to see Kilkenny beat Tipperary by 5-8 to 3-4 in 1948. The Wexford-Tipperary clash in 1955 attracted fifteen thousand fans. In contrast, the Kilkenny-Clare game in Wembley in 1958 attracted thirty-three thousand. The biggest number came to see Tipperary and Kilkenny fight it out in 1963, when forty-two thousand turned up. In the seventies the numbers began to decrease; over thirteen thousand attended the final contest, but it was not enough to justify holding it in the stadium.

The tournament attracted great interest and was cherished by participating teams. Tipperary took part more often than any other team and had most victories. Other teams that participated include Cork, Kilkenny, Dublin, Wexford, Galway, Clare, and Limerick. Over the years the format for participation changed several times.

The Walsh and Kehoe Cups

The competitions for the Walsh and Kehoe Cups are confined to hurling teams from Leinster. The Walsh Cup is named after Tom Walsh TD

(Minister for Agriculture from 1951 to 1954), who was chairman of Kilkenny County Board from 1944 until his sudden death in 1956. He also held the chairmanship of the Leinster Council from 1948 to 1950.

In 1954 the Leinster Council began a competition to boost the Players' Injury Fund in the province. The first winners were Wexford, who defeated Dublin by 1-8 to 0-2 in the final at Enniscorthy. Two years later, on the death of Tom Walsh, the Kilkenny firm of Mahon and McPhillips donated a cup in his honour to be used in the competition, which then became known as the Walsh Cup tournament. The format of the competition changed at different times. On some occasions it was a tournament for the stronger hurling counties and at other times for the weaker counties. It was played regularly from 1954 to 1970 but irregularly after that.

A second cup for the same purpose was put up for competition in 1977. In that year, on the death of Michael Kehoe of Wexford, president of the GAA from 1949 to 1952, a cup in his memory was presented to the Leinster Council. It was decided to alternate it with the Walsh Cup between the stronger and the weaker counties for the Players' Injury Fund. In the first year it was for competition between the stronger counties, and Wexford beat Kilkenny. After some years the Kehoe Cup was used exclusively for competition among the weaker counties and the Walsh Cup for the stronger counties, and so it remains to this day.

16

The Geography of Hurling

There is no doubt that hurling was in a precarious state when Michael Cusack turned his attention to it. The game had been widespread during the eighteenth century but had suffered drastic decline during the nineteenth, when landlord, priest and magistrate turned against it. It did survive in certain places; but because it was not organised, had not got standard rules and was played by the lower classes, it did not get much coverage in the newspapers.

There were two forms of the traditional game. The first of these, 'commons', was played generally in winter on a restricted field of play. It resembled hockey or the Scottish game of shinty (and in fact was known as 'shinny' in County Antrim) in that it used a thin crooked stick and a hard ball and was played solely with the stick. This was the game in the north of the county and of the common people. The second type, called *iomáin* or *báire*, played largely in the south, was a summer game that used what would now be regarded as a typical hurling stick, the broad camán, and a softer ball of hair that might be lifted by the hand to be struck with the stick. The game needed a large area and might be played across country. It was an aristocratic game, often associated with violence and even death.

Maurice Davin was given the task of drafting the rules of hurling at the second meeting of the GAA on 27 December 1884. He must already have been working on them, however, for he presented his draft to the third meeting, at Thurles on 17 January 1885. The draft, which was adopted, contained twelve rules; and while Davin did adopt elements of the two traditional forms of the game, the new rules more closely resembled those of *iomáin* or *báire*. Gradually the rules were accepted throughout the country and replaced the old rules, where these existed. In fact as a result of the adoption of the rules, hurling activity increased considerably.

In spite of the decline from the time of the Famine, hurling continued to be played in certain areas. In 1876 Carrigaline played a challenge match against St Finbarr's, who won and played Blackrock later in the year in a more notable encounter. A lively newspaper controversy followed the victory, the last letter of which came from a St Finbarr's scribe:

> It was madness for the Blackrock men to say their hurleys were taken away from them by outsiders and the ball kicked. The people coming onto the field prevented us from striking the ball towards our own coole. However, through sound judgement and manly play we took the ball away from them and won one of the best matches ever played in Cork. But, if Blackrock wish to try our strength again, we will play them in Corker's Inch, Inishannon, on any weekday they please to avoid overcrowding.[1]

The game was also thriving in north Cork and in County Limerick. As we have seen from the visit of Cusack's Metropolitans to Ballinasloe, it was strong in south-east Galway, with some spill-over in Clare. It was also alive and well in Tipperary, especially in the parishes of Moycarkey, Toomevara, Boherlahan, and Thurles. Tullaroan and Carrickshock, where they beat the title-holders with their camáns, were noted for hurling. Places like New Ross and Tullagher in Wexford were still playing the game. Other counties where hurling of some form was being played before the foundation of the GAA were Antrim, Derry, Donegal, Meath, and of course Dublin, where Cusack's efforts had resulted in the formation of clubs.

The teams that participated in the first All-Ireland championship are an indication of where the game was played at the time of the foundation of the GAA. Twelve teams were included in the first draw, and while a number of them did not take part because of a variety of difficulties, their entry gives us some indication of the state of hurling in 1887. The draw was as follows: Wexford v. Galway, Tipperary v. Dublin, Clare v. Wicklow, Limerick v. Meath, Cork v. Kilkenny, and Waterford v. Louth. Significantly, nine of these teams (the exceptions being Wicklow, Meath, and Louth) have won 101 of the 107 All-Irelands played to date. The teams that won the other All-Irelands were Offaly, with three, and Laois, Kerry, and London, with one each.

It is significant that successful counties are in what was earlier the *iomáin* area. But mention must be made of isolated hurling pockets elsewhere. Whereas Davin's rules revived the game of hurling in the south, they were to sound the death knell of the old game of commons in the north.

Gradually the old game faded away and was replaced by hurling. For a number of years in some rural districts the 'old' rules struggled on, but in Newry and other towns the new rules were used.[2] During the eighteen-eighties and nineties GAA in Down usually meant Gaelic football only, but a revival came after the Parnell split.

> It was to hurling that the young men turned as though they wanted
> to express their Irishness through the most distinctive national
> game.[3]

A poster for the first Feis an Dúin in Newcastle in 1902 includes an advertisement for a hurling match. The game never spread far, however, and is today confined to the south of the Ards Peninsula and three clubs: Ballycran, Ballygalget, and Portaferry.

Another place where commons persisted was County Donegal, where cross-country commons—a more spectacular form of the game—was played. Not until the Donegal County Board of the GAA was formed in 1906 and an attempt was made to organise hurling did cross-country hurling cease to be a feature of the game in Ardara in south-west Donegal.

Ordinary commons games, played on Sundays with teams from different townlands and approximately seventeen players on each, took place during the winter months, when the fields were cleared of crops. The playing fields would be similar in size to the present pitches but unmarked. Two sticks or branches about the height of a man served as goalposts. Points were unknown, and there were neither sidelines nor referee. Every player made his own camán of ash, holly, black sallow, or hazel. The handle was of uniform thickness, about two inches in diameter. The boss was roughly three inches wide with a depth of two inches at the heel and a half-inch ridge on each side to give the ball elevation when striking off the ground. Some forwards fashioned camáns with a hollow in the boss so that the ball could be carried with greater ease and speed.

The ball used was known in Ardara as a 'bool' and was made of briar root, rounded under the embers of the turf fire until it was round and hard on the outside. This 'bool' was three inches in diameter and weighed half a pound or more and had a life span of less than two months. Other 'bools' made of hazel were lighter but had a shorter life span. Sometimes the 'bool' was covered in leather, and this ensured a longer life. The games lasted for three to four hours and were tests of speed, strength, and endurance.[4]

With the formation of the county board, hurling was promoted, and Donegal, represented by Burt, defeated Carey, County Antrim, in the first Ulster final (in either hurling or football), that of 1906, played in July 1907.

The Burt hurlers were the most skilful and proficient in Donegal in the early years and seemed to have adapted earlier and faster to the game as it was played in Munster. They used a distinctive type of hurley, about twice as heavy as today's and much narrower at the boss, with a grooved inner side or ridge along the heel for the purpose of giving the ball elevation when struck on the ground.

The promise shown by the hurlers of Donegal in the first decade was not fulfilled, and the county's great tradition of commons was never translated into a successful hurling tradition.[5]

In the north of Antrim there is plenty of historical and traditional evidence of a form of hurling or 'shinny' having being played for centuries. By the nineteenth century this had become informally organised into inter-parish contests on suitable beaches on such holidays as New Year's Day. The geography of the county, with its dominating plateau, has determined the location of the hurling grounds and, as a consequence, the hurling clubs. They are mainly near the seashore or the shore of Lough Neagh or, in modern times, in urban areas. Several pitches are to be found just above the high-tide mark, on the first stretch of ground on which grass can be grown. Such pitches are virtually all-weather because of their sandy base; the best examples are the grounds of Glenariff Ossians at Waterfoot and Cushendun Emmets at Leac an Airgid.

The first north Antrim GAA team was established in Glenarm in 1903 by F. J. Bigger, James McRann, and John 'Benmore' Clarke. This club, under a different name, flourishes to this day. It wasn't long before clubs were founded in Carey, Ballycastle, Cushendun, and Loughguile. However, the first big event was at the Glen Feis in Glenariff in 1904. This match was contested by Glenarm Shauns and Carey Faughs. Dan Dempsey of Loughguile was the referee, and Roger Casement was one of the umpires. Bigger presented the shield; Carey won it and treasure it to this day.[6] Earlier five teams had been formed in Belfast in the eighteen-eighties, and these dominated the county championship for the first few years. But in 1906 Carey Faughs became the first team from north Antrim to win the hurling championship, and teams from that area have dominated the competition ever since. It is an interesting example of the old 'shinny' tradition adapting to the new hurling rules and carrying on a tradition centuries old.

Outside those isolated hurling areas the traditional area is quite compact. The heartland comprises the three hurling counties of Tipperary, Kilkenny, and Cork, with a number of counties enclosing them, such as Wexford, Limerick, Waterford, Clare, Galway, Offaly, and Laois. As Dr Kevin Whelan points out, the boundaries are surprisingly well defined. To the north the midland bogs ... act as a buffer zone resolutely impervious to the spread of cultural influences from further south. The western edge of the hurling region can be traced over a long distance. In County Galway, for example, its boundaries run from Ballinasloe to the city ... In County Clare the boundary runs from Tubber on the Galway border through Corofin and Kilmaley to Labasheeda on the Shannon estuary ... Across the Shannon in Limerick the football-hurling divide runs clearly along the scarp dividing hilly west Limerick from the lush limestone lowlands of east Limerick. West of this is the enclave of hurling parishes in the footballing kingdom of Kerry in the area north of Tralee, in Ardfert, Ballyheigue, Causeway, and Ballyduff ... From Limerick the hurling boundary loops through County Cork from Mallow to the city and then to the coast at Cloyne, home of the maestro, Christy Ring ...[7]

The strength of hurling in north Kerry is an interesting phenomenon. The area is bounded by the rivers Cashen, Feale, and Smearlagh, which enclose a number of clubs where hurling is king. It is not clear why hurling should have survived here in an otherwise football environment. It has the larger fields where the game can be played in comfort, and it has a supply of ash. There is another important ingredient, which may be the real reason: there is tremendous club commitment and great inter-club rivalry, and consequently little support for the inter-county teams.

The persistence of hurling in its core region can be seen from the map illustrating gentry patronage of hurling in the eighteenth century (see p. 14). The landlords of the day were great supporters of hurling and kept teams of hurlers to challenge other landlords for substantial wagers. Three such matches that we know about were played in Wexford, one in south Wicklow, two in Carlow, one in Kilkenny, two in Laois, one in Offaly, three in Galway, four in Tipperary, and four in Cork. Apart from this hurling heartland there were two in Kerry and one in Donegal.

Predominantly a rural game, hurling has not transplanted to the cities. In the early days of the GAA at least five hurling teams were formed in Belfast. This development was due to the presence in the city of a substantial number of civil servants, teachers, shopkeepers and artisans from rural areas; but over the decades many of these teams went into oblivion. Dublin has never been a hurling area; and Castlegar is the nearest the game ever got to the city of Galway. Rugby is the popular game in Limerick.

In only two cities has hurling found a home. It has always been strong in Cork, where two great teams, Blackrock and St Finbarr's, have long been rivals. Waterford has also proved a powerhouse of hurling, with no less than eight of the successful 1959 team and eleven of the 1963 team coming from the city.[8]

Many reasons are put forward for the confinement of the game to its present region. The game does not travel well, and unless a person has acquired the essential skills of the hurling stick and sliotar in early childhood it is virtually impossible to acquire them at all. 'Attempts to master hurling in later years merely fill hospital casualty wards.'[9] Another explanation is that hurling is an intensely regional sport, and if it is not native to a parish or barony it will not be played.

The baronies and parishes where it is played are in fact those that experienced heavy settlement by fourteenth-century invaders from England. The implication of this—that hurling is a Norman import—may sound heretical to those who regard the game as quintessentially Irish. In support of this argument is the fact that there is no single word for the game in Irish (*báire, camánacht/camánaíocht, iomáin/iománaíocht*) and that the sport is virtually absent in the Irish-speaking districts of the Atlantic seaboard. Of a group of hurlers in the seventeenth century an observer wrote:

> They have a sort of jargon speech peculiar to themselves and understand not one word of Irish.[10]

One alternative explanation may be the Norman practice of adopting exciting cultural and sporting practices in the areas they conquered and becoming better exponents of them than the natives themselves. And an obvious argument against finding hurling on the Atlantic seaboard is the total absence of timber, let alone ash.

It is true that the landlords supported hurling between 1600 and 1800 (see chapter 2). They sponsored teams, arranged inter-parish and inter-baronial matches, and wagered heavy stakes on the outcome. In the hurling heartland of the south this patronage was at its strongest. It may be said to have been responsible for the preservation of the game in the area, and for the converse being true for the areas in which the game was not under patronage. Many of the players on the barony and parish teams were mediaeval Norman and English settlers who had been hibernicised over the centuries. 'Since then the colonists have been assimilated completely, but even today their connection with hurling is evident in the English and Norman surnames which tend to be more common in the areas where the game is played.'[11] Whelan sees the hurling heartland as the area where 'in the late medieval period, the Norman and Gaelic worlds fused to produce a vigorous culture … It coincides with well-drained, level terrain, seldom moving too far off the dry sod of the limestone areas, which also happen to produce the best materials for hurls—ash. It is closely linked to the distribution of big farms, where the relatively comfortable lifestyle afforded the leisure to pursue the sport.'[12] Another commentator adds: 'These same arguments should also apply to Meath and Kildare, but these counties were probably too close to the Pale and too dominated by the English influence.'[13]

Many attempts have been made in the last hundred years to extend the hurling area. They have not been successful. The game may now indeed be played in all thirty-two counties, but it continues to be played well only in the traditional heartland. Three of the teams in this heartland— Tipperary, Kilkenny, and Cork—have between them won 76 of the 107 All-Ireland championships. The peripheral teams—Limerick, Wexford, Galway, Waterford, Offaly, Laois, Clare, and Kerry—have won 24 of the remaining 31. Dublin won 6 up to 1938, when there was a big influx of rural players into the city; and London surprised Cork in 1901. It is unlikely that either Dublin or London will be successful in the future, and of the remainder of the counties, Antrim, where the traditional game of commons did translate to hurling at the turn of the century, is the only one with the slightest chance.

17

Hurling Styles

Writing in his *Annual* in 1939, Carbery stated that the GAA, having found hurling in a precarious state, had nurtured and improved the game so that it was then on 'sound national foundations'. As a thrilling outdoor sporting spectacle it had few equals and no peers. However, he went on to claim that there had been no improvement in pure hurling technique to correspond to the remarkable growth in the game's popularity. In contemporary hurling he recognised a 'baneful tendency' to depart from fundamental principles and to evolve a game that had lost some of its best characteristics.[1]

For Carbery hurling was essentially a manly game. Speed, skill, stamina and courage were all demanded, and the last was the most important. The art of hurling had not kept pace with its renaissance; even the best of contemporary players couldn't hit a ball as truly as the Tubberadora, Blackrock, Mooncoin or Tulla men of the previous generation. They were no longer capable of tackling, parrying, sidestepping, hooking, pulling, driving or 'dropping' a ball on the sod, doubling with direction on ground or overhead, or striking a flying 'drop' with any degree of accuracy. He blamed these developments on a want of sound tutors and a desire for speed at all cost, as well as a contemporary craze for the spectacular.

Students of the game had to become proficient in hitting on the sod, off left and right hands, before they attempted to raise or handle the ball. 'Handling' was the bane of contemporary hurling, and if Carbery had his way it would be prohibited from a direct lift. Instructors should insist on ground hurling as the basis of proficiency. The beginner must be taught to lift and hit away without catching. Blackrock and Tubberadora hurlers would not deign to lift a ball into their hands, as it was a sign of want of skill. Wrist-work was another important acquirement. In it was to be found the secret of true, sweet striking. Shoulders must open up for power, but it is the dexterous work with the wrists that brings true command of the hurley. The follow-through was also important, and all the best players of the past practised this with assiduity. According to Carbery, previous generations of hurlers cultivated style on the models of their elders, but it was at a discount in his time.

Carbery concluded by saying: 'Future instructors of the young "hurling idea" must recover this smooth style with firm yet flexible wrists, and an easy swing of body to aid length. Weight must always bear on the front leg at the time of ball-impact; concentration on the approaching sphere is the essential for accurate "doubling" so important in all match play.'[2]

What Carbery was describing were the essential characteristics of hurling as practised in the early decades of this century. By the late thirties there were changes that he believed diluted the pure style practised previously.

Interestingly, Con Murphy of Cork, whose playing career spanned the forties and began when Carbery noted such detrimental changes, would see hurling deteriorating from a high point in the forties to a drop in the overall level of skills in the seventies.[3] In the forties it was played much more on a man-to-man basis than to a set pattern; it was a contest of individual skill and courage. He instances the great duels between Limerick's Mick Mackey and Waterford's John Keane. Individual contests were a significant part of the match and an attraction in themselves. People came to see them. And if one player won the contest today, spectators looked forward to a return bout to see how the defeated player responded.

Starting in the seventies, there were certain negative developments. Certain skills well nigh disappeared. Grand overhead striking, à la Timmy Ryan of Limerick, and long-distance striking gradually went out of the game. The introduction of the hand-pass was detrimental; it reached the stage where top inter-county players were dropping the hurley altogether to play the ball with the hand. Murphy would not agree that it speeded up the game: he admits that it looks more 'classy', but it cannot be as economical of energy or part of the great skill of hurling in the way that driving the ball is.

Certain developments were welcome. Some of the activity associated with the goal area had to be excluded from the game; but too much was lost. Powerful striking of the ball, stick-work and wrist-work that had been traditionally associated with the game were dramatically reduced. As an illustration Murphy mentions John Fenton's famous goal in Thurles from fifty yards out, when he pulled on a ground ball and sent it searing all the way to the net. It was regarded as a unique spectacle and was played over and over again on television; but it was nothing more than a traditional skill, part and parcel of the hurler's repertoire of skills, that had disappeared with the new developments. Another example is a spectacular goal scored by Jimmy Barry Murphy in an All-Ireland semi-final against Galway, when he doubled on an overhead ball and buried it in the net. That stroke also attracted inordinate attention, because the player was using a skill, traditional to the game, that had fallen into disuse. What had been the practice and the pattern on one occasion now called for special comment.

Con Murphy is particularly vocal against what he describes as 'soft-option scoring'—by this he means players going for a point when a goal was a real possibility. He cites the player putting the ball over the bar when his side is five points down and time is running out. Another undesirable development in his eyes is 'pattern hurling', which involves transferring the ball to a nearby colleague in the backs when the player himself is in a position to make an effective long clearance, or swinging the ball around from player to player either as a tactic or the abdicating by each player of the direct approach, which is more effective and rewarding and more difficult for backs and goalkeeper to cope with.

Another baneful development is running with the ball. As a result, many players cannot last the seventy minutes. Why should they carry the ball when long-distance striking can achieve the same result? Many of these developments have tended to refine the game out of its traditional form.

One of the most detrimental developments is the gradual decline in the use of the body. Con Murphy believes that hurling is a proper combination of body use with traditional hurling skills. The game cannot have one without the other. Players are no longer taught the proper use of the body, which is a vital characteristic of the traditional game. He believes that traditional skills are being replaced by gimmicks. Palming the ball was regarded at one time as a reflection on the player's ability and was frowned on: the stick, not the hand, was for striking the ball. Good striking and strong hurling are rarely seen in the modern game. The use of the shoulders and the wrists has nearly disappeared; the real cut-and-thrust of the traditional game is to be seen no more.

Some of this comment may appear severe or unwarranted. Every game changes and develops; rules are changed to meet new demands. But with the advent of television the rate of change has become more precipitate, and sometimes the rules are being changed to suit the television audience rather than the game itself. Television demands speed, excitement, and glamour. There is a great emphasis on presentation and on the trivial and ephemeral; with its action replays and close-ups it exposes mercilessly every aspect of the game. One can imagine close-ups of some of the goal-mouth happenings from the days when the goalkeeper was bundled unceremoniously into the back of the net!

There are other agents of change. The improvement in playing areas and field maintenance has speeded up the game. There is a huge difference between the well-kept stadium with its smooth and level surface, regularly cut and properly maintained, and the field of fifty years ago that was a hurling field only part of the time and a field for grazing cattle or sheep most of the time. And playing areas could vary between counties. One of the reasons put forward for Antrim's poor performance in the 1943 All-Ireland against Cork, after impressive performances against Galway and Kilkenny in Corrigan Park, is that they were unable to adjust to the faster run of the ball in Croke Park.

Another area of change has been that of playing gear. The footwear of the modern hurler is a lighter and better-fitting piece of equipment than the hurling boot used by his ancestors. The sliotar is smaller, lighter, and water-resistant, unlike the bigger, baggier and heavier ball used in the past. The stick has changed also, predominantly from one with a heavy rounded boss, suited to moving the ball along the ground, to the lighter, sharper-turned head, more suited to picking the sliotar off the ground. And what about the jersey and shorts? There's an enormous difference in quality and comfort between the old woollen jerseys and the modern ones of light materials. A seamstress in Castleconnell used to make shorts out of well-bleached flour bags for Mick Mackey so that he would be well togged out for important games!

Then there is the change in training methods. The modern coach with his charts and programmes, his schedules and personal training plans, his dietary advice and medical back-up is a far cry from the 'few rounds of the field, lads' of an evening and a couple of raw eggs a day for a fortnight before the game.

All these developments have led to a faster game and a much faster movement of the ball than in the past. They have ensured that the modern player has achieved a level of fitness much higher than his predecessor of a generation or more ago could have imagined. On top of that the modern player does not endure the same level of physical punishment as his predecessor: he is protected by changing rules that have eliminated much of the physical element from the game and by referees who see their primary role as the protection of the players. And yet, ironically, the prevalence of injuries among modern players seems greater than in the past. It seems incredible today that John Doyle of Tipperary, during a career that spanned eighteen championships, never failed to turn out for a game and never went off because of injury. Admittedly the occupations of many players in the thirties, forties and fifties led to tougher physical specimens than are produced by the sedentary occupations of today.

While all these changes have brought about a faster game, they have done nothing to improve the fundamental characteristics of hurling. These involve propelling a four-ounce ball with an ash stick from one end of a field to the other with the purpose of scoring a goal or a point and preventing one's opponents doing the same thing. That can be achieved by striking the ball, passing to an opponent, going on a solo run, striking on the ground or in the air, and doubling on the ball either on the ground or in the air. The team that carries out these actions with the greatest skill and efficiency wins. The training of teams involves getting the players to the highest level of fitness and improving their skill and efficiency. After that the team with the best players, the best match plan and the highest level of motivation is successful. Some coaches try out 'gimmicks', ruses and other deceptions to achieve success, but they can be used only once.

Traditionally it was believed that different counties had different styles: one spoke of the Cork style or the Wexford style. A reporter remarked after Tubberadora had won the 1895 Munster final:

> The style of the Tipperary hurlers was fast, free and open, and their positional work perfect. In every unit there was sting and dash; in every line there was ability and method. With such a gallant combination, it looks as if Tipperary is going to make some history in the ancient pastime.[4]

There is no longer much difference in the way different counties play. There are variations in style, but each county borrows and learns from the next. In general it may be said that the counties of Munster favour the direct style of play, while Kilkenny favour a game of possession. The present Galway style appears to be a mixture of all the styles at different times; and different players on a team may use different styles. Waterford at their best used a mixture of the Kilkenny and Cork styles, which was very effective.

The word 'dash' recurs again and again in accounts of Tipperary hurling in the thirties: it was regarded as an essential ingredient of the Tipperary style. Jimmy Butler Coffey, who played for the county during that decade, was asked what was meant by the term. He believed it was the practice of all the team moving in unison up the field in a spirited and determined attack, throwing everything at the opposition in an attempt to score.[5] It sounds more like a run for the line in rugby than anything that might be termed 'style'.

An important ingredient of Tipperary hurling during the fifties and sixties was physical strength. But it was more than brawn. Allied to physical strength was the leaven of superb skill, typified by the hurling of Jimmy Kennedy, Tony Wall, Jimmy Doyle, and Mick Roche, to name a few. Today the cry is that the strength is gone and that without it the skill level has made little progress against teams such as Galway and Kilkenny, who appear to have worked out the proper relationship between controlled aggression and the playing of the game.

Tipperary's greatest rivals in Munster typify in their play another important aspect of style: tradition. Every time Cork go into a Munster championship game they know that they have beaten their opponents more often than their opponents have beaten them. This gives them the confidence that goes with being the first in the province; that confidence enables them to play with greater élan and sparkle than many of their opponents. A team in the habit of winning can express itself better; and when Cork are at their best there can be no better hurling sight to see. For many, Cork hurling found its best expression in Christy Ring. He was the embodiment of genius, skill, and craft. Nothing seemed impossible to him. So often he exemplified in his play the old dictum that Cork were never beaten until the final whistle. Perhaps this is the greatest characteristic of Cork hurling: a tremendous belief that no matter how things are going against them in a game they have the time and the will and the cuteness to pull victory from the jaws of defeat. This was apparent during the years when Tipperary were physically stronger than Cork. The Rebel County always had ways round that impediment, and they frustrated Tipperary's prospects so often that the prayer of the Premier County became 'The hay saved and Cork bet!'

Writing in the *Cork Examiner* in 1994, Justin McCarthy, one of the most articulate analysts of the game, said of Kilkenny hurling: 'Kilkenny are a joy to watch. Hurling is their game and they are the specialists—it's the number one sport in the county. They have great stickmen always watching the ball, use every trick in the book, are thinking ahead all the time and are always comfortable on the ball. Each man, no matter what grade he plays, can play his position well. Their hurling is in their heads and in their hands, left or right. They are not an athletic looking team sturdily built, but they have staying power and can run well over short distances and can always time their runs.'[6]

Over fifty years earlier Carbery pronounced on Kilkenny hurling: 'Kilkenny hurlers from Tullaroan, Mooncoin, and the Marble City introduced neat quick hitting and wrist work; soon the spectacular side of the game won fresh acclaim. Skill and brain replaced to some extent strength and brawn. The happy medium triumphed without any loss of dash, daredevilry or vigour.'[7]

But the game in Kilkenny has not remained static. According to Paddy Buggy, 'it evolves and develops and is subject to change. The doing away with the third-man tackle, and the change in rules giving greater protection to the goalkeeper, probably suited Kilkenny hurling. Other changes, as in the sliotar—now almost rimless, the development of the hand-pass and so on Kilkenny adopted very quickly, so that change made very little difference to the performance of its team.' Kilkenny hurling and its mentors are prepared to experiment with new ideas while at the same time maintaining the natural craft style and artistry of their hurling. In the face of these changes, however, he has regrets: 'On a personal basis, I would have to say that I miss the excitement of the schmozzle in the square, the direct play by way of the overhead stroke, the reduction in the playing of the ball on the ground, and the use of hip and shoulder. Nowadays, if a player falls to the ground the referee invariably awards a free, even though the tackle was perfectly legitimate under the existing rules.'[8]

According to another commentator, one of the great exponents of Kilkenny hurling, Eddie Keher, 'the Kilkenny style was ideally suited to the smaller man with speed and skill who was knacky enough to beat bigger opponents.'[9] However, Kilkenny had to adjust their style with the advent of the great Wexford team in the fifties. According to Keher they introduced a new skill to the game, 'the spectacular high catch, which left commentators gasping for new words to describe the fearless, cavalier approach of the Wexford giants. They used their height and skill to command the area where the ball was dropping and used their hurley to protect the "catching" hand. Opponents were left pulling on fresh air as the Wexford men surged out with the ball to set up another attack. Possession was the name of the new game.'

Kilkenny hurling had to adjust to this new phenomenon, and Eddie Keher gives Father Tommy Maher the credit for coming up with an appropriate response. According to him there was 'no need to change the style, just change what you do with the ball. Play it low, across the field. Every ball must be used to the advantage of your colleague. Develop the hand-pass. Put a few strong men in central positions.' And Kilkenny were back on track with an All-Ireland victory in 1957 and a near miss in 1959. Kilkenny learned much from their encounters with Tipperary during the sixties and eventually won through in 1967. By then the old style of skill and wrist-work was still there, and the big men in the middle were able to catch like the Wexford men of the fifties. Keher concludes: 'The 1970 rule changes opened up the play in front of goal, and the new Kilkenny style was best positioned to take advantage of them. Hence the amazing run of success in the early seventies. Dillon, Henderson, Cummins, Delaney and Purcell were some backbone for a team, and it was easy to deal with the crumbs that fell to the wings.'

Billy Quirke of Enniscorthy believes that Wexford hurling style is a mongrel breed, a little of the best of everything. 'Big brave-hearted men moulded these skills together and immediately set themselves the task of becoming the best.'[10] He would concur with Eddie Keher's assessment of Wexford style and believes the style of play was copied, altered and used to suit the physique of the players. 'These big men enjoyed a robust game. They made full use of sprinting power that is part of the make-up of big men; they used their weight in the legitimate shoulder-charge and their height under the dropping ball.' Players like Morrissey, Wheeler, Codd and Cummins became famous for their overhead striking. All of them perfected the art of raising the ball and striking in one movement, and they could also use first-time striking when the occasion demanded it.

Probably the greatest change in style in any county has occurred in Galway. The tradition at club level in former times was of a robust, rugged, unadorned style with little scope given to the fast, stylish ball-player who liked the open spaces. The hurling was close and hard, with lots of body contact. But this did not imply that the tradition did not also throw up players whose first touch was fast and sure, who could double on a fast-running ground ball, who could carry the ball at speed and strike without handling or changing step, who could double on a fast overhead ball or flick it into the net. Two of the greatest exponents of this level of skill were Mick King and Josie Gallagher, but Galway teams always had a number of them.

One of the great Galway players of the forties, Father Paddy Gantley, believes that the traditional Galway style often found itself wanting in the open spaces of Croke Park, 'the testing-ground that separates the good from the less good. Galway teams did indeed play with dash and vigour, with first-time striking and daredevil feats of courage and determination. Time after time they brought their cheering supporters to their feet. But the great, unsubtle strength and long-driving power play of a Mattie Burke was no match for the cunning artistry of his contemporary Mick Mackey. The result was that many Galway teams became the much-admired gallant losers, who gave great entertainment to the crowds, who put up a great fight but lacked the skill that paid dividends on the scoreboard or the cool-headed determination that would sustain the effort right to the end of the game.'[11]

Galway hurling, for all its entertainment value, did not adequately reward its players or supporters until the seventies and eighties, according to Father Gantley. A number of developments were responsible. Better organisation at club and board level, improved fields, good juvenile competitions, an increase in the number of second-level schools and somewhat better refereeing all contributed to a higher level of good-quality players coming through. The advent of the under-21 grade gave players invaluable experience, and the teams of the seventies and eighties began to play the kind of hurling that brought the long-delayed rewards. They played with the vigour, dash and spirit of their predecessors but with more craft and combination, more self-assurance and, above all, with forwards who had the skill and style to pick off points at vital stages of the game.

Hurling purists, observing the changes in Galway hurling, complain of too much hand-passing, too much possession hurling, too much carrying of the ball. One could retort that these very skills have contributed their share in bringing about the county's present-day success. Also, it can be added, the general trend in hurling, aided by the rule changes that have made the game less physical, is towards more possession. Probably the greatest exponents of possession hurling at the moment are Offaly. Their players, whether in back or upfield, are extremely effective in finding their man when they strike the ball; not for them the long, raking clearance to relieve pressure. However, the weakness of over-elaboration and too much possession was underlined for Galway when Cork's first-time pulling put the men of the west off their stride in Croke Park in 1986.

It can be said with reasonable certainty that the style of hurling played in the less successful counties is of a slower variety. Commenting on Clare hurling and on the desire of so many that the county make the breakthrough, Justin McCarthy had this to say: 'When I went there in the 70's I tried to introduce a faster hurling style and a greater will to win. It worked to a fair extent and with some degree of success. But now they may have to start all over again and develop a snappier style of hurling, better footwork and wrist work and make up for the fact that they have been losers for the most part.'[12]

In the same vein, in an earlier period Carbery described the Antrim style as slow and cumbersome. This derived, especially in the Glens, from the use of a heavy ground hurl, a shinny, driving a wooden ball or crag on poor, unprepared grounds. Records relate that Antrim teams looked ponderous when faced with the likes of Kilkenny or Tipperary, playing with their broad camáns and leather-covered sliotar. The influence of the southern hurlers and the general adoption of the sliotar improved the game. The old style of the long, slow ground hit gave way to lift, handle, and strike. The change was gradual, however, and the big difference in standards between the north and the hurling core area was emphasised in the 1943 All-Ireland between Antrim and Cork.

A slow and cumbersome style is a recipe for failure, and with continued failure the opportunity to speed up the game never comes. Success on the other hand comes with the quickness of the striking action and the speed of the player's mental and physical reflexes. Anyone who has observed top-class hurlers will immediately be conscious of how little time and space they need to execute a hurling action. Responses can be speeded up with plenty of top-class play, and the quicker the responses the greater the chance of success. Ultimately the successful players and the successful teams are those who most effectively get the ball from one end of the field to the other, requiring the minimum of space and time to do so.

One traditional skill, the drop shot, is now scarcely ever seen. It was used to lethal effect in a close-in free when, properly executed, the ball would leave the ground at a rapid speed and rise in a trajectory to the roof of the net. Paddy Phelan of Kilkenny was a noted exponent; another Kilkenny man, Terry Leahy, was one of the last great masters of the skill. Pat Stakelum of Tipperary also made effective use of it. According to him it was a skill one inherited and practised until it was perfect. It was very difficult to hook or block down a player using the drop puck, and the ball shot off 'like a swallow out a barn door.' One of the few players using it today is Pat Fox of Tipperary, who employs it occasionally to get in his shot when closely marked.

Free-taking is a most important skill. Close to half of all scores, especially in winter conditions, come from placed balls. The penalty is a modern innovation in hurling, but the traditional 21-yard free with six defenders between the posts was an important shot. Any team who had a striker capable of scoring in this situation had an important asset. Such strikers used different techniques. Paddy Kenny of Tipperary favoured a strike from above the waist to the feet of the defenders, and in fact his shot was so lethal that some of his opponents in Tipperary clubs were afraid of the shot and the damage it might do to a body. Nicky Rackard depended on sheer power, and with his size and strength behind it a shot from him was difficult to stop. He had a higher level of success in 21-yard frees than anyone else. Christy Ring was another master, and he favoured the ball hit low and rising towards the roof of the net. Eddie Keher, a very effective free-taker, liked to aim head-high with his shots. Among today's players D. J. Carey throws the ball ahead of him, gaining a number of yards before striking it.

Scoring points can be equally important, and it's a skill that is called on more often in a game. A good free-taker is one of the most important players. Some would go so far as to suggest that any team should carry a specialist free-taker, even if he is not capable of much else. Such a player is one with the ability to score a placed ball ninety per cent of the time from centrefield to the twenty-metre mark. Jimmy Kennedy of Tipperary was that kind of player in the early fifties. Nearer the present John Fenton of Cork was probably the player with the best success rate from placed balls. Eddie Keher was in the same league.

Mention of John Fenton introduces another skill, the sideline puck, which can be another extremely valuable asset. Fenton could hit a sideline puck sixty yards or more. One of the most exciting exponents was Mick Moroney of Clare. He could score points on the ground from the centre of the field, with great length, height and direction in his shots. Theo English of Tipperary could also hit this shot effectively, as could Liam 'Chunky' O'Brien of Kilkenny; and there are others, too numerous to mention. Interestingly, this is a skill that has many good exponents today. Sideline pucking is still very effective, even though the shape of the modern hurley would appear to be against effective striking on the ground.

Another area of contrasting styles is the way the hurley is gripped. The general principle is that it should be gripped with the stronger hand further up the handle. The fact that some outstanding right-handed hurlers—such as Jim English of Wexford, Seán Kenny of Tipperary, and Martin Coogan and Paddy Moran of Kilkenny—gripped with the left hand on top does not deny the rule: all it means is that they succeeded in spite of this rather than because of it. 'Beginners who grip the hurley with their weaker hand on top start with a disadvantage which often precludes any chance of greatness.'[13] Two of the greatest exponents of the left hand on top (because they were left-handed players) were Jimmy Doyle and Paddy Kenny of Tipperary.

All players ought to be able to strike the ball on their bad side as well as their good. A few players succeeded so well on their bad side that it became more effective than their 'good' side. Such players as Paddy Barry of Cork, Jimmy Smith of Clare, Séamus Power and Frankie Walsh of Waterford, Fran Whelan of Dublin and Ned Wheeler of Wexford, although they played with their right hand on top, had very strong left-handed strokes—'so strong in fact that I suspect that most of them are really ciotógs who hurl with the right hand on top.'[14] The complete hurler is able to swing at a ball on the left or the right with equal skill. It matters not whether the ball is on the ground, overhead, or at any height in between. The ideal is to have both hands equally strong, and if they are it doesn't matter which is on top when gripping the hurley. Otherwise the stronger should be on top, and efforts should be made to strengthen the other side.

Thirty years ago Tony Wall wrote a short critical analysis of hurling in which he touched on all aspects of the game. He wrote: 'In hurling the end result is more important than how it is achieved. In other words it is more important to score a goal than to hit the ball perfectly, and many players are able to achieve the same result by different methods. However, the more technically correct a player is in his movements, the greater chance he will have of obtaining maximum certainty with the greatest possible speed and the minimum expenditure of energy ... The ability to hit the ball surely, and as quickly as possible, needs no explaining. Playing with the least expenditure of energy hardly needs explaining either. At the end of a game when players are tired the man who can drive the ball seventy yards with a flick of his wrists will be in better shape than the man who has to put all his strength into the swing.'[15]

18

The Future of Hurling

A degree of pessimism surrounds the future of hurling. In an emotional contribution on the subject at the 1994 Congress the chairman of the Kilkenny County Board of the GAA, Nicky Brennan, used the word 'crisis' to describe the state of the game and warned that there was a danger that it would disappear from areas of the country traditionally regarded as the hurling strongholds. He said that while we have had some good competitions in hurling, the overall state of the game and its standing within the GAA were being eroded, and serious actions needed to be taken.[1]

The fears this member was expressing were not just his own but arose from the findings of a working group set up by the GAA to report on the state of hurling. This report did not receive the publicity or the attention it deserved, and so Nicky Brennan felt obliged to speak out. His drawing attention to the state of hurling was not too well received in Croke Park, although he was speaking as the winner of two All-Ireland medals and an administrator of the game in one of the strong hurling counties.

One of the most effective forwards of the past decade, John Fitzgibbon of Cork, has recently expressed even greater gloom. 'I'm very pessimistic about hurling. Look at Cork. The main city clubs are not producing the hurlers. Carbery won the championship last year. Yet, the club teams of the '60's and '70's—the Rockies, the Barr's and the Glen would hammer any of the present teams by fifteen points or more. In my humble opinion, only D. J. Carey and Michael Cleary have real star quality. The rest are all good hurlers at intercounty level, but nothing compared to the past. I'm talking now strictly about the skill factor. There are other fellows then like Tomás Mulcahy who are great hurlers, inspirational, but in a different way ...'[2]

Tomás Ó Baróid, county secretary of Tipperary GAA, who served with Nicky Brennan on the hurling working group, is also pessimistic. He is particularly trenchant in his belief that despite all the coaching, the skill level is falling behind rather than improving. He is well placed to observe the state of things, as he watches many school and under-age games.

It is generally accepted that the numbers playing the game have declined. There are several reasons for this development. Hurling has to compete for players to a much greater degree today than ever before. There is a supermarket of choices for the young; hurling has to fight for players with Gaelic football, soccer, rugby, badminton, tennis, and many more. This is a modern phenomenon and something the promoters of hurling have not yet come to terms with.

For years, hurling and Gaelic football had the field virtually to themselves. They were well organised and had the backing of a powerful group of supporters in the Christian Brothers, who saw the promotion of Gaelic games as an essential part of their educational philosophy and who inculcated the idea that Irish games were the proper games for Irish boys. They backed this belief with an authoritarian approach that saw whole classes playing the games whether they liked them or not. Nobody called their regime into question, and they provided a steady stream of hurlers and footballers to fill the teams.

That era is now passed. The Brothers have departed from the scene so rapidly and completely that they have become little more than a memory. But the GAA as a body has not yet come to terms with this development. Most clubs were not geared to the promotion of hurling; and while the Brothers were there the clubs did not have to devote any time or personnel to the teaching of skills. When they did become aware of the problem they had not got the personnel with the time or the ability to teach the skills; and in the meantime many of their potential players had drifted into other games.

Belatedly, clubs are getting organised and coming to grips with the fact that they have to take the young players at an early age and teach them the game. With the departure of the Christian Brothers from primary education as well, fewer national schools are nurseries of hurling. Primary schools now have a preponderance of female teachers, and this has also taken attention away from the promotion of the game. Although many primary schools in the strong hurling counties still promote hurling, there are numerous instances where the lack of male teachers makes this impracticable.

More and more the club has to fill the gap and get the young players together at weekends to teach them the skills and to organise them for competitions. In doing this it has to contend with other sports that have become equally well organised in recent years and in some instances offer more exciting prospects to the younger player. Often the young player keeps his options open and plays several games, becoming proficient in all of them but not achieving the level of development required in any one. This 'dabbling' in many games and becoming a master of none is particularly detrimental to hurling, which requires hours of training and practice.

Coaching has become increasingly important in recent years; in some counties elaborate coaching schemes are in operation, and coaches regularly visit schools and clubs to teach the skills of the game. This is laudable, but it is not enough. It is not sufficient to spend one or two hours a week in formal coaching sessions and expect to become a master of hurling skills: many more hours of practice are required. And this is not forthcoming, because the nature of today's society is not conducive to hours of practice. Not too many years ago it was possible to see groups of young lads practising their skills, pucking about in the local field. Less and less does one see that now, and more and more players depend on the weekly coaching session.

A crucial development in the last decade or so has been the impact of soccer. With the success of the Irish team since the arrival of Jack Charlton as manager, soccer has had an enormous impact on the minds and imagination of the youth; the game has suddenly achieved a glamour and excitement that League of Ireland football on a Sunday afternoon could never offer. Ireland's international players have taken the place of the hurling heroes of yore. The aim and the expectation of many a young sportsman is to wear the green shirt of Ireland and to get international recognition, which has become a more desirable goal than winning an All-Ireland medal. In many ways identification with the country has taken over from local patriotism, where the dominant identification was with one's club or county. On top of this is the tremendous development of soccer at local level, where it is organised as extensively and effectively as the GAA. Soccer competitions, leagues and championships are now organised for all age groups. Virtually every parish has its soccer team, affiliated to the local league, and there are plenty of competitions to suit all levels.

Many parents are also opting for soccer, for a number of reasons. There is a perception that it is less dangerous than hurling. Less gear is required: boots and togs are all that are needed, while hurling requires a camán, which may break easily enough, and a helmet, which can cost over twenty pounds. (It could be said that soccer does not come cheaply either. No follower of the game is without his favourite team. All teams have home and away strips, and they change regularly, driving the parents to ever greater expense to keep their sons 'up to date'.)

The media attention given to soccer is another and perhaps a decisive factor. A truly international sport, soccer offers a generous weekly diet of games, national and international, which both whets and satisfies the appetite for the game. These matches are presented at peak viewing times and in an exciting and glamorous manner: they have build-ups, previews, interviews, and post-mortems. In contrast, hurling makes little media impact, with televised games few and far between. Apart from the fact that there are not more than a dozen championship games in the year, the GAA is not too keen on live television coverage, because of the fear of loss of revenue at the gate and the effect the televised game might have on attendance at other games played at the same time. The result is that hurling cannot compete with the glamour or impact of soccer, although the game itself is so much more exciting.

The result of all this is that fewer boys are taking up hurling today than ten or twenty years ago, and fewer of those who take it up are achieving the level of skill possessed by their predecessors.

A further detrimental development is the increasing drop-out rate among those who do take it up. There was a time when this occurred between minor and under-21 level, but the age level has dropped to between under-16 and under-18, and even lower. There is no single explanation for this development. Educational pressure is one reason: after the Junior Cert the pressure to get as many points as possible in the Leaving begins to build up, and sport is forced to take a back seat. There is opposition by parents to children playing hurling anywhere near examination time. Another cause is the changing life-style in the country, the greater affluence and the greater desire for the easier options in life. Many young people give up the life of active participation in sports in favour of that of the television sportsman.

Finally there is the enormously increased participation in third-level education and the resulting pressure to get high qualifications. Exams are held during a peak time in the hurling season, and competitions such as the minor and under-21 are brought to a halt between early May and late June. There is the additional fact of thousands of third-level students going abroad to work during the summer, during the height of the hurling season, and thus being lost to the game.

The quality of hurling played today is another matter of constant discussion. In every age there is a tendency to regard the play of yesteryear as better and more heroic. This applies in all areas of life: few people are capable of taking an objective stance and assessing the merits of today's play vis-à-vis yesterday's. Kevin Cashman sounds a warning note: 'Of standards, as of numbers, it is dangerous to generalise. The notion of a measurable "standard of hurling" is most commonly subscribed to by persons who see little of it, and/or those who are mind-locked in the conviction that change equals decline.'[3] The difference between top-class hurling today and that played by Blackrock a century earlier, he continues, was as great as that between the Rockies and the teams sponsored by the landlords a further century before. 'Natural evolution was helped along by changes of rules through all of those years. Which is as good as any other reason for experimenting when idealists perceive change to be necessary. Stasis is as impossible in hurling as in every other minutest facet of life in this evolving universe.'[4]

People of a certain age are inclined to look back and see hurling of a particular period—especially if it was a successful time for their county—as the golden age of hurling, against which every other time must be judged. Tipperary and Cork supporters will look back to the fifties as a time when their counties were locked in mortal combat for hurling supremacy; they will recall the exploits of their heroes through rose-tinted glasses and remember epic contests between men of legendary prowess. In like manner Wexford followers will remember the age of the Rackards; and the same can be said of other counties.

There is a hurling video that contains the highlights of All-Ireland finals from 1952 to 1967. It shows the 'heroic' players of that period as they really were. They are fine hurlers, capable of great displays; but they too have feet of clay: they make mistakes, miss shots, fail to take chances, make the wrong decisions, and in short behave very much as players do today. Watching it is a chastening experience for all who would make these players larger than life. And the games are in many instances very ordinary, in some cases not even that. Watching this record bears out Kevin Cashman's contention that of the fifty Munster finals he has seen, only fourteen were memorable. Enough said!

Perhaps what supporters of the 'golden age of hurling' theory are saying is that they preferred the kind of game that was played at a particular time. The type of hurling they remember as the best is a game in which physical contact and personal courage played a greater part. For them, today's game has been emasculated. What they forget is that whereas the game has been 'tamed' somewhat it is still one that demands a high level of personal courage and at its best is no place for the tender-hearted. (It is ironic that rule changes that have reduced physical contact have not reduced the number of injuries. There is a spate of injuries today of the ligament, tendon and hamstring variety that were unknown in the past.

'The only hamstring we knew anything about was the piece we got on the plate after the match,' quipped a Tipperary player and holder of five All-Irelands, Mickey Byrne. The higher level of physical fitness achieved by contemporary players is the likely cause.)

Rule changes have also done a lot to speed up the game and to make it an even more exciting spectacle. Anyone who watched the Kilkenny-Waterford under-21 All-Ireland semi-final in Semple Stadium in 1994 and studied the display of P. J. Delaney will agree that it was one of the finest displays of hurling ever seen and that it would stand beside any other display at any time or place in the history of hurling. Indeed it is probable that this and similar displays at the present time will become the standard by which present supporters will judge hurling in years to come.

As well as the decline in numbers and the evolution of the game through rule changes, with the result that hurling is a different spectacle today from what it was in the fifties, there is another aspect of the future of hurling that needs to be discussed. It would seem that there will be no significant extension of the area in which the game is played. Over the past century attempts have been made to spread hurling to counties outside the traditional areas. These attempts have resulted in greater numbers playing the game and in all counties fielding hurling teams; but that's as much as can be said about the success of the efforts. The standard of hurling achieved in these non-traditional areas is so far behind that in the core counties of Cork, Kilkenny and Tipperary that they have virtually no chance of winning an All-Ireland championship. In fact, as has been shown by the domination of the championship by the three core counties, the chances of the counties in the immediate area surrounding the core are as slim as one in four. That is not to take from the emergence of Galway and Offaly as serious challengers since 1980 and the possibility that Clare and Waterford may join that category in the not too distant future. But apart from these four counties the only other realistic challengers are Limerick and Wexford. This situation does not differ very much in fact from a hundred years ago, and there is no reason to believe that the balance will shift dramatically in the next century.

This may appear a pessimistic assessment of the future of hurling, but it may be the only realistic one. If one were to make a similar statement at the time of the first All-Ireland it might have appeared as if hurling had only a short future; but it survived, and is stronger today than it was then. Is there any reason to fear that it has less of a future today? Surely it is all the greater reason for it to be cherished and protected in the core area. Hurling is a significant game in about ten counties, and it should be cultivated and developed in them. This would be a better policy than dissipating scarce resources in trying to cultivate the game outside that area. It may be heresy to say that the game cannot travel, but the experience of the past century would seem to confirm the belief. The skill level of the game is so demanding that unless the essentials are learned at a very early age it is virtually impossible to acquire them later in life. Because of the impossibility of *making* hurlers, therefore, one has to depend on breeding them, and this is why concentration on the core area is of such importance.

There is another important consideration in any discussion of the future of hurling. The game will not live by itself but, to compete satisfactorily with other sports, must be packaged and presented in the best possible way. It must be made appear as attractive as possible, and this can only happen if it is played in the best conditions and on the best of pitches. This has to mean summer hurling, when the sun is at the back and the ball bounces as high as a house. There is also a great need for top-class hurling games. People must be exposed more and more to this marvellous game, with its high level of skill and its demands on personal courage. As matters stand, there are far too few inter-county games. The only new competition in the last twenty-five years was the club championship; this has proved a great success, is immensely popular with players and spectators alike, and seems set for a long future. Side by side with its rise has been the almost total eclipse of that once-great competition, the Railway Cup. The league too has lost some of its appeal, and this may be because it is played at a time of the year not conducive to good hurling.

When one discusses the organisation and presentation of hurling, the governing body of the game, the GAA, comes into focus. At present it is the governing body not only of hurling but also of Gaelic football, handball, and camogie. There is a strong argument that the organisation is too unwieldy and is stretched too far to do justice to hurling. Since football is the most popular of the games under its control, it gets most of the attention. The GAA over a century has failed to realise Cusack's desire to 'bring back the hurling.' It succeeded in making Gaelic football popular and widespread beyond the dreams of the founders, but the spread of hurling has never been as great. It needs special treatment to ensure its survival, and perhaps only a separate organisation can provide that. From the players' point of view also there are urgent reasons for a separate body. Many of the people who sit on important GAA committees are football-oriented and have not got hurling at heart. At the moment many hurlers play football also, because the GAA promotes both games. With so much pressure on their time, they cannot give hurling the attention needed to perfect the skills. In some cases football is taking over, because it does not demand the level of training that hurling does. The sooner hurling goes it alone, the sooner this drift to football in hurling areas will be halted.

Eamon Rea of Limerick is flanked by Kilkenny men Tom McCormack (left) and Nicky Orr during the All-Ireland final of 1974.

The Galway team that won the National Hurling League in 1975. **BACK ROW** (LEFT TO RIGHT): S. SILKE, P. J. QUALTER, N. McINERNEY, M. CONNEELY, J. McDONAGH, PAT LALLY, I. CLARKE. **FRONT ROW** (LEFT TO RIGHT): J. CLARKE, P. FAHY, F. BURKE, J. CONNOLLY, S. MURPHY, P. J. MOLLOY, M. BARRETT, G. COONE.

Action from the All-Ireland final of 1976 with Martin Quigley of Wexford (left) and John Horgan of Cork.

The Kilkenny side that won the championship in 1979. **BACK ROW** (LEFT TO RIGHT): F. LARKIN, N. BRENNAN, P. PRENDERGAST, F. CUMMINS, M. CROTTY, B. FITZPATRICK, R. REID, M. RUTH. **FRONT ROW** (LEFT TO RIGHT): M. BRENNAN, J. HENNESSY, L. O'BRIEN, G. FENNELLY, N. SKEHAN, J. HENDERSON, G. HENDERSON.

Joe McKenna of Limerick following their victory in the Munster final of 1980.

The agony and joy of beating Cork in the 1989 Munster senior final is illustrated in this picture of Willie Fitzmaurice (Limerick) and Noel Drumgoole, formerly of Dublin.

All-Ireland final, 1980, Galway v. Limerick. **LEFT TO RIGHT**: JOHN CONNOLLY (GALWAY), JOE
CONNOLLY (GALWAY), SEÁN FOLEY (LIMERICK), DOMINIC PUNCH (LIMERICK).

The Galway side that bridged a 57-year gap by winning the championship in 1980. **BACK
ROW** (LEFT TO RIGHT): CONOR HAYES, STEVE MAHON, JOHN CONNOLLY, MICHAEL CONNOLLY, FRANK
BURKE, NOEL LANE, SEÁN SILKE. **FRONT ROW** (LEFT TO RIGHT): NIALL McINERNEY, SÉAMUS COEN, JIMMY
COONEY, JOE CONNOLLY, SYLVIE LINNANE, P. J. MOLLOY, BERNIE FORDE.

The 1981 championship brought an even bigger breakthrough than 1980, as Offaly finally secured their first senior title. Here the rival captains, Seán Silke (Galway) and Pádraig Horan (Offaly), engage in a little repartee before the throw-in.

The Offaly team that made history by winning the 1981 championship. **BACK ROW** (LEFT TO RIGHT): PAT KIRWIN, CHRISTY KING, PAT FLEURY, JOACHIM KELLY, LIAM CURRAMS, PAT DELANEY, EUGENE COUGHLAN, AODH HORAN, JIM TROY, TOM CONNEELY, MICK KENNEDY, AIDAN FOGARTY. **SECOND ROW** (LEFT TO RIGHT): BRENDAN KEESHAN, TOM DONOGHUE, JOHNNY FLAHERTY, DAMIEN MARTIN, PÁDRAIG HORAN, GER COUGHLAN, PAT CARROLL, MARK CORRIGAN, DANNY OWENS, MARTIN CASHIN, BRENDAN BERMINGHAM. **FRONT ROW** (LEFT TO RIGHT): SEÁN O'MEARA, SEÁN WHITE.

The Limerick side that won the National League in 1984. **BACK ROW** (LEFT TO RIGHT): JOE McKENNA, MATT REA, PADDY KELLY, SEÁN FOLEY, TOMMY QUAID, PA FOLEY, LIAM O'DONOGHUE, PAT HERBERT. **FRONT ROW** (LEFT TO RIGHT): OLLIE O'CONNOR, PAUDIE FITZMAURICE, M. J. COFFEY, LEONARD ENRIGHT, JIMMY CARROLL, DANNY FITZGERALD, JOHN FLANAGAN.

The Centenary final of 1984 was played at Semple Stadium, Thurles, between Cork, the winners, and Offaly. Here Seánie O'Leary of Cork heads for goal.

The Cork side that won the Centenary championship of 1984. **BACK ROW** (LEFT TO RIGHT): DONAL O'GRADY, TOMÁS MULCAHY, TIM CROWLEY, KEVIN HENNESSY, GER CUNNINGHAM, JIMMY BARRY MURPHY, JOHN CROWLEY. **FRONT ROW** (LEFT TO RIGHT): TONY O'SULLIVAN, DENIS MULCAHY, DERMOT McCURTAIN, TOM CASHMAN, JOHN FENTON (CAPT.), JOHN HODGINS, PAT HARTNETT, SEÁNIE O'LEARY.

Jubilation on the Cork bench at the end of the All-Ireland final of 1986. Frank Murphy, County Secretary, John 'Kid' Cronin, masseur, Cathal Casey, Frank O'Sullivan (partly hidden) and John O'Callaghan, at back, race onto the pitch to congratulate the heroes.

Nicholas English, one of the most stylish and effective hurlers of modern times, was the linchpin of the Tipperary attack from the mid-eighties on.

Galway All-Ireland champions, 1988. **BACK ROW** (LEFT TO RIGHT): B. LYNSKEY, P. McINERNEY, M. COLEMAN, A. CUNNINGHAM, J. COMMINS, T. KEADY, M. NAUGHTON, P. MALONE. **FRONT ROW** (LEFT TO RIGHT): M. McGRATH, J. COONEY, C. HAYES, S. LEENANE, G. MCINERNEY, O. KILKENNY, E. RYAN.

Action from the 1990 final between Cork and Galway.

The Cork side that defeated Galway by 5-15 to 2-21 to win the All-Ireland final, 1990.

The early nineties brought a series of thunderous games between Tipperary and Galway, not least the 1991 All-Ireland semi-final, which Tipperary won en route to their second championship in three years.

The Down side that won the Ulster hurling championship in 1992. **BACK ROW** (LEFT TO RIGHT): MARTIN BAILIE, GERARD COULTER, KEVIN COULTER, GERARD McGRATTAN, NOEL KEITH, DANNY HUGHES, GARY SAVAGE, GREG BLANEY. **FRONT ROW** (LEFT TO RIGHT): MARTIN MALLON, PAUL COULTER, PADDY BRANNIF, PAUL McMULLAN, NOEL SANDS (CAPT.), DERMOT WOODS, MICK BLANEY.

The most romantic story in modern hurling was the triumph of Clare in the 1995 championship after a wait of eighty-one years. They had won their first Munster championship since 1932 a few weeks earlier. **BACK ROW** (LEFT TO RIGHT): BRIAN LOHAN, MICHAEL O'HALLORAN, FRANK LOHAN, CONOR CLANCY, DAVID FITZGERALD, SEÁN McMAHON, GER O'LOUGHLIN. **FRONT ROW** (LEFT TO RIGHT): LIAM DOYLE, P. J. O'CONNELL, OLLIE BAKER, ANTHONY DALY, JAMES O'CONNOR, FERGAL HEGARTY, FERGUS TUOHY, STEPHEN McNAMARA.

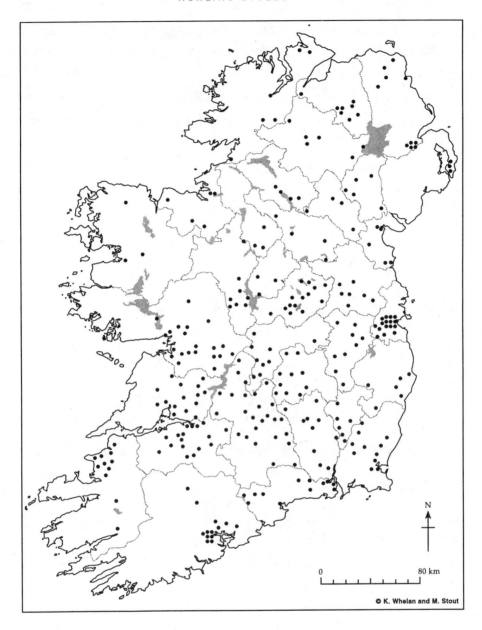

Senior hurling clubs

A separate body to control hurling would be able to devote its attention exclusively to the game, to its organisation and development, to its protection and welfare, and to catering for its specific needs and requirements. Such a body would have no need to accommodate other games by providing space for them during the best hurling months of the year.

The future of hurling will depend also on looking after players properly. Any obstacles to a player taking up the game or remaining in it should be removed. If the gear is too expensive or beyond the reach of a player, there should be subsidies for hurleys and helmets and anything else required. Players should have the benefit of a good insurance scheme and should not be fearful for Monday's job when playing Sunday's game: the controlling body should realise how important a job is to a player and that playing the game should not be a factor in losing it.

Side by side with a good insurance scheme must be good refereeing. Standards of refereeing must be improved, and the referee must realise that his primary role is the protection of the players. Equally, the players must feel fully confident that they have that protection.

There must be a proper games structure, so that the player has a regular series of games. At present there is a dreadful imbalance between the playing chances of the top-class player and the ordinary one with aspirations that will never reach higher than the club junior Bs. Too much emphasis is put on the inter-county structures, with the ordinary player standing by the wayside waiting for club competitions to be concluded at the tail end of the season.

The introduction of professionalism might be another way to guarantee the future of hurling. The example of ice hockey in Canada is often quoted as a model. The demands on the top-class player have become so great that he needs to be paid for it. Such a player may have commitments to a club, county, college or company team, and if all are going well the number of matches and training sessions he must find time for is incredible. At present if he is successful the perks are generous. Clothes and gear, meals and holidays and in some cases 'expenses' are part of the scene; the really successful players can command substantial fees for 'appearances'. All this smacks of professionalism but is regarded as acceptable because of the demands made on players. How players would react to full-blown professionalism is difficult to assess. It does seem as if it would run counter to the traditional club and county rivalry that is so much part of hurling. If these problems were overcome and a professional or semi-professional game came into existence, it might give the game the publicity and the impact it deserves. It would also transform it.

As things are, there is not as much thought put into the nature and the potential of the game as there might be. Perhaps it could be better played with thirteen or eleven players a side. Already one of the fastest of games, perhaps it could become still faster and more exciting. Under professional control it could be more intensely explored as a game. Hurling is getting lost in the world around it. It is not making the impact it should, and unless something dramatic is done it may be squeezed out of existence.

Hurling is the oldest recorded field game. It is a link with our heroic past, part of our cultural heritage and part of what we are. It is still a strong and virile game, a game worth going a long way to see and one that is well worth preserving. It is as much a part of our heritage as our language and our music, and just as the Government considers itself duty bound to preserve them and to expend money in doing so, any help or subsidisation required for the preservation of hurling should be forthcoming from the same source.

The survival of hurling has always caused concern, and that concern has been expressed at the most unlikely times. Looking back from the perspective of 1995, the game seems to have been alive and well in 1958; and yet a contemporary newspaper report had this to say:

> Delegates to the annual GAA Congress today are sure to get warmed-up when they consider the General Secretary's statement on the revival of hurling. Listen to this extract: 'It is time to stop the talk about spreading hurling and get down to the work of having it done.' Challenging and true. Remember Mr O'Keeffe's 'appointment' speech made on the eve of the Cork-Galway All-Ireland final in 1927. It was hurling then. After 30 years in office it is the same story.[5]

Within a couple of years a new attendance record for a Munster final was created. Dublin nearly won an All-Ireland. Galway and Offaly made the breakthrough to All-Ireland honours. Hurling today, however, does not appear to have such a rosy future.

Epilogue

Incredible as Offaly's victory over Limerick seemed, Clare's arrival in 1995 was sensational. No county had so many disappointments in a long hurling history, particularly during the previous thirty years. Beaten in nine Munster senior finals and numerous deciders at other levels, the Clare team and its supporters had come to believe that a Munster final would never come to the Banner County and that the winning of the Liam McCarthy Cup was in the realm of fantasy.

Their only previous All-Ireland success was in 1914, when a team captained by Amby Power from Quin beat Laois in the final. They were back in the final in 1932 but lost to Kilkenny in the decider. On that occasion the captain of the team was John Joe 'Goggles' Doyle; and he and the other two survivors from the team, Mick Falvey and Tom 'Fowler' McInerney, were present on 3 September 1995 to witness Clare's breakthrough.

There wasn't much to presage the events of 1995. Admittedly Clare had defeated Tipperary and Kerry to qualify for the 1994 Munster final, but they had been humiliated by Limerick in the decider. Again after an impressive showing in the 1994/95 National League, losing only one game on their way to the final, they failed against Kilkenny in a game that showed a big difference in class between the two sides. Somehow the manager, Ger Loughnane, was able to see some light at the end of the tunnel, but few after the defeat were inclined to believe his prediction, 'We will win the Munster championship this summer.'

Loughnane believed that the successes achieved over the years by St. Flannan's College and the great work being done at under-age level were about to be reflected in senior success. He also believed that Clare could compete with any team as far as midfield and that if he could raise the performance level of the forwards he would have a team to compete with the best. This lack of forward power was all too evident against Kilkenny in the league final, when Clare scored nine points to the winners' 2-12. Four points of Clare's total came from the stick of the centre-back, Seánie McMahon, who scored from placed balls. A point for each of the full-forward line during the first half was supplemented by a completely inadequate two points after the interval. Before a tight Kilkenny defence, Clare's forwards had neither the technique nor the penetration to succeed.

How justified Loughnane's hopes were would be seen in the Munster semi-final against Cork in Limerick on 4 June. Together with the selectors, Mike McNamara and Tony Considine, the manager and the team continued their preparations during the four intervening weeks. Little more than fourteen thousand turned up for the game, an interesting comment on the faith of Clare's supporters. And those of little faith lived to rue their decision to stay at home. A match of very poor standard came alive in the closing five minutes, during which three goals were scored, each of which seemed to have irrefutably altered the match's course. With five minutes to go, 'Sparrow' O'Loughlin completed a fine Clare move with a goal to bring the sides level; within a minute P. J. O'Connell had edged them ahead with a point. But Cork were not dead. Mark Mullins got possession and, though pursued by Frank Lohan, got the ball to Alan Browne, whose flick-on was despatched to the net by Kevin Murray. If Cork could do it, why not Clare? In injury time Fergus Tuohy sent in a line ball that dropped in on Cork's goal and was finished to the net by Ollie Baker. In the seconds remaining a desperate Cork attack nearly succeeded; Alan Browne's shot hit the Clare post, and Ger Manley's rebound was splendidly blocked by Frank Lohan, to leave Clare victorious, 2-13 to 3-9.

The game will be remembered for a number of things. The most obvious was the appalling shooting of the forwards. Clare shot no less than twenty wides, and Cork made their own contribution of fourteen. Jamesie O'Connor, who was switched to centrefield at the start of the game, was magnificent and eclipsed his marker, Barry Egan. Above all the game will be remembered for Clare's spirit: it was fantastic. During the last twenty minutes—when they were reduced to fourteen men, having used up their three subs; Seán McMahon, who had injured his collarbone, had nobody to replace him—they gave a heroic display and drew on reserves of courage and purpose that had to be admired.

The Munster final in Thurles on 9 July will long be remembered, not for the game itself, which was mediocre and one-sided, but for the scenes of enthusiasm that greeted the final whistle. The opposition was Limerick, the same outfit who had dished out a nine-point drubbing to the Banner County the previous year. Clare had the perfect build-up to the game, low-key, with little expected of them. They were cool and calm coming into the match, which allowed them to play their natural game. But it was difficult for their supporters to erase the memory of forty years previously, when the same sides met. On that occasion Clare had gone into the game roaring-hot favourites after victories over Cork and Tipperary, only to collapse miserably on the day.

After the first twenty minutes the result was never really in doubt. With the advantage of the wind, Limerick pulled away into a 0-5 to 0-2 lead. The possibility existed that the champions might extend their lead, but this was the furthest in front they were to get. Clare gradually established themselves, and a dramatic goal from a penalty by the goalie, David Fitzgerald, in about the thirtieth minute helped them to a 1-5 to 0-7 lead at the interval. They maintained their momentum in the second half, and though Limerick threatened occasionally they hadn't got the finish against a determined Clare defence. Limerick's big names—Ciarán Carey, Mike Houlihan, and Gary Kirby—did not perform to their best, and with their efforts below par, Limerick were in big trouble. In the end Clare won by 1-17 to 0-11, a victory of nine points and a perfect retaliation for their defeat in 1994. The history-making side was: David Fitzgerald, Michael O'Halloran, Brian Lohan, Frank Lohan, Liam Doyle, Seán McMahon, Anthony Daly, Jamesie O'Connor, Ollie Baker, Fergus Tuohy, P. J. O'Connell, Fergal Hegarty, Stephen McNamara, Conor Clancy, and Ger 'Sparrow' O'Loughlin; subs: Jim McInerney for Tuohy, Cyril Lyons for Clancy. The referee was Johnny McDonnell of Tipperary.

The next step for Clare to the highest honour in hurling was the All-Ireland semi-final encounter with Galway in Croke Park on 6 August. Having properly celebrated their great Munster victory, they got back to the important business of preparing for the next game and returned to the discipline of training. They were helped on the day by a very poor Galway performance, especially in the first half, when they appeared to be disorganised and disoriented. Matters improved for them in the second half, but by this time they had conceded too much to Clare, who led by 2-6 to 0-7. A goal was added two minutes into the second half when O'Loughlin completed a great Clare move; but Galway were soon back with a Francis Forde goal, and points were then exchanged. Then Clare went through a period of lassitude for about fifteen minutes and failed to score. Galway got four points; then in the twenty-first minute P. J. O'Connell got a long-range point. This appeared to rouse Clare again: they scored three more before the final whistle, to Galway's one. The result was 3-12 to 1-13 in favour of the Munster champions.

The third of September 1995 is a date that will for ever be etched on the hurling consciousness of Clare. Supporters came from near and far to cheer their heroes in the All-Ireland encounter against Offaly, the team that had so stunningly snatched victory from the jaws of defeat just twelve months previously. The Liam McCarthy Cup, presented in 1923, had never been won by Clare. The general expectation was that Offaly should win: they had the experience of the previous year's victory to cushion them, and, it was believed, you had to lose one to win one. And Offaly were brilliant against Kilkenny in the Leinster final. However, this prognosis failed to take into consideration the unmeasurable resolve, spirit and purpose that filled the Clare team and the unrelenting refusal to accept defeat that imbued Ger Loughnane.

The game was one in which backs dominated. The Clare defence suffocated the Offaly forward line and reduced a sparkling set of players to dull plodders. This was reflected in the fact that during the entire second half the team managed only one score from play, a goal by Johnny Pilkington in the fifty-fourth minute. In fact the scoring was the lowest in an All-Ireland since 1987. And if Clare backs were superb in reducing the Offaly forwards to ineptitude, the champions' defence was equally brilliant. Under sustained pressure for most of the second half, they held out against the best efforts of the Banner County, with Kevin Kinihan at full-back having a mighty game. It was unfortunate for this brave player that, four minutes from time, a ball he batted down from a long-distance free by Anthony Daly should fall in the path of the sub Éamonn Taaffe, who sent it crashing to the net and the lead for Clare.

Offaly led 1-6 to 0-7 at half time, Clare having got two valuable points in the last two minutes of the half. Opinion was now divided between those who saw Clare's ability to fight and their closeness on the scoreboard as signs in their favour and those who expected Offaly to snap out of their lethargy and up their performance dramatically in the second half. It was Clare who had the answers, and particularly in the performance of Fergus Tuohy, who scored three great points during the half. The Clare effort was temporarily halted by the Offaly goal in the fifty-fifth minute but received a tremendous boost with the Taaffe goal four minutes from time. That score put Clare a point in front; then a Johnny Dooley free immediately brought Offaly level. Two minutes from time a great sixty-five by Anthony Daly, who played a captain's part, put the Banner County in front, and in the final minute Jamesie O'Connor clinched it for Clare with a point from a free: 1-13 to 2-8.

The scenes of jubilation were unprecedented. In a fine victory speech Anthony Daly said that there had been better Clare teams down the years and that the current side was accepting the All-Ireland on their behalf also. He then paid tribute to Offaly, who, he said, had inspired Clare hurling by breaking the grip of tradition fourteen years previously. It was a generous speech, on a par with everything the team did on the road to the All-Ireland. A well-behaved and disciplined bunch of players, they set standards of behaviour and attitude that were a credit to the players and their management.

The first Clare team to win the McCarthy Cup were: David Fitzgerald, Michael O'Halloran, Brian Lohan, Frank Lohan, Liam Doyle, Seán McMahon, Anthony Daly (captain), Jamesie O'Connor, Ollie Baker, Fergus Tuohy, P. J. O'Connell, Fergal Hegarty, Stephen McNamara, Conor Clancy, and Ger O'Loughlin; subs: Éamonn Taaffe for McNamara, Cyril Lyons for Clancy, Anthony Neville for Taaffe.

'There is nothing that cannot be achieved with the proper approach, together with dedication and commitment,' Ger Loughnane said on the morning after the All-Ireland. The Clare hurlers of 1995 were proof of that belief, and their success must do something to inspire other teams, whether from Waterford or Wexford, Antrim or Down, to dedicate themselves with the same commitment that saw Clare overcome decades of defeat and achieve such a great victory.

Appendix 1

All-Ireland Senior Championship (Liam McCarthy Cup), 1887–1996

1887 (1 Apr. 1888): Tipperary (Thurles) 1-1, Galway (Meelick) 0-0.
Tipperary: J. Stapleton (capt.), M. Maher, T. Maher, A. Maher, T. Burke, M. McNamara, E. Murphy, J. Dwyer, T. Stapleton, N. Bowe, T. Healy, D. Ryan, J. Ryan, P. Leahy, T Dwyer, J. Mockler, J. Dunne, T. Carroll, J. Leahy, M. Carroll, P. Lambe.

1888: Unfinished because of American 'invasion' by GAA athletes.

1889 (3 Nov.): Dublin (Kickhams) 5-1, Clare (Tulla) 1-6.
Dublin: N. O'Shea (capt.), F. Coughlan, P. Butler, J. Lambe, D. Kerwick, J. D. O'Byrne, T. McKenna, W. J. Spain, J. Harper, C. Hackett, T. Maher, J. Bishop, T. Belton, P. Ryan, J. Cahill, E. Gilligan, F. Palmer, S. Riordan, P. O'Shea, P. Riordan, M. Madigan.

1890 (16 Nov.): Cork (Aghabullogue) 1-6, Wexford (Castlebridge) 2-2. Unfinished; Cork awarded match.
Cork: D. Lane (capt.), J. Henchion, J. Buckley, D. Lenihan, D. Looney, D. Drew, T. O'Connor, T. Twomey, M. Horgan, P. Buckley, T. Kelleher, J. Kelleher, J. Reilly, P. O'Riordan, D. O'Sullivan, T. Good, D. Horgan, J. Lenihan, J. O'Sullivan, E. Reilly, P. O'Riordan.

1891 (28 Feb. 1892): Kerry (Ballyduff) 2-3, Wexford (Crossbeg) 1-5 (after extra time).
Kerry: J. O'Mahoney, M. Kelly, J. Pierce, P. Carroll, M. Wynne, M. J. O'Sullivan, R. Kissane, F. Crowley, J. Crowley, J. O'Sullivan, T. Dunne, J. Murphy, M. Fitzmaurice, J. McDonnell, T. D. McCarthy, T. E. McCarthy, M. Riordan, P. Quane, J. Quane, P. Rourke, P. Kirby.

1892 (26 Mar. 1893): Cork (Redmonds) 2-4, Dublin (Flag-Davitts) 1-1. Unfinished; Dublin withdrew after fifty minutes' play.
Cork: W. O'Callaghan (capt.), J. Kenneally, M. Casserly, J. Keegan, J. Leahy, M. Sheehan, C. O'Callaghan, D. Halloran, T. Irwin, J. Conway, J. O'Connor, W. O'Connor, D. Scannell, J. Cashman, D. Coughlan, D. Drew, P. Buckley. (Teams reduced to seventeen a side.)

1893 (24 June 1894): Cork (Blackrock) 6-8, Kilkenny (Confederation) 0-2.
Cork: J. Murphy, J. Norberg, D. Scannell, M. Murphy, D. Hayes, P. Coughlan, J. Young, S. Hegarty, M. Cronin, P. O'Keeffe, J. Cullinane, J. O'Leary, J. Delea, M. O'Connor, J. Cashman, W. J. O'Connell, P. Flaherty.

1894 (24 Mar. 1895): Cork (Blackrock) 5-20, Dublin (Rapparees) 2-0.
Cork: S. Hayes (capt.), D. Hayes, P. Coughlan, J. O'Leary, M. Murphy, J. Cashman, J. Kidney, J. Delea, M. Cronin, D. Coughlan, J. Kelleher, J. Norberg, S. Hegarty, J. Cullinane, J. O'Connor, J. Young, W. O'Connell.

1895 (15 Mar. 1896): Tipperary (Tubberadora) 6-8, Kilkenny (Tullaroan) 1-0.
Tipperary: M. Maher (capt.), E. Maher, P. Byrne, W. Kerwick, J. Maher, D. Walsh, J. Walsh, P. Maher, T. Flanagan, J. Flanagan, P. Riordan, J. Gleeson, F. Moriarty, J. Connolly, J. Maher, E. Brennan, W. Devane.

1896 (27 Mar. 1898): Tipperary (Tubberadora) 8-14, Dublin (Commercials) 0-4.
Tipperary: M. Maher (capt.), J. Maher (F), P. Byrne, W. Devane, M. Wall, E. Maher, E. Brennan, J. Walsh, T. Condon, J. Connolly, J. Flanagan, T. Ryan, P. Scanlon, T. Flanagan, E. Ryan, P. Doherty, D. Walsh.

1897 (20 Nov. 1898): Limerick (Kilfinnane) 3-4, Kilkenny (Tullaroan) 2-4.
Limerick: D. Grimes (capt.), J. 'Seán Óg' Hanly, M. Flynn, P. Flynn, M. Finn, P. O'Brien, T. Brazill, J. Condon, J. Catteral, J. Hynes, P. Butler, J. Flood, P. Mulcahy, M. Downes, J. Reidy, J. Finn, P. Buskin.

1898 (25 Mar. 1900): Tipperary (Tubberadora) 7-13, Kilkenny (Threecastles) 3-10.
Tipperary: M. Maher (capt.), E. Maher, E. Brennan, J. Walsh, J. Connolly, T. Ryan, W. Devane, E. Ryan, P. Byrne, W. Dunne, T. Condon, J. O'Keeffe, J. Maher (M), D. Walsh, J. Maher (F), D. O'Keeffe.

1899 (24 Mar. 1901): Tipperary (Moycarkey) 3-12, Wexford (Blackwater) 1-4.
Tipperary: T. Condon (capt.), J. O'Keeffe, W. 'Big Bill' Gleeson, J. Gleeson, R. O'Keeffe, J. O'Keeffe, D. Walsh, M. Maher, J. Walsh, J. Flanagan, J. Ryan, M. Wall, W. Dunne, P. Byrne, J. Maher, W. 'Little Bill' Gleeson, T. Ryan.

1900 (26 Oct. 1902): Tipperary (Twomileborris) 2-5, London (Desmonds) 0-6.
Tipperary: E. Hayes (capt.), P. Hayes, M. Ryan, M. Purcell, T. Allen, P. Maher, W. Maher, M. Maher, J. Walsh, T. Ryan, E. Maher, W. 'Big Bill' Gleeson, W. 'Little Bill' Gleeson, J. O'Keeffe, M. Wall, T. Semple, J. Gleeson.

Home final (21 Oct. 1902): Tipperary 6-3, Galway (Ardrahan) 1-5.
Tipperary: E. Hayes (capt.), P. Hayes, M. Ryan, M. Purcell, T. Allen, W. Maher, J. Walsh, T. Ryan, E. Maher, W. Gleeson (2), M. Wall, J. O'Keeffe, P. Maher, J. Gleeson, T. Semple, M. Maher.

1901 (2 Aug. 1903): London (selection) 1-5, Cork (Redmonds) 0-4.
London: J. Coughlan (capt.), P. King, J. King, P. Crowe, J. Fitzgerald, J. O'Brien, T. Barry, J. Barry, J. Connell, D. Horgan, M. Horgan, S. Lynch, T. Doody, M. McMahon, E. Barrett, J. Kelleher, J. Crowley.

Home final (14 June 1903): Cork 2-8, Wexford (Blackwater) 0-6.
Cork: P. Cantillon (capt.), J. Delea, D. McGrath, T. Irwin, J. Leonard, D. O'Keeffe, T. Powell, C. Young, J. Kelleher, J. Ronayne, J. O'Neill, T. Hallinan, P. Sullivan, J. O'Leary, D. Daly, W. Sheehan, M. O'Reilly.

1902 (11 Sep. 1904): Cork (Dungourney) 3-13, London 0-0.
Cork: J. Kelleher (capt.), J. Ronayne, J. Desmond, J. O'Shea, W. Daly, J. Daly, T. Mahoney, T. Lynch, J. Leahy, T. Coughlan, W. Moloney, C. Young, W. Parfrey, P. Cantillon, D. McGrath, D. O'Keeffe, W. O'Neill.

Home final (3 July 1904): Cork 1-7, Dublin (Faughs) 1-7. Replay (17 July 1904): Cork 2-6, Dublin 0-1.
Cork: J. Kelleher (capt.), J. Ronayne, J. Desmond, J. O'Shea, W. Daly, J. Daly, T. Mahoney, M. O'Shea, J. Leahy, T. Coughlan, D. Coughlan, S. Riordan, W. Parfrey, W. Fitzgibbon, D. McGrath, D. O'Keeffe, W. O'Neill.

1903 (12 Nov. 1905): Cork (Blackrock) 3-16, London (Hibernians) 1-1.
Cork: S. Riordan (capt.), T. Coughlan, J. Coughlan, D. Kidney, L. Flaherty, J. Kelleher, J. Desmond, J. O'Leary, W. Mackessy, A. Buckley, D. Buckley, W. Hennessy, W. O'Neill, P. O'Sullivan, M. O'Leary, D. O'Keeffe, D. McGrath.

Home final (16 July 1905): Cork 8-9, Kilkenny (Threecastles) 0-8.
Cork: as above, except J. Leary in place of J. Coughlan.

1904 (24 June 1906): Kilkenny (Tullaroan) 1-9, Cork (St Finbarr's) 1-6.
Kilkenny: J. Doheny (capt.), P. Maher, S. Walton, J. Hoyne, P. Saunders, J. Lawlor, R. Doyle, E. Doyle, P. Fielding, R. Walsh, J. Rochford, D. Grace, R. Brennan, D. Stapleton, P. Lanigan, J. Anthony, M. Lawlor; sub: J. Dunne.

1905: In a disputed match on 14 Apr. 1907 the score was Cork 5-10, Kilkenny 3-13. Replay (30 June 1907): Kilkenny (Erin's Own) 7-7, Cork (St Finbarr's) 2-9.
Kilkenny: D. J. Stapleton, J. Hoyne, T. Kenny, D. Kennedy, J. Anthony, J. J. Brennan, R. Walsh, E. Teehan, D. Grace, S. Walton, J. Kelly, P. Lanigan, E. Doyle, M. Lawlor, J. Lawlor, R. Doyle, J. Rochford.

1906 (27 Oct. 1907): Tipperary (Thurles) 3-16, Dublin (Faughs) 3-8.
Tipperary: T. Semple (capt.), J. Hayes, J. O'Brien, P. Burke, M. O'Brien, T. Kerwick, P. Brolan, H. Shelley, J. Mockler, T. Kenna, P. Riordan, T. Allen, P. Maher, J. Burke, J. Gleeson, J. O'Keeffe, T. Gleeson.

1907 (21 June 1908): Kilkenny (Mooncoin) 3-12, Cork (Dungourney) 4-8.
Kilkenny: R. 'Drug' Walsh (capt.), R. Doyle, M. Doyle, E. Doyle, R. Doherty, J. Kelly, T. Kenny, M. Gargan, D. Stapleton, D. Kennedy, J. Keoghan, J. Rochford, D. Grace, P. Lanigan, J. Power, J. Anthony, S. Walton.

1908 (25 Apr. 1909): Tipperary (Thurles) 2-5, Dublin (Kickhams) 1-8. Replay (27 June 1909): Tipperary 3-15, Dublin 1-5.
Tipperary: T. Semple (capt.), T. Kerwick, J. Mockler, J. O'Brien, H. Shelley, A. Carew, J. Mooney, T. Kenna, P. Burke, P. Brolan, J. Moloughney, J. Burke, T. Gleeson, M. O'Dwyer, J. Fitzgerald, P. Fitzgerald, M. O'Brien. (J. Gleeson, J. O'Keeffe, B. Mockler and W. Herns played in the drawn game for Tipperary. M. O'Dwyer, J. Fitzgerald, P. Fitzgerald and J. Burke came in for the replay.)

1909 (12 Dec.): Kilkenny (Mooncoin) 4-6, Tipperary (Thurles) 0-12.
Kilkenny: R. 'Drug' Walsh, E. Doyle, M. Doyle, R. Doherty, J. Kelly, W. Henebry, J. Delahunty, J. Dunphy, D. Kennedy, J. Keoghan, S. Walton, J. Rochford, M. Gargan, M. Shortall, J. Ryan, P. Lanigan, R. Doyle; sub: R. Grace.

1910 (20 Nov.): Wexford (Castlebridge) 7-0, Limerick (Castleconnell) 6-2.
Wexford: R. Doyle (capt.), R. Fortune, M. Cummins, P. Mackey, M. Parker, J. Mythen, J. Shortall, A. Kehoe, J. Kennedy, S. Donohue, P. Roche, D. Kavanagh, J. Fortune, W. McHugh, P. Corcoran, M. Neville, W. Devereux.

1911 Limerick, the Munster champions, refused to play the final match in Thurles. Kilkenny played Tipperary, nominated by the Munster Council, in a subtitute contest on 28 July 1912 and beat them 3-3 to 2-1 with the same team that won the 1912 championship.

1912 (17 Nov.): Kilkenny (Tullaroan) 2-1, Cork (Blackrock) 1-3.
Kilkenny: S. Walton (capt.), J. T. Power, P. Grace, D. Kennedy, J. J. Brennan, P. Lanigan, J. Keoghan, R. Walsh, R. Grace, J. Rochford, E. Doyle, T. McCormack, R. Doyle, M. Doyle, M. Gargan, J. Kelly, R. Doherty.

1913 (2 Nov.): Kilkenny (Mooncoin) 2-4, Tipperary (Toomyvara) 1-2.
Kilkenny: R. 'Drug' Walsh (capt.), J. Power, J. Keoghan, J. Rochford, J. Lennon, D. Kennedy, R. Grace, M. Gargan, J. J. Brennan, P. Grace, R. Doherty, R. Doyle, S. Walton, M. Doyle, J. Kelly. (Teams reduced to fifteen a side.)

1914 (18 Oct.): Clare (Quin) 5-1, Laois (Kilcotton) 1-0.
Clare: A. Power (capt.), J. Power, M. Flanagan, E. Grace, T. McGrath, P. McInerney, J. Shalloo, W. Considine, B. Considine, M. Moloney, R. Doherty, J. Fox, J. Clancy, J. Guerin, J. Spellisey.

1915 (24 Oct.): Laois (Ballygeehan) 6-2, Cork (Redmonds) 4-1.
Laois: J. Finlay (capt.), J. Walsh, T. Finlay, J. Carroll, J. Carroll, J. Daly, P. Campion, J. Phelan, J. Hiney, J. Phelan, E. McEvoy, R. O'Keeffe, J. Dunphy, P. Ryan.

1916 (21 Jan. 1917): Tipperary (Boherlahan) 5-4, Kilkenny (Tullaroan) 3-2.
Tipperary: J. Leahy (capt.), T. Dwan, J. Doherty, W. Dwyer, T. Shanahan, J. Power, J. Fitzpatrick, J. Collison, P. Leahy, H. Shelly, J. Murphy, R. Walsh, D. Walsh, W. Dwyer, A. O'Donnell.

1917 (28 Oct.): Dublin (Collegians) 5-4, Tipperary (Boherlahan) 4-2.
Dublin: T. Daly, J. Ryan (capt.), S. Hyde, S. O'Donavan, H. Burke, C. Stuart, J. Phelan, R. Mockler, T. Moore, J. Cleary, F. Burke, M. Neville, M. Hackett, M. Hayes, P. Kenefick; sub: B. Considine.

1918 (26 Jan.): Limerick (Newcastle West) 9-5, Wexford (selection) 1-3.
Limerick: W. Hough (capt.), P. McInerney, D. Lanigan, R. McConkey, W. Gleeson, J. Keane, M. Rochford, D. Troy, T. McGrath, M. Murphy, P. Barry, W. Ryan, R. Ryan, J. Humphries, P. Kennedy.

1919 (21 Sep. 1920): Cork (selection) 6-4, Dublin (Collegians) 2-4.
Cork: J. Kennedy (capt.), E. Gray, J. O'Keeffe, S. Óg Murphy, P. Aherne, C. Lucy, J. J. Hassett, T. Nagle, P. O'Halloran, M. Murphy, F. Kelleher, D. Ring, C. Sheehan, R. Gorman, J. B. Murphy.

1920 (14 May 1922): Dublin (Faughs) 4-9, Cork (selection) 4-3.
Dublin: R. Mockler (capt.), M. Hayes, M. Neville, T. Moore, T. Hayes, J. Cleary, E. Tobin, R. Doherty, J. Walsh, T. Daly, F. Burke, J. J. Callanan, J. Phelan, J. Ryan, J. Clune.

1921 (4 Mar. 1923): Limerick 8-5, Dublin (Faughs) 3-2.
Limerick: R. McConkey (capt.), M. Murphy, W. Gleeson, J. Humphries, D. Lanigan, D. Marnane, W. Hough, J. Keane, W. Ryan, G. Howard, P. McInerney, T. Mangan, M. Mullane, C. Ryan, T. McGrath.

1922 (9 Sep. 1923): Kilkenny 4-2, Tipperary 2-6.
Kilkenny: W. Dunphy (capt.), E. Dunphy, M. McDonald, J. Holohan, J. Tobin, T. Carroll, R. Grace, W. Kenny, P. Glendon, P. Aylward, M. Lawlor, J. Roberts, P. Donohue, M. Power, R Tobin.

1923 (14 Sep. 1924): Galway 7-3, Limerick 4-5.
Galway: M. Kenny (capt.), J. Mahoney, M. Derivan, I. Harney, J. Power, A. Kelly, B. Gibbs, E. Gilmartin, J. Morris, M. King, T. Fleming, R. Morrissey, L. McGrath, M. Gill, J. Garvey.

1924 (14 Dec.): Dublin 5-3 ,Galway 2-6.
Dublin: T. Daly, J. Bannon, T. Kelly, W. Small, M. Gill, J. Walsh, R. Mockler, P. Aylward, R. Doherty, M. Holland, D. O'Neill, G. Howard, T. Barry, W. Banim, T. Finlay (non-playing captain: F. Wall).

1925 (6 Sep.): Tipperary 5-6, Galway 1-5.
Tipperary: J. Leahy (capt.), A. O'Donnell, M. Mockler, M. D'arcy, J. J. Hayes, M. Kennedy, S. Hackett, J. Power, P. Leahy, P. Cahill, T. Duffy, J. D'Arcy, W. Ryan, P. Power, P. O'Dwyer.

1926 (24 Oct.): Cork 4-6, Kilkenny 2-0.
Cork: S. Óg Murphy (capt.), J. Coughlan, M. Murphy, E. O'Connell, D. B. Murphy, M. Murphy, J. O'Regan, J. Hurley, E. Coughlan, W. Higgins, P. Delea, J. Kearney, M. Murphy, M. Ahearne, P. Ahearne.

1927 (4 Sep.): Dublin 4-8, Cork 1-3.
Dublin: M. Gill (capt.), P. McInerney, W. Phelan, E. Tobin, J. Gleeson, T. O'Rourke, G. Howard, M. Power, E. Fahy, T. Daly, T. Barry, J. Walsh, D. O'Neill, J. Bannon, M. Hayes.

1928 (9 Sep.): Cork 6-12, Galway 1-0.
Cork: S. Óg Murphy (capt.), E. O'Connell, J. Hurley, E. Coughlan, P. Ahearne, P. Delea, M. Ahearne, M. Leahy, M. Burke, M. Madden, D. B. Murphy, J. O'Regan, T. Barry, P. O'Grady, M. O'Connell.

1929 (1 Sep.): Cork 4-9, Galway 1-3.
Cork: D. Barry Murphy (capt.), J. Burke, M. Madden, P. Collins, T. Barry, J. O'Regan, M. O'Connell, J. Kenneally, M. Ahearne, P. Ahearne, P. Delea, J. Hurley, E. Coughlan, P. O'Grady, E. O'Connell; sub: D. McCarthy.

1930 (7 Sep.): Tipperary 2-7, Dublin 1-3.
Tipperary: J. J. Callanan (capt.), J. O'Loughlin, J. Maher, M. Ryan, J. Harney, J. Lanigan, T. O'Meara, M. Kennedy, P. McKenna, P. Purcell, P. Cahill, M. F. Cronin, T. Butler, T. Leahy, T. Treacy; sub: J. Heeney.

1931 (6 Sep.): Cork 1-6, Kilkenny 1-6. Replay (11 Oct. 1931): Cork 2-5, Kilkenny 2-5. Second replay (1 Nov. 1931): Cork 5-8, Kilkenny 3-4.
Cork: J. Coughlan, M. Madden, E. O'Connell, P. 'Fox' Collins, D. Barry Murphy, J. O'Regan, T. Barry, J. Hurley, M. O'Connell, E. Coughlan (capt.), M. Ahearne, P. O'Grady, P. Delea, P. Ahearne, W. Clancy. (The same team played in all three matches. G. Garret came on as a sub in the second and third matches.)

1932 (4 Sep.): Kilkenny 3-3, Clare 2-3.
Kilkenny: J. Dermody, P. Larkin, P. O'Reilly, J. Carroll, P. Phelan, P. Byrne, E. Doyle, E. Byrne, L. Meagher, J. Walsh (capt.), M. Power, T. Leahy, D. Dunne, M. White, M. Power.

1933 (3 Sep.): Kilkenny 1-7, Limerick 0-6.
Kilkenny: E. Doyle (capt.), J. Dunne, J. Dermody, L. Meagher, P. Phelan, P. Larkin, M. White, P. O'Reilly, P. Byrne, J. Walsh, J. Fitzpatrick, E. Byrne, T. Leahy, M. Power, M. Power; subs: J. Duggan, J. O'Connell.

1934 (2 Sep.): Limerick 2-7, Dublin 3-4. Replay (30 Sep. 1934): Limerick 5-2, Dublin 2-6. Limerick: T. Shinny, E. Cregan, T. McCarthy, M. Kennedy, M. Cross, P. Clohessy, G. Howard, T. Ryan (capt.), M. Ryan, J. Mackey, M. Mackey, J. Roche, J. O'Connell, D. Clohessy, J. Close; sub: M. Condon in drawn game. (P. Scanlan and B. McConkey played in the drawn game, with T. Shinny and J. O'Connell replacing them for the replay.)

1935 (1 Sep.): Kilkenny 2-5, Limerick 2-4. Kilkenny: J. O'Connell, P. Larkin, P. O'Reilly, P. Blanchfield, E. Byrne, P. Byrne, P. Phelan, L. Meagher (capt.), T. Leahy, J. Walsh, J. Duggan, M. White, J. Dunne, L. Byrne, M. Power; subs: L. Duggan, J. Dunne.

1936 (6 Sep.): Limerick 5-6, Kilkenny 1-5. Limerick: P. Scanlan. T. McCarthy, P. O'Carroll, M. Kennedy, M. Cross, P. Clohessy, G. Howard, T. Ryan, M. Ryan, J. Mackey, M. Mackey (capt.), J. Roche, D. Clohessy, P. McMahon, J. Power.

1937 (5 Sep.): Tipperary 3-11, Kilkenny 0-3. Tipperary: T. Butler, D. O'Gorman, G. Cornally, J. Lanigan (capt.), J. Ryan, J. Maher, W. Wall, J. Cooney, J. Gleeson, J. Coffey, T. Treacy, T. Doyle, W. O'Donnell, D. Murphy, P. 'Sweeper' Ryan; subs: D. Mackey, T. Kennedy.

1938 (4 Sep.): Dublin 2-5, Waterford 1-6. Dublin: M. Daniels (capt.), C. Forde, T. Teehan, M. Butler, C. McMahon, M. Gill, P. Farrell, J. Byrne, H. Gray, R. Ryan, M. McDonnell, P. Doody, M. Brophy, M. Flynn, W. Loughnane; sub: J. Kilmartin.

1939 (3 Sep.): Kilkenny 2-7, Cork 3-3. Kilkenny: J. O'Connell, P. Grace, P. Larkin, P. Blanchfield, R. Hinks, W. Burke, P. Phelan, J. Walsh (capt.), J. Kelly, J. Langton, T. Leahy, J. Gargan, J. Mulcahy, J. O'Brien, J. Phelan; sub: R. Branagan.

1940 (1 Sep.): Limerick 3-7, Kilkenny 1-7. Limerick: P. Scanlan, J. McCarthy, M. Hickey, M. Kennedy, T. Cooke, P. Clohessy, P. Cregan, T. Ryan, J. Roche, J. Mackey, M. Mackey (capt.), R. Stokes, E. Chawke, P. McMahon, J. Power; sub: T. Herbert.

1941 (28 Sep.): Cork 5-11, Dublin 0-6. Cork: J. Buttimer, W. Murphy, B. Thornhill, A. Lotty, W. Campbell, C. Cottrill, D. J. Buckley, S. Barrett, J. Lynch, C. Ring, C. Buckley (capt.), J. Young, J. Quirke, T. O'Sullivan, M. Brennan; subs: J. Ryng, P. O'Donovan.

1942 (6 Sep.): Cork 2-14, Dublin 3-4. Cork: E. Porter, W. Murphy, B. Thornhill, C. Murphy, A. Lotty, D. J. Buckley, J. Young, J. Lynch (capt.), P. O'Donovan, C. Ring, S. Condon, M. Kenefick, C. Tobin, J. Quirke, D. Beckett; sub: J. Buttimer.

1943 (5 Sep.): Cork 5-16, Antrim 0-4.
Cork: T. Mulcahy, W. Murphy, B. Thornhill, C. Murphy, A. Lotty, D. J. Buckley, J. Young, J. Lynch, C. Cottrell, S. Condon, C. Ring, M. Kenefick (capt.), J. Quirke, T. O'Sullivan, M. Brennan; subs: P. O'Donovan, B. Murphy.

1944 (3 Sep.): Cork 2-13, Dublin 1-2.
Cork: T. Mulcahy, W. Murphy, B. Thornhill, D. J.Buckley, P. O'Donovan, C. Murphy, A. Lotty, J. Lynch, C. Cottrell, C. Ring, S. Condon (capt.), J. Young, J. Quirke, J. Morrison, J. Kelly; sub: P. Healy.

1945 (2 Sep.): Tipperary 5-6, Kilkenny 3-6.
Tipperary: J. Maher, J. Devitt, G. Cornally, F. Coffey, M. Murphy, J. Maher (capt.), T. Purcell, H. Goldsboro, T. Wall, M. Ryan, T. Doyle, E. Gleeson, J. Coffey, A. Brennan, P. 'Sweeper' Ryan.

1946 (1 Sep.): Cork 7-5, Kilkenny 3-8.
Cork: T. Mulcahy, W. Murphy, C. Murphy, D. J.Buckley, P. O'Donovan, A. Lotty, J. Young, J. Lynch, C. Cottrell, P. Healy, C. Ring (capt.), C. Murphy, M. O'Riordan, G. O'Riordan, J. Kelly.

1947 (7 Sep.): Kilkenny 0-14, Cork 2-7.
Kilkenny: J. Donegan, P. Grace, P. 'Diamond' Hayden, M. Marnell, J. Kelly, P. Prendergast, J. Mulcahy, D. Kennedy (capt.), J. Heffernan, T. Walton, T. Leahy, J. Langton, S. Downey, W. Cahill, L. Reidy; sub: E. Kavanagh.

1948 (5 Sep.): Waterford 6-7, Dublin 4-2.
Waterford: J. Ware (capt.), A. Fleming, J. Cusack, J. Goode, M. Hickey, V. Baston, M. Hayes, J. O'Connor, E. Carew, K. O'Connor, J. Keane, C. Moylan, W. Galvin, E. Daly, T. Curran.

1949 (4 Sep.): Tipperary 3-11, Laois 0-3.
Tipperary: T. Reddan, M. Byrne, A. Brennan, J. Doyle, P. Stakelum (capt.), F. Coffey, T. Doyle, S. Kenny, P. Shanahan, T. Ryan, M. Ryan, J. Kennedy, J. Ryan, S. Maher, S. Bannon; sub: P. Kenny.

1950 (3 Sep.): Tipperary 1-9, Kilkenny 1-8.
Tipperary: T. Reddan, M. Byrne, A. Brennan, J. Doyle, J. Finn, P. Stakelum, T. Doyle, S. Bannon, P. Shanahan, E. Ryan, M. Ryan, S. Kenny (capt.), P. Kenny, S. Maher, J. Kennedy; sub: T. Ryan.

1951 (2 Sep.): Tipperary 7-7, Wexford 3-9.
Tipperary: T. Reddan, M. Byrne, A. Brennan, J. Doyle, J. Finn (capt.), P. Stakelum, T. Doyle, P. Shanahan, J. Hough, E. Ryan, M. Ryan, T. Ryan, P. Kenny, S. Maher, S. Bannon; sub: S. Kenny.

1952 (7 Sep.): Cork 2-14, Dublin 0-7.
Cork: D. Creedon, G. O'Riordan, J. Lyons, A. O'Shaughnessy, M. Fouhy, V. Twomey, S. O'Brien, J. Twomey, G. Murphy, W. Griffin, W. J. Daly, C. Ring, L. Abernethy, L. Dowling, P. Barry (capt.); subs: M. O'Riordan, J. Lynam.

1953 (6 Sep.): Cork 3-3, Galway 0-8.
Cork: D. Creedon, G. O'Riordan, W. O'Neill, J. Lyons, A. O'Shaughnessy, M. Fouhy, D. Hayes, V. Twomey, J. Twomey, G. Murphy, W. J. Daly, J. Hartnett, C. Ring (capt.), T. O'Sullivan, L. Dowling, P. Barry.

1954 (5 Sep.): Cork 1-9, Wexford 1-6.
Cork: D. Creedon, G. O'Riordan, J. Lyons, A. O'Shaughnessy, M. Fouhy, V. Twomey, D. Hayes, G. Murphy, W. Moore, W. J. Daly, J. Hartnett, C. Ring (capt.), J. Clifford, E. Goulding, P. Barry; sub: T. O'Sullivan.

1955 (4 Sep.): Wexford 3-13, Galway 2-8.
Wexford: A. Foley, R. Rackard, N. O'Donnell (capt.), M. O'Hanlon, J. English, W. Rackard, M. Morrissey, J. Morrissey, S. Hearne, P. Kehoe, E. Wheeler, P. Kehoe, T. Ryan, N. Rackard, T. Flood; subs: O. Gough, D. Aherne.

1956 (23 Sep.): Wexford 2-14, Cork 2-8.
Wexford: A. Foley, R. Rackard, N. O'Donnell, M. Morrissey, J. English (capt.), W. Rackard, J. Morrissey, S. Hearne, E. Wheeler, P. Kehoe, M. Codd, T. Flood, T. Ryan, N. Rackard, T. Dixon.

1957 (1 Sep.): Kilkenny 4-10, Waterford 3-12.
Kilkenny: O. Walsh, T. Walsh, J. Walsh, J. Maher, P. Buggy, M. Walsh, J. McGovern, M. Brophy, J. Sutton, D. Heaslip, M. Kenny, M. Kelly (capt.), R. Rockett, W. Dwyer, S. Clohessy; sub: W. Walsh.

1958 (7 Sep.): Tipperary 4-9, Galway 2-5.
Tipperary: J. O'Grady, M. Byrne, M. Maher, K. Carey, J. Finn, A. Wall (capt.), J. Doyle, J. Hough, T. English, D. Nealon, T. Larkin, J. Doyle, L. Keane, L. Devaney, L. Connolly.

1959 (6 Sep.): Waterford 1-17, Kilkenny 5-5. Replay (4 Oct. 1959): Waterford 3-12, Kilkenny 1-10.
Waterford: E. Power, J. Harney, A. Flynn, J. Barron, M. Lacey, M. Óg Morrissey, J. Condon, S. Power, P. Grimes, M. Flannely, T. Cheasty, F. Walsh (capt.), L. Guinan, T. Cunningham, J. Kiely; subs: M. O'Connor, D. Whelan. (D. Whelan and C. Ware played in the drawn game and were replaced by T. Cunningham and M. Flannely for the replay.)

1960 (4 Sep.): Wexford 2-15, Tipperary 0-11.
Wexford: P. Nolan, J. Mitchell, N. O'Donnell (capt.), T. Neville, J. English, W. Rackard, J. Nolan, E. Wheeler, J. Morrissey, J. O'Brien, P. Kehoe, S. Quaid, O. McGrath, J. Harding, T. Flood; subs: S. Power, M. Morrissey.

1961 (3 Sep.): Tipperary 0-16, Dublin 1-12.
Tipperary: D. O'Brien, M. Hassett (capt.), M. Maher, K. Carey, M. Burns, A. Wall, J. Doyle, M. O'Gara, T. English, J. Doyle, L. Devaney, D. Nealon, J. McKenna, W. Moloughney, T. Moloughney; subs: T. Ryan, J. Hough, S. McLoughlin.

1962 (2 Sep.): Tipperary 3-10, Wexford 2-11.
Tipperary: D. O'Brien, J. Doyle, M. Maher, K. Carey, M. O'Gara, A. Wall, M. Burns, T. English, L. Devaney, J. Doyle (capt.), T. Ryan (Killenaule), D. Nealon, T. Moloughney, S. McLoughlin; subs: L. Connolly, T. Ryan (Toomyvara).

1963 (1 Sep.): Kilkenny 4-17, Waterford 6-8.
Kilkenny: O. Walsh, P. Larkin, C. Whelan, M. Treacy, S. Cleere (capt.), T. Carroll, M. Coogan, P. Moran, S. Clohessy, D. Heaslip, J. McGovern, E. Keher, T. Walsh, W. Dwyer, T. Murphy; sub: O. Gough.

1964 (6 Sep.): Tipperary 5-13, Kilkenny 2-8.
Tipperary: J. O'Donoghue, J. Doyle, M. Maher, K. Carey, M. Burns, A. Wall, M. Murphy (capt.), T. English, M. Roche, J. Doyle, L. Kiely, M. Keating, D. Nealon, J. McKenna, S. McLoughlin; subs: M. Lonergan, L. Devaney.

1965 (5 Sep.): Tipperary 2-16, Wexford 0-10.
Tipperary: J. O'Donoghue, J. Doyle, M. Maher, K. Carey, M. Burns, A. Wall, L. Gaynor, T. English, M. Roche, J. Doyle (capt.), L. Kiely, L. Devaney, D. Nealon, J. McKenna, S. McLoughlin.

1966 (4 Sep.): Cork 3-9, Kilkenny 1-10.
Cork: P. Barry, P. Doolan, T. O'Donoghue, D. Murphy, A. Connolly, J. O'Sullivan, P. Fitzgerald, J. McCarthy, M. Waters, S. Barry, J. O'Halloran, G. McCarthy (capt.), C. McCarthy, C. Sheehan, J. Bennett.

1967 (3 Sep.): Kilkenny 3-8, Tipperary 2-7.
Kilkenny: O. Walsh, T. Carroll, P. Dillon, J. Treacy (capt.), S. Cleere, P. Henderson, M. Coogan, P. Moran, J. Teehan, E. Keher, T. Walsh, C. Dunne, J. Bennett, J. Lynch, M. Brennan; subs: R. Blanchfield, J. Kinsella, P. Carroll.

1968 (1 Sep.): Wexford 5-8, Tipperary 3-12.
Wexford: P. Nolan, T. Neville, E. Kelly, E. Colfer, V. Staples, D. Quigley (capt.), W. Murphy, P. Wilson, D. Bernie, P. Lynch, A. Doran, C. Jacob, J. O'Brien, S. Whelan, J. Berry; sub: J. Quigley.

1969 (7 Sep.): Kilkenny 2-15, Cork 2-9.
Kilkenny: O. Walsh, T. Carroll, P. Dillon, J. Treacy, W. Murphy, P. Henderson, M. Coogan, F. Cummins, M. Lawler, C. Dunne, P. Delaney, E. Keher (capt.), J. Millea, M. Brennan, T. Murphy; subs: P. Kavanagh, P. Moran, S. Buckley.

1970 (6 Sep.): Cork 6-21, Wexford 5-10.

Cork: P. Barry (capt.), T. Maher, P. McDonnell, J. Horgan , D. Clifford, P. Hegarty, C. Roche, G. McCarthy, S. Looney, T. Ryan, W. Walsh, C. Cullinane, C. McCarthy, R. Cummins, E. O'Brien; sub: S. Murphy.

1971 (5 Sep.): Tipperary 5-17, Kilkenny 5-14.

Tipperary: P. O'Sullivan, L. King, J. Kelly, J. Gleeson, T. O'Connor (capt.), M. Roche, L. Gaynor, P. J. Ryan, S. Hogan, F. Loughnane, N. O'Dwyer, D. Ryan, J. Flanagan, R. Ryan. M. Keating; subs: J. Doyle, P. Byrne.

1972 (3 Sep.): Kilkenny 3-24, Cork 5-11.

Kilkenny: N. Skehan (capt.), P. Larkin, P. Dillon, J. Treacy, P. Lalor, P. Henderson, E. Morrissey, F. Cummins, L. O'Brien, M. Crotty, P. Delaney, J. Kinsella, E. Byrne, K. Purcell, E. Keher; subs: M. Murphy, M. Coogan, P. Moran.

1973 (2 Sep.): Limerick 1-21, Kilkenny 1-14.

Limerick: S. Horgan, W. Moore, P. Hartigan, J. O'Brien, P. Bennis, E. Cregan, S. Foley, R. Bennis, E. Grimes (capt.), B. Hartigan, M. Dowling, L. O'Donoghue, F. Nolan, E. Rea, J. McKenna; sub: T. Ryan.

1974 (1 Sep.): Kilkenny 3-1, Limerick 1-13.

Kilkenny: N. Skehan, N. Orr (capt.), J. Treacy, P. Lalor, P. Henderson, T. McCormack, L. O'Brien, F. Cummins, M. Crotty, P. Delaney, B. Fitzpatrick, M. Brennan, K. Purcell, E. Keher.

1975 (7 Sep.): Kilkenny 2-22, Galway 2-10.

Kilkenny: N. Skehan, P. Larkin, N. Orr, B. Cody, P. Lalor, P. Henderson, T. McCormack, L. O'Brien, F. Cummins, M. Crotty, P. Delaney, B. Fitzpatrick (capt.), M. Brennan, K. Purcell, E. Keher.

1976 (5 Sep.): Cork 2: 21, Wexford 4-11.

Cork: M. Coleman, B. Murphy, P. McDonnell, M. Doherty, P. Barry, J. Crowley, D. Coughlan, G. McCarthy, P. Moylan, M. Malone, B. Cummins, J. Barry Murphy, C. McCarthy, R. Cummins (capt.), S. O'Leary; subs: E. O'Donoghue, J. Horgan.

1977 (4 Sep.): Cork 1-17, Wexford 3-8.

Cork: M. Coleman, B. Murphy, M. Doherty (capt.), J. Horgan, D. MacCurtain, J. Crowley, D. Coughlan, T. Cashman, T. Crowley, M. Malone, G. McCarthy, J. Barry Murphy, C. McCarthy, R. Cummins, S. O'Leary; subs: P. Moylan, T. Murphy.

1978 (3 Sep.): Cork 1-15, Kilkenny 2-8.

Cork: M. Coleman, B. Murphy, M. Doherty, J. Horgan, D. MacCurtain, J. Crowley, D. Coughlan, T. Cashman, P. Moylan, J. Barry Murphy, G. McCarthy, T. Crowley, C. McCarthy (capt.), R. Cummins, S. O'Leary; subs: J. Allen, E. O'Donoghue.

1979 (2 Sep.): Kilkenny 2-12, Galway 1-8.
Kilkenny: N. Skehan, P. Larkin, P. Prendergast, J. Henderson, R. Reid, G. Henderson, N. Brennan, J. Hennessy, F. Cummins, G. Fennelly (capt.), B. Fitzpatrick, L. O'Brien, M. Brennan, M. Crotty, M. Ruth; subs: K. Fennelly, D. O'Hara.

1980 (7 Sep.): Galway 2-15, Limerick 3-9.
Galway: M. Conneely, C. Hayes, N. McInerney, J. Cooney, S. Linnane, S. Silke, S. Coen, M. Connolly, S. Mahon, F. Burke, J. Connolly (capt.), P. J. Molloy, B. Forde, J. Connolly, N. Lane; subs: F. Gantley, J. Ryan.

1981 (6 Sep.): Offaly 2-12, Galway 0-15.
Offaly: D. Martin, T. Donoghue, E. Coughlan, P. Fleury, A. Fogarty, P. Delaney, G. Coughlan, J. Kelly, L. Currams, P. Kirwan, B. Bermingham, M. Corrigan, P. Carroll, P. Horan (capt.), J. Flaherty; subs: B. Keeshan, D. Owens.

1982 (5 Sep.): Kilkenny 3-18, Cork 1-13.
Kilkenny: N. Skehan, J. Henderson, B. Cody (capt.), D. O'Hara, N. Brennan, G. Henderson, P. Prendergast, J. Hennessy, F. Cummins, R. Power, K. Brennan, G Fennelly, B. Fitzpatrick, C. Heffernan, L. Fennelly.

1983 (4 Sep.): Kilkenny 2-14, Cork 2-12.
Kilkenny: N. Skehan, J. Henderson, B. Cody, D. O'Hara, J. Hennessy, G. Henderson, P. Prendergast, F. Cummins, G. Fennelly, R. Power, K. Brennan, H. Ryan, B. Fitzpatrick, C. Heffernan, L. Fennelly (capt.); sub: P. Lannon.

1984 (2 Sep.): Cork 3-16, Offaly 1-12.
Cork: G. Cunningham, D. Mulcahy, D. O'Grady, J. Hodgins, T. Cashman, J. Crowley, D. MacCurtain, J. Fenton (capt.), P. Hartnett, K. Hennessy, T. Crowley, T. O'Sullivan, T. Mulcahy, J. Barry Murphy, S. O'Leary.

1985 (1 Sep.): Offaly 2-11, Galway 1-12.
Offaly: J. Troy, A. Fogarty, E. Coughlan, P. Fleury (capt.), T. Conneely, P. Delaney, G. Coughlan, D. Owens, J. Kelly, P. Corrigan, B. Bermingham, M. Corrigan, P. Cleary, P. Horan, J. Dooley; subs: D. Fogarty, B. Keeshan.

1986 (7 Sep.): Cork 4-13, Galway 2-15.
Cork: G. Cunningham, D. Mulcahy, R. Brown, J. Crowley, P. Hartnett, T. Cashman (capt.), D. Walsh, J. Fenton, J. Cashman, T. McCarthy, T. Mulcahy, T. O'Sullivan, G. Fitzgerald, J. Barry Murphy, K. Hennessy; sub: K. Kingston.

1987 (6 Sep.): Galway 1-12, Kilkenny 0-9.
Galway: J. Commins, S. Linnane, C. Hayes (capt.), O. Kilkenny, P. Finnerty, T. Keady, G. McInerney, S. Mahon, P. Malone, M. McGrath, J. Cooney, M. Naughton, E. Ryan, B. Lynskey, A. Cunningham; subs: N. Lane, P. J. Molloy, T. Kilkenny.

1988 (4 Sep.): Galway 1-15, Tipperary 0-14.
Galway: J. Commins, S. Linnane, C. Hayes (capt.), O. Kilkenny, P. Finnerty, T. Keady, G. McInerney, M. Coleman, P. Malone, A. Cunningham, B. Lynskey, M. Naughton, M. McGrath. J. Cooney, E. Ryan; subs: T. Kilkenny, N. Lane, G. Burke.

1989 (3 Sep.): Tipperary 4-24, Antrim 3-9.
Tipperary: K. Hogan, J. Heffernan, C. O'Donovan, N. Sheedy, C. Bonnar, B. Ryan, J. Kennedy, C. Bonnar, D. Carr, J. Leahy, D. Ryan, M. Cleary, P. Fox, C. Bonnar, N. English; subs: A. Ryan, J. Hayes, D. O'Connell.

1990 (2 Sep.): Cork 5-15, Galway 2-21.
Cork: G. Cunningham, J. Considine, D. Walsh, S. O'Gorman, S. McCarthy, J. Cashman, K. McGuckian, B. O'Sullivan, T. McCarthy, G. Fitzgerald, M. Foley, T. O'Sullivan, T. Mulcahy (capt.), K. Hennessy, J. Fitzgibbon; subs: D. Quirke, C. Casey.

1991 (1 Sep.): Tipperary 1-16, Kilkenny 0-15.
Tipperary: K. Hogan, P. Delaney, N. Sheedy, M. Ryan, C. Bonnar, B. Ryan, C. Bonnar, D. Carr (capt.), A. Ryan, M. Cleary, D. Ryan, J. Leahy, P. Fox, C. Bonnar, N. English; subs: C. Stakelum, D. O'Connell.

1992 (6 Sep.): Kilkenny 3-10, Cork 1-12 .
Kilkenny: M. Walsh, E. O'Connor, P. Dwyer, L. Simpson, L. Walsh, P. O'Neill, W. O'Connor, M. Phelan, B. Hennessy, L. McCarthy, J. Power, D. J. Carey, E. Morrissey, L. Fennelly (capt.), J. Brennan; subs: C. Heffernan, A. Ronan.

1993 (5 Sep.): Kilkenny 2-17, Galway 1-15.
Kilkenny: M. Walsh, E. O'Connor (capt.), P. Dwyer, L. Simpson, L. Keoghan, P. O'Neill, W. O'Connor, B. Hennessy, M. Phelan, L. McCarthy, J. Power, D. J. Carey, E. Morrissey, P. J. Delaney, A. Ronan; subs: J. Brennan, T. Murphy, C. Heffernan.

1994 (4 Sep.): Offaly 3-16, Limerick 2-13.
Offaly: J. Troy, S. McGuckin, K. Kinahan, M. Hanamy (capt.), B. Whelahan, H. Rigney, K. Martin, J. Pilkington, D. Regan, J. Dooley, J. Troy, J. Dooley, B. Dooley, B. Kelly, D. Pilkington; subs: J. Errity, P. O'Connor, M. Duignan.

1995 (3 Sep.): Clare 1-13, Offaly 2-8.
Clare: D. Fitzgerald, M. O'Halloran, B. Lohan, F. Lohan, L. Doyle, S. McMahon, A. Daly (capt.), J. O'Connor, O. Baker, F. Tuohy, P.J. O'Connell, F. Hegarty, S. McNamara, C. Clancy, G. O'Loughlin; subs: E. Taaffe for McNamara, C. Lyons for Clancy, A. Neville for Taaffe.

1996 (1 Sep.): Wexford 1-13, Limerick 0-14
Wexford: D. Fitzhenry, C. Kehoe, G. Cush, J. O'Connor, R. Guiney, L. Dunne, L. O'Gorman, A. Fenlon, G. O'Connor, R. McCarthy, M. Storey (capt.), L. Murphy, E. Scallan, G. Laffan. T. Dempoey; subs: B. Byrne for Murphy, P. Finn for Guiney, P. Codd for Laffan.

Appendix 2

All-Ireland Junior Championship, 1912–94

1912: Cork 3-6, Westmeath 2-1.
Cork: C. Hallahan (capt.), J. Long, J. Hallahan, W. Finn, D. Aherne, P. Prior, J. Murphy, W. Lombard, S. Salmon, J. O'Brien, T. O'Riordan, J. Cahill, J. McDonnell, D. Singleton, W. Fitzgerald, P. Vaughan, C. O'Connell.

1913: Tipperary 2-2, Kilkenny 0-0.
Tipperary: J. Ryan-Lanigan (capt.), J. Ryan-Lanigan, T. Delaney, J. Hammonds, T. Dwyer, T. Dwan, P. Purcell, M. Hammonds, N. McGrath, P. Leahy, A. O'Donnell, D. Walsh, J. Power, J. Fitzpatrick, T. Shanahan, P. Dargan, J. Murphy.

1914: Clare 6-5, Laois 1-1.
Clare: D. Minogue (capt.), P. Minogue, D. Flannery, P. Hannon, M. Bolton, T. Daly, J. Quinn, E. Lucia, J. Spellacy, P. Gordon, M. Baker, A. Glesson, D. Crowe, J. Marrinan (14).

1915: Tipperary 1-6, Offaly 2-2.
Tipperary: T. Dwan (capt.), W. Quinn, M. Leahy, J. Fitzpatrick, J. Campbell, J. Kennedy, J. Hammonds, W. Dwyer, T. Shanahan, F. Cronin, Horan, Wilson, Corcoran, Fahy, Donovan.

1916: Cork 4-6, Kilkenny 3-4.
Cork: J. McCarthy (capt.), C. Twomey, F. O'Donoghue, P. Healy, C. Neenan, D. Long, P. Kelleher, T. Livesey, E. Frizelle, J. Barry Murphy, E. O'Connell, M. O'Driscoll, D. Sullivan, R. Hunter, M. Brophy.

1917–22: Championship suspended.

1923: Offaly 3-4, Cork 3-2.
Offaly: M. Cordial, W. Cordial, A. Cordial, J. Halligan, E. Hayes, P. Lyons, W. Fox, P. Fox, W. Ryan, M. Whelan, M. White, M. Carroll, J. Murphy, J. Horan, J. Carroll.

1924: Tipperary 5-5, Galway 1-2.
Tipperary: P. Purcell (capt.), W. O'Brien, J. O'Loughlin, S. Dwan, J. Costelloe, J. Gleeson, T. O'Meara, M. Flanagan, J. Hickey, M. Ryan, T. F. Meagher, P. Kennedy, B. O'Meara, M. Kennedy, R. Nealon, M. Aherne.

1925: Cork 5-6, Dublin 1-0.
Cork: M. Kenny (capt.), J. Seymour, E. Lynch, J. Kearney, C. Cronin, J. Desmond, J. Barry, D. Barry Murphy, D. Geaney, S. Noonan, J. Burke, M. Aherne, J. Hurley, L. Brady, J. Egan.

1926: Tipperary 6-2, Galway 2-3.
Tipperary: T. Butler, J. Moylan, P. Hogan, T. Crowe, P. Harty, J. Hayes, M. Ryan (Newport), M. Ryan (Boherlahan), T. Leahy, T. Treacy, E. Browne, T. Cleary, E. Walsh, J. O'Gorman, M. F. Cronin.

1927: Meath 2-3, Britain 1-1.
Meath: L. Mitchell (capt.), R. Collins, J. Doherty, T. Brown, M. Cluskey, C. Dolan, T. Irwin, E. Giles, J. Griffin, M. Madden, W. Smith, J. Loughran, T. Loughran, T. Carrigy, S. Ó Finn; sub: C. Curley.

1928: Kilkenny 4-6, Tipperary 4-4.
Kilkenny: M. Bergin, J. O'Carroll, T. Mullins (capt.), P. Kelly, J. McNamara, T. Grace, P. Butler, T. Cronin, J. Walsh, D. Duggan, M. Brennan, P. Dowling, P. Walsh, P. Dwan, J. Fitzpatrick.

1929: Offaly 6-1, Cork 2-3.
Offaly: M. Corrigan, M. Nolan, J. Kinneary, W. Guinan, N. Dooley, J. Dooley, T. Dooley, T. Carroll, J. Kearney, M. Coughlan, M. Hogan, J. Carroll, P. J. Grogan (capt.), J. King, W. Cordial.

1930: Tipperary 6-8, Kilkenny 2-3.
Tipperary: P. Harty (capt.), T. Harty, W. Ryan, T. Connolly, M. McCann, M. Browne, E. Wade, T. Rainey, J. Dwyer, M. Ryan, D. Looby, J. Furlong, W. Gorman, J. Fletcher, S. Harrington.

1931: Waterford 10-7, Lancashire 1-2.
Waterford: M. Curley, J. O'Donnell, N. Condon, N. Flynn, G. Kehoe, A. Sandford, W. Sheehan, T. Greaney, P. Hannigan, P. Gough, D. Goode, R. Morrissey, J. Ormond, J. Hunt, R. Condon.

1932: Dublin 8-4, London 2-0.
Dublin: O'Brien, O'Hara, Gleeson, Reynolds, Kavanagh, Scally, Aherne, Sexton, Sheehan, J. Flanagan, Flanagan, Moran, O'Dwyer, Higgins, Elebert.

1933: Tipperary 10-1, London 1-4.
Tipperary: D. Roche, W. Roche, P. O'Mahoney, M. O'Toole, J. Cooney, E. Wade, P. O'Keeffe, D. Looby, D. Hayes, J. Tynan, J. Duggan, D. Gorman, D. Murphy, W. Ryan, D. Gleeson.

1934: Waterford 3-5, London 3-3.
Waterford: M. Curley, W. Hanley, J. Keane, J. Whelan, J. O'Gorman, M. Regan, J. Healy, G. Kehoe, W. Shanahan, B. Doyle, M. Creed, P. Sheehan, J. Murphy, J. Walsh, D. Mahoney.

1935: Limerick 4-9, London 3-3.
Limerick: J. McCarthy, J. Curtin, P. O'Carroll, J. Ryan, T. McCarthy, M. Power, M. Cross (capt.), P. McCarthy, J. Sullivan, T. McCarthy, M. Butler, W. Daly, P. McSweeney, J. Curtin, J. O'Sullivan.

1936: Westmeath 2-5, Waterford 3-1.
Westmeath: P. Fahy, W. Doyle, J. Mulligan, F. Monaghan, T. Nugent, F. White, T. Gavagan, F. Moynihan, P. Lenihan, P. Morgan, M. McCarthy, J. Skehal, T. McNeice, T. McGrath, C. Boland; sub: J. Leonard.

1937: Dublin 7-8, London 3-6.
Dublin: J. Hennessy, P. Tolan, M. Butler, P. Crowley, P. Horan, D. Hurley, S. Barrett, T. Leahy, R. Ryan, M. Fletcher, P. McCormack, J. Byrne, P. Maher, P. McMahon, P. Doody.

1938: London 4-4, Cork 4-1.
London: J. Shaughnessy, J. Dunne, T. Walker, E. Eade, J. Hickey, E. Foulds, L. Moran, J. Dwyer (capt.), J. Farrell, M. Regan, J. Hardiman, T. Reaney, B. Hickey, N. Noonan, D. Hoyne.

1939: Galway 2-6, London 2-2.
Galway: Nolan, Donnellan, T. Fahy, Flaherty, Hanley, Connor, M. Lowry, W. Lambert, K. Costello, Hanniffy, Hogan, Cunningham, Forde, M. Connaire, P. Fahy.

1940: Cork 3-3, Galway 3-1.
Cork: E. Porter, T. O'Connell, C. Kelly, W. Holton, H. O'Callaghan, G. Sadlier, R. Walsh, P. Aherne, J. Barry Murphy, E. Riordan, P. J. Riordan, L. Tully, C. Radley, D. Lynch, P. Corbett.

1941: Limerick 8-2, Galway 4-1.
Limerick: H. Wilson, J. O'Donoghue, S. Riordan, A. O'Donoghue, P. Walsh, T. McCarthy, P. McCarthy, J. Tobin, T. Toomey, O. O'Brien, T. Murphy, J. Foley, J. Madden, P. McCarthy, K. Foley.

1942–45: Championship suspended.

1946: Kilkenny 5-4, London 2-2.
Kilkenny: J. Egan, M. Marnell, P. Hayden, P. Prendergast, P. Cahill, M. Kenny, W. Cahill, E. Doyle, P. Dack (capt.), P. Stapleton, P. McEvoy, B. Maher, H. Giles, P. O'Connor, N.Maher.

1947: Cork 3-10, London 2-3.
W. Barry, B. Murphy, W. Holton, D. O'Donovan, D. Lyons, M. Nestor, D. O'Mahoney, S. Twomey, J. Thornhill, J. West, M. O'Toole (capt.), W. J. Daly, M. Kearney, T. O'Sullivan, P. Abernathy; sub: J. O'Grady.

1948: Meath 3-5, London 3-5. Replay: Meath 2-7, London 2-5.
Meath: R. Grogan, P. Kane, O. O'Reilly, N. Collier, S. Kelly, A. Donnelly, M. Kane, D.Mulligan, P. Donnelly, D. O'Mahoney, P. Kelly, F. Foran, L. Wright, M. O'Brien, B. Smith. (D. Clarke, J. Clarke, T. Carolan, P. Tuite and P. Mitchell played in the drawn game.)

1949: London 3-7, Clare 3-6.
London: W. Ryan, T. Hayse, T. O'Mahoney, S. O'Riordan, H. O'Shea, W. Brophy, S. Fogarty, S. Costelloe, R. Hobson, P. Fitzpatrick, F. Hogan, J. Duggan, B. Boyle, P. Madden, J. Lawton; subs: Lewis, C. Burke, P. Connors.

1950: Cork 5-5, London 1-4.
Cork: F. Daly, D. Barry, J. Walsh, V. Twomey, P. Walsh, W. O'Neill, M. Cashman, G. Power, C. O'Neill, D. O'Driscoll, P. Healy, S. Fleming, A. Aherne, M. O'Donoghue, P. O'Riordan.

1951: Kilkenny 3-9, London 3-5.
Kilkenny: R. Rockett, J. Lynch, S. Hickey (capt.), W. Bolger, T. Walsh, P. Fitzgerald, J. McGovern, J. Sutton, P. Stapleton, P. Johnston, P. Hennebry, M. Gardiner, T. Ryan, H. Burke, J. Barron.

1952: Dublin 3-4, London 2-6.
Dublin: S. Murphy, J. Duggan, W. Holmes, J. Young, J. Manton, C. Hayes, D. Kelly, L. Skelly, L. Harding, J. Rodgers, T. Ryan, M. Ryan, W. Fletcher, J. Griffin, S. Daly.

1953: Tipperary 4-10, Warwickshire 3-3.
Tipperary: W. Fogarty, T. Kennedy, M. Doheny, S. Kelly, J. Callanan, S. Organ, T. Sweeney, J. Ryan, M. Conway, T. English, M. Kenny (capt.), J. Hannon, T. Foran, R. Hayes, K. McKenna.

1954: Limerick 4-6, London 2-4.
Limerick: P. Cuneen, J. O'Sullivan, J. Keogh, P. O'Neill, J. Dooley, S. Murphy, J. Quaid, J. Quaid, W. Dooley, A. Raleigh, M. Carmody (capt.), V. Cobbe, M. Sheehan, C. Daly, J. Barry.

1955: Cork 6-10, Warwickshire 0-5.

Cork: L. Ó Tuama, N. Looney, G. Mulcahy, L. Young, J. O'Mahoney, C. Moynihan, P. Dowling, C. Cooney, J. Deasy, J. Browne, M. O'Toole, C. O'Shea, M. Quane, J. Cooney, P. O'Leary.

1956: Kilkenny 5-2, London 2-8.

Kilkenny: J. Murphy, T. Walsh, J. 'Link' Walsh, S. Tyrell (capt.), P. Murphy, R. O'Neill, J. Burke, F. McCarthy, D. Gorey, D. Heaslip, D. Bolger, J. Dunne, M. Fleming, W. Costigan, D. Hogan; subs: J. Coyne, P. Fleming, P. Browne, P. Leacy.

1957: Limerick 5-12, London 2-5.

Limerick: G. Casey, T. O'Donnell (capt.), P. O'Connor, T. O'Dwyer, D. McCarthy, J. Dooley, J. Heilan, L. Hogan, M. Savage, M. O'Shea, J. Shanahan, M. Sheehan, P. Ryan, J. Enright, J. Barry; sub: D. McGrath.

1958: Cork 7-10, Warwickshire 4-2.

Cork: J. Dempsey, S. French, F. Maxwell, A. O'Regan, J. Browne, N. Lynam, M. Thompson, C. Cooney, N. Gallagher, W. Galligan, M. O'Brien, S. Kelly, L. McGrath, F. Daly, M. Quane.

1959: London 5-10, Antrim 2-10.

London: A. Morrissey, J. Kearns, M. Kersse, P. Murphy, M. Carmody, P. Dwyer, M. Kelly, E. Murray, W. Dargan, S. Sullivan, W. Duffy, D. Dillon, L. Healy, J. Rabbitte, C. Hickey; subs: J. O'Halloran, W. Ryan, J. Hickey, P. Ryan.

1960: London 2-4, Carlow 2-4. Replay: London 4-8, Carlow 2-11.

London: A. Morrissey, J. Kearns, M. Kersse, P. Murphy, F. Spillane, P. O'Dwyer, A. Muldowney, L. Dargan, E. Morrissey, P. Wilson, W. Duffy, N. Murphy, P. Ryan, J. Hickey, L. Healy (W. Ryan, J. Fitzgerald and J. Redmond played in the drawn game); sub: S. Somers.

1961: Kerry 4-14, London 2-4.

Kerry: J. O'Donovan, N. Sheehy, N. Quill, T. Kirby, M. Hennessy, R. McElligott, K. Dermody, S. Lovett, C. Healy, J. Barry, J. Hennessy, P. Sullivan, J. Cullloty, B. McCarthy, E. Sullivan.

1962: Kildare 4-7, London 2-4.

Kildare: P. Dunny, P. Morris, A. Whelan, P. Sharpe, D. Noonan, T. O'Connell, A. Sullivan, P. Curley, F. Fogarty, K. O'Malley, M. Wall, J. Barker, M. Leahy, L. Kiely; subs: S. Schwer, P. Cummins.

1963: London 4-7, Antrim 3-6.

London: A. Fayard, T. Connolly, M. Butler, M. O'Brien, M. O'Connor, M. Connolly, V. O'Halloran, T. Sheehan, M. Murphy, J. J. Browne, B. Murray, J. Barrett, P. Carmody, J. Hickey, J. O'Reilly; sub: M. Diggins.

1964: Down 3-2, London 1-3.
Down: A. Falloona, P. Branniff, H. O'Prey, F. Gilmore, H. Dorrian, W. Smith, E. Falloona, P. Branniff, S. Savage, C. McMullan (capt.), D. Crawford, S. Fitzgerald, H. Sloan, T. McGovern; subs: G. Gilmore, P. McGratton.

1965: Roscommon 3-9, Warwickshire 2-11.
Roscommon: T. Gavin, J. Moylette, P. Lyons, T. Murphy, B. Mitchell, J. Kenny, M. Keane, S. Cormican, M. Laffey, G. O'Malley, J. Boland, R. Fallon, M. Hoare, T. Boyle, J. McDonnell.

1966: Kildare 4-6, Warwickshire 2-9.
Kildare: J. Curran, K. O'Malley, P. Sharpe, J. Wall, J. Fogarty, P. Dunny, T. Carew, D. Burke, T. Christain, J. Lalor, D. O'Keeffe, M. Dwane, N. Behan, W. Quinn, M. O'Brien; sub: A. Byrne.

1967: Wicklow 3-15, London 6-6. Replay: Wicklow 3-15, London 4-4.
Wicklow: J. Torpey, T. Collins, J. Fogarty, L. Collins, J. Kearns (capt.), T. Kelly, R. O'Shea, S. Doyle, T. Doyle, P. Dwyer, L. Jordan, T. Morrissey, M. Jordan, T. Scott, W. Hilliard; sub: C. Keddy.

1968: Warwickshire 1-14, Kerry 1-9.
Warwickshire: D. Breen, J. Dineen, J. Quinn, D. Hayes, T. Timmons, D. Dillane, P. Cullen, S. O'Keeffe, C. Danagher, W. Hogan, T. Ryan, M. O'Sullivan, C. Crowe, J. Cronin, D. Dunne.

1969: Warwickshire 3-6, Kerry 0-11.
Warwickshire: M. McCarthy, J. O'Brien, P. Grimes, P. Heffernan, M. Hanley, L. Dalton, L. Moore, T. Crowley, L. Moloney, B. Collins, M. Brennan, J. Gilligan, J. McLaughlin, J. Browne (capt.), V. Coffey; sub: P. Hallinan.

1970: Meath 4-6, Hertfordshire 4-6. Replay: Meath 3-14, Hertfordshire 3-7.
P. McGovern, T. Troy, T. Reilly, M. Doherty, F. Cosgrove, G. Baugh, P. Priest, F. McGann, P. Christie, R. Melia, M. McCabe, S. Kearney, F. Gleeson, S. Gohery, N. Costello; subs: S. Curtis, J. Doherty.

1971: Wicklow 3-11, Hertfordshire 4-9. Dispute; replay ordered. Replay: Wicklow 3-9, Hertfordshire 2-12. Second replay: Wicklow 4-6, Hertfordshire 3-8.
Wicklow: J. Byrne, L. O'Loughlin, T. Reilly, J. O'Shaughnessy, J. Doyle, F. Byrne, M. O'Reilly, P. Reilly (capt.), P. Berkerry, P. Sheehan, T. McCarthy, T. Kennedy, G. Delaney, E. Murray, G. Gibbons; subs: A. Byrne, D. O'Sullivan, P. O'Connell.

1972: Kerry 5-5, Warwickshire 2-9.
Kerry: A. Casey, B. Fitzgerald, E. B. Fitzgerald, B. Kenny, E. Canty, T. Cronin, T. Hussey, J. Bunyan, P. Finnegan, C. Nolan, T. Kenny, P. Costello, J. McCarthy, P. Donegan, J. Flanagan; subs: J. Fitzgerald, B. O'Connell.

1973: Warwickshire 6-9, Louth 3-8.
  Warwickshire: O. Cuddy, V. McKenna, T. Conroy, P. Doherty, L. Dalton, D. Dillane, J. Scanlon, J. Madden, N. McLean, M. Murphy, L. Moloney, C. Crowe, E. Bergin, J. Ryan, J. Cronin; subs: T. Crowley, T. Timmons.

From 1974 to 1982 the original format of the championship was abandoned and the competition was incorporated in division 3 of the National Hurling League. The original format, including the strong hurling counties, was reintroduced in 1983.

1974: Roscommon 2-11, Derry 2-9.
  Roscommon: P. Dolan, T. Healy, O. Hanley, T. Shaughnessy, C. McGann, S. Farrell, J. Dolan, J. Coyne, F. Mitchell, H. Cox, B. Tansey, D. Cox, B. Mitchell, M. Murphy, R. Farran; sub: J. Kilroy.

1975: Derry 5-12, Louth 3-5.
  Derry: B. Taylor, P. McGill, L. Hinphey, A. Ó'Hara, J. O'Kane, S. Stevenson (capt.), P. Stevenson, M. McCloskey, S. Kealey, J. McGurk, P. Mellon, C. Hinphey, F. Kennedy, C. Ferris, L. Moore.

1976: Louth 6-8, Mayo 4-9.
  Louth: P. Hartnett, J. McGuinness, J. Delaney, S. Walsh, D. Callan, P. Fahy, A. Byrne, L. McKillian, L. Toal, S. McEney, T. Rice, P. Murphy, T. Melia, T. Lowry, S. Mulcairns; subs: M. McGarry, D. Hegarty.

1977: Louth 1-14, Fermanagh 2-4.
  Louth: P. Hartnett, M. Begley, J. Delaney, C. McGinley, D. Callan, P. Fahy, S. Walsh, P. Murphy, A. Kerrigan, T. Ryan, T. Rice, T. Melia, S. Mulkearns, T. Lowry, O. Reilly; sub: J. McGuinness.

1978: Armagh 5-15, Mayo 2-6.
  Armagh: P. Lavery, S. King, L. McKenna, I. Beattie, D. Devlin, M. Smith, E. Kinsella, C. Casey, B. McNally, J. McCormack, P. Devlin, J. Short, F. Malon, C. McKeown, J. Corvan.

1979: Armagh 2-13, Derry 2-1.
  Armagh: P. Lavery, S. King, D. McBride, I. Beattie, G. Devlin, M. Smith, F. Kinsella, C. Casey, B. McNally, J. McCormack, P. Devlin, J. Short, J. Christie, F. Mallon, C. McKeown.

1980: Mayo 2-13, Monaghan 2-7.
  Mayo: M. Nolan, E. Freeman, M. Keane, M. Walshe, P. Clarke, T. Henry, P. Lynsky, J. Cunnane, V. Henry, J. J. Hoban, C. Conlon, C. Murphy, J. Henry, M. Ryan, W. Kelly.

1981: Mayo 2-13, Louth 1-8.
  Mayo: D. Sinnott, M. Walshe, M. Kenny, T. Phillips, P. Clarke, T. Henry, P. Lynsky, V. Henry, J. Cunnane, P. Delaney, J. Henry, C. Murphy, J. J. Hoban, D. Healy, C. Conlon.

1982: Derry 1-10, Monaghan 0-8.
Derry: T. Tracey, J. McCullagh, A. O'Hara, G. McCullagh, C. Kelly, P. Stevenson, D. O'Hara, G. Murphy, B. McGilligan, E. Kealy, S. McCloskey, D. Kealy, P. O'Donoghue, P. Murphy, J.A. Mullan.

Resumed in original format.

1983: Cork 3-14, Galway 2-15.
Cork: J. Cronin, F. Walsh, E. Flynn, D. Relihan, B. Coleman, P. Madigan, N. Crowley, W. Walsh, M. Fitzgibbon (capt.), P. O'Connell, D. Walsh, N. Brosnan, R. O'Connor, S. O'Gorman, G. Hanley; subs: A. Jagoe, M. McDonnell.

1984: Kilkenny 0-13, Galway 2-5.
Kilkenny: A. McCormack, W. Dwyer, B. Ryan, F. Morgan, L. O'Brien, T. Lennon, P. Fennelly, B. Ayres, D. Mullan, L. Egan, J. Power, P. McEvoy, G. Drennan, B. Cleere, L. Dowling; sub: D. O'Rourke.

1985: Wexford 3-9, Tipperary 1-13.
Wexford: S. Dunne, J. Prendergast, W. Dunphy, B. Bernie, L. Finn, J. Furlong, J. Weafer, J. Barron, P. Dooley, R. Murphy, J. Walsh, M. Murphy, S. Murphy, B. O'Connor, T. Byrne; subs: P.Barden, P. Daly, V. Murphy.

1986: Kilkenny 1-17, Limerick 0-15.
Kilkenny: M. Walsh, J. Lennon, D. Dunne, W. Wall, J. Power, M. Cleere, G. Kerins, M. Morrissey, K. Hennessy, T. Bawle, T. Lennon, T. Carroll, D. Walsh, L. McCarthy, J. Meaney; sub: L. Cleere.

1987: Cork 3-11, Wexford 2-13.
Cork: T. Kingston, B. O'Sullivan, P. Redmond, D. Murphy, S. McCarthy, L. Lynch, J. Moynihan, D. Sheehan, M. Fitzpatrick (capt.), T. Burke, L. Kelly, T. Barry Murphy, M. Foley, P. Cahill, P. Crowley; subs: D. McCarthy, D. Relihan, R. O'Connor.

1988: Kikenny 1-12, Tipperary 0-10.
Kilkenny: D. Burke, J. Marnell, P. Holden, J. Lennon, M. Caulfield, P. O'Dwyer, T. McCluskey, G. Ryan, P. Ryan, T. Bawle, J. Walsh, D. Carroll, M. Rasper, J. O'Dwyer, J. Ronan; subs: D. McCarthy, P. Gannon.

1989: Tipperary 0-12, Galway 0-8.
Tipperary: J. Grace, M. Stapleton, M. Ryan, D. Quinlan, J. O'Brien, R. Quirke, L. Sheedy, E. Kelly, K. Laffan (capt.), D. Ryan, P. Everard, D. Flannery, M. McCormack, J. Sheedy, S. Nealon.

1990: Kilkenny 4-21, Tipperary 2-11.
Kilkenny: M. Walsh, T. Byrne, P. Holden (capt.), L. Simpson, J. Murphy, P. Walsh, J. Mahon, P. Ryan, T. Bawle, M. Dunphy, T. Murphy, C. Carter, M. Wrafter, J. Lennon, M. Walsh; subs: M. Hogan, M. Walsh.

1991: Tipperary 4-17, London 1-5.
   Tipperary: J. Leamy, M. Ryan, M. Stapleton, D. Quinlan, P. McGuire, G. O'Brien, S. McManus, O. Cummins, C. Byron, L. Stokes, L. Sheedy, E. Maher, J. Harrington, E. Kelly, S. Nealon; subs: P. O'Keeffe, J. Ryan, D. Fogarty.

1992: Wexford 2-7, Cork 0-13. Replay: Wexford 0-13, Cork 1-8.
   Wexford: M. Quigley, D. Morris, P. McGrath, J. Furlong, P. Nolan, G. Cody, D. Guiney, P. Owley, R. Guiney, R. O'Callaghan, P. Byrne, R. Quigley, J. Byrne, J. Bolger, S. Conroy; subs: E. Scallan. (B. Kavanagh came on as a sub in the drawn game.)

1993: Clare 3-10, Kilkenny 0-8.
   Clare: N. Considine, L. Doyle, F. Corey, B. Lynch, S. Power, T. Kennedy, N. Raner (capt.), D. Considine, C. Chaplin, P. O'Rourke, C.O'Neill, B. Quinn, V. Donnellan, B. McNamara, G. Rogers; subs: J. McKenna, C. Lynch.

1994: Cork 2-13, Kilkenny 2-11.
   Cork: T. O'Donovan, A. White, J. O'Driscoll, J. Walsh, J. O'Sullivan, J. O'Mahoney, V. Murray (capt.), M. Downing, G. Cummins, M. Sheehan, P. Kenneally, F. McCormack, A. O'Driscoll, K. Morrison, D. O'Connell; subs: R. Sheehan, B. Sheehan.

Appendix 3

All-Ireland Minor Championship, 1928–94

1928: Cork 1-8, Dublin 3-2. Replay: Cork 7-6, Dublin 4-0.
Cork: L. Horgan (capt.), J. Galvin, F. Cronin, D. Coughlan, C. Sheehan, J. Lee, D. Cogan, C. Murphy, D. Lynch, D. Lynch, M. Lewis, M. Moloney, M. Finn, G. O'Connor, J. Ryng. (C. Duggan, J. Mannix, J. Healy and J. O'Connor played in the drawn game.)

1929: Waterford 5-0, Meath 1-1.
Waterford: P. Rellis, F. Pinkert, L. Byrne, D. Wyse, P. Ryan, P. Donnelly (capt.), J. Butler, A. Noonan, J. Dwyer, N. Faraday, T. Sheehan, D. Goode, J. Goode, J. Houlihan, J. Murphy.

1930: Tipperary 4-1, Kilkenny 2-1.
Tipperary: M. Maher, J. Russell (capt.), M. Coffey, W. O'Neill, L. Burke, G. Heavey, J. Lanigan, T. Coffey, J. Dunne, J. Semple, E. Wade, P. Ryan, J. Close, T. Harney, J. Quinlan.

1931: Kilkenny 4-7, Galway 2-3.
Kilkenny: M. Doyle, D. Hughes, A. Cullen, M. Tyrell, T. Shortall, M. Brennan, A. N. Other, J. Phelan, P. Kelly, J. Shortall (capt.), J. Dwyer, C. Barry, W. Walsh, B. Ayres, P. Shortall.

1932: Tipperary 8-6, Kilkenny 5-1.
Tipperary: T. O'Keeffe, J. Looby, J. O'Dwyer, M. Burke, P. Leahy, C. Downes, J. Cooney, P. Bowe, N. Barry, P. Purcell, T. Burke, J. Fletcher, D. O'Gorman (capt.), W. Nolan, J. Maher.

1933: Tipperary 4-6, Galway 2-3.
Tipperary: J. Moloney, J. Mooney, T. Doyle, M. Ryan, M. Condon, M. Everard, P. Duggan, P. Dwyer, T. Brennan, P. Frazer, M. Burke, J. Farrell, P. Callaghan, T. Maher, J. Fletcher (capt.).

1934: Tipperary 4-3, Laois 3-5.
Tipperary: C. Maher (capt.), T. Lanigan, J. Noonan, J. Mooney, J. Moloney, J. Coffey, D. Ryan, P. O'Neill, T. English, T. Brennan, P. Callaghan, M. Loughnane, M. Mockler, T. Cawley, P. O'Dwyer.

1935: Kilkenny 4-2, Tipperary 3-3.
Kilkenny: T. Delaney, R. Hinks, P. Grace (capt.), W. Holohan, P. Boyle, P. Walsh, M. McEvoy, T. Leahy, J. Cahill, E. Tallent, B. Brannigan, J. Langton, J. Mulcahy, T. Prendergast, S. O'Brien; sub: P. Long.

1936: Kilkenny 2-4, Cork 2-3.
Kilkenny: T. Delaney, R. Hinks, P. Kavanagh, E. Fitzpatrick, N. Hyland, J. O'Neill, T. Waldron, B. Brannigan, P. Giles, J. Langton, T. Mahon, E. Tallent (capt.), J. Mulcahy, M. Grace, S. O'Brien.

1937: Cork 8-5, Kilkenny 2-7.
Cork: D. Coughlan, R. Murphy, R. Dineen, D. O'Sullivan, J. Duggan, J. O'Shea, D. Lynch, J. Burrows, M. Goggin (capt.), K. McGrath, J. Hackett, J. P. Creedon, J. O'Mahoney, K. McMahon, M. Emphy.

1938: Cork 7-2, Dublin 5-4.
Cork: P. J. Quinn, J. O'Mahoney, A. Lotty, G. Sadlier, C. Ring, P. Hogan, W. Cummins, E. Young, J. Looney, W. Aherne, T. Foley, L. O'Sullivan, T. Ryan, K. McGrath (capt.), T. O'Sullivan.

1939: Cork 5-2, Kilkenny 2-2.
Cork: T. McGrath, W. Cummins, D. O'Driscoll, W. Holton, P. Hayes, G. Sadlier, S. Murphy, E. Young, T. Crowley, M. Cody, T. Barry (capt.), J. White, P. Keohane, D. Cahalane, K. McGrath.

1940: Limerick 6-4, Antrim 2-4.
Limerick: P. Healy, K. O'Donoghue, J. Crotty, P. Murphy, M. Culhane, T. Hogan, T. Cregan, M. Fenton, P. McCarthy (Newcastle West) (capt.), P. McCarthy (Mungret), J. Hayes, W. Deere, A. O'Rourke, C. Birrane, J. Blackwell.

1941: Cork 3-11, Galway 1-1.
Cork: T. Mulcahy, J. Murphy, J. Looney, D. Lyons, J. Aherne, M. Murphy, C. Flaherty, P. Hill, S. Condon (capt.), D. Twomey, M. Kenefick, P. O'Leary, J. McCarthy, J. Morrison, J. Kelly.

1942–44: championship suspended.

1945: Dublin 3-14, Tipperary 4-6.
Dublin: S. Copeland, P. Whelan, S. McLoughlin, G. Jennings, J. Prendergast, T. McLysaght, B. Clancy, S. McEntaggert, D. Healy (capt.), P. Donnelly, L. Donnelly, N. Maher, F. Tormey, P. McCarthy, P. Lynch; sub: S. O'Neill.

1946: Dublin 1-6, Tipperary 0-7.
Dublin: G. Sutton (capt.), P. Whelan, J. Lavin, S. McLoughlin, J. Butler, N. Fingleton, B. Clancy, J. Guinea, C. McHale, N. Maher, L. Donnelly, J. Finnan, A. Young, C. Kavanagh, W. Fletcher; sub: S. Molumby.

1947: Tipperary 9-5, Galway 1-5.
Tipperary: J. O'Grady, J. Doyle, J. J. McCormack, B. Mockler, C. Keane, J. Ryan, S. Twomey, M. Ryan, J. Farrell, D. Butler, D. McNulty, P. Kenny (capt.), T. O'Meara, M. Butler, S. McDonnell.

1948: Waterford 3-8, Kilkenny 4-2.
Waterford: S. O'Flynn, M. Morrissey, S. Hayden, M. Hogan, V. Walsh, M. Kelleher, T. Cunningham, S. Conlon, T. Gallagher, L. Conway, M. Flannelly (capt.), M. O'Connor, M. McHugh, P. O'Connor, M. Browne.

1949: Tipperary 6-5, Kilkenny 2-4.
Tipperary: J. O'Grady (capt.), Jim Moloney, John Moloney, S. Browne, D. Maher, J. Finn, S. McGrath, R. Holden, W. Perkins, A. McDonnell, L. Keane, T. Aherne, M. Buckley, M. Maher, J. Doyle.

1950: Kilkenny 3-4, Tipperary 1-5.
Kilkenny: J. Murphy, J. Doherty, J. Maher, P. Lyng, P. Lennon (capt.), J. Walsh, J. McGovern, P. Johnston, D. Gorey, M. Gardiner, M. Brophy, T. O'Hanrahan, S. O'Brien, J. Brennan, R. Brennan; sub: C. Gough.

1951: Cork 4-5, Galway 1-8.
Cork: J. Dempsey, J. Coffey, M. Sheehan, P. Dreivers, P. Gaffney, S. O'Regan, F. O'Regan, F. O'Mahoney, P. Duggan, P. Crowley, J. O'Donoghue, J. Clifford (capt.), T. Kelly, S. O'Sullivan, E. Goulding; sub: V. Dorgan.

1952: Tipperary 9-9, Dublin 2-3.
Tipperary: E. McLoughney, D. Quinn, E. McGrath, E. Burke, F. Dyer, W. Hayes, L. Quinn, P. Hennessy, B. Quinn, L. Devaney, T. Wall (capt.), S. McLoughlin, M. Butler, J. Browne, P. Cleary; sub: S. McGovern.

1953: Tipperary 8-6, Dublin 3-6.
Tipperary: T. McCormack, M. Cleary, T. Kelly, P. Barry, L. Quinn, R. Reidy, S. Kenny, B. Quinn (capt.), M. Kennedy, L. Devaney, S. Murphy, S. McLoughlin, S. Corcoran, M. Stapleton, L. Connolly; sub R. Ryan.

1954: Dublin 2-7, Tipperary 2-3.

Dublin: S. O'Neill, C. Moore, T. O'Neill, M. Bohan, M. Meagher, B. Boothman (capt.), F. Whelan, T. Brackan, P. McGurk, A. Kavanagh, V. Bell, P. Delaney, P. Hyland, E. Kelly, P. Farnan; sub: M. Mannion.

1955: Tipperary 5-15, Galway 2-5.

Tipperary: S. Ryan, T. Gleeson, R. O'Donnell, M. Craddock, D. Ryan, R. Reidy (capt.), S. Wrren, C. Foyle, M. Burns, J. Doyle, A. Leahy, M. Gilmartin, L. O'Grady, P. Ryan, P. Dorney; subs: S. Small, M. O'Gara.

1956: Tipperary 4-16, Kilkenny 1-5.

Tipperary: A. Tierney, T. Gleeson, M. Dorney, B. Maher, M. Craddock, P. Reynolds, J. Mulooly, S. Warren, S. Mackey, J. Doyle, P. Ryan (capt.), W. O'Grady, T. Flynn, J. Scott, S. Dalton.

1957: Tipperary 4-7, Kilkenny 3-7.

Tipperary: T. Moloney, M. Craddock, M. Lonergan, P. Kearns, M. Stapleton, P. Reynolds, A. Croke, M. Murphy, P. Kennedy, S. Ryan, L. Kiely, J. Doyle (capt.), P. Doyle, M. Hogan, P. Butler; subs: W. Hogan, P. Woodlock.

1958: Limerick 5-8, Galway 3-10.

Limerick: T. Hanley, J. McDonagh, J. Guinane, C. O'Connell, J. J. Bresnihan, J. Leonard, M. Hanrahan, B. Kelleher, P. Hartnett, P. Cobbe (capt.), L. Canty, P. Murphy, E. Carey, J. Hayes, S. Sexton; sub: D. Dillane.

1959: Tipperary 2-8, Kilkenny 2-7.

Tipperary: J. O'Donoghue, P. Griffin, G. Kinnane, M. Lonergan, J. Carroll, A. Croke, R. Slevin, T. Ryan (Killenaule), T. Ryan (Toomyvara), P. Doyle, B. Carey, M. Duggan, M. Nolan, L. Kiely (capt.), J. Ryan; subs: S. Gleeson, P. Crampton.

1960: Kilkenny 7-12, Tipperary 1-11.

Kilkenny: D. Kinsella, N. Roughan, J. Ayres, P. Dempsey, R. Walsh, O. Ryan, P. Brett, T. Murphy, T. Barry, P. Freaney, W. Grace (capt.), J. Nyhan, S. O'Brien, P. Ryan, A. McGrath.

1961: Kilkenny 3-13, Tipperary 0-15.

Kilkenny: P. Foley, J. McGrath, N. Forrestal, P. Cullen, S. O'Brien, P. Henderson, S. Hanrahan, T. Barry, J. Murphy, T. Walsh, D. Kinsella, P. Freaney, J. Dunphy (capt.), M. Aylward, J. Delaney.

1962: Kilkenny 3-6, Tipperary 0-9.

Kilkenny: N. Skehan, S. Treacy, T. Phelan, J. Walsh, S. Hanrahan, P. Drennan, W. Burke, J. Byrne, S. Muldowney, S. Cooke, T. Walsh, J. Delaney, J. Dunphy (capt.), P. Walsh, M. Aylward; sub: T. Ryan.

1963: Wexford 6-12, Limerick 5-9.
Wexford: L. Byrne, J. Hartley, M. Nolan, E. O'Connor, J. Murphy, M. Kinsella, V. Staples, L. Bernie (capt.), C. Rafferty, C. Dowdall, T. Doran, F. Swords, W. Carley, S. Barron, P. Quigley; sub: B. Gaule.

1964: Cork 10-7, Laois 1-4.
Cork: H. O'Brien, T. Murphy, G. Aherne, P. O'Sullivan, J. O'Callaghan, B. Wylie, W. Murphy, P. O'Riordan, C. Roche, D. Clifford, L. McAuliffe, K. Cummins (capt.), C. McCarthy, A. O'Flynn, M. Kenneally.

1965: Dublin 4-10, Limerick 2-7.
Dublin: P. Cunningham, A. Fletcher, L. Deegan, C. Brennan, W. Markey, P. Kennedy, L. Martin (capt.), H. Dalton, F. McDonald, J. Fetherson, E. Davey, T. Grealish, T. McCann, B. Whelan, M. Kinsella; sub: P. Cassels.

1966: Wexford 6-7, Cork 6-7 (draw). Replay: Wexford 4-1, Cork 1-8.
Wexford: H. Butler, J. Quigley, E. Murphy, W. Butler, E. McDonald, E. Buggy, M. Fitzpatrick, D. Howell, T. Kavanagh, T. Furlong, L. Bent, P. Byrne, T. Royce, M. Browne, P. Bernie (capt.). (Subs J. Nagle, J. Ryan and M. Butler played in the drawn game; T. Kavanagh came on as a sub in the drawn game.)

1967: Cork 2-15, Wexford 5-3.
Cork: W. Galvin, M. McCarthy, B. Tobin, M. Bohane, T. O'Brien, J. Horgan, M. Aherne, P. Moylan (capt.), J. Barrett, S. Murphy, M. Malone, C. Kelly, T. Buckley, B. O'Connor, P. Ring; subs: M. Ryan, K. Fitzgerald.

1968: Wexford 2-13, Cork 3-7.
Wexford: P. Cox, G. O'Connor, J. Russell, P. O'Brien, A. Kerrigan, L. Byrne, L. Bennett, P. Kennedy, T. Byrne (capt.), M. Quigley, P. Walsh, J. Murphy, M. Butler, M. Casey, M. Byrne; subs: L. Kinsella, B. Walsh.

1969: Cork 2-15, Kilkenny 3-6.
Cork: P. Lawton, P. Casey, J. Rothwell, J. O'Sullivan, K. Murray, M. O'Doherty, S. Collins (capt.), N. Crowley, S. O'Farrell, P. Kavanagh, T. Crowley, T. Sheehan, F. Coughlan, G. Hanley, S. O'Leary; sub: J. Buckley.

1970: Cork 5-19, Galway 2-9.
Cork: D. O'Brien, B. Murphy, L. Kelly, M. Corbett, V. Twomey, M. O'Doherty, J. Buckley, P. Kavanagh (capt.), N. Crowley, G. Hanley, S. O'Farrell, T. Sheehan, D. Relihan, T. Crowley, S. O'Leary.

1971: Cork 2-11, Kilkenny 1-11.
Cork: F. O'Sullivan, M. Corbett, L. McNally, D. J. Foley, D. Coakley, J. Buckley (capt.), D. O'Keeffe, T. Canavan, D. O'Dwyer, P. Buckley, A. Creagh, V. Twomey, T. Fogarty, J. Barry Murphy, E. O'Sullivan; subs: S. Coughlan, B. Cotter, J Ryan.

1972: Kilkenny 8-7, Cork 3-9.
Kilkenny: K. Fennelly, J. Ryan, J. Burke, P. O'Brien, K. Robinson, B. Cody (capt.), J. Dowling, G. Woodcock, G. Fennelly, S. O'Brien, M. Tierney, W. Fitzpatrick, P. Butler, M. McCarthy, B. Sweeney; sub: J. O'Sullivan.

1973: Kilkenny 4-5, Galway 3-7.
Kilkenny: P. Dunphy, D. O'Hara, G. Doheny, K. Robinson (capt.), J. Hennessy, J. Marnell, O. Bergin, G. Devane, B. Waldron, P. Lannon, P. Mulhall, J. Lyng, P. Treacy, S. O'Brien, M. Lyng; subs: J. Purcell, M. Lanigan.

1974: Cork 1-10, Kilkenny 1-8.
Cork: J. Cronin, P. Coughlan, L. Geaney (capt.), J. Crowley, C. Brassil, T. Cashman, D. MacCurtain, R. O'Mahoney, F. Delaney, K. O'Driscoll, D. Ryan, G. McEvoy, T. Murphy, T. Cullinane, D. Buckley; subs: D. Keane, D. Murphy, P. Horgan.

1975: Kilkenny 3-19, Cork 1-14.
Kilkenny: E. Mahon, R. Power, P. Prendergast, J. Henderson, H. Ryan (capt.), D. O'Hara, G. Stapleton, P. Lannon, J. O'Brien, K. Brennan, J. Wall, K. O'Shea, S. Hennessy, P. Brennan, J. Ryan.

1976: Tipperary 2-20, Kilkenny 1-7.
Tipperary: V. Mullins, P. Loughnane, P. J. Maxwell, T. Slattery, M. Stapleton, G. Stapleton, J. O'Dwyer, J. Hogan (capt.), P. Ryan, E. O'Shea, M. Doyle, T. Grogan, M. Murphy, J. Stone, P. Power; sub: P. Looby.

1977: Kilkenny 4-8, Cork 3-11 (draw). Replay: Kilkenny 1-8, Cork 0-9.
Kilkenny: L. Ryan, C. Mackey, M. Meagher, B. O'Hara, T. Lennon, S. Fennelly (capt.), D. Connolly, G. Ryan, J. Mulcahy, E. Deegan, R. Murphy, E. Crowley, M. Nash, E. Wallace; subs: J. Waters (drawn game), J. Heffernan (drawn game and replay). (R. Murphy did not play in the drawn game.)

1978: Cork 1-15, Kilkenny 1-8.
Cork: G. Cunningham, W. Cashman, P. Murphy (capt.), J. Hodgins, B. O'Driscoll, J. Murphy, T. McCarthy, D. Walsh, J. Hartnett, L. Lynch, T. Aherne, G. O'Regan, D. Murphy, S. O'Gorman, S. Cashman.

1979: Cork 2-11, Kilkenny 1-9.
Cork: G. Cunningham, W. Cashman, C. O'Connor, J. Hodgins, C. Marshall, K. O'Driscoll, C. Coughlan (capt.), D. Scanlon, D. Walsh, T. O'Sullivan, K. Hennessy, J. Greally, A. Coyne, M. O'Sullivan, T. Coakley; sub: R. Hegarty.

1980: Tipperary 2-15, Wexford 0-10.
Tipperary: K. Hogan, M. Conway, P. Maher, E. Hogan, I. Conroy, J. Maher (capt.), D. Finnerty, J. Hayes, P. Kenny, G. O'Neill, , M. McGrath, J. Darcy, A. Browne, W. Peters, N. English; subs: V. Dooley, J. Treacy.

1981: Kilkenny 1-20, Galway 3-9.

Kilkenny: D. Burke, G. O'Neill, E. Kennedy (capt.), E. Wall, D. Hoyne, M. Morrissey, J. O'Hara, P. Ryan, T. Bawle, J. McDonald, D. Carroll, R. Heffernan, L. McCarthy, S. Delahunty, S. Rafter; subs: S. Whearty, P. Cleere, J. Donnelly.

1982: Tipperary 2-7, Galway 0-4.

Tipperary: J. Leamy, J. Flannery, J. Bergin, C. Bonnar, B. Everard, D. Kealy, W. Hayes, J. Kennedy (capt.), G. Bradley, N. Sheehy, M. Cunningham, S. Slattery, J. Cormack, L. Stokes, M. Scully; subs: M. Corcoran, G. Ryan, A. Ryan.

1983: Galway 0-10, Dublin 0-7.

Galway: J. Commins, M. Killeen, P. Dervan, S. Treacy, P. Brehony, P. Malone, G. McInerney, D. Jennings, J. J. Broderick, T. Monaghan, T. Moloney, J. Cooney, S. Keane, A. Cunningham (capt.), P. Higgins; subs: M. Shiel, G. Elwood, N. Brody.

1984: Limerick 3-8, Kilkenny 1-14 (draw). Replay: Limerick 2-5, Kilkenny 2-4.

Limerick: V. Murnane, A. Madden, P. Carey, J. Fitzgerald, G. Hegarty, A. O'Riordan (capt.), A. Cunneen, A. Carmody, M. Reale, T. Byrnes, G. Kirby, G. Ryan, J. O'Neill, P. Davern, B. Stapleton; subs: M. O'Brien, B. Flynn (draw), C. Coughlan (both games), D. Marren (replay).

1985: Cork 3-10, Wexford 0-12.

Cork: T. Kingston, C. Connery, P. Cahalane, P. Coutts, C. Casey, B. Murphy, K. McGuckian, M. O'Mahoney (capt.), L. Kelly, G. O'Riordan, B. Harte, J. Fitzgibbon, G. Manley, M. Foley, M. Mullins.

1986: Offaly 3-12, Cork 3-9.

Offaly: J. Errity, P. Nallan, R. Mannion, D. Sherlock, J. Kilmartin, M. Hogan (capt.), B. Kelly, D. Geoghegan, A. Kelly, A. Cahill, D. Regan, R. Byrne, T. Moylan, M. Duignan, D. Pilkington; sub: B. Dooley.

1987: Offaly 2-8, Tipperary 0-12.

Offaly: J. Troy, B. Whelehan, D. Geoghegan, B. Hennessy, J. Dooley, J. Errity, A. Cahill, J. Pilkington, T. Dooley, S. Morkam, B. Dooley, K. Egan, T. Moylan (capt.), J. Troy, D. Pilkington.

1988: Kilkenny 3-13, Cork 0-12.

Kilkenny: J. Conroy, G. Henderson, P. J. O'Connor, D. Roche, P. O'Neill, P. Brophy (capt.), J. Conlon, D. Dooley, D. Bradley, W. O'Keeffe, B. Ryan, P. O'Grady, A. Ronan, C. Carter, D. J. Carey; subs: P. Treacy, J. Buggy.

1989: Offaly 2-16, Clare 1-12.

Offaly: J. Troy, M. Hogan, F. Cullen, H. Rigney, D. Barron, B. Whelehan (capt.), D. Franks, A. Cahill, R. Dooley, J. Dooley, S. Grennan, O. O'Neill, R. McNamara, N. Hand, K. Flynn; sub: R. Deegan.

1990: Kilkenny 3-14, Cork 3-14 (draw). Replay: Kilkenny 3-16, Cork 0-11.

Kilkenny: A. Behan, M. Holohan, L. Mahoney, J. Carroll, D. O'Neill, C. Brennan, P. Larkin, J. McDermott (capt.), P. Long, A. Comerford, J. Shefflin, P. Farrell. P. J. Delaney, S. Ryan, D. Lawlor; subs: A. Cleere, B. Power. (C. Brennan and J. Carroll came on as subs in the drawn game. S. Meally, D. Beirne and A. Cleere played in the drawn game.)

1991: Kilkenny 0-15, Tipperary 1-10.

Kilkenny: M. Carey, S. Meally, L. Mahoney, B. Power, A. O'Sullivan, E. Dwyer, D. O'Neill (capt.), D. Maher, J. Hickey, S. Dollard, P. J. Delaney, G. Walsh, D. Byrne, M. Owens, R. Shorthall; subs: P. Davis.

1992: Galway 1-13, Waterford 2-4.

Galway: L. Donoghue, T. Healy, M. Spellman, C. Moore, N. Shaughnessy, C. Donavan (capt.), M. Donoghue, F. Forde, S. Walsh, M. Lynskey, D. Coen, P. Kelly, S. Corcoran, C. O'Doherty, D. Walsh; subs: J. Murray, J. Kerins.

1993: Kilkenny 1-17, Galway 1-12.

Kilkenny: O. Blanchfield, T. Hickey, S. Doyle (capt.), J. Ayres, V. O'Brien, B. Lonergan, B. Bolger, K. Grogan, S. Kealy, D. Cleere, L. Smith, E. Mackey, B. Dalton, D. Buggy, O. O'Connor; sub: J. Young.

1994: Galway 2-10, Cork 1-10.

Galway: A. Kerins, G. Kennedy (capt.), P. Huban, O. Canning, M. Healy, F. Gantley, L. Madden, L. Hogan, G. Glynn, K. Broderick, R. Farrell, F. Healy, E. Brady, R. Gantley, D. Fahy.

Appendix 4

All-Ireland Intermediate Championship, 1961–73

1961: Wexford 3-15, London 4-4.
Wexford: J. O'Neill, J. Hyland, B. Ryan, M. Collins, B. Doran, J. Crean, P. Sullivan, L. Byrne (capt.), P. Lynch, J. Walsh, N. Newport, T. Hawkins, L. Crean, J. Coady, S. Whelan.

1962: Carlow 6-15, London 3-3.
Carlow: J. O'Connell, W. Walsh, M. Hogan, A. Fortune, P. McGovern, P. Somers, T. Nolan, M. Morrissey, M. O'Brien, L. Walsh, W. Hogan, P. O'Connell, W. Walsh, E. Gladney, C. Hynes.

1963: Tipperary 1-10, London 1-7.
Tipperary: P. O'Sullivan, T. Burke, M. Barry, P. Crampton, W. Boyle, P. Gleeson, P. Dawson, M. Roche, J. Fogarty, M. Kearns, J. Collison, M. Keating, T. Flynn, T. Larkin, J. Lanigan.

1964: Wexford 4-7, London 1-11.
Wexford: S. Boggan, N. O'Gorman, N. O'Brien, A. Carty, L. Butler, O. Hearne, J. Murphy, M. Delaney, B. Murray, O. Culen, S. Whelan, P. Murphy, L. Delaney, L. Kehoe, N. O'Brien.

1965: Cork 2-20, London 5-5.
Cork: T. Monatghan, D. Murphy, J. Ryan, M. Garde, J. O'Keeffe, J. Barry Murphy, F. Sheehan, O. O'Keeffe, J. Hogan, S. Barry, W. Galigan, J. K. Coleman, D. O'Brien, D. O'Keeffe, W. Fitton.

1966: Tipperary 4-11, Dublin 2-12.
Tipperary: S. Shinnors, P. Kenny, N. Ryan, A. Burke, J. Drohan, N. O'Gorman, P.

Dawson, W. O'Grady, J. Fogarty, S. Kenny, M. O'Grady, M. Jones, L. Connolly, S. Noonan, T. Brennan.

1967: London 1-9, Cork 1-5.
London: W. Barneville, M. Hassett, L. Walsh, F. Healy, R. Cashin, M. Kirwan, P. Fahy, S. Lambe, T. Connolly, T. Cleary, F. Condon, M. Loughnane, J. Organ, D. O'Keeffe, E. Murray.

1968: London 4-15, Dublin 0-3.
London: W. Barneville, M. Hassett, L. Walsh, C. Wiley, P. Fahy, M. Connolly, R. Cashin, M. Meaney, R. O'Neill, S. Lambe, F. Condon, P. Connolly, M. Loughnane, M. Kirwan, T. Cleary.

1969: Kildare 2-8, Cork 3-4.
Kildare: P. Connolly, S. Malone, C. O'Malley, N. Burke, A. Carew, P. Dunny, M. O'Brien, R. Burke, J. O'Connell, T. Christian, T. Carew, M. Duane, J. Wall, M. Mullins, N. Brehan.

1970: Antrim 4-18, Warwickshire 3-6.
Antrim: J. Coyle, E. Elliot, K. Donnelly, E. Hamill, N. Wheller, T. Connolly, A. McCamphill, S. Burns, S. Collins, S. Richmond, E. Donnelly, A. Hamill, B. McGarry, P. McShane, A. McCallin; sub: A. Connolly.

1971: Tipperary 3-16, Wicklow 3-13.
Tipperary: W. Barneville, J. Dunlea, P. Kennedy, J. Keogh, D. Crowe, P. Quinlan, B. Teehan, O. Quinn, J. P. McDonnell, S. Power, J. Noonan, M. Brennan, E. Butler, P. Lowry, J. Barry.

1972: Tipperary 2-13, Galway 1-9.
Tipperary: S. Cahalane, J. Costigan, J. Keogh, S. Fitzpatrick, M. Fitzgibbon, N. Seymour, J. Keane, T. Moloney, B. Ferncombe, J. Connor, J. Kennedy, M. Ryan, O. Killeen, J. Seymour, S. Mackey.

1973: Kilkenny 5-15, London 2-9.
Kilkenny: P. Grace, M. Mason, K. Mahon, M. Hoyne, J. Dunne, T. Murphy, T. Foley, P. Kavanagh, D. Burke, J. Doyle, P. Holden, J. O'Connor, F. Cleere, J. Walsh, S. Muldowney.

Appendix 5

All-Ireland B Championship, 1974–94

1974: Kildare 1-26, Antrim 3-13.
Kildare: J. Curran, R. Cullen, P. Dunny, M. O'Brien, M. Moore, A. Carew, M. Dunne, R. Burke, J. O'Connell, J. Walsh, T. Carew, J. O'Leary, E. Walsh, J. Wall, M. Deeley.

1975: Westmeath 4-16, London 3-19. Replay: Westmeath 3-23, London 2-7.
Westmeath: O. Gallagher, F. Shields, P. Jackson, M. Cosgrave, S. Fagan, M. Fagan, W. Shanley, P. Curran, G. Whelan, C. Connaghton, J. Keary, M. Kilcoyne, E. Fagan, M. Flanagan, E. Clarke; sub: N. Fitzsimmons. (J. Burke played in the drawn game.)

1976: Kerry 0-15, London 1-10.
Kerry: J. Conway, J. Fitzgerald, R. Dineen, J. Brick, M. Carrol, P. Cronin, D. Brassil, J. M. Brick, M. Brick, T. Nolan, J. Bunyan, P. J. Houlihan, P. Moriarity, G. Scollard, F. Donovan; subs: P. Bunyan, J. Carroll.

1977: Laois 3-21, London 2-9.
Laois: J. Carroll, M. Bolger, P. Ging, R. Moloney, J. Doran, M. Mahon, E. Moore, M. Walsh, F. Bates, M. Aherne, P. Kelly, J. Mahon, A. Lanham, M. Cuddy, P. Dillon; sub: J. Delahunty.

1978: Antrim 1-16, London 3-7.
Antrim: J. Corr, S. Collins, E. Hamill, F. Ward, C. Ward, S. Donnelly, D. Donnelly, J. Fegan, D. McNaughton, P. Boyle, J. Crossey, M. O'Connell, D. McNaughton, P. McDonnell, P. McIlhatton.

1979: Laois 2-13, London 3-10. Replay: Laois 1-20, London 0-17.
Laois: J. Carroll, P. Ging, M. Carroll, J. Bohane, P. Dowling, C. Jones, M. Mahon, W. Bohane, J. Killeen, M. Walsh, M. Cuddy, M. Brophy, F. Keenan, C. Wall, J. Mahon. (M. Cuddy played in the drawn game and came on as a sub in the replay.)

1980: Kildare 2-20, London 2-14.
Kildare: R. Bryan, T. Burke, R. Cullen, L. Hogan, P. Dooley, M. Moore, F. Johnson, T. Johnson, J. O'Connell, J. Walsh, E. Walsh, T. White, J. Tomkins, T. Carew, D. Maguire; sub: L. Shinnors.

1981: Antrim 2-17, London 3-14.
Antrim: N. Patterson, S. McNaughton, D. McKinley, F. Ward, S. Donnelly, T. Donnelly, S. Collins, G. Cunningham, M. O'Connell, B. Donnelly, J. Crossey, P. Boyle, E. Donnelly, P. McFall, D. Donnelly; sub: B. Laverty.

1982: Antrim 2-16, London 2-14.
Antrim: N. Patterson, S. Reynolds, S. McNaughton, F. Ward, S. Donnelly, T. Donnelly, B. Gormley, S. Boyle, S. Collins, M. O'Connell, B. Donnelly, P. Boyle, D. Donnelly, P. McFall, G. Rogan.

1983: Kerry 2-8, London 1-7.
Kerry: J. Conway, C. Nolan, M. Leahy, J. Lucid, M. Burke, T. Canty, J. McElligot, D. J. Leahy, F. Dineen, J. M. Brick, J. O'Connell, J. Hennessy, P. Stack, T. Nolan, J. O'Regan; subs: M. Allen, B. Neenan.

1984: Westmeath 4-10, London 1-16.
Westmeath: S. Greville, N. Fitzsimmons, J. Doyle, R. Shaw, R. Gavin, W. Burke, G. Jackson, D. McCormack, W. Shanley, M. Daly, J. Fitzsimmons, E. Gallagher, D. Kilcoyne, M. J. Corrigan, M. Kilcoyne; subs: P. Curran, M. Kennedy, P. Browne.

1985: London 1-8, Meath 1-6.
London: L. Shanahan, G. Kelleher, M. Headd, T. O'Donoghue, T. Nallan, N. Daly, L. Walsh, K. White, N. Uniacke, P. Hoctor, M. Burke, M. Maher, J. Power, S. O'Neill, J. Cormack; subs: T. Lawlor, B. Grealish.

1986: Kerry 3-10, London 1-9.
Kerry: J. Conway, M. Burke, M. Leahy, M. Casey, J. O'Sullivan, D. J. Leahy, J. McCarthy, P. O'Donoghue, C. Walsh, S. Sheehan, C. Nolan, P. McMahon, T. Nolan, G. McCarthy, S. Flaherty; subs: J. O'Connell, E. Murphy.

1987: London 0-20, Carlow 1-15.
London: L. Shanaghan, T. O'Donoghue, M. Headd, T. Whelan, P. O'Donoghue, N. Daly, D. Crotty, T. Nallan, C. Spain, P. Lynch, G. Ryan, P. Hoctor, J. Murphy, P. Butler, M. Jordan; subs: M. Burke, K. Dealy, C. Aherne.

1988: London 2-6, Down 1-7.
London: L. Shanahan, T. Whelan, L. Long, C. White, D. McKenna, N. Daly, D. Crotty, J. Leahy, P. O'Shea, K. Morrissey, M. Conneely, J. O'Donoghue, P. Hoctor, J. Murphy, J. Quinn; subs: J. Dillon, C. Spain, P. Butler.

1989: Kildare 1-13, London 1-12.

    Kildare: L. Deering, J. Riedy, C. Kelly, J. O'Donnell, P. Hayden, P. Kelly, J. O'Connell, G. Deering, K. Flynn, J. Byrne, E. Kelly, G. Ennis, R. Byrne, M. Moore, N. Byrne; sub: C. Guiney.

1990: London 1-15, Kildare 2-10.

    London: L. Shanahan, T. Whelan, J. Coady, M. Daly, D. McKenna, A. Woulfe, M. Cunningham, P. O'Donoghue, A. Moylan, M. Connolly, J. Donoghue, P. Hoctor, J. Murphy, J. Quinn, T. Kennedy; subs: J. Morrissey, C. Spain, J. Ryan.

1991: Westmeath 2-12, London 2-6.

    Westmeath: S. Greville, P. O'Brien, P. Connaghton, G. Reilly, A. Weir, B. McCabe, M. Kennedy, P. Clancy, S. McLoughlin, R. Galvin, D. Gillen, A. Devine, J. Donoghue, D. Kilcoyne, J. Kennedy; sub: E. Gallagher.

1992: Carlow 2-15, London 3-10.

    Carlow: R. Kielty, C. Kealy, T. English, B. Lawlor, J. English, J. Nevin, J. Carey, B. Hayden, P. Brennan, D. Doyle, M. Mullins, J. McDonald, T. Murphy, J. Byrne, J. Hayden; sub: C. Jordan.

1993: Meath 2-16, London 1-16.

    Meath: M. Gannon, A. O'Neill, J. Andrews, M. Ennis, J. Gorry, P. Donnelly, S. Kealy, P. Cahill, P. Potterton, M. Cole, P. Kelly, M. Massey, R. Kelly, M. Smith, I. McCaffrey; sub: D. Murray.

1994: Roscommon 1-10, London 1-9.

    Roscommon: A. Tully, M. Hussey, A. Kelly, N. Cunningham, T. Killian, K. McGeeney, P. Mannion, P. Feeney, M. Cunniffe, L. Murray, D. Coyle, R. Mulroy, J. Mannion, G. Coyle, P. Tiernan.

Appendix 6

All-Ireland Under-21 Championship, 1964–94

1964: Tipperary 8-9, Wexford 3-1.
Tipperary: P. O'Sullivan, J. Smith, N. O'Gorman, M. O'Meara, O. Killoran, C. O'Dwyer, L. Gaynor, M. Roche, J. Fogarty, N. Lane, M. Keating, F. Loughnane (capt.), J. Dillon, T. J. Butler, T. Brennan; sub: P. J. Ryan.

1965: Wexford 3-7, Tipperary 1-4.
Wexford: M. Jacob, W. O'Neill (capt.), D. Quigley, A. Somers, V. Staples, M. Kinsella, W. Murphy, E. Ryan, J. Doran, C. Dowdall, P. Quigley, S. Barron, T. Maher, T. Doran, J. Berry; sub: C. Jacob.

1966: Cork 3-12, Wexford 5-6. Replay: Cork 4-9, Wexford 4-9. Second replay: Cork 9-9, Wexford 5-9.
Cork: J. Mitchell, W. Murphy, T. Falvey, P. O'Sullivan, C. Roche, J. Russell, D. Coughlan, J. McCarthy, G. McCarthy (capt.), S. Barry, T. Browne, P. Curley, C. McCarthy, A. O'Flynn, E. O'Brien; subs: A. Maher, B. McKeown. (B. Wylie played in both draws; K. Farrell, D. McKeown, D. Clifford and P. O'Riordan played in the first draw.)

1967: Tipperary 1-8, Dublin 1-7.
Tipperary: H. Condron, S. Ryan, J. Kelly, D. Grady, M. Esmonde, T. O'Connor, S. Hogan, P. J. Ryan (capt.), C. Davitt, N. O'Dwyer, J. Ryan, J. Walsh, P. O'Connor, P. Lowry, J. Flanagan; subs: M. Nolan, T. Delaney.

1968: Cork 2-18, Kilkenny 3-9.
Cork: B. Hurley, W. Murphy, B. Tobin, F. Norberg, N. Dunne, W. Walsh, R. Cummins, D. Clifford, P. Moylan, B. Meade, S. Murphy, P. Hegarty (capt.), H. O'Sullivan, P. Curley, P. Ring; subs: M. McCarthy, R. Lehane, J. Murphy.

1969: Cork 5-13, Wexford 4-7.
   Cork: B. Hurley, M. McCarthy, B. Tobin, F. Norbert, S. Looney, D. Clifford (capt.), T. O'Brien, S. Murphy, P. Moylan, B. Meade, W. Walsh, N. Dunne, F. Keane, R. Cummins, B. Cummins; sub: P. McDonnell.

1970: Cork 3-8, Wexford 2-11. Replay: Cork 5-17, Wexford 0-8.
   Cork: M. Coleman, M. McCarthy, P. McDonnell, B. Tobin, S. Murphy, J. Horgan, T. O'Brien (capt.), S. Looney, P. Moylan, C. Kelly, B. Cummins, K. McSweeney, S. O'Leary, J. Barrett, P. Ring. (M. Malone and J. Nodwell played in the drawn game.)

1971: Cork 7-8, Wexford 1-11.
   Cork: M. Coleman, J. Horgan, P. McDonnell (capt.), B. Murphy, S. O'Farrell, M. O'Doherty, B. Coleman, S. Looney, N. Crowley, E. Fitzgerald, M. Malone, K. McSweeney, B. Cummins, J. Rothwell, S. O'Leary; subs: P. Casey, D. Collins, P. Kavanagh.

1972: Galway 2-9, Dublin 1-10.
   Galway: E. Campbell, L. Glynn, G. Kelly, L. Shields, I. Clarke (capt.), F. Donoghue, T. Brehony, G. Glynn, F. Burke, M. Coen, A. Fenton, M. Donoghue, M. Barrett, T. O'Donoghue, G. Holland; subs: P. J. Molloy, J. Duggan.

1973: Cork 2-10, Wexford 4-2.
   Cork: F. O'Sullivan, M. Corbett, L. Kelly, B. Murphy, M. O'Doherty (capt.), J. Buckley, D. Burns, T. Crowley, B. Cotter, P. Kavanagh, S. O'Farrell, Tony Murphy, D. Relihan, T. Fogarty, S. O'Leary; subs: T. Sheehan, J. Barry Murphy

1974: Kilkenny 3-8, Waterford 3-7.
   Kilkenny: K. Fennelly, T. McCormack, M. Hogan, J. Dunne, G. Henderson, B. Cody, M. Tierney, J. Dowling, S. Brophy, N. Brennan, G. Woodcock, G. Fennelly (capt.), P. Kearney, T. Teehan, W. Fitzpatrick; subs: B. Sweeney, P. Mulcahy.

1975: Kilkenny 5-13, Cork 2-19.
   Kilkenny: K. Fennelly (capt.), J. Marnell, J. Moran, D. O'Hara, G. Henderson, B. Cody, J. Grace, J. Dowling, G. Fennelly, J. Hennessy, M. Tierney, J. Lyng, T. Brennan, B. Sweeney, W. Fitzpatrick; subs: K. Robinson, J. O'Sullivan, G. Woodcock.

1976: Cork 2-17, Kilkenny 1-8.
   Crok: J. Cronin, J. Crowley, B. Geaney, D. MacCurtain, J. Fenton, T. Cashman, F. Delaney, S. O'Mahony, C. Brassil, J. Allen, R. McDonnell, P. Horgan, T. Murphy (capt.), K. Murphy, D. Buckley; sub: B. Reidy.

1977: Kilkenny 2-9, Cork 1-9.
   Kilkenny: E. Mahon, J. Lennon, J. Henderson, P. Prendergast, J. Hennessy, D. O'Hara, R. Reid, P. Lannon, M. Kennedy, R. Power, M. Lyng (capt.), B. Waldron, B. Fennelly, G. Tyrell, J. Wall; sub: K. Brennan.

1978: Galway 3-5, Tipperary 2-8. Replay: Galway 3-15, Tipperary 2-8.
Galway: G. Smith, C. Hayes, M. Headd, P. J. Burke, J. Greaney, M. Earls, S. Coen, S. Mahon, M. Kilkenny, G. Kennedy, J. Good, P. Ryan, B. Forde (capt.), M. Conneely, J. Ryan; subs: T. Brehony, J. Coen, S. Forde (draw), G. Kennedy (replay). (G. Linnane played in the drawn game.)

1979: Tipperary 2-12, Galway 1-9.
Tipperary: V. Mullins, P. Loughnane, J. Ryan, E. Hogan, T. Slattery, J. O'Dwyer, G. Stapleton, G. O'Connor, P. Fox, M. Murphy, E. O'Shea, T. Grogan, B. Mannion, M. Doyle (capt.), P. Looby; sub: P. Ryan.

1980: Tipperary 2-9, Kilkenny 0-14.
Tipperary: V. Mullins, M. Ryan, C. Bonnar, P. Fox, B. Heffernan, J. O'Dwyer, P. McGrath, M. Kennedy, P. Kennedy (capt.), M. Murphy, B. Ryan, A. Buckley, J. Kennedy, D. O'Connell, P. Power; sub: A. Kinsella.

1981: Tipperary 2-16, Kilkenny 1-10.
Tipperary: J. Farrell, M. Ryan, P. Brennan, P. Fox, I. Conroy, J. McIntyre, P. McGrath, A. Kinsella, P. Kennedy (capt.), N. English, B. Ryan, M. McGrath, G. O'Neill, D. O'Connell, A. Buckley.

1982: Cork 0-12, Galway 0-11.
Cork: G. Cunningham, M. McCarthy (capt.), M. Boylan, J. Hodgins, W. Cashman, K. O'Driscoll, C. O'Connor, K. Hennessy, D. Curtin, T. O'Sullivan, T. Coyne, D. Walsh, E. Brosnan, M. O'Sullivan, G. Motherway; subs: G. McCarthy, P. Deasy, T. Mulcahy.

1983: Galway 0-12, Tipperary 1-6.
Galway: T. Coen, B. Derivan, P. Casserly (capt.), M. Donaghue, P. Finnerty, T. Keady, O. Kilkenny, A. Moylan, P. Healy, A. Staunton, M. Coleman, M. Costelloe, G. Burke, J. Murphy, M. McGrath; subs: E. Ryan, M. Kenny, C. Hennebry.

1984: Kilkenny 1-12, Tipperary 0-11.
Kilkenny: D. Burke, E. Wall, E. O'Connor, B. Young, D. Hoyne, L. Cleere, L. Walsh, T. Phelan, R. Heffernan, D. Carroll, P. Walsh, J. McDonald, L. McCarthy, R. McCarthy, S. Delahunty (capt.); subs: P. Ryan, M. Rafter.

1985: Tipperary 1-10, Kilkenny 2-5.
Tipperary: J. Leamy, N. McDonnell, P. O'Donoghue, C. Bonnar, M. Corcoran, D. Kealy, P. Delaney, J. Kennedy, A. Ryan, M. Cunningham, J. McGrath, N. Sheehy, J. Cormack, L. Stokes, M. Scully (capt.); sub: M. Bryan.

1986: Galway 0-14, Wexford 2-6.
Galway: J. Commins, P. Dervan, M. Kelly, M. Flaherty, M. Helebert, P. Malone, G. McInerney, T. Monaghan, D. Jennings, M. Connolly, A. Cunningham (capt.), A. Davoren, P. Nolan, Joe Cooney, P. Higgins; subs: G. Elwood, S. Keane.

1987: Limerick 2-15, Galway 3-6.
Limerick: V. Murnane, A. Madden, P. Carey, D. Flynn, D. Nash, A. O'Riordan, M. Reale, G. Hegarty, J. O'Neill, G. Kirby, A. Carmody, G. Ryan (capt.), P. Barrett, J. O'Connor, L. O'Connor; sub: D. Marren.

1988: Cork 4-11, Kilkenny 1-5.
Cork: T. Kingston, C. Connery (capt.), D. Irwin, S. O'Leary, C. Casey, P. Kenneally, T. O'Keeffe, L. Kelly, T. Cooney, J. Corcoran, G. Manley, F. Horgan, D. O'Connell, M. Foley, J. Fitzgibbon.

1989: Tipperary 4-10, Offaly 3-11.
Tipperary: B. Bane, L. Sheedy, M. Ryan, G. Frend, J. Madden, C. Bonnar, S. Maher, J. Leahy, D. Ryan (capt.), P. Hogan, C. Stakelum, D. Ryan, M. Nolan, D. Quirke, T. Lanigan; subs: J. Cahill, D. Lyons, K. Ryan.

1990: Kilkenny 2-11, Tipperary 1-11.
Kilkenny: J. Conroy, J. Houlihan, P. O'Neill, D. Carroll, P. Brophy, T. Murphy, J. Conlon, J. Brennan (capt.), B. McGovern, A. Ronan, J. Lawlor, T. Shefflin, D. J. Carey, P. Treacy, C. Carter; subs: P. O'Grady, J. Walton.

1991: Galway 2-17, Offaly 1-9.
Galway: R. Burke, C. Helebert, B. Feeney (capt.), M. Killalea, G. McGrath, P. Hardiman, N. Power, B. Keogh, N. Larkin, L. Burke, J. Campbell, T. O'Brien, B. Larkin, J. Rabbitte, C. Moran; subs: P. Egan, M. Curtin.

1992: Waterford 4-4, Offaly 0-16. Replay: Waterford 0-12, Offaly 2-3.
Waterford: R. Barry, K. O'Gorman, O. Dunphy, M. O'Sullivan, T. Browne (capt.), P. Fanning, F. Hartley, T. Fives, J. Brenner, A. Fitzgerald, M. Hubbard, K. McGrath, N. Dalton, S. Daly, P. Flynn; subs: P. Flynn, M. Geary (drawn game). (P. Power played in the drawn game and came on as a sub in the replay.)

1993: Galway 2-14, Kilkenny 3-11. Replay: Galway 2-9, Kilkenny 3-3.
Galway: M. Darcy, T. Headd, W. Burke, D. Canning, R. Walsh, R. Walsh, N. Shaughnessy, M. Donaghue, L. Burke (capt.), M. Kearns, F. Forde, J. McGrath, T. Kirwan, P. Kelly, D. Coleman, M. Headd; subs: C. O'Doherty, C. O'Donavan, M. Kilkelly (M. Kilkelly played in the drawn game. C. O'Doherty and P. Coyne came on as subs in the drawn game.)

1994: Kilkenny 2-10, Galway 0-11.
Kilkenny: M. Carey, S. Meally, E. Drea, B. Power, A. O'Sullivan, E. Dwyer, P. Larkin, B. McEvoy, D. Maher, S. Dollard, P. Barry, P. J. Delaney, B. Ryan, D. Byrne, R. Shortall; subs: O. O'Connor, D. O'Neill.

Appendix 7

All-Ireland Club Championship, 1971–95

1971: Roscrea (Tipperary) 4-5, St Rynagh's (Offaly) 2-5.
Roscrea: T. Murphy, M. Hogan, K. Carey, B. Maher, P. Rowland, T. O'Connor, J. Crampton, M. Minogue, D. Moloney (capt.), F. Loughnane, J. Hannon, J. Cunningham, J. Tynan, M. Nolan, W. Stapleton.

1972: Blackrock (Cork) 5-13, Rathnure (Wexford) 6-9.
Blackrock: B. Hurley, P. Casey, P. Geary, J. Horgan (capt.), S. Murphy, F. Cummins, F. Norberg, M. Murphy, P. Kavanagh, D. Collins, R. Cummins, P. Moylan, B. Cummins, J. Rothwell, D. Prendergast.

1973: Glen Rovers (Cork) 2-18, St Rynagh's (Offaly) 2-8.
Glen Rovers: F. O'Neill. D. O'Riordan, M. O'Doherty, P. Barry, J. O'Sullivan, D. Coughlan (capt.), M. O'Halloran, J. J. O'Neill, P. O'Doherty, P. Harte, R. Crowley, T. Buckley, M. Ryan, T. Collins, J. Young; sub: M. Corbett.

1974: Blackrock (Cork) 2-14, Rathnure (Wexford) 3-11. Replay: Blackrock 3-8, Rathnure 1-9.
Blackrock: T. Murphy, J. Rothwell, P. Geary, J. Horgan (capt.), F. Cummins, C. O'Brien, F. Norberg, J. Russell, P. Moylan, P. Kavanagh, J. O'Halloran, D. Collins, D. Prendergast, R. Cummins, E. O'Donoghue; subs S. Kearney, D. Buckley. (B. Cummins played in the first game.)

1975: St Finbarr's (Cork) 3-8, Fenians (Kilkenny) 1-6.
St Finbarr's: J. Power (capt.), T. Maher, S. Canty, C. Barrett, B. O'Brien, D. O'Grady, T. Butler, G. McCarthy, C. Roche, E. Fitzpatrick, J. Barry Murphy, S. Gillen, C. McCarthy, S. Looney, J. O'Shea; sub: C. Cullinane.

1976: James Stephens (Kilkenny) 2-10, Blackrock (Cork) 2-4.
James Stephens: M. Moore, P. Neary, P. Larkin (capt.), N. Morrissey, T. McCormack, B. Cody, J. O'Brien, D. McCormack, M. Taylor, J. Hennessy, L. O'Brien, J. McCormack, M. Crotty, M. Leahy, G. Tyrell; sub: M. Neary.

1977: Glen Rovers (Cork) 2-12, Camross (Laois) 0-8.
Glen Rovers: F. O'Neill, J. O'Sullivan, M. O'Doherty (capt.), T. O'Brien, F. O'Sulivan, D. Clifford, D. Coughlan, R. Crowley, J. J. O'Neill, P. Harte, P. Horgan, P. O'Doherty, M. Ryan, T. Collins, V. Marshall; subs: L. McAuliffe, T. O'Neill, F. Cunningham.

1978: St Finbarr's (Cork) 2-7, Rathnure (Wexford) 0-9.
St Finbarr's: J. Power, C. Barrett, T. Maher, D. Burns (capt.), D. O'Grady, N. Kennefick, J. Murphy, G. McCarthy, J. Cremin, J. Allen, J. Barry Murphy, B. Wiley, E. Fitzpatrick, C. Ryan, C. McCarthy; sub: B. Meade.

1979: Blackrock (Cork) 5-7, Shamrocks (Kilkenny) 5-5.
Blackrock: T. Murphy, F. Norberg, C. O'Brien, J. Horgan (capt.), D. MacCurtain, F. Cummins, A. Creagh, T. Cashman, J. O'Grady, P. Moylan, T. Lyons, D. Collins, E. O'Sullivan, R. Cummins, E. O'Donoghue; sub: D. Buckley.

1980: Castlegar (Galway) 1-11, Ballycastle (Antrim) 1-8.
Castlegar: T. Grogan, T. Murphy, P. Connolly, J. Coady, G. Glynn, J. Connolly, M. Glynn, T. Murphy, S. Fahy, J. Francis, J. Connolly, P. O'Connor, G. Connolly, M. Connolly (capt.), L. Mulryan; sub: P. Burke.

1981: Ballyhale Shamrocks (Kilkenny) 1-15, St Finbarr's (Cork) 1-11.
Ballyhale Shamrocks: K. Fennelly, W. Phelan, L. Dalton, R. Reid (capt.), F. Holohan, M. Mason, D. Connolly, J. Walsh, S. Fennelly, M. Fennelly, P. Holden, G. Fennelly, B. Fennelly, L. Fennelly, M. Kelly; sub: D. Fennelly.

1982: James Stephens (Kilkenny) 3-13, Mount Sion (Waterford) 3-8.
James Stephens: M. Moore, P. Neary, B. Cody, P. Larkin, J. Hennessy, M. Hennessy, J. O'Brien (capt.), T. McCormack, D. McCormack, A. Egan, E. Kelly, B. Walton, J McCormack, M. Crotty, J. J.Cullen; sub: D. Collins.

1983: Loughguile Shamrocks (Antrim) 1-8, St Rynagh's (Offaly) 2-5. Replay: Loughguile Shamrocks 2-12, St Rynagh's 1-12.
Loughguile Shamrocks: N. Patterson (capt.), M. Carey, P. J. Mullen, S. Carey, E. Connolly, P. McIlhatton, A. McNaughton, M. O'Connell, G. McGinley, P. Carey (jr), D. McGinley, B. Laverty, P. Carey (sr), A. McGarry, S. McNaughton. (M. Coyle and B. McGarry played in the drawn game. P. Carey (sr) and P. Carey (jr) were subs in the drawn game.)

1984: Ballyhale Shamrocks (Kilkenny) 1-10, Gort (Galway) 1-10. Replay: Ballyhale Shamrocks 1-10, Gort 0-7.

Ballyhale Shamrocks: O. Harrington, F. Holohan, L. Dalton, W. Phelan, M. Fennelly, M. Mason, S. Fennelly, J. Walsh, T. Phelan, B. Fennelly, G. Fennelly, M. Kelly, D. Fennelly, K. Fennelly (capt.), L. Fennelly; sub: L. Long. (L. Long and D. Connolly played in the drawn game; L. Fennelly and R. Kenneally were subs in the drawn game.)

1985: St Martin's (Kilkenny) 2-9, Castlegar (Galway) 3-6. Replay: St Martin's 1-13, Castlegar 1-10.
St Martin's: B. Shore, J. Kelly, T. Maher, J. J. Dowling, T. Walsh, J. Moran, M. Maher, P. Lawlor, J. Moran, J. Morrissey, J. Brennan (capt.), P. Moran, D. Coonan, T. Moran, R. Moloney; sub: E. Morrissey (both games).

1986: Kilruane McDonaghs (Tipperary) 1-15, Buffer's Alley (Wexford) 2-10.
Kilruane McDonaghs: T. Sheppard (capt.), J. Cahill, D. O'Meara, S. Gibson, J. Branaghan, J. O'Meara, G. Williams, E. Hogan, D. Cahill, J. Williams, J. Williams, E. O'Shea, P. Quinlan, P. Quinlan; sub: S. Hennessy.

1987: Borrisoleigh (Tipperary) 2-9, Rathnure (Wexford) 0-9.
Borrisoleigh: N. Maher, F. Spillane, T. Stapleton, M. Ryan (capt.), R. Stakelum, G. Stapleton, B. Ryan, T. Ryan, F. Collins, C. Stakelum, N. O'Dwyer, J. McGrath, M. Coen, P. Kenny, A. Ryan; sub: B. Kenny.

1988: Midleton (Cork) 3-8, Athenry (Galway) 0-9.
Midleton: G. Power (capt.), D. Mulcahy, M. Boylan, S. O'Mahoney, E. Cleary, S. O'Brien, P. Hartnett, T. McCarthy, M. Crotty, J. Fenton, J. Hartnett, J. Boylan, G. Fitzgerald, C. O'Neill, K. Hennessy; subs: G. Galvin, C. O'Neill, A. Smyth.

1989: Buffer's Alley (Wexford) 2-12, O'Donovan Rossa (Antrim) 0-12.
Buffer's Alley: H. Butler, B. Murphy, P. Kenny (capt.), J. O'Leary, P. Gahan, M. Foley, C. Whelan, E. Sinnott, S. Whelan, T. Dempsey, M. Casey, P. Donoghue, M. Butler, T. Doran, S. Ó Laoire.

1990: Ballyhale Shamrocks (Kilkenny) 1-16, Ballybrown (Limerick) 0-16.
Ballyhale Shamrocks: K. Fennelly, M. Fennelly, F. Holohan, W. Phelan (capt.), R. Walsh, P. Phelan, S. Fennelly, G. Fennelly, T. Shefflin, T. Phelan, J. Lawlor, D. Fennelly, B. Fennelly, L. Fennelly, B. Mason.

1991: Glenmore (Kilkenny) 1-13, Patrickswell (Limerick) 0-12.
Glenmore: M. Deady, E. O'Connor, E. Aylward, P. J. O'Connor, L. Walsh, W. O'Connor, D. Ennett, R. Heffernan (capt.), D. Mullally, M. Phelan, P. Barron, J. Heffernan, C. Heffernan, J. Flynn; subs: S. Dollard, M. Phelan, M. Aylward.

1992: Kiltormer (Galway) 0-15, Birr (Offaly) 1-8.
Kiltormer: S. McKeigue, B. McManus, C. Hayes, K. Tierney, F. Curley, P. Dervan, G. Kelly, T. Larkin, A. Staunton (capt.), J. Campbell, T. Kilkenny, D. Curley, D. Cox, M. Staunton, S. Kelly; subs: T. Furey, T. Hanrahan.

1993: Sarsfields (Galway) 1-17, Kilmallock (Limerick) 2-7.
Sarsfields: T. Kenny, P. Cooney (capt.), B. Cooney, M. Cooney, P. Kelly, D. Keane, W. Earls, N. Morrissey, J. Cooney, M. McGrath, J. McGrath, A. Donoghue, P. Kelly, M. Kenny, P. Cooney.

1994: Sarsfields (Galway) 1-14, Toomyvara (Tipperary) 3-6.
Sarsfields: T. Kenny, P. Cooney (capt.), B. Cooney, M. Cooney, P. Kelly, D. Keane, W. Earls, N. Morrissey, J. Cooney, M. McGrath, J. McGrath, A. Donohue, P. Kelly, M. Kenny, P. Cooney.

1995: Birr (Offaly) 0-9, Dunloy (Antrim) 0-9. Replay: Birr 3-13, Dunloy 2-3.
Birr: R. Shields, M. Hogan, J. Errity, B. Hennesy, B. Whelehan, G. Cahill, N. Hogan, J. Pilkington (capt.), C. McGlone, O. O'Neill, P. Murphy, D. Pilkington, A. Cahill, D. Regan, S. Whelehan; subs: R. Landy (both games), L. Vaughan, M. Finnane.

Appendix 8

National Hurling League, 1926–95

1925/26: Cork 3-7, Dublin 1-5.

1926/27: None.

1927/28: Tipperary winners on points system: 8 games, 14 points.

1928/29: Dublin 7-4, Cork 5-5.

1929/30: Cork 3-5, Dublin 3-0.

1930/31: None.

1931/32: Galway 4-5, Tipperary 4-4.

1932/33: Kilkenny 3-8, Limerick 1-3.

1933/34: Limerick 3-6, Dublin 3-3.

1934/35: Limerick winners on points system: 8 games, 15 points.

1935/36: Limerick winners on points system: 8 games, 15 points.

1936/37: Limerick winners on points system: 8 games, 13 points.

1937/38: Limerick 5-2, Tipperary 1-1.

1938/39: Dublin 1-8, Waterford 1-4.

1939/40: Cork 8-9, Tipperary 6-4.

1940/41: Cork 4-11, Dublin 2-7.

1942–45: League suspended.

1945/46: Clare 1-6, Dublin 1-6. Replay: Clare 2-10, Dublin 2-5.

1946/47: Limerick 4-5, Kilkenny 2-11. Replay: Limerick 3-8, Kilkenny 1-7.

1947/48: Cork 3-3, Tipperary 1-2.

1948/49: Tipperary 3-5 Cork 3-3.

1949/50: Tipperary 1-12, New York 3-4. Home final: Tipperary 3-8, Kilkenny 1-10.

1950/51: Galway 2-11, New York 2-8. Home final: Galway 6-7, Wexford 3-4.

1951/52: Tipperary 6-14, New York 2-5. Home final: Tipperary 4-7, Wexford 4-6.

1952/53: Cork 2-10, Tipperary 2-7.

1953/54: Tipperary 3-10, Kilkenny 1-4.

1954/55: Tipperary 3-5, Wexford 1-5.

1955/56: Wexford 5-9, Tipperary 2-14.

1956/57: Tipperary 3-11, Kilkenny 2-7.

1957/58: Wexford 5-7, Limerick 4-8.

1958/59: Tipperary 0-15, Waterford 0-7.

1959/60: Tipperary 2-15, Cork 3-8.

1960/61: Tipperary 6-6, Waterford 4-9

1961/62: Kilkenny 1-16, Cork 1-8.

1962/63: Waterford 3-6, New York 3-6. Replay: Waterford 3-10, New York 1-10. Home final: Waterford 2-15, Tipperary 4-7.

1963/64: Tipperary 4-16, New York 6-6. Home final: Tipperary 5-12, Wexford 1-4.

1964/65: First leg: Tipperary 4-10, New York 2-11. Second leg: New York 3-9, Tipperary 2-9. Aggregate: Tipperary 6-19, New York 5-20. Home final: Tipperary 3-14, Kilkenny 2-8.

1965/66: First leg: Kilkenny 3-10, New York 2-7. Second leg: Kilkenny 7-5, New York 0-8. Aggregate: Kilkenny 10-15, New York 2-15. Home final: Kilkenny 0-9, Tipperary 0-7.

1966/67: Wexford 3-10, Kilkenny 1-9.

1967/68: First leg: New York 2-14, Tipperary 2-13. Second leg: Tipperary 4-14, New York 2-8. Aggregate: Tipperary 6-27, New York 4-22. Home final: Tipperary 3-9, Kilkenny 1-13.

1968/69: Cork 3-12, Wexford 1-14.

1969/70: First leg: Cork 4-11, New York 4-8. Second leg: New York 2-8, Cork 1-10. Aggregate: Cork 5-21: New York 6-16. Home final: Cork 2-17, Limerick 0-7.

1970/71: Limerick 3-12, Tipperary 3-11.

1971/72: Cork 3-14, Limerick 2-14.

1972/73: Wexford 4-13, Limerick 3-7.

1973/74: Cork 6-15, Limerick 1-12.

1974/75: Galway 4-9, Tipperary 4-6.

1975/76: Kilkenny 6-14, Clare 1-14.

1976/77: Clare 2-8, Kilkenny 1-9.

1977/78: Clare 3-10, Kilkenny 1-10.

1978/79: Tipperary 3-15, Galway 0-8.

1979/80: Cork 2-10, Limerick 2-10. Replay: Cork 4-15, Limerick 4-6.

1980/81: Cork 3-11, Offaly 2-8.

1981/82: Kilkenny 2-14, Wexford 1-11.

1982/83: Kilkenny 2-14, Limerick 2-12.

1983/84: Limerick 3-16, Wexford 1-9.

1984/85: Limerick 3-12, Clare 1-7.

1985/86: Kilkenny 2-10, Galway 2-6

1986/87: Galway 3-12, Clare 3-10.

1987/88: Tpperary 3-15, Offaly 2-9.

1988/89: Galway 2-16, Tipperary 4-8.

1989/90: Kilkenny 0-18, New York 0-9. Home final: Kilkenny 3-12, Wexford 1-10.

1990/91: Offaly 2-6, Wexford 0-10.

1991/92: Limerick 0-14, Tipperary 0-13.

1992/93: Cork 2-11, Wexford 2-11. Replay: Cork 0-18, Wexford 3-9. Second replay: Cork 3-11, Wexford 1-12.

1993/94: Tipperary 2-14, Galway 0-12.

1994/95: Kilkenny 2-12, Clare 0-9.

Appendix 9

Inter-provincial Championship (Railway Cup)

1927: Leinster 1-11, Munster 2-6.

1928: Munster 2-2, Leinster 1-2.

1929: Munster 5-3, Leinster 3-1.

1930: Munster 4-6, Leinster 2-7.

1931: Munster 1-12, Leinster 2-6.

1932: Leinster 6-8, Munster 4-4.

1933: Leinster 4-6, Munster 3-6.

1934: Munster 6-3, Leinster 3-2.

1935: Munster 3-4, Leinster 3-0.

1936: Leinster 2-8, Munster 3-4.

1937: Munster 1-9, Leinster 3-1.

1938: Munster 6-2, Leinster 4-3.

1939: Munster 4-4 Leinster 1-6.

1940: Munster 4-9, Leinster 5-4.

1941: Leinster 2-5, Munster 2-4.

1942: Munster 4-9, Leinster 4-5.

1943: Munster 4-3, Leinster 3-5.

1944: Munster 4-10, Connacht 4-4.

1945: Munster 6-8, Ulster 2-0.

1946: Munster 3-12, Connacht, 4-8.

1947: Connacht 2-5, Munster 1-1.

1948: Munster 3-5, Leinster 2-5.

1949: Munster 5-3, Connacht 2-9.

1950: Munster 0-9, Leinster 1-3.

1951: Munster 4-9, Leinster 3-6.

1952: Munster 5-11 Connacht 4-2.

1953: Munster 5-7, Leinster 5-5.

1954: Leinster 0-9, Munster 0-5.

1955: Munster 6-8, Leinster 3-4.

1956: Leinster 5-11, Munster 1-7.

1957: Munster 5-7, Leinster 2-5.

1958: Munster 3-7, Leinster 3-5.

1959: Munster 7-11, Connacht 2-6.

1960: Munster 6-6, Leinster 2-7.

1961: Munster 4-12, Leinster 3-9.

1962: Leinster 1-11, Munster 1-9.

1963: Munster 5-5, Leinster 5-5. Replay: Munster 2-8, Leinster 2-7.

1964: Leinster 3-7, Munster 2-9.

1965: Leinster 3-11, Munster 0-9.

1966: Munster 3-13, Leinster 3-11.

1967: Leinster 2-14, Munster 3-5.

1968: Munster 0-14, Leinster 0-10.

1969: Munster 2-9, Connacht 2-9. Replay: Munster 3-13, Connacht 4-4.

1970: Munster 2-15, Leinster 0-9.

1971: Leinster 2-17, Munster 2-12.

1972: Leinster 3-12, Munster 1-10.

1973: Leinster 1-13, Munster 2-8.

1974: Leinster 2-15, Munster 1-11.

1975: Leinster 2-9, Munster 1-11.

1976: Munster 4-9, Leinster 4-8.

1977: Leinster 2-17, Munster 1-13.

1978: Munster 2-13, Leinster 1-11.

1979: Leinster 1-13, Connacht, 1-9.

1980: Connacht 1-5, Munster 0-7.

1981: Munster 2-16, Leinster 2-6.

1982: Connacht 3-8, Leinster 2-9.

1983: Connacht 0-10, Leinster 1-5.

1984: Munster 1-18, Leinster 2-9.

1985: Munster 3-6, Connacht 1-11.

1986: Connacht 3-11, Munster 0-11.

1987: Connacht 2-14, Leinster 1-14.

1988: Leinster 2-14, Connacht 1-12.

1989: Connacht 4-16, Munster 3-17.

1990: No competition.

1991: Connacht 1-13, Munster 0-12.

1992: Munster 3-12, Ulster 1-8.

1993: Leinster 1-15, Ulster 2-6.

1994: Connacht 1-11, Leinster 1-10.

1995: Munster 0-13, Ulster 1-9.

Appendix 10

Oireachtas Tournament (Corn Thomáis Ághas), 1939–94

1939: Limerick 4-4, Kilkenny 2-5.

1940: Kilkenny 7-11, Cork 1-6.

1941–43: Run as a football tournament.

1944: Dublin 6-6, Galway 3-6.

1945: Tipperary 4-6, Galway 2-6.

1946: Run as a football tournament.

1947: Kilkenny 2-12, Galway 2-6.

1948: Dublin 3-6, Waterford 2-6.

1949: Tipperary 2-8, Laois 1-6.

1950: Galway 2-9, Wexford 2-6.

1951: Wexford 4-7, Kilkenny 3-7.

1952: Galway 3-7, Wexford 1-10.

1953: Wexford 5-11, Clare 4-5.

1954: Clare 2-8, Wexford 2-8. Replay: Clare 3-6, Wexford 0-12.

1955: Wexford 3-11, Kilkenny 3-4.

1956: Wexford 0-16, Kilkenny 1-9.

1957: Kilkenny 4-10, Waterford 3-5.

1958: Galway 5-16, Wexford 2-4.

1959: Kilkenny 6-6, Galway 5-8.

1960: Tipperary 4-11, Cork 2-10.

1961: Tipperary 3-6, Wexford 2-9. Replay: Tipperary 2-13, Wexford 3-4.

1962: Waterford 4-12, Tipperary 3-9.

1963: Tipperary 4-15, Wexford 3-12.

1964: Tipperary 5-7, Kilkenny 4-8.

1965: Tipperary 2-12, Kilkenny 2-7.

1966: Kilkenny 4-7, Wexford 1-7.

1967: Kilkenny 4-4, Clare 1-8.

1968: Tipperary 1-9, Cork 1-6.

1969: Kilkenny 4-14, Cork 3-10.

1970: Tipperary 1-12, Cork 0-8.

1971: Limerick 4-12, Wexford 3-8.

1972: Tipperary 2-13, Wexford 2-13. Replay: Tipperary 2-13, Wexford 1-8.

1973: Cork 1-8, Kilkenny 1-6.

1974: Cork 3-15, Waterford 1-5.

1975: Cork 3-13, Wexford 2-7.

1976: Galway 1-15, Cork 2-9.

1977: Galway 2-8, Cork 2-8. (No replay.)

1978: Wexford 0-18, Galway 1-10.

1979: Wexford 3-17, Offaly 5-8.

1980: Wexford 1-19, Offaly 3-5.

1981: Galway 1-15, Wexford 1-7.

1982: Clare 3-9, Limerick 2-9.

1983: Clare 1-12, Kilkenny 1-11.

1984: Kilkenny 1-11, Cork 1-7.

1985: Cork 2-11, Galway 1-10.

1986: Wexford 3-17, Galway 1-22 (after extra time).

1987: No competition.

1988: Galway 4-15, Wexford 3-11.

1989: Galway 1-19, Tipperary 0-8.

1990: Tipperary 1-15, Galway 0-7.

1991: Galway 2-12, Wexford 3-5.

1992: Galway 1-13, Waterford 0-10.

1993: Galway 2-19, Clare 3-9.

1994: Wexford 2-8, Cork 1-8.

Appendix 11

Thomond Tournament, 1913–56

1913: Limerick 4-0, Tipperary 3-1.

1914: Cork 5-5, Tipperary 5-3.

1915: Tipperary 4-5, Clare 1-0.

1916: Tipperary 5-5, Limerick 2-2.

1917–19: No competition.

1920: Limerick 7-5, Cork 1-4.

1921: No competition.

1922: Limerick 8-3, Clare 3-3.

1923: No competition.

1924: Tipperary 9-3, Limerick 0-3.

1925: Limerick 4-4, Cork 1-8.

1926: Cork 2-4, Limerick 2-2.

1927: Tipperary 4-4, Limerick 4-3.

1928: Limerick 1-8, Clare 2-2.

1929: Clare 2-6, Tipperary 2-4.

1930: Tipperary 5-4, Cork 1-4.

1931: Tipperary 7-6, Cork 4-11.

1932: Limerick 2-6, Clare 2-4.

1933: Limerick 4-2, Tipperary 2-2.

1934: Limerick 3-6, Cork 3-4.

1935: Limerick 4-7, Tipperary 1-5.

1936: Cork 4-5, Tipperary 4-4.

1937: Limerick 6-2, Clare 1-2.

1938–39: No competition.

1940: Limerick 3-1, Tipperary 0-2.

1941: Cork 4-7, Tipperary 3-3.

1942–43: No competition.

1944: Limerick 4-9, Cork 3-1.

1945: Limerick 7-5, Cork 5-8.

1946: Clare 4-5, Tipperary 2-6.

1947: Limerick 4-3, Clare 2-5.

1948: Cork 6-10, Tipperary 1-7.

1949: Tipperary 5-9, Cork 3-7.

1950: Cork-Tipperary decider not played.

1951: Tipperary 5-13, Clare 3-4.

1952: Cork 6-9, Limerick 2-4.

1953: Competition not completed.

1954: Cork 5-11, Limerick 3-5.

1955: No competition.

1956: Clare 4-7, Limerick 3-3.

Appendix 12

Wembley Tournament (Monaghan Cup), 1927–75

(Venues: Herne Hill, 1927–30; Woolwich, 1931–35, 1956–57; Mitcham Stadium, 1936–55; Wembley, 1958–75.)

1927 (6 June): Cork 4-5, Tipperary 0-3.

1928 (28 May): Cork 4-5, Dublin 3-3.

1929 (20 May): Cork 3-2, Kilkenny 1-2.

1930 (2 June): Dublin 3-5, Cork 2-4.

1931 (25 May): Tipperary 9-5, Dublin 2-6.

1932 (16 May): Cork 9-3, Tipperary 4-1.

1933 (5 June): Kilkenny 4-5, Cork 4-2.

1934 (21 May): Limerick 5-4, Kilkenny 4-5.

1935 (10 June): Limerick 6-5, Dublin 5-1.

1936 (1 June): Kilkenny 4-2, Galway 2-2.

1937 (17 May): Limerick 3-5, Kilkenny 3-3.

1938 (6 June): Tipperary 5-7, Limerick 3-1.

1939 (28 May): Tipperary 4-6, Dublin 1-7.

1940 (12 May): Tipperary 6-6, Kilkenny 4-5.

1941–45: No competition.

1946 (5 Aug.): Tipperary 4-7, Galway 1-13.

1947 (25 May): Tipperary 3-8, Cork 3-8.

1948 (17 May): Kilkenny 5-8, Tipperary 3-4.

1949 (5 June): Tipperary 5-14, Kilkenny 2-4.

1950 (28 May): Tipperary 8-5, Cork 4-5.

1951 (14 May): Tipperary 1-12, Galway 3-3.

1952 (2 June): Tipperary 2-4, Galway 1-7.

1953 (25 May): Tipperary 2-7, Cork 2-6.

1954 (7 June): Tipperary 5-6, Kilkenny 1-5.

1955 (30 May): Tipperary 4-7, Wexford 3-4.

1956 (21 May): Tipperary 6-4, Wexford 2-5.

1957 (10 June): Kilkenny 3-6, Tipperary 1-5.

1958 (24 May): Kilkenny 6-10, Clare 5-7.

1959 (16 May): Cork 7-9, Kilkenny 3-8.

1960 (6 June): Kilkenny 6-16, Waterford 2-16.

1961 (22 May): Tipperary 3-4, Wexford 1-6.

1962 (9 June): Tipperary 3-11, Dublin 2-10.

1963 (1 June): Tipperary 5-8, Kilkenny 2-10.

1964 (16 May): Tipperary 2-10, Kilkenny 0-7.

1965 (6 June): Kilkenny 2-12, Tipperary 1-8.

1966 (30 June): Cork 2-15, Wexford 3-7.

1967 (10 June): Cork 4-8, Kilkenny 2-10.

1968 (1 June): Wexford 3-16, Cork 1-8.

1969 (24 Apr.): Tipperary 2-10, Wexford 1-2.

1970 (23 May): Cork 5-13, Kilkenny 4-6.

1971 (29 May): Cork 3-17, Tipperary 2-9.

1972 (29 May): Tipperary 8-7, Limerick 4-12.

1973 (26 May): Carroll's All-Stars 1-18, Tipperary 0-16.

1974 (26 May): Kilkenny 2-15, Limerick 1-13.

1975 (1 June): Kilkenny 2-18, Limerick 2-13.

Appendix 13

Walsh Cup Tournament, 1954–94

1954: Wexford 1-8, Dublin 0-2.

1955 (15. Apr. 1956): Kilkenny 2-10, Westmeath 3-6.

1956 (14 Oct.): Wexford 2-10, Kilkenny 1-8.

1957 (6 Oct.): Kilkenny 1-18, Dublin 4-5.

1958 (7 Dec.): Kilkenny 3-4, Dublin 2-5.

1959 (13 Sep.): Kilkenny 4-3, Wexford 3-4.

1960 (16 Oct.): Dublin 2-13, Kilkenny 2-6.

1961 (1 Oct.): Kilkenny 3-11, Wexford 0-11.

1962 (30 Oct.): Kilkenny 2-6, Wexford 0-5.

1963 (8 Sep.): Kilkenny 4-10, Wexford 3-9.

1964 (9 May): Dublin 5-4, Kilkenny 2-12.

1965 (10 Oct.): Wexford 1-12, Kilkenny 2-7.

1966 (27 Nov.): Dublin 3-10, Offaly 3-9.

1967 (28 July): Wexford 8-16, Kilkenny 3-7.

1968 (24 Nov.): Wexford 3-15, Kilkenny 0-5.

1969 (23 Aug. 1970): Wexford 6-13, Dublin 3-18.

1970: Kilkenny won.

1971 (27 Feb. 1972): Kilkenny 3-9, Wexford 1-10.

1972: No competition.

1973 (12 Aug.): Kilkenny 2-21, Wexford 2-11.

1974 (23 Mar.): Kilkenny 4-11, Offaly 0-7.

1975: No competition.

1976: No competition.

1977 (4 Dec.): Offaly 7-7, Dublin 1-7.

1978: No competition.

1979: No competition.

1980 (16 July): Laois 2-12, Carlow 2-10.

1981 (11 Apr.): Offaly 4-13, Laois 4-4.

1982 (2 May): Westmeath 2-9, Wicklow 1-10.

1983–86: No competition.

1987 (17 May): Wexford 3-11, Offaly 1-12.

1988 (15 May): Kilkenny 4-20, Laois 2-8.

1989 (14 May): Kilkenny 1-12, Wexford 0-5.

1990 (13 May): Offaly 2-13, Kilkenny 2-9.

1991 (15 May): Laois 2-12, Kilkenny 1-12.

1992 (28 Nov.): Kilkenny 1-12, Wexford 1-7.

1993 (28 Feb.): Offaly 1-16, Kilkenny 1-12.

1994 (27 Mar.): Offaly 0-14, Meath 0-6.

1995: Final between Offaly and Wexford not played at time of publication.

Appendix 14

Kehoe Cup Tournament, 1977–95

1977 (21 Aug.): Wexford 2-13, Kilkenny 1-15.

1978 (13 Apr.): Westmeath 0-13, Dublin 0-9.

1979: No competition.

1980 (11 May): Kilkenny 4-15, Offaly 2-9.

1981 (3 May): Dublin 6-10, Meath 1-5.

1982 (2 May): Laois 2-7, Dublin 1-9.

1983 (8 May): Westmeath 1-14, London 1-13. Home final (24 Apr.): Westmeath 2-12, Dublin 2-11.

1984: No competition.

1985: No competition.

1986 (29 Mar.): Carlow 2-11, Meath 1-7.

1987 (31 May): London 1-15, Meath 0-10. Home final (26 Apr.): Meath 1-14, Carlow 3-5.

1988 (22 May): London 4-8, Meath 1-10. Home final (7 May): Meath 1-12, Wicklow 0-3.

1989 (7 May): Wicklow 1-8, Meath 1-6.

1990 (20 May): Carlow 1-10, Meath 0-12

1991 (11 May): Wicklow 2-8, Carlow 1-6.

1992 (3 May): Carlow 0-17, Kildare 1-9.

1993 (14 Feb.): Meath 3-9, Wicklow 2-10.

1994 (1 Oct.): Westmeath 1-9, Carlow 0-5.

1995 (9 Apr.): Westmeath 1-10, Wicklow 2-5.

Appendix 15

All-Stars, 1971–94

Teams

1971: D. Martin (Offaly), T. Maher (Cork), P. Hartigan (Limerick), J. Treacy (Kilkenny), T. O'Connor (Tipperary), M. Roche (Tipperary), M. Coogan (Kilkenny), F. Cummins (Kilkenny), J. Connolly (Galway), F. Loughnane (Tipperary), M. Keating (Tipperary), E. Keher (Kilkenny), M. Bermingham (Dublin), R. Cummins (Cork), E. Cregan (Limerick).

1972: N. Skehan (Kilkenny), T. Maher (Cork), P. Hartigan (Limerick), J. Treacy (Kilkenny), P. Lawlor (Kilkenny), M. Jacob (Wexford), C. Roche (Cork), F. Cummins (Kilkenny), D. Coughlan (Cork), F. Loughnane (Tipperary), P. Delaney (Kilkenny), E. Keher (Kilkenny), C. McCarthy (Cork), R. Cummins (Cork), E. Cregan (Limerick).

1973: N. Skehan (Kilkenny), P. Larkin (Kilkenny), P. Hartigan (Limerick), J. O'Brien (Limerick), C. Doran (Wexford), P. Henderson (Kilkenny), S. Foley (Limerick), R. Bennis (Limerick), F. Loughnane (Tipperary), P. Delaney (Kilkenny), E. Grimes (Limerick), M. Quigley (Wexford), K. Purcell (Kilkenny), E. Keher (Kilkenny).

1974: N. Skehan (Kilkenny), P. Larkin (Kilkenny), P. Hartigan (Limerick), J. Horgan (Cork), G. Loughnane (Clare), P. Henderson (Kilkenny), C. Roche (Cork), L. O'Brien (Kilkenny), J. Galvin (Waterford), J. McKenna (Limerick), M. Quigley (Wexford), M. Crotty (Kilkenny), J. Quigley (Wexford), K. Purcell (Kilkenny), E. Keher (Kilkenny).

1975: N. Skehan (Kilkenny), N. McInerney (Galway), P. Hartigan (Limerick), B. Cody (Kilkenny), T. O'Connor (Tipperary), S. Silke (Galway), I. Clarke (Galway), L. O'Brien (Kilkenny), G. McCarthy (Cork), M. Quigley (Wexford), J. McKenna

311

(Limerick), E. Grimes (Limerick), M. Brennan (Kilkenny), K. Purcell (Kilkenny), E. Keher (Kilkenny).

1976: N. Skehan (Kilkenny), P. Larkin (Kilkenny), W. Murphy (Wexford), J. McMahon (Clare), J. McDonagh (Galway), M. Jacob (Wexford), D. Coughlan (Cork), F. Burke (Galway), P. Moylan (Cork), M. Malone (Cork), M. Quigley (Wexford), J. Barry Murphy (Cork), M. Brennan (Kilkenny), T. Doran (Wexford), S. O'Leary (Cork).

1977: S. Durack (Clare), J. McMahon (Clare), M. O'Doherty (Cork), J. Horgan (Cork), G. Loughnane (Clare), M. Jacob (Wexford), D. Coughlan (Cork), T. Cashman (Cork), M. Moroney (Clare), C. Keogh (Wexford), J. Barry Murphy (Cork), P. J. Molloy (Galway), C. McCarthy (Cork), R. Cummins (Cork), S. O'Leary (Cork).

1978: S. Durack (Clare), P. Larkin (Kilkenny), M. O'Doherty (Cork), J. Horgan (Cork), J. Hennessy (Kilkenny), G. Henderson (Kilkenny), D. Coughlan (Cork), T. Cashman (Cork), I. Clarke (Galway), J. Barry Murphy (Cork), N. Casey (Clare), C. Honan (Clare), C. McCarthy (Cork), J. McKenna (Limerick), T. Butler (Tipperary).

1979: P. McLoughney (Tipperary), B. Murphy (Cork), M. O'Doherty (Cork), T. O'Connor (Tipperary), D. MacCurtain (Cork), G. Henderson (Kilkenny), I. Clarke (Galway), J. Connolly (Galway), J. Hennessy (Kilkenny), J. Callinan (Clare), F. Burke (Galway), L. O'Brien (Kilkenny), M. Brennan (Kilkenny), J. McKenna (Limerick), N. Buggy (Wexford).

1980: P. McLoughney (Tipperary), N. McInerney (Galway), L. Enright (Limerick), J. Cooney (Galway), D. MacCurtain (Cork), S. Silke (Galway), I. Clarke (Galway), J. Kelly (Offaly), M. Walsh (Waterford), J. Connolly (Galway), P. Horgan (Cork), P. Carroll (Offaly), B. Forde (Galway), J. McKenna (Limerick), E. Cregan (Limerick).

1981: S. Durack (Clare), B. Murphy (Cork), L. Enright (Limerick), J. Cooney (Galway), L. O'Donoghue (Limerick), S. Stack (Clare), G. Coughlan (Offaly), S. Mahon (Galway), L. Currams (Offaly), J. Callinan (Clare), G. O'Connor (Wexford), M. Corrigan (Offaly), P. Carroll (Offaly), J. McKenna (Limerick), J. Flaherty (Offaly).

1982: N. Skehan (Kilkenny), J. Galvin (Waterford), B. Cody (Kilkenny), P. Fleury (Offaly), A. Fogarty (Offaly), G. Henderson (Kilkenny), P. Prendergast (Kilkenny), T. Crowley (Cork), F. Cummins (Kilkenny), T. O'Sullivan (Cork), P. Horgan (Cork), R. Power (Kilkenny), B. Fitzpatrick (KIlkenny), C. Heffernan (Kilkenny), J. Greene (Waterford).

1983: N. Skehan (Kilkenny), J. Henderson (Kilkenny), L. Enright (Limerick), D. O'Hara (Kilkenny), J. Hennessy (Kilkenny), G. Henderson (Kilkenny), T. Cashman (Cork), F. Cummins (Kilkenny), J. Fenton (Cork), N. English (Tipperary), G. Fennelly (Kilkenny), N. Lane (Galway), B. Fitzpatrick (Kilkenny), J. Barry Murphy (Cork), L. Fennelly (Kilkenny).

1984: G. Cunningham (Cork), P. Fitzmaurice (Limerick), E. Coughlan (Offaly), P. Fleury (Offaly), J. Hennessy (Kilkenny), J. Crowley (Cork), D. MacCurtain (Cork), J. Fenton (Cork), J. Kelly (Offaly), N. English (Tipperary), K. Brennan (Kilkenny), P. Kelly (Limerick), T. Mulcahy (Cork), N. Lane (Galway), S. O'Leary (Cork).

1985: G. Cunningham (Cork), S. Coen (Galway), E. Coughlan (Offaly), S. Linnane (Galway), P. Finnerty (Galway), P. Delaney (Offaly), G. Coughlan (Offaly), P. Critchley (Laois), J. Fenton (Cork), N. English (Tipperary), B. Lynskey (Galway), J. Cooney (Galway), P. Cleary (Offaly), P. Horan (Offaly), L. Fennelly (Kilkenny).

1986: G. Cunningham (Cork), D. Mulcahy (Cork), C. Hayes (Galway), S. Linnane (Galway), P. Finnerty (Galway), T. Keady (Galway), B. Ryan (Tipperary), R. Power (Kilkenny), J. Fenton (Cork), T. O'Sullivan (Cork), T. Mulcahy (Cork), J. Cooney (Galway), D. Kilcoyne (Westmeath), J. Barry Murphy (Cork), K. Hennessy (Cork).

1987: K. Hogan (Tipperary), J. Hennessy (Kilkenny), C. Hayes (Galway), O. Kilkenny (Galway), P. Finnerty (Galway), G. Henderson (Kilkenny), J. Conran (Wexford), S. Mahon (Galway), J. Fenton (Cork), M. McGrath (Galway), J. Cooney (Galway), A. Ryan (Tipperary), P. Fox (Tipperary), N. English (Tipperary), L. Fennelly (Kilkenny).

1988: J. Commins (Galway), S. Linnane (Galway), C. Hayes (Galway), M. Hanamy (Offaly), P. Finnerty (Galway), T. Keady (Galway), B. Ryan (Tipperary), C. Bonnar (Tipperary), G. O'Connor (Wexford), D. Ryan (Tipperary), C. Barr (Antrim), M. Naughton (Galway), M. McGrath (Galway), N. English (Tipperary), T. O'Sullivan (Cork).

1989: J. Commins (Galway), A. Fogarty (Offaly), E. Cleary (Wexford), D. Donnelly (Antrim), C. Bonnar (Tipperary), B. Ryan (Tipperary), S. Treacy (Galway), M. Coleman (Galway), D. Carr (Tipperary), E. Ryan (Galway), J. Cooney (Galway), O. McFetridge (Antrim), P. Fox (Tipperary), C. Bonnar (Tipperary), N. English (Tipperary).

1990: G. Cunningham (Cork), J. Considine (Cork), N. Sheehy (Tipperary), S. O'Gorman (Cork), P. Finnerty (Galway), J. Cashman (Cork), L. Dunne (Wexford), M. Coleman (Galway), J. Pilkington (Offaly), M. Cleary (Tipperary), J. Cooney (Galway), T. O'Sullivan (Cork), E. Morrissey (Kilkenny), B. McMahon (Dublin), J. Fitzgibbon (Cork).

1991: M. Walsh (Kilkenny), P. Delaney (Tipperary), N. Sheehy (Tipperary), S. Treacy (Galway), C. Bonnar (Tipperary), J. Cashman (Cork), C. Casey (Cork), T. McNaughton (Antrim), J. Leahy (Tipperary), M. Cleary (Tipperary), G. Kirby (Limerick), D. J.Carey (Kilkenny), P. Fox (Tipperary), C. Bonnar (Tipperary), J. Fitzgibbon (Cork).

1992: T. Quaid (Limerick), B. Corcoran (Cork), P. Dwyer (Kilkenny), L. Simpson (Kilkenny), B. Whelehan (Offaly), C. Carey (Limerick), W. O'Connor (Kilkenny), M. Phelan (Kilkenny), S. McCarthy (Cork), G. McGrattan (Down), J. Power (Kilkenny), T. O'Sullivan (Cork), M. Cleary (Tipperary), L. Fennelly (Kilkenny), D. J.Carey (Kilkenny).

1993: M. Walsh (Kilkenny), E. O'Connor (Kilkenny), S. O'Gorman (Cork), L. Simpson (Kilkenny), L. Dunne (Wexford), P. O'Neill (Kilkenny), P. Kelly (Galway), P. Malone

(Galway), P. McKillen (Antrim), M. Storey (Wexford), J. Power (Kilkenny), D. J. Carey (Kilkenny), M. Cleary (Tipperary), J. Rabbitte (Galway), B. Egan (Cork).

1994: J. Quaid (Limerick), A. Daly (Clare), K. Kinahan (Offaly), M. Hanamy (Offaly), D. Clarke (Limerick), H. Rigney (Offaly), K. Martin (Offaly), C. Carey (Limerick), M. Houlihan (Limerick), J. Dooley (Offaly), G. Kirby (Limerick), J. Leahy (Tipperary), B. Dooley (Offaly), D. J. Carey (Kilkenny), D. Quigley (Limerick).

Results of All-Stars matches in United States and Canada

1972: (26 Mar., San Francisco) Tipperary, 6-10 All-Stars 6-7; (2 Apr., San Francisco) All-Stars 5-17, Tipperary 2-16.

1973: (25 Mar., San Francisco) All-Stars 5-10, Kilkenny 3-14; (1 Apr., San Francisco) Kilkenny 4-9, All-Stars 1-7.

1974: (24 Mar., San Francisco) All-Stars 4-20, Limerick 6-8; (29 Mar., Los Angeles) Limerick 4-6, All-Stars 3-8; (31 Mar., San Francisco) Limerick 4-8 All-Stars 2-13.

1975: (6 Apr., San Francisco) All-Stars 5-8, Kilkenny 3-10; (11 Apr., Los Angeles) Kilkenny 4-12, All-Stars 3-14; (13 Apr., San Francisco) Kilkenny 3-15, All-Stars 1-16; (20 Apr., New York) Kilkenny 2-9, All-Stars 1-4.

1976: (16 May, Los Angeles) All-Stars 4-13, Kilkenny 2-18; (23 May, San Francisco) All-Stars 5-18, Kilkenny 6-5; (30 May, New York) All-Stars 4-17, Kilkenny 3-11.

1977: (29 Apr., Chicago) Cork 5-7, All-Stars 3-10; (1 May, Los Angeles) All-Stars 2-15, Cork 1-7; (8 May, San Francisco) Cork 2-17, All-Stars 1-15; (15 May, New York) All-Stars 4-12, Cork 2-7.

1978: (14 May, Boston) Cork 3-14, All-Stars 1-12; (21 May, San Francisco) All-Stars 4-15, Cork 3-10; (28 May, Los Angeles) All-Stars 5-12, Cork 3-6.

Sponsorship of the All-Stars passed from Carroll's to Bank of Ireland at this stage.

1979: (14 Oct., New York) Kilkenny 1-16, All-Stars 3-7; (16 Oct., Chicago) All-Stars 2-17, Kilkenny 2-17; (21 Oct., San Francisco) All-Stars 1-18, Kilkenny 0-7; (28 Oct., Los Angeles) Kilkenny 1-15, All-Stars 2-10.

1980: (19 Oct., New York) Galway 2-16, All-Stars 3-11; (22 Oct., Chicago) Galway 3-16, All-Stars 2-15; (26 Oct., Los Angeles) All-Stars 1-15, Galway 1-14.

1981: No tour.

1982: (2 May, New York) All-Stars 3-9, Offaly 1-11; (9 May, San Francisco) Offaly 2-20, All-Stars 1-19.

1983: (1 May, New York) Kilkenny 1-16, All-Stars 0-13; (8 May, San Francisco) Kilkenny 5-10, All-Stars 1-15.

1984: No tour.

1985: (12 May, San Francisco) Cork 6-9, All-Stars 3-17; (19 May, New York) Cork 2-12, All-Stars 1-11.

1986: (18 May, New York) All-Stars 2-17, Offaly 0-6; (25 May, Los Angeles) All-Stars 7-18, Offaly 4-15.

1987: (10 May, San Francisco) Cork 1-20, All-Stars 2-9; (17 May, Chicago) Cork 5-14, All-Stars 3-15.

1988: (1 May, Boston) Galway 1-19, All-Stars 1-11; (8 May, San Francisco) All-Stars 4-15, Galway 1-20.

1989: (7 May, New York) All-Stars 3-20, Galway 2-13; (14 May, New York) All-Stars 3-11, Galway 1-13.

1990: (18 Mar., Toronto) Tipperary 5-15, All-Stars 3-11.

1991: (17 Mar., Toronto) All-Stars 5-13, Cork 0-6.

1992–94: No tour.

Appendix 16

Colleges Championship (Fitzgibbon Cup), 1912–96

In 1912 Dr Edwin Fitzgibbon, a Capuchin priest who was professor of philosophy in UCC from 1911 to 1936, presented the trophy for a hurling championship between the constituent colleges of the NUI. Later the championship was extended to include other third-level institutions.

1912: University College, Dublin.

1913: University College, Cork.

1914: University College, Cork.

1915: University College, Dublin.

1916: University College, Dublin.

1917: University College, Dublin.

1918: University College, Cork.

1919: University College, Galway.

1920: University College, Cork.

1921: Not played.

1922: University College, Cork.

1923: University College, Dublin.

1924: University College, Dublin.

1925: University College, Cork.

1926: University College, Galway.

1927: University College, Dublin.

1928: University College, Cork.

1929: University College, Cork.

1930: University College, Cork.

1931: University College, Dublin.

1932: University College, Dublin.

1933: University College, Cork.

1934: University College, Dublin.

1935: University College, Dublin.

1936: University College, Dublin.

1937: University College, Cork.

1938: University College, Dublin.

1939: University College, Cork.

1940: University College, Cork.

1941: University College, Dublin.

1942: University College, Galway.

1943: University College, Cork.

1944: University College, Dublin.

1945: University College, Galway.

1946: University College, Galway.

1947: University College, Cork.

1948: University College, Dublin.

1949: University College, Galway.

1950: University College, Dublin.

1951: University College, Dublin.

1952: University College, Dublin.

1953: Queen's University, Belfast.

1954: University College, Galway.

1955: University College, Cork.

1956: University College, Cork.

1957: University College, Dublin.

1958: University College, Cork.

1959: University College, Dublin.

1960: University College, Dublin.

1961: University College, Cork.

1962: University College, Cork.

1963: University College, Dublin.

1964: University College, Dublin.

1965: University College, Dublin.

1966: University College, Cork.

1967: University College, Cork.

1968: University College, Dublin.

1969: University College, Dublin.

1970: University College, Galway.

1971: University College, Cork.

1972: University College, Cork.

1973: St Patrick's College, Maynooth.

1974: St Patrick's College, Maynooth.

1975: University College, Dublin.

1976: University College, Cork.

1977: University College, Galway.

1978: University College, Dublin.

1979: University College, Dublin.

1980: University College, Galway.

1981: University College, Cork.

1982: University College, Cork.

1983: University College, Cork.

1984: University College, Cork.

1985: University College, Cork.

1986: University College, Cork.

1987: University College, Cork.

1988: University College, Cork.

1989: University of Limerick.

1990: University College, Cork.

1991: University College, Cork.

1992: Waterford RTC.

1993: University College, Dublin.

1994: University of Limerick.

1995: Waterford RTC.

1996: University College, Cork.

Appendix 17

Secondary Schools

All-Ireland results, 1944–95
(Only Leinster and Munster took part from 1944 to 1948.)

1944: St Flannan's.

1945: St Flannan's.

1946: St Flannan's.

1947: St Flannan's.

1948: St Kieran's.

1949–56: Suspended.

1957: St Flannan's.

1958: St Flannan's.

1959: St Kieran's.

1960: North Monastery, Cork.

1961: St Kieran's.

1962: St Peter's.

1963: St Finbarr's, Cork.

1964: Limerick CBS.

1965: St Kieran's.

1966: Limerick CBS.

1967: St Peter's.

1968: St Peter's.

1969: St Finbarr's, Cork.

1970: North Monastery, Cork.

1971: St Kieran's.

1972: St Finbarr's.

1973: St Peter's.

1974: St Finbarr's.

1975: St Kieran's.

1976: St Flannan's.

1977: St Colman's.

1978: Templemore CBS.

1979: St Flannan's.

1980: North Monastery, Cork.

1981: Kilkenny CBS.

1982: St Flannan's.

1983: St Flannan's.

1984: St Finbarr's, Farranferris.

1985: North Monastery, Cork.

1986: Birr Community School.

1987: St Flannan's.

1988: St Kieran's.

1989: St Kieran's.

1990: St Kieran's.

1991: St Flannan's.

1992: St Kieran's.

1993: St Kieran's.

1994: North Monastery, Cork.

1995: St Raphael's, Loughrea.

Ulster Senior Hurling, 1953–95

Until 1963 the trophy was the Ulster Colleges Shield. In that year the Mageean Cup was presented, and it has been played for since then.

1953: St Malachy's, Belfast.

1954: St Macnissi's, Garron Tower.

1955: St Macnissi's, Garron Tower.

1956: St Malachy's, Belfast.

1957: St Macnissi's, Garron Tower.

1958: St Malachy's and St Macnissi's shared the title.

1959: St Michael's, Omeath.

1960: St Macnissi's, Garron Tower.

1961: St Macnissi's, Garron Tower.

1962: St Macnissi's, Garron Tower.

1963: St Macnissi's, Garron Tower.

1964: St Macnissi's, Garron Tower.

1965: St Mary's CBS, Belfast.

1966: St Mary's CBS, Belfast.

1967: St Mary's CBS, Belfast.

1968: St Mary's CBS, Belfast.

1969: St Mary's CBS, Belfast.

1970: St Mary's CBS, Belfast.

1971: St Mary's CBS, Belfast.

1972: St Mary's CBS, Belfast.

1973: St Mary's CBS, Belfast.

1974: St Mary's CBS, Belfast.

1975: St Mary's CBS, Belfast.

1976: St Mary's, CBS, Belfast.

1977: Cross and Passion, Ballycastle.

1978: Cross and Passion, Ballycastle.

1979: St Mary's CBS, Belfast.

1980: St Mary's CBS, Belfast.

1981: St Mary's CBS, Belfast.

1982: Armagh CBS.

1983: St Patrick's, Maghera.

1984: St Patrick's, Maghera.

1985: St Patrick's, Maghera.

1986: St Mary's CBS, Belfast.

1987: St Mary's CBS, Belfast.

1988: St Louis, Ballymena.

1989: St Patrick's, Maghera.

1990: St Mary's, Belfast.

1991: St Patrick's, Maghera.

1992: St Patrick's, Maghera.

1993: Cross and Passion, Ballycastle.

1994: Cross and Passion, Ballycastle.

1995: St Mary's CBS, Belfast.

Munster Senior Hurling (Dr Harty Cup), 1918–95

1918: Rockwell College.

1919: North Monastery, Cork.

1920: Limerick CBS.

1921: None.

1922: St Munchin's.

1923: Rockwell College.

1924: Rockwell College.

1925: Limerick CBS.

1926: Limerick CBS.

1927: Limerick CBS.

1928: No competition.

1929: North Monastery, Cork.

1930: Rockwell College.

1931: Rockwell College.

1932: Limerick CBS.

1933: Thurles CBS.

1934: North Monastery, Cork.

1935: North Monastery, Cork.

1936: North Monastery, Cork.

1937: North Monastery, Cork.

1938: Thurles CBS.

1939: Thurles CBS.

1940: North Monastery, Cork.

1941: North Monastery, Cork.

1942: North Monastery, Cork.

1943: North Monastery, Cork.

1944: St Flannan's.

1945: St Flannan's.

1946: St Flannan's.

1947: St Flannan's.

1948: St Colman's.

1949: St Colman's.

1950: Thurles CBS.

1951: Thurles CBS.

1952: St Flannan's.

1953: Mount Sion.

1954: St Flannan's.

1955: North Monastery, Cork.

1956: Thurles CBS.

1957: St Flannan's.

1958: St Flannan's.

1959: Tipperary CBS.

1960: North Monastery, Cork.

1961: North Monastery, Cork.

1962: Ennis CBS.

1963: St Finbarr's, Farranferris.

1964: Limerick CBS.

1965: Limerick CBS.

1966: Limerick CBS.

1967: Limerick CBS.

1968: Coláiste Chríost Rí.

1969: St Finbarr's, Farranferris.

1970: North Monastery, Cork.

1971: St Finbarr's, Farranferris.

1972: St Finbarr's, Farranferris.

1973: St Finbarr's, Farranferris.

1974: St Finbarr's, Farranferris.

1975: Coláiste Iognáid Rís.

1976: St Flannan's.

1977: St Colman's.

1978: Templemore CBS.

1979: St Flannan's.

1980: North Monastery, Cork.

1981: North Monastery, Cork.

1982: St Flannan's.

1983: St Flannan's.

1984: St Finbarr's, Farranferris.

1985: North Monastery, Cork.

1986: North Monastery, Cork.

1987: St Flannan's.

1988: Midleton CBS.

1989: St Flannan's.

1990: St Flannan's.

1991: St Flannan's.

1992: St Colman's.

1993: Limerick CBS.

1994: North Monastery, Cork.

1995: Midleton CBS.

Leinster Senior Hurling, 1918–95

1918: Castleknock College, Dublin.

1919: No competition.

1920: Mount St Joseph's.

1921: Mount St Joseph's.

1922: St Kieran's.

1923: Mount St Joseph's.

1924: Mount St Joseph's.

1925: St Kieran's.

1926: St Kieran's.

1927: St Kieran's.

1928: St Kieran's.

1929: St Kieran's.

1930: Coláiste Chaoimhín, Dublin.

1931: St Kieran's.

1932: St Kieran's.

1933: St Kieran's.

1934: Coláiste Chaoimhín, Dublin.

1935: Blackrock College, Dublin.

1936: Kilkenny CBS.

1937: St Kieran's.

1938: St Kieran's.

1939: St Kieran's.

1940: St Kieran's.

1941: St Kieran's.

1942: Ballyfin PBS.

1943: St Kieran's.

1944: St Kieran's.

1945: St Joseph's, Marino.

1946: O'Connell Schools, Dublin.

1947: Mount St Joseph's.

1948: St Kieran's.

1949: St Kieran's.

1950: St Kieran's.

1951: St Kieran's.

1952: Ballyfin PBS.

1953: St Kieran's.

1954: O'Connell Schools, Dublin.

1955: Knockbeg College.

1956: Ballyfin PBS.

1957: St Kieran's.

1958: St Kieran's.

1959: St Kieran's.

1960: St Peter's.

1961: St Kieran's.

1962: St Peter's.

1963: Ballyfin PBS.

1964: St Peter's.

1965: St Kieran's.

1966: St Kieran's.

1967: St Peter's.

1968: St Peter's.

1969: St Kieran's.

1970: Kilkenny CBS.

1971: St Kieran's.

1972: St Kieran's.

1973: St Peter's.

1974: St Kieran's.

1975: St Kieran's.

1976: Kilkenny CBS.

1977: St Kieran's.

1978: St Peter's.

1979: Presentation College, Birr.

1980: Birr Community School.

1981: Kilkenny CBS.

1982: St Peter's.

1983: Kilkenny CBS.

1984: St Kieran's.

1985: Birr Community School.

1986: Birr Community School.

1987: St Kieran's.

1988: St Kieran's.

1989: St Kieran's.

1990: St Kieran's.

1991: St Kieran's.

1992: St Kieran's.

1993: St Kieran's.

1994: St Kieran's.

1995: Good Counsel, New Ross.

Connacht Senior Hurling, 1938–95

1938: Roscommon CBS.

1939: Roscommon CBS.

1940: St Mary's, Galway.

1941: St Mary's, Galway.

1942: St Mary's, Galway.

1943: None.

1944: None.

1945: None.

1946: St Mary's, Galway.

1947: St Mary's, Galway.

1948: De La Salle, Loughrea.

1949: St Mary's, Galway.

1950: St Mary's, Galway.

1951: St Mary's, Galway.

1952: St Mary's, Galway.

1953: St Mary's, Galway.

1954: St Mary's, Galway.

1955: St Mary's, Galway.

1956: St Mary's, Galway.

1957: St Mary's, Galway.

1958: St Joseph's, Garbally.

1959: St Joseph's, Garbally.

1960: St Mary's, Galway.

1961: St Molaise's, Portumna.

1962: St Molaise's, Portumna.

1963: St Mary's, Galway.

1964: St Mary's, Galway.

1965: St Mary's, Galway.

1966: St Mary's, Galway.

1967: St Mary's, Galway.

1968: St Joseph's, Garbally.

1969: Our Lady's, Gort.

1970: Presentation, Athenry.

1971: Presentation, Athenry.

1972: Our Lady's, Gort.

1973: Our Lady's, Gort.

1974: Our Lady's, Gort.

1975: Our Lady's, Gort.

1976: Presentation, Athenry.

1977: Presentation, Athenry.

1978: Our Lady's, Gort.

1979: St Mary's, Galway.

1980: St Joseph's, Garbally.

1981: Our Lady's, Gort.

1982: Our Lady's, Gort.

1983: St Joseph's, Garbally.

1984: Our Lady's, Gort.

1985: St Joseph's, Garbally.

1986: St Joseph's, Garbally.

1987: St Joseph's, Garbally.

1988: St Mary's, Galway.

1989: St Mary's, Galway.

1990: St Mary's, Galway.

1991: St Raphael's, Loughrea.

1992: St Raphael's, Loughrea.

1993: Our Lady's, Gort.

1994: St Mary's, Galway.

1995: St Raphael's, Loughrea.

Vocational Schools, 1961–95

1961: Limerick (city).

1962: North Tipperary.

1963: Kilkenny.

1964: North Tipperary.

1965: North Tipperary.

1966: North Tipperary.

1967: North Tipperary.

1968: North Tipperary.

1969: North Tipperary.

1970: Cork.

1971: Antrim.

1972: Kilkenny.

1973: Kilkenny.

1974: North Tipperary.

1975: Kilkenny.

1976: Kilkenny.

1977: Kilkenny.

1978: North Tipperary.

1979: Clare.

1980: Galway.

1981: Galway.

1982: Galway.

1983: Galway.

1984: Galway.

1986: Galway.

1987: Galway.

1988: Tipperary.

1989: Kilkenny.

1990: Tipperary.

1991: Kilkenny.

1992: Galway.

1993: Galway.

1994: Galway.

1995: Galway.

Individual schools

1978: Gort.

1979: Ennis.

1980: Roscrea.

1981: New Inn.

1982: Johnstown.

1983: Portumna.

1984: Nenagh.

1985: Banagher.

1986: Banagher.

1987: Thomastown.

1988: Moneenageisha.

1989: Banagher.

1990: Moneenageisha.

1991: Roscrea.

1992: Athenry.

1993: Athenry.

1994: Athenry.

1995: Loughrea.

Notes

Chapter 1 [pp. 1-9]

1. *Irish Sagas*, ed. Myles Dillon (Dublin: Stationery Office 1959), 27.
2. Ibid.
3. Ó Maolfabhail, *Camán*, 8.
4. Ó Caithnia, Liam P., 'Hurling in early Irish law', *The Book of Gaelic Games* (Kilkenny), 30.
5. Ó Maolfabhail, *Camán*, 14.
6. Ibid.
7. Quoted by Ó Maolfabhail, *Camán*, 15, 16.
8. Ibid.
9. Ó Caithnia, *Scéal na hIomána*, 385.

Chapter 2 [pp. 10-24]

1. *Journal of the Royal Society of Antiquaries of Ireland*, 1909, 74.
2. W. J. Hayes, 'The Purcells of Loughmore' (manuscript).
3. Ó Caithnia, Liam P., 'Landlords and hurling', *The Book of Gaelic Games*, 55–9.
4. Ó Maolfabhail, *Camán*.
5. Edward MacLysaght, *Irish Life in the Seventeenth Century* (London 1939), 135.
6. Quoted by Ó Maolfabhail, *Camán*, 19.
7. Peter Burke, *Popular Culture in Early Modern Europe* (Aldershot 1978).
8. Ó Maolfabhail, *Camán*, 20.
9. 'The present state of Ireland', *Journal of the Royal Society of Antiquaries of Ireland*, vol. 5, 179.
10. *Journal of the Royal Society of Antiquaries of Ireland*, vol. 4, 144.
11. MacLysaght, op. cit., 363–4.

12. *Kildare Archaeological Journal*, vol. 5, 179.
13. Quoted by Ó Maolfabhail, *Camán*, 28.
14. Quoted by Ó Maolfabhail, *Camán*, 29–30.
15. Ó Laoi, *Annals of the GAA in Galway*: vol. I, 1.
16. Ó Maolfabhail, *Camán*, 30.
17. Ó Maolfabhail, *Camán*, 30.
18. Ó Maolfabhail, *Camán*, 138.
19. J. T. Collins, 'An old time hurling match near Blarney', *The Rebel: Diamond Jubilee, County Corkmen's Association of New York* (New York 1959) 106–7.
20. Burke, op. cit., 271.

Chapter 3 [pp. 25-37]

1. Quoted in *The Book of Gaelic Games*, ed. Seán Courtney (Kilkenny), 163.
2. Op. cit., 86.
3. Op. cit., 165.
4. Ó Laoi, *Annals of the GAA in Galway*: vol. 2, 10.
5. *United Irishman*, 7 Feb. 1885.
6. T. F. O'Sullivan, *Story of the GAA* (Dublin 1983), 10.
7. Ó Caithnia, op. cit., 190.
8. A. T. Lucas, 'Hair hurling balls', *Journal of the Cork Historical and Archaeological Society*, 1952.
9. Lucas, op. cit., 104.
10. Bob Stakelum, *Gaelic Games in Holycross-Ballycahill, 1884–1990* (Midleton 1990), 17.
11. *Official Guide*, 1919–1920 (Wexford 1920), 129.
12. The Sam Melbourne Collection can be seen in 'Lár na Páirce', an interpretative centre for Gaelic games in Thurles, Co. Tipperary.
13. *Official Guide*, 1943 (Dublin 1943), 139.
14. *Official Guide*, 1988 (Dublin 1988), 79.

Chapter 4 [pp. 38-53]

1. De Búrca, *Michael Cusack and the GAA*, 96.
2. Op. cit., 97.
3. Op. cit., 98.
4. The Sunday Observance Act, 1695, had stipulated that 'no person or persons whatsoever shall play, use or practise any hurling, commoning, football playing, cudgels, wrestling or any other games, pastimes or sports on the Lord's Day, or any part thereof: and if any person or persons shall offend therein, and be thereof convicted in such manner as herein after directed, every such person and persons shall forfeit the sum of five pennies for every such offence ...'

5. A. M. Sullivan, *New Ireland*, 68.

6. Michael Doheny, 'Part of the autobiography of an agitator', *Irish American*, 19 Feb. 1859.

7. P. F. O'Brien, *Messenger of St. Joseph*, Apr. 1884.

8. De Búrca, *The GAA: a History*, 5.

9. O'Sullivan, *Story of the GAA*, 7.

10. Fogarty, *Tipperary's GAA Story*, 21.

11. Kevin Whelan, *History Ireland*, spring 1993, 30.

12. Ibid.

13. Newspaper reports, 17 and 20 Feb.

14. Fogarty, op. cit., 22.

15. O'Sullivan, op. cit., 56.

16. Ibid.

17. *Tipperary Star*, 25 Jan. 1913.

18. Whelan, op. cit.

19. O'Sullivan, op. cit., 58.

20. Whelan, op. cit., 30.

Chapter 5 [pp. 54–70]

1. O'Sullivan, *Story of the GAA*, 79.

2. Fogarty, *Tipperary's Hurling Story*, 23.

3. *Cashel Sentinel*, 14 Sep. 1895.

4. Carbery, *History of Hurling*, 107.

5. Fogarty, op. cit., 66.

6. Because of the delay in completing competitions, the Central Council decided that the Croke Cup for 1898 would be given to the All-Ireland champions of that year.

7. Jim Cronin, *Cork GAA: a History*, 1886–1986, 40.

8. Fogarty, op. cit., 129.

9. P.F. O'Brien, *Messenger of St Joseph*, Apr. 1884.

10. In *The Mackey Story* by Séamus Ó Ceallaigh and Seán Murphy (p. 23) Andrew 'Doorick' Buckley is credited with 7-4 in the same match.

11. Quoted by O'Sullivan, op. cit., 186.

12. I am indebted to two books in particular for information used in this chapter: *Kilkenny: the GAA Story*, 1884–1984 by Tom Ryall and *Famous Tullaroan*, ed. Antóin Ó Dúill.

13. Dónal Shanahan, *The Green and Golden Years of Toomevara GAA*, 1885–1985 (Brosna Press 1985), 3.

Chapter 6 [pp. 71–81]

1. O'Sullivan, *Story of the GAA*, 79.
2. John Power, *A Story of Champions*.
3. O'Neill, *Twenty Years of the GAA*, 26.
4. *Centenary Tribute to the GAA in Wexford*, 31.
5. I am indebted to Ó Ceallaigh and Murphy, *One Hundred Years of Glory*, for much of the information in this section.
6. Raymond Smith, *The Hurling Immortals* (Dublin 1988), 131.
7. Ó Laoi, *Annals of the GAA in Galway*, vol. 2, 10.
8. Op. cit., 174.
9. *Sunday Tribune*, 12 Nov. 1995
10. Op. cit., 175.

Chapter 7 [pp. 82–89]

1. Seán Kilfeather, *Irish Times*, 15 July 1995.
2. 'Pato', quoted by O'Neill, *Twenty Years of the GAA*, 293.
3. Quoted in Cronin, *Munster GAA Story*, 146.
4. Horgan, *Cork's Hurling Story*, 66.
5. Op. cit., 67.

Chapter 8 [pp. 90–102]

1. Ó Laoi, *Annals of the GAA in Galway*, vol. II, 249.
2. Quoted in Raymond Smith, *The Hurling Immortals* (Dublin 1969), 147.
3. Ryall, *Kilkenny: the GAA Story*, 51–2.
4. *Post* (Kilkenny), 4 Sep. 1935.
5. *Limerick Echo*, 3 Aug. 1939.
6. *Post* (Kilkenny), 6 Sep. 1940.

Chapter 9 [pp. 103–114]

1. Fullam, *Giants of the Ash*, 15.
2. Ó Ceallaigh and Murphy, *One Hundred Years of Glory*, 110–11.
3. Ó Ceallaigh and Murphy, *The Mackey Story*, 125.
4. Ryall, *Kilkenny*, 66.
5. Fullam, *Giants of the Ash*, 126.

Chapter 11 [pp. 128–138]

1. Fullam, *Giants of the Ash*, 203.
2. Furlong, *Greatest Hurling Decade*, 137.

NOTES

NOTES

Chapter 12 [pp. 139–154]

1. *Sunday Independent*, 4 Sep. 1960.
2. *Daily Mail*, 4 Sep. 1967.

Chapter 15 [pp. 198–218]

1. J. J. Ó Ceallaigh, *History of* GAA.

Chapter 16 [pp. 219–225]

1. Quoted by Puirséal, *The GAA in its Time*, 26.
2. Nic an Ultaigh, *An Dún*, 45.
3. Nic an Ultaigh, *An Dún*, 42.
4. P. J. McGill, 'Cross-country hurling in south-west Donegal', *Donegal GAA Annual*, 1967, 30–2.
5. Pádraig Mac an Ghoill, *Early Years of* GAA *in Donegal*, 110–11.
6. Brendan Harvey, *Irish News*, 1 Sep. 1989.
7. Kevin Whelan, 'The geography of hurling', *History Ireland*, spring 1993, 31.
8. Proinsias Breathnach, *History Ireland*, summer 1993, 8.
9. *Economist*, 10 July 1993.
10. Op. cit.
11. Op. cit.
12. Kevin Whelan, 'The geography of hurling', *History Ireland*, spring 1993, 31.
13. Liam Ryan, 'Hurling heresy', Fitzgibbon Cup Final programme, 5 Mar. 1995.

Chapter 17 [pp. 226–237]

1. *Carbery's Annual*, 1939, 21.
2. *Carbery's Annual*, 1939, 23.
3. Conversation with the author.
4. Maher and Ryan, *Boherlahan and Dualla*, 31.
5. Conversation with the author.
6. *Cork Examiner*, 3 Feb. 1994.
7. *Carbery's Annual*, 1942.
8. Letter to the author.
9. Letter to the author.
10. Letter to the author.
11. Letter to the author.
12. *Cork Examiner*, 10 Feb. 1994.
13. Wall, *Hurling*, 24.
14. Wall, *Hurling*, 30.
15. Wall, *Hurling*, 116.

Chapter 18 [pp. 238–247]

1. Congress report, 1994.
2. Interview by Marty Morrissey, *Sunday Independent*, 5 Mar. 1995.
3. *Sunday Independent*, 8 Jan. 1995.
4. *Sunday Independent*, 8 Jan. 1995.
5. *Sunday Independent*, 6 Apr. 1958.

Select Bibliography

Beecher, Seán, *The Blues: a History of the St Finbarr's National Hurling and Football Club*, Cork 1984.

The Book of Gaelic Games, Kilkenny 1986.

Breheny, Martin, and Farrell, Cyril, *The Right to Win*, Dublin 1994.

Carbery [P. D. Mehigan], *History of Hurling*, Tralee 1946.

Carbery's *Annuals*.

County Wexford Centenary Year Committee, *Centenary Tribute to the GAA in Wexford*, Wexford 1984.

Courtney, Pat, *Famous All-Irelands*, Dublin 1984.

Courtney, Pat, *Classic Munster Finals*, Galway 1993.

Cronin, Jim (ed.), *Munster GAA Story*, Cork: Munster Council, GAA, 1986.

Cumann Lúthchleas Gael, *A Century of Service*, Dublin 1984.

Davin, P., *Recollections of a Veteran Irish Athlete: the Memoirs of Pat Davin, World's All-Round Athletic Champion*, Dublin 1939.

de Búrca, Marcus, *The GAA: a History*, Dublin 1980.

de Búrca, Marcus, *Gaelic Games in Leinster, 1904–1984*, Leinster Council GAA 1984.

de Búrca, Marcus, *One Hundred Years of Faughs Hurling*, Tralee 1985.

de Búrca, Marcus, *Michael Cusack and the GAA*, Dublin 1989.

Devlin, P., *Our Native Games*, Dublin 1935.

Dooley, William, *Champions of the Athletic Arena*, Dublin 1946.

Dorgan, Val, *Christy Ring: a Personal Portrait*, Dublin 1980.

Doyle, Tommy, *A Lifetime in Hurling*, London 1955.

Fennelly, Teddy, 100 Years of the GAA in Laois, Port Laoise 1984.

Fogarty, Canon Philip, Tipperary's GAA Story, Thurles 1960.

Freeman, Norman, Classic Hurling Matches, 1956–1975, Dublin: Gill & Macmillan 1993.

Freeman, Norman, Classic Hurling Matches, 1976–1991, Dublin: Gill & Macmillan 1993.

Fullam, Brendan, Giants of the Ash, Dublin: Wolfhound 1991.

Fullam, Brendan, Hurling Giants, Dublin 1994.

Furlong, Nicholas, The Greatest Hurling Decade: Wexford and the Epic Teams of the '50s, Dublin: Wolfhound 1993.

GAA Official Guide (various editions).

History Committee, Doire: a History of the GAA in Derry, Derry County Board 1984.

Horgan, Tim, Cork's Hurling Story, Tralee: Anvil 1977.

Hutchinson, Roger, Camanachd: the Story of Shinty, Edinburgh 1989.

King, Séamus. J., Tipperary's GAA, 1935–1984, Tipperary County Board 1988.

Leahy, Christy, James Stephens GAA Club, Club Centenary Committee 1987.

McCann, Owen, The Shell Book of the McCarthy Cup, Dublin 1993.

Macken, Ultan, Eddie Keher's Hurling Life, Cork 1978.

MacLennan, Hugh D., Not an Orchid, Inverness 1993.

MacLennan, Hugh D., Shinty!: Celebrating Scotland's Game, Inverness 1993.

Madden, Paddy, A History of Blackrock Hurling Club, Blackrock National Hurling Club 1984.

Maher, J. G., and Ryan, P. F., Boherlahan and Dualla: a Century of Gaelic Games, Midleton: Boherlahan-Dualla GAA Club 1987.

Mandle, W. F., The Gaelic Athletic Association and Irish Nationalist Politics, 1884–1924, Dublin 1987.

Morrison, Tim, Cork's Glorious Years, Midleton 1975.

Nic an Ultaigh, Sighle, An Dún: the GAA Story, Newry: Down County Board 1988

North American County Board GAA, Our Story Reviewed, 1884–1993, North American Board 1993.

Ó Caithnia, Liam P., Scéal na hIomána, Baile Átha Cliath 1980.

Ó Ceallacháin, Seán Óg, Seán Óg: His Own Story, Dublin 1988.

Ó Ceallaigh, Séamus, History of Limerick GAA, 1884–1908, Tralee 1937.

Ó Ceallaigh, Séamus, Gaelic Athletic Memories, Dublin 1945.

Ó Ceallaigh, Séamus, Story of the GAA, Gaelic Athletic Publications 1977.

Ó Ceallaigh, Séamus, and Murphy, Seán, *One Hundred Years of Glory: a History of Limerick* GAA, Limerick: Limerick GAA Publications Committee 1987.

Ó Ceallaigh, Séamus, and Murphy, Seán, *The Mackey Story*, Limerick: Limerick GAA Publications Committee 1987.

Ó Dúill, Antóin, *Famous Tullaroan*, 1884–1984, Tullaroan GAA Club 1984.

O'Hehir, Micheál, *The GAA: 100 Years*, Dublin 1984.

Ó Laoi, Pádraic, *Annals of the GAA in Galway: vol. I*, 1884–1901, Galway: Connaught Tribune 1983.

Ó Laoi, Pádraic, *Annuals of the GAA in Galway: vol. II*, 1902–1934, Galway: Connaught Tribune 1992.

Ó Maolfabhail, Art, *Camán: Two Thousand Years of Hurling in Ireland*, Dundalk 1973.

O'Neill, Phil, *Twenty Years of the GAA*, 1910–1930, Kilkenny 1931.

Ó Riain, Séamus, *Maurice Davin*, 1842–1927, Dublin 1994.

O'Sullivan, T. F., *Story of the GAA*, Dublin 1916.

O'Toole, Pádraig, *The Glory and the Anguish*, Loughrea 1984.

Puirséal, Pádraig, *The GAA in Its Time*, Dublin 1982.

Quinn, Jerome, *Ulster Football and Hurling*, Dublin 1993.

Ryall, Tom, *Kilkenny: the GAA Story*, 1884–1984, Kilkenny 1984.

Scully, R., and Cunningham, P. J., *Uíbh Fhailí: the Faithful County*, 1884–1984, Offaly County Board 1984.

Smith, Raymond, *The Clash of the Ash*, Dublin 1981.

Smith, Raymond, *A Century of Gaelic Games*, Dublin 1987.

Smith, Raymond, *Complete Handbook of Gaelic Games*, Dublin 1988, 1993.

Smith, Raymond, *The Greatest Hurlers of Our Time*, Dublin 1990.

Smith, Raymond, *The Hurling and Football Annual*, Dublin, 1992–95

Wall, Tony, *Hurling*, Dublin 1965.

Whelan, Seán, *Wexford GAA Memories*, 1884–1984, Enniscorthy 1984.

Yearbooks: Clare, Cork, Dublin, Down, Galway, Kilkenny, Limerick, Tipperary, Wexford.

Index

A History of Hurling